PUBLIC FOLKLORE

Public Folklore

Edited by Robert Baron and Nick Spitzer

University Press of Mississippi Jackson

www.upress.state.ms.us

The University Press of Mississippi is a member
of the Association of American University Presses.

Manufactured in the United States of America
Originally published by the Smithsonian Institution, 1992, 1996.

First University Press of Mississippi edition 2008

Library of Congress Cataloging-in-Publication Data

Public folklore / edited by Robert Baron and Nicholas R. Spitzer.
    p. cm.
  Originally published: Washington : Smithsonian Institution Press, c1992, in series: Publications
of the American Foklore Society. New series.
  Includes bibliographical references.
  ISBN-13: 978-1-934110-40-9 (pbk. : alk. paper)
  ISBN-10: 1-934110-40-X (pbk. : alk. paper) 1. Public folklore—United States. 2. Public
folklore—United States—Bibliography. I. Baron, Robert, 1951– II. Spitzer, Nicholas R.
  GR105.P84 2007
  398.20973—dc22   2007022172

British Library Cataloging-in-Publication Data available

Contents

Cultural Continuity and Community Creativity in a New Century

Preface to the Third Printing

This book came to life at an expansive moment for the field of folklore when its public dimension became more fully realized as both a social practice and accepted domain of scholarship. During the 1980s a national infrastructure of public folklore and folklife programs crystalized. They quickly grew into a well-articulated network of federal, state, and local programs situated mostly within government arts, historic preservation, and humanities agencies, not-for-profit folklife organizations, and a few private-sector entities. Folklorists directing these programs or working independently with them began to generate scholarship about their endeavors. The effect was to challenge the discipline of folklore studies to integrate the practicing profession. We viewed our practice as inherently collaborative in its engagement with communities that were themselves increasingly interested in safeguarding, presenting, and documenting local cultural expressions. Our commitment as folklorists to cultural equity and pluralism resonated at a time when cultural activists reshaped the politics of culture in their advocacy for multiculturalism.

The national network of public folklore programs continued to expand and solidify through the early 1990s even as public funding was severely reduced. While opportunities for academic employment diminished, the "public sector" emerged as a primary locus for the practice of folklore by academically trained folklorists. Recognizing a need to foster discourse about public folklore practice and theory throughout the discipline of folklore studies, we organized a series of sessions at the annual meeting of the American Folklore Society's (AFS) annual meeting in Albuquerque in 1987 which brought together folklorists from both the academic and public sectors—still identified as largely separate by political economy and practice. Speakers at these sessions spoke of the inherently public nature of folklore studies throughout the discipline's history and called for rapprochement between the academic and public sectors. We viewed public folklore as bringing into high relief conceptual issues at the heart of contemporary folkloristics, including intervention, ideology, and the theorization of practice as well as the authority and aesthetics of cultural representation. The Albuquerque AFS sessions resulted in this volume, first published by Smithsonian Institution Press in 1992.

Public folklore, as conceptualized and defined in this book, is by nature collaborative and dialogical, involving folklore applied and/or presented in new contexts within and beyond the communities where it originates. We eschewed the term "applied folklore," with its associations of folklorists determining objectives, agendas, and interpretive frameworks, whether for beneficent ends of social amelioration or malevolent purposes well documented in studies of the manipulation of folklore by extremist regimes. We were also concerned that, in contrast, academic practitioners not be labeled "unapplied," as Joe Wilson of the National Council for Traditional Arts once quipped. Further we wanted to encourage the public dialogic aspects of college and university-based work that does indeed involve passing knowledge (teaching), writing (publication), and engagement with communities in its fullest realization. At the same time, we viewed public folklore as communicating symbolically to broad audiences of community members, colleagues, students, institutions and the general public—even while highly specific local applications of folklore theory and practice were engaged with traditional artists and community members working through cultural issues of modern life. Following David Whisnant's view that all folklore study is interventionist by nature and must be transparent about its motivations, ends and objectives, *Public Folklore* incorporates a number of reflexive case studies about relationships between folklorists and the "tradition-bearers" and communities with whom we work. These essays are forthright about issues of folklorist's power to represent and create dialogue about the direction of projects and the impact—both positive and negative—of exposure to new audiences and markets, health care facilities and educational institutions.

As presenters of traditional expressive culture in social and historical contexts to new audiences, public folklorists invent and refine methodologies appropriate to those varied settings. The "performance" paradigm in folklore studies developed in the 1970s, that views folklore as situated behavior and emergent in performance, shaped the professional and intellectual formation of most of the contributors to *Public Folklore*. Recontextualization, a paramount concern for public folklorists, meant grounding presentations to new audiences in the modes of presentation occurring in a "natural" context. New contexts for presentations occurring outside of customary community contexts are necessarily artifices constructed by folklorists, and *Public Folklore* sought to advance presentational practice by exploring the construction of formats in aesthetically organic or at least appropriate ways, as well as examining the consequences for artists, communities and their art forms of engaging them. They include such venues as museum exhibition, concert stage, and festival workshop; media formats include films, documentary photography, sound recordings and radio broadcasts. Framing presentations and extending cultural symbols into these new settings incorporates conceptual, interpretive and practical dimensions. In *Public Folklore,* we see greater understanding of traditions and their varied contextual meanings fostered through signage, commentary, design, editorial and other devices in print, broadcast or exhibition and film production, and through spoken introductions and colloquies with performers. Through such interpretation, folklore field research and scholarship reaches much wider audiences—traditions are more readily understood as part of modernity rather than apart from it. Local and global concerns about culture can help create a new space in public discourse. Contributors to *Public Folklore* also contend that making folk traditions accessible to wide audiences demands mastery, within folkloristic frameworks, of physical settings and techniques for presentations and technologies of lighting, sound reinforcement, film and audio production, design and stage management, as well as in scholarly understanding.

Viewed in historical perspective, the essays in *Public Folklore* served as a manifesto and blueprint for future action. Many called for full integration of the practicing profession of public folklore within the discipline of folklore studies. Contributors underscored the public character of folklore studies throughout its history, resisting dichotomization of "academic and applied," and calling for graduate training that embraced public folklore as central to the standard curricula for folklore studies. Since the initial publication of this book, a number of graduate folklore programs either introduced or expanded training in the history and theory of folklore practice from a public perspective. At Indiana University, candidates for master's degree may produce educational materials or intern at a museum as an alternative to a master's thesis. A public folklore course at the University of Oregon deals with both the intellectual history and practice of public folklore, as students engage in project and proposal development, and creation of a fieldwork plan. Partnerships and close working relationships are maintained between many graduate folklore programs and state folk arts programs. Folklorists practicing primarily outside of the academy now represent over half of all members of the American

Folklore Society (AFS), many academic folklorists consult for public folklore programs, and three folklorists who mainly work outside of the academy have served as presidents of the American Folklore Society since 1995.

In the past fifteen years, scholarship has addressed new issues while continuing to focus on the concerns raised in *Public Folklore* about representation, dialogical approaches towards engagement with communities, and the theorization of practice. Advocacy was considered in several of the essays, with Barbara Kirshenblatt-Gimblett contending that advocacy can distort inquiry, Archie Green describing the fruits of his efforts lobbying for the establishment of the American Folklife Center, and Robert Baron relating spirited disagreements at the 1950 Mid-Century International Folklore Conference about whether folklorists should be advocates for the presentation and perpetuation of traditions. Advocacy is a recurrent matter of contention in folklore studies, and it has resurfaced as an issue in recent years. An entire issue of the *Journal of Folklore Research* (*JFR*) in 2004 was devoted to advocacy, with several authors arguing for the obligation of a folklorist to advocate for the tradition-bearers and communities he or she studies, a position supported by the *Statement of Ethics of the American Folklore Society*. It argues that the primary responsibility of folklorists "is to those they study," and stipulates that when "there is a conflict of interest, these individuals come first." Elliot Oring contended in the same issue of *JFR* that folklorists should not be expected to advocate for traditions that are morally reprehensible to them, and argued that there are situations where advocacy for one community may conflict with advocacy for another. Oring's objections seem overdrawn. Advocacy may entail appropriate representation of the interests of a community, rather than explicit political advocacy. It need not only involve representing a community as it sees itself, which Oring views as inherent in folkloristic representations of cultures. It could also entail conflict resolution when folklorists have worked with multiple communities with competing interests.

Intellectual property has come to forefront of advocacy by folklorists. Rights to traditional cultural expressions and knowledge became a major international issue over the past decade, engaging lawyers, global organizations, folklorists, and other cultural specialists as never before. In a globalized world of instantaneous virtual communication, no community is immune to appropriation and use of its traditions. Biopiracy through the commercial exploitation of traditional medicinal plants, use of motifs and patterns in indigenous textiles by non-Native designers, and appropriation of traditional music through sampling in "world" music led to efforts to protect traditional communities left uncompensated and with no patent or copyright to the products of their traditional creativity. The World International Property Organization (WIPO) organized multiple convenings to discuss rights to traditional cultural expressions, and a number of nations and nation groups initiated legislation to protect the intellectual property of traditional communities (see http://www.wipo.int/tk/en/laws/folklore.html).

The American Folklore Society also weighed in on intellectual property issues with a list of recommendations to the WIPO Intergovernmental Committee on Intellectual Property and Genetic Resources, Traditional Knowledge and Folklore, supporting the rights of indigenous and traditional communities. It called on WIPO to recognize that the needs of its member nations do not necessarily coincide with the "indigenous and traditional communities" within their borders—and may, in fact run counter to them, urged recognition of the knowledge and folklore of both indigenous and non-indigenous traditional groups, and recommended technical assistance and leadership training in documentation and conservation directed towards traditional and indigenous communities. The AFS recommendations also insisted on recognition of intangible as well as tangible values, and indicated that "commodification and privatization of these values may run counter to the rights and desires of holders of traditional knowledge and folklore" (2004: 299).

The international dialogue on rights to traditional cultural expressions and knowledge places in sharp focus fundamental questions of critical importance to public folklore: "Who owns folklore?"; "Who speaks for a culture or community?"; "What happens when culture is viewed as a commodity?"; "How do traditional cultural creativity and issues of collective vs. individual rights to folklore relate to interest in local, national, or global economic development?" Valdimar Hafstein, in an article in the *Journal of American Folklore*, called into question an official United States position that folklore is "always individually created and then adopted by the community." He emphasized that traditional creativity is a social process and characterized the act of creation as a social act, contending that "individual creators of folklore are in most cases mere postulates." Tracing contemporary Western notions of intellectual property to ideas of originality and personality associated with Hegel and Kant as well as Locke's theory of possessive individualism, Hafstein called for recognition of "a social concept of creativity," with the "common dynamic" of folklore being "communal origination through individual recreation."

Copying should be viewed as a "creative act," and "creation as an act of reproduction" (2004: 300, 306–8, 310).

The protection of traditional cultural expressions and knowledge are in-
tegrally related to a vibrant international discourse about the safeguarding of
intangible cultural heritage (ICH). This dialogue has occurred in large part
under the aegis of UNESCO, with federal cultural agencies assuming a dominant role. The convention for the safeguarding of intangible cultural heritage
has been signed by seventy-seven countries as of May 2007, but not by the U.S.
Intangible cultural heritage consists in large part of folklore by another name,
although it also involves such areas as language, digital media, and scientific
processes (see the special issue of *Museum International* "Views and Visions
of the Intangible," 2004). While the current UNESCO ICH initiative grew out
of UNESCO conventions and projects involving "traditional folklore," negative associations of the term "folklore" among some member states led to the
adoption of the term "intangible cultural heritage." In international discourse
about intangible cultural heritage, the use of the term "safeguarding" rather
than "preservation" represents another critical change in nomenclature. This
shift is explained by concern for emphasizing the dynamic qualities of ICH, in
contrast with the stasis suggested by preservation. The replacement of "preservation" with "safeguarding" is probably more in sync with the practice and
world view of most American public folklorists. However, neither safeguarding nor preservation should be viewed as necessarily requiring legal enforce-
ment to maintain any dimension of traditional culture by state regulatory
authorities.

In some circles where traditional arts and skills, and the communities
in which they originate, are imperiled by economic or social pressures, environmental and engineering catastrophes (as with the New Orleans floods),
or more broadly adapted to new circumstance, the notion of cultural conservation has changed to "cultural continuity." While it may often be impos-
sible and not desirable to legally enforce cultural conservation or continuity
of community life—much less the boundaries of traditional intangible intellectual property—the very notion of public folklore, as much a symbolic as
applied practice and discourse, offers the promise of urging space in the social
order for traditional creativity as a matter of policy rather than law. Policies
backed by incentives of grants and programs that stimulate and widely present traditional arts and artists can respond to the idea that creolized and other
forms of vernacular creativity may also embed cultural conservation with ap-

propriate transformations that reflect new social conditions. Public discourse among local, national, and global spheres should aim for an appropriate balance between tradition and transformation. The result can be characterized as an ongoing process that yields cultural continuity. In this perspective, cultural continuity is allied with concepts of an "authentic future"—where traditional forms of creativity enable new ways of generating the intimacies and freedoms of community-based culture under current and future conditions (Spitzer: 308, 320).

The international ICH conversation addresses fundamental issues concerning the protection and safeguarding of folklore, most of which are familiar to American public folklorists. Critical writing and scholarship about ICH views transmission, field research, publication, and presentation as primary vehicles for the safeguarding of traditions. Apprenticeships, for example, are a critically important vehicle of transmission, and the American experience with folk arts apprenticeships could serve as a model for other countries and UNESCO's efforts to operationalize ICH objectives. The Convention for the Safeguarding of the Intangible Cultural Heritage places strong emphasis upon the establishment of institutions for documentation, widely accessible field research, and national ICH inventory initiatives. The process of creating a national inventory is quite open-ended, especially since ICH is such a broad—and even amorphous—category.

A primary objective of this research is the identification of candidates for designation as "Masterpieces of Oral and Intangible Heritage of Humanity," which, in contrast to the recognition of individuals through the National Endowment for the Arts's National Heritage Fellowships, designates collective traditions. Barbara Kirshenblatt-Gimblett contends that the ICH masterpieces initiative "places considerable faith—too much faith, according to some participants in the process—in the power of valorization to effect revitalization" (2004: 57).

Wend Wendland, a lawyer who directs the WIPO's Traditional Creativity and Cultural Expressions section, raises a cautionary note about ICH field research by scholars. He contends that the "very process of preservation (such as the recording or documentation and publication of traditional cultural materials) can trigger concerns about the lack of intellectual property protection and can run the risk of unintentionally placing the materials in the 'public domain' from the perspective of the intellectual property system," and "may potentially . . . undercut" the intellectual property interests of the very communities "whose intangible cultural heritage is documented and made accessible" (2004: 102).

American public folklorists have much to share about our experience safeguarding and encouraging traditions, and we could benefit from greater international awareness and engagement. While UNESCO functions as a primary medium of exchange for ideas and resources about culture everywhere else in the world, American public folklore—as practiced outside of the Beltway and beyond national public media of recording and broadcast—largely exists as an archipelago of self-contained community and regional universes. Further, in a time of global communication and contact where community members are increasingly documenting themselves, and affected by worldwide forms of art, entertainment, information, and systems of economic production, our efforts may be increasingly oriented to looking at the "World in Creolisation" as Ulf Hannerz (1987, see also Baron and Cara 2003, Spitzer 2003) would have it. The implications are that rather than necessarily seeking legal or policy redress of intellectual property violations, our conjoined critical and celebratory foci may depend just as much on how communities generate new aspects of production and symbol systems that resonate within their group. Group consciousness about this process can lead to economic sustainability through cultural production and services to local and outside markets. This perspective more fully integrates economies of scale into perspectives on how cultures and communities sustain themselves by selectively retaining their traditional practices and greatest practitioners in arts and culture. It also opens up for public discussion which economic means are most appropriate to sustain a better quality of life in local cultural terms.

Communities are ever more frequently in interaction with one another and their ancestral regions and countries in our globalized world. Any American folklorist working with an immigrant community knows well how transnationalism is a major, accelerating force, serving both to safeguard older traditions and introduce new forms of popular culture through YouTube and other web sites, e-mail, DVDs, inexpensive international phone calls, and frequent air travel between the homeland and a new home in an immigrant American neighborhood.

Public folklore is an American invention, and as Barbara Kirshenblatt-Gimblett notes, for German-speaking countries there is "No German term or adequate translation for the term "public folklore. . . . It has never existed" in the form it has in the United states "nor is it likely to emerge in the foreseeable future" (2000: 1). Throughout Europe as well as on other continents, public practitioners often work in a domain wholly apart from the academy. At the 1998 symposium in Bad Homburg, Germany, "Public Folklore: Forms of Intellectual Practice in Society," Konrad Köstlin observed, in response to a paper by Robert Baron, that he and his colleagues in German-speaking countries study the institutions represented by Baron, but do not participate in them (Burkhardt-Seebass 1999, Baron 1999). In Germany, "applied folklore" carries especially negative resonances deriving from the historic relationship of German folklore studies to National Socialism. While folklorists in many countries may not speak of practicing "public folklore" as such, global implementation and operationalization of the ICH convention is engaging folklorists within and outside of the academy in many of the kinds of initiatives American public folklorists pursue.

"Applied folklore" in the U.S. has historically been associated with specific acts of social justice and other ameliorative agendas in realms like community health, economy, ecology, and education. Some applied folklorists see "public folklore" as encompassed by applied folklore and refuse to identify themselves as public folklorists, distinguishing their work by its social agenda (Payne 2004: 341). Diana Baird N'Diaye, however, suggests that public folklore employs an applied approach when supporting traditional artists in maintaining and transmitting their culture as a "means" for folklorists to "work with community members to support their efforts to use traditional knowledge to deal with practical issues effecting their lives" (1999: 94). We remain committed to the term public folklore and its larger symbolic inclusion within whole social orders across nations and the globe as well as its manifestations among specific peoples and localities. As Archie Green originally indicated in this volume, "the very word 'public' resonates positively: commonweal, general welfare, external service," as he rejects the "binary pair 'pure' and 'applied.'" Nevertheless, we are in accord with the value of the ameliorative objectives of applied folklorists, which are shared within the larger domain of public folklore.

Since the initial publication of *Public Folklore*, scholars have explored issues of mediation, representation, and dialogical approaches to engagement with communities related to the concerns of this book. Richard Kurin's *Reflections of a Culture Broker: A View from the Smithsonian* considers various examples of the work of cultural brokers, who "study, understand, and represent someone's culture (sometimes even their own) to non-specialized others

through various means and media," through representations "to some degree
. . . negotiated, dialogical, and driven by a variety of interests on behalf of
the involved parties" (1997: 19). The Smithsonian Folklife Festival (formerly
known as the Festival of American Folkllife) is viewed as a highly contested
ethnographic terrain in critical studies by other scholars.

A team of Indiana University folklorists led by Richard Bauman conducted a study of the Michigan program area at the 1987 Festival, *Reflections
on the Folklife Festival: An Ethnography of Participant Experience*, published
the same year as this volume. It looked at how participants framed the festival
through their "presentation of self, their representation of group, and in their
recreation of tradition" (1992: 61). Responding to critical analysis of the relationship of presenters to participants at the festival, the presenters and fieldworkers from Michigan discussed their curatorial choices and relationships
with participants, distinguished their role from the Smithsonian Festival's
administration, and noted in "Folk Festivals: Michigan on the Mall," a special
issue of *Folklore in Use* (1994), that the Indiana University team did not interview them.

Anthropologists Richard and Sally Price published a highly critical account of their experience as presenters of Caribbean Maroon cultural communities at the 1992 Smithsonian Festival, viewing the event as an objectification of culture—a perspective on public folklore also variously embodied
in the work of other scholars like Handler (1988) and Kirshenblatt-Gimblett
(this volume and her book *Destination Culture*, 1998). While the Prices extensively discuss their role as cultural brokers, the work lacks a certain reflexiv-
ity (and irony) about their own power and authority to interpret another's
culture as experts. In contrast, Robert Cantwell's book *Ethnomimesis* (1993)
includes reflections about his participant-observer status, in a study that explores the Smithsonian Festival's "complex traffic in representations, mediated
by guides, texts, presenters, and other agents," which he compares to tourism
while acknowledging that it provides a kind of "intimate, authentic encounter
with the other" that "recreational or commercial tourism can only promise"
(1993: 274–75). Cantwell's book is a fascinating extension of his thoughtful essay originally published in *Public Folklore*.

Perhaps owing to its budget, visibility, and enduring issues surrounding
finance, management and content, the Smithsonian Folklife Festival received
disproportionate attention in public folklore scholarship of the mid- and late
1990s, a time when scores of public folklore programs nationwide continued

to expand. While these studies were carried out by university-based scholars, public folklore practitioners generated a number of analytic, self-critical, and empirical publications about their own work. James Bau Graves's *Cultural Democracy: The Arts, Community and the Public Purpose* draws from—and contributes to—public folklore scholarship in its analysis of the give and take of collaborative programming initiatives with immigrant communities, reflections of his meditative role in producing these programs, and discussion of the interplay of the local and global. He proposes the development of initiatives "global in scope while remaining devoted to the locally specific cultural knowledge that informs traditional heritage" (2005: 188). The needs of refugee and immigrant artists were among the topics of a series of convenings and publications of the Fund for Folk Culture (available at www.folkculture. org) which also dealt with small not-for-profit traditional arts organizations, the needs of individual artists, and the interrelationships between the conservation of natural and cultural resources and its implications for sustainable livelihoods. These convenings involved scholars and practitioners from a variety of disciplines, who developed public policy recommendations which are being implemented in Fund for Folk Culture funding programs. Folk arts in education, cultural tourism, the conservation of places of local folk cultural significance, international development, marketing, and public foodways programs are among other topics of works by public folklore practitioners since the initial publication of this volume (Hufford 1994; Jones 1994; *Southern Folklore* 1992; Wells 1996, 2006).

Interest in sustaining traditional forms of expressive culture and varied communities that create and identify with forms of music, food, ritual, festival, dance, material culture, narrative, language, and other forms may be at a high point in a world where the freedom to live within the culture of a community defined by ties of family, neighborhood, ethnicity, work, and belief sometimes feels imperiled. While new communications technologies appear to contract world diversity and portend the loss of intimacy with their speed and sometimes impersonal qualities, there are also those cultural groups in places like French Louisiana, Northern New Mexico, or urban neighborhoods resisting gentrification that may purposefully use the very technologies, economies, and information that overwhelm others to reinforce cultural continuity. In the end our concern must be human agency first at the community level to advocate for appropriate culture continuity as a fundamental freedom and means to a better quality of life. Whether one is part of a community or culture newly in diaspora from a disaster or political depredations, or long-settled on a landscape imperiled by changing economies and ecologies, the possibilities of sustainable cultural diversity expressed aesthetically at special performative moments, through material creations or simply lived in the aesthetics of daily life, should be a concern of all people.

Sadly, in this very moment that folk art, folklife, folklore, and related forms of larger shared vernacular culture are seen as increasingly important by community leaders, policy makers, government agencies, private foundations, and the private sector, many colleges and universities have been less and less able to sustain folklore programs. Fewer major universities grant Ph.D.'s in folklore. A slowly growing number of MA programs produce practitioners—many of them excellent, but still far below the numbers needed to truly reflect public concern for and student interest in traditional cultures and related aesthetic forms as a means of shaping the future of human community life for the better. We applaud those discerning academic institutions, departments, and programs that have been able to bring folklore into a variety of curricular settings—American studies, anthropology, ethnic and regional studies, ethnomusicology, urban studies, and so on. We hope that nascent academic programs devoted to "public culture" and "public humanities" learning will embrace the vernacular perspectives and aesthetics that community cultures and studies of informal and intangible knowledge have to offer to society as a whole. Our desire is that this third printing of *Public Folklore* will encourage discussion about a pluralistic future where the quest for cultural continuity and creativity is framed by concern for balancing tradition and transformation in human communities worldwide.

Robert Baron, New York
Nick Spitzer, New Orleans
2007

References

American Folklore Society. 1988. *A Statement of Ethics for the American Folklore Society.* http://af snet.org/aboutAFS/ethics.cfm. First published in *AFS News* 17 (1), February 1988.

American Folklore Society. 2004. "American Folklore Society Recommendations to the WIPO Intergovernmental Committee on Intellectual Property and Genetic Resources, Traditional Knowledge and Folklore." *Journal of American Folklore* 117 (465): 296–99.

Baron, Robert. 1999. "Theorizing Public Folklore Practice—Documentation, Genres of Representation, and Everyday Competencies." *Journal of Folklore Research* 36 (2–3): 185–201.

Baron, Robert, and Ana Cara. 2003. "Introduction: Creolization and Folklore—Cultural Creativity in Process." *Journal of American Folklore* 116 (459): 4–8.

Bauman, Richard, Patricia Sawin, and Inta Gale Carpenter. 1992. *Reflections on the Folklife Festival: An Ethnography of Participant Experience.* Special Publications of the Folklore Institute. Indiana University. Special Publications, No. 2.

Burckhardt-Seebass, Christine. 1999. "The Role of Expert in Public Folklore: Response to Robert Baron." *Journal of Folklore Research* 36 (2–3): 201–5.

Cantwell, Robert. 1993. *Ethnomimesis.* Chapel Hill: University of North Carolina Press.

Graves, James Bau. 2005. *Cultural Democracy: The Arts, Community and the Public Purpose.* Urbana and Chicago: University of Illinois Press.

Hafstein, Valdimar. 2004. "The Politics of Origin: Collective Creation Revisited." *Journal of American Folklore* 117 (465): 300–315.

Handler, Richard. 1988. *Nationalism and the Politics of Culture in Quebec.* Madison: University of Wisconsin Press.

Hufford, Mary, ed. 1994. *Conserving Culture: A New Discourse on Heritage.* Urbana and Chicago: University of Illinois Press.

Hannerz, Ulf. 1987. "The World in Creolisation." *Africa* 57 (4): 546–58.

Jones, Michael Owen, ed. 1994. *Putting Folklore to Use.* Lexington: University Press of Kentucky.

Journal of Folklore Research. 2004. Special Double Issue: "Advocacy Issues in Folklore" 41 (2/3).

Kirshenblatt-Gimblett, Barbara. 1998. *Destination Culture: Tourism, Museums and Heritage.* Berkeley: University of California Press.

———. 2000. "Folklorists in Public: Reflections on Cultural Brokerage in the United States and Germany." *Journal of Folklore Research* 37 (1): 1–21.

———. 2004. "Intangible Heritage as Metacultural Production." *Museum International* 56 (1–2): 52–64.

Kurin, Richard. 1997. *Reflections of a Culture Broker: A View from the Smithsonian.* Washington: Smithsonian Institution Press.

Museum International. 2004. Special Issue: "Views and Visions of the Intangible" 56 (1–2).

N'Diaye, Diana Baird. 1999. "Public Folklore as Applied Folklore: Community Collaboration in Public Service Practice at the Smithsonian." *Journal of Applied Folklore* 4 (1): 91–114.

Oring, Elliot. 2006. "Folklore and Advocacy: A Response." *Journal of Folklore Research* 41 (2/3): 259–67.

Payne, Jessica M. 2004. "Critical Historiography of the Present: A Response to 'Looking Back, Moving Forward' by Peggy Bulger." *Journal of American Folklore* 117 (465): 337–43.

Price, Richard and Sally. 1994. *On the Mall: Presenting Maroon Tradition Bearers at the 1992 Festival of American Folklife.* Special Publications of the Folklore Institute. Indiana University. Special Publications, No. 4.

Sommers, Laurie Kay, ed. 1994. "Folk Festivals: Michigan on the Mall." *Folklore in Use: Applications in the Real World* 2 (2).

Southern Folklore. 1992. Special Issue: "Promoting Southern Cultural Heritage" 29 (3).

Spitzer, Nick. 2006. "Rebuilding the 'Land of Dreams' with Music." In *Rebuilding Urban Places after Disaster: Lessons from Hurricane Katrina,* 305–28. Edited by Eugenie L. Birch and Susan M. Wachter. Philadelphia: University of Pennsylvania Press.

———. 2004. "Monde Créole: The Cultural World of French Louisiana Creoles and the Creolization of World Cultures." *Journal of American Folklore* 116 (459): 57–72.

Wells, Patricia Atkinson, ed. 1996. *Keys to the Marketplace: Problems and Issues in Cultural and Heritage Tourism.* Enfield Lock, Middlesex, U.K.: Hisarlik Press.

———. ed. 2006. "Working for and with the Folk: Public Folklore in the Twenty-First Century." Special Issue: *Journal of American Folklore* 471 (119).

Whisnant, David. 1988. "Public Sector Folklore as Intervention: Lessons from the Past: Prospects for the Future." In *The Conservation of Culture: Folklorists and the Public Sector,* edited by Burt Feintuch, 233–47. Lexington: University Press of Kentucky.

Wendland, Wend. 2004. "Intellectual Heritage and Intellectual Property: Challenges and Future Prospects." *Museum International* 56 (1–2): 97–106.

World Intellectual Property Organization. *Legislative Texts on the Protection of Traditional Cultural Expressions (Expressions of Folklore).* http://www.wipo.int/tk/en/laws/folklore.html.

Acknowledgments

The making of this volume embodied, sometimes painfully, the conditions under which public folklorists often work. Much of our conceptualization, editing, and writing of the book occurred in stolen moments away from the everyday commitments of our work in public agencies. Midnight telephone conversations from rural motel rooms, lap-top editing on rattling Amtrak trains, napkin note-taking in sequestered corners at folk festival parties, are among the delights of the public scholar operating outside the academy. Lest we seem to suffer too much, our burden was diminished not just by the excitement of the topic, but by the many hands that have aided us. Our primary scholarly inspirations are the lives and work of Archie Green and Bess Hawes. We also owe a debt to the authors and others involved in the 1987 American Folklore Society sessions on "practice," who, although not in the volume, participate in its spirit: Hal Cannon, Susi Jones, Debora Kodish, Diana N'Diaye, and Charles Perdue. At the Smithsonian Institution Press, Daniel Goodwin encouraged this project, and Duke Johns and Tom Ireland helped guide us through the occupational folklore of publication. We are also grateful to the Smithsonian Institution's Office of Folklife Programs, for its assistance at various phases of the project. In addition to the authors, other folklorists with whom we have had fruitful discussion include Barry Ancelet, Dick Bauman, Anna Lomax Wood, Camilla Collins, Joe Hickerson, George Holt, Alan Lomax, Helen Hubbard Marr, Thomas Vennum, Jr., Joe Wilson, and Steve Zeitlin.

Fifteen years later, with this third printing, we recall the warm reception of this book by our colleagues in public folklore. It is used for many courses in folklore and its sister disciplines, and we are pleased that it has generated a more informed practice as well as critical scholarship.

The authors are deeply grateful to Craig Gill of the University Press of Mississippi for his support for the reprinting of this volume. The friendly and incisive advice of Craig and his staff enabled us to publish this book again at a highly opportune time. We thank our ever patient families with special gratitude—Lise Korson and Violet Baron; and Margaret Howze, and Perry and Gardner Spitzer.

We remember with sorrow the passing of our friend and colleague Gerald L. Davis in 1997. His important contribution to this volume endures, and we dedicate this reprinting to his memory.

Contributors

ROGER D. ABRAHAMS, Hum Rosen Professor of Folklore and Folklife, Emeritus at the University of Pennsylvania, was involved in a good number of public folklore programs and projects. These include the establishment of the American Folklife Center at the Library of Congress, the Festival of American Folklife at the Smithsonian Institution, the Folk Arts and the Interarts Programs at the National Endowment for the Arts, the East Texas Dialect Project, and the Philadelphia Folklore Project. Teaching in the folklore programs at the University of Texas and the University of Pennsylvania, he supervised at least fifteen dissertations in the general area of public folklore, including those of the editors of this volume.

ROBERT BARON is the director of the Folk Arts Program of the New York State Council on the Arts. He is a Non-Resident Fellow of the W. E. B. Du Bois Institute for African and American Research of Harvard University, and he has served as a Fulbright Senior Specialist at the University of Turku, Finland, and a past president of the Middle Atlantic Folklife Association. Baron received the Benjamin A. Botkin prize of the American Folklore Society for Outstanding Achievement in Public Folklore. As a Smithsonian Fellow in Museum Practice, he is currently engaged in a research and publication project on the idea and practice of curation in museums, with an emphasis upon public programs. A special issue of the *Journal of American Folklore* on creolization which he edited with Ana Cara will appear in an expanded form as a book. Baron received his Ph.D. in folklore and folklife from the University of Pennsylvania.

ROBERT CANTWELL is professor of American studies at the University of North Carolina–Chapel Hill. He is the author of *Bluegrass Breakdown: The Making of the Old Southern Sound* (1984); *Ethnomimesis: Folklife and the Representation of Culture* (1993); and *When We Were Good: The Folk Revival* (1996). A collection of essays on the forms of "ethnomimesis" or the culture power, is due in 2008.

GERALD L. DAVIS (1941–97), a folklorist, was professor of American studies at the University of New Mexico. Previously he was associate professor and chairperson of the Department of Africana Studies at Rutgers University. He was the author of *"I Got the Word in Me and I Can Sing It, You Know": A Study of the Performed African American Sermon* and articles on African American folklore and aesthetics. A Fellow of the American Folklore Society, he was the co-founder of the Association of African and African American folklorists and an associate editor of the *Journal of American Folklore*. At the time of his death, he was engaged in a work in progress on African American male "resocialization/re-gendering" challenging patriarchal theory constructions, a book-length study of African American folklorist Thomas W. Talley, and a field study and book project, "A Moor in the 16th Century American Southwest: Esteban Remembered in Southwest Pueblo Oral Tradition."

ARCHIE GREEN is professor emeritus of folklore at the University of Texas. A former San Francisco shipwright and union shop steward, he has published extensively in the areas of occupational folklore, labor history, labor folksong, and public folklore. He lobbied for nearly a decade for the creation of the Library of Congress's American Folklife Center. Green received his Ph.D. in folklore and folklife from the University of Pennsylvania.

JIM GRIFFITH worked until his retirement as a public folklorist for the University of Arizona in Tucson. Concentrating on the traditional cultures found in southern Arizona and Sonora, Mexico, he produced books, articles in popular and professional journals, radio and TV series, concerts, CDs, audio and videotapes, and museum exhibitions, and started the annual folklife festival "Tucson Meet Yourself," now in its thirty-fourth year. He is currently concentrating on the traditional religious art and *vaquero* (cowboy) culture of the neighboring state of Sonora, Mexico.

BESS LOMAX HAWES was director of the Folk Arts Program at the National Endowment for the Arts from 1977 to 1992. She has also served as director of the Smithsonian's Festival of American Folklife. Hawes has written about family song and play traditions and is coauthor with Bessie Jones of *Step It Down*, a collaborative study and guide to African American ritual, festival, and play traditions of the Georgia Sea Islands. Her films include *Pizza Pizza Daddy-o* and *Say, Old Man, Can You Play the Fiddle?*

BARBARA KIRSHENBLATT-GIMBLETT is university professor, professor of performance studies, and affiliated professor of Hebrew and Judaic studies at New York University, and past president of the American Folklore Society. She is currently chairing the Core Exhibition Development Team of the Museum of the History of Polish Jews, in Warsaw, Poland. Her books include *Destination Culture: Tourism, Museums, and Heritage* and *Image before My Eyes: A Photographic History of Jewish Life in Poland, 1864–1939*, with Lucjan Dobroszycki. *They Called Me Mayer July: Painted Memories of a Jewish Childhood in Poland before the Holocaust*, in collaboration with her father, Mayer Kirshenblatt, will appear in September 2007.

RICHARD KURIN is the director of the Smithsonian Center for Folklife and Cultural Heritage and also the director of Smithsonian National Programs. A former Fulbright Fellow with a Ph.D. in cultural anthropology from the University of Chicago, he is the author of *Hope Diamond: The Legendary History of a Cursed Gem, Reflections of a Cultural Broker: A View from the Smithsonian, Smithsonian Folklife Festival: Culture Of, By, and For the People*, and scores of scholarly articles. He serves on the U.S. Commission for UNESCO and is a recipient of the American Folklore Society's Botkin Prize for his work in public folklore.

ROBERT S. McCARL is professor in the Sociology Department of Boise State University. Previously, he was director of the Folk Arts Program at the Idaho Commission on the Arts. He received his doctorate in folklore from Memorial University in Newfoundland. McCarl has worked extensively with occupational groups, labor unions, and ethnic communities in the production of public folklore projects. His most recent publication is "Lessons of Work," a special issue of *Western Folklore*.

FRANK PROSCHAN is a folklorist and linguistic anthropologist specializing in mainland Southeast Asian oral traditions. Since October 2006, he has been a programme specialist in UNESCO's Intangible Cultural Heritage Section, assisting in the implementation of the 2003 Convention for the Safeguarding of the Intangible Cultural Heritage.

SUSAN ROACH is professor of English and folklorist for the Louisiana Regional Folklife Program at Louisiana Tech University, where she serves the northeast Louisiana parishes. She has been involved in a variety of research and public folklore projects, including fieldwork on north Louisiana traditions, Louisiana quilt documentation, museum exhibitions, state and national folklife festivals, and folk architecture restoration. Her exhibition catalog for the touring exhibit *On My Way: The Arts of Sarah Albritton*, received the 1999 Elli Köngas Maranda award from the American Folklore Society Women's Section. She received her doctorate in anthropology (folklore) from the University of Texas at Austin and Ph.A. and M.A. in English from the University of Arkansas.

DANIEL SHEEHY is the director of Smithsonian Folkways Recordings, director of Smithsonian Global Sound, and curator of the Smithsonian Institution's Folkways Collection. He served as director of Folk & Traditional Arts at the National Endowment for the Arts from 1992 to 2000 and as staff ethnomusicologist and assistant director from 1978 to 1992. A Fulbright-Hays scholar in Veracruz, Mexico, he earned his Ph.D. in ethnomusicology from UCLA. He served as co-editor of the *South America, Mexico, Central America, and the Caribbean* volume of the *Garland Encyclopedia of World Music* and authored *Mariachi Music in America: Experiencing Music, Expressing Culture*, published by Oxford University Press in 2006.

STEVE SIPORIN is professor of English and history (folklore) at Utah State University, where he has taught folklore classes, including Public Folklore/ Applied Folklore, for over twenty years. Previously he worked as folk arts coordinator for the Idaho Commission on the Arts and the Oregon Arts Commission. He is the author of *American Folk Masters: The National Heritage Fellows* (Abrams, 1992) and co-editor of *Worldviews and the American West: The Life of the Place Itself* (Utah State University Press, 2000). His translation of *Augusto Segre's Memories of Jewish Life: Casale Monferrato, Rome, Jerusalem, 1918–1960*, from the Italian, is due to be published in 2008 (University of Nebraska Press).

NICK SPITZER is professor of folklore and cultural conservation at the University of New Orleans, and has also served as Mellon Professor in the Humanities at Tulane University. He received his Ph.D. in anthropology from the University of Texas. A commentator and producer for ABC's *Nightline*, NPRs *All Things Considered*, and PBS's *Great Performance*, Nick also produced the ethnographic film *Zydeco: Creole Music and Culture in Rural Louisiana.* He served as founding director of the Louisiana Folklife Program, senior folklife specialist at the Smithsonian, and artistic director of the *Folk Masters* series at Carnegie Hall and Wolf Trap, and the *American Roots Independence Day* concerts broadcast from the National Mall (1992–2001).A former scholar at the School of American Research in Santa Fe and a Fellow of the American Folklore Society, Nick has received the Botkin Prize for Outstanding Achievement in Public Folklore, an ASCAP Deems Taylor Award for *American Routes*, a New Orleans Mayor's Arts Award, and was named Louisiana Humanist of the Year for cultural recovery efforts after the catastrophe of 2005. He received a Guggenheim fellowship in 2007 for work on traditional creativity in Louisiana Creole communities.

. Introduction

ROBERT BARON AND
NICHOLAS R. SPITZER

P ublic folklore is the representation and application of folk traditions in new contours and contexts within and beyond the communities in which they originated, often through the collaborative efforts of tradition bearers and folklorists or other cultural specialists. When the Cowboy Poetry Gathering is held before ten thousand people in Elko, Nevada, in the dead of winter; when several African American girls from the South Carolina Low Country are state folk arts program apprentices with a master Sea Grass basketmaker; when a scholar writes about the occupational traditions of fire fighters in the District of Columbia for colleagues and the workers themselves—all these are acts of public folklore (McCarl 1985). They involve folklorists purposefully reframing and extending tradition in collaboration with folk artists, native scholars, and other community members.

While folklore is private and intimately shared by groups in informal settings, it is also the most public of activities when used by groups to symbolize their identity to themselves and others. With the naming of "folklore" in the mid-nineteenth century and its emergence as a field of study, coincided the increasing use of folk traditions by groups to represent themselves beyond their immediate communities. Indeed, a good deal of this outside "sharing" has been done by university-based folklore scholars who have collected, analyzed, and published their findings for audiences broad and narrow.

To be a folklorist is inescapably to have one's work evaluated by some form of public. We all share our representations of folklore with others, whether culture group members, students and colleagues, or broader audiences. Being a conscious and conscientious public folklorist depends less upon employment venue than the primacy of collaboration with traditional artists and communities in the representation of their cultural expression. Public folklorists do many or all of the following over the arc of a career: research and writing to describe and interpret folk cultures; teaching students to know, respect, and further research diverse cultural expressions; producing media documents and curating exhibits and festivals that present traditional communities and the issues they face; addressing public policy and market conditions that affect access to tangible and intangible resources necessary for the sustenance of traditional culture; working with native scholars to assist groups in documenting their own cultures. All of these acts are carried out by professional folklorists who may be employed in arts councils and historic preservation commissions, hospitals and social service agencies, museums, and independent recording companies, as well as universities and colleges.

Public folklore is not, and never was, a merely vocational endeavor subordinate to the main business of folklore studies. At its best, the study of public folklore brings into high relief the issues of representation, ideology, and practice at the center of the discipline.

Yet paradoxes surround the scholarship about public representation and popular understanding of folk cultures in America. Folklore today is widely viewed as fragile, withering tradition that must be preserved from the forces of mass culture and protected within the communities from which it originates. However, many groups have constructed representations of their traditional cultural expression for public and private consumption—their folklore has never seemed stronger. In America's idealized self-image, an array of groups referred to as the "folk"—Indians, cowboys, bluesmen, mountaineers, mill workers, Cajuns, lumberjacks—have historically been used to evoke national identity in much of the twentieth century. At the same time, these groups have often been stereotyped as illiterate, backward, and marginal to the nation's progress.

Now in the waning years of the century, many Americans find themselves unbound from traditions of group, place, work, and play as never before. In the same historical moment, there are movements to rediscover cultural traditions and seek renewed identification with community. Still, some groups in America, whether new immigrants from the third world, African Americans in the Mississippi Delta, or Native American traditionalists, remain "other," the "folk"—isolated or enclaved by social and geographic factors. These groups, in varying relationships to the elusive American mainstream, may have less of an opportunity for cultural self-determination. They instead find their long-term cultural life torn asunder by rapidly changing patterns of education, economy, land use, amusement, mass media, and related forces of modernity.

Folklorists have long been concerned with the place of tradition in modern life. Contemporary public folklorists have turned this concern to activism in countering the forces that disrupt and threaten traditional cultures. This activism is centered upon working with artists and community members to develop strategies for maintaining and creatively adapting their traditions to new social circumstances. The contributors in this volume include a constellation of folklorists and ethnomusicologists engaged in discourse about and practice of public folklore. We straddle the academic, public, and private sectors of folklore. We play multiple roles as practitioners—concert producers, scholars, teachers, administrators, ethnographers, curators, and filmmakers.

The stories of our endeavors are framed by the ongoing redefinition of what constitutes the professional practice of folklore. Why and how should folk cultures be represented? Who has the authority to represent them? What are the ideologies that inform such representations? The essayists here present a variety of personal, intellectual, and programmatic responses to these questions.

Most of the essays came about as a result of a series of sessions devoted to "practice" in public folklore at the 1987 American Folklore Society (AFS) meeting in Albuquerque, New Mexico. Other essays are original contributions that resonate with and complement the themes set out at the practice sessions. These sessions provided critical reflection upon the central role of public folk cultural programming throughout the history of the discipline. Practice was seen to entail both activities carried out within academic settings and presentations to broader audiences based upon scholarly research. We sought to explore emerging paradigms of practice as integrated scholarly and public activity carried out in partnership with traditional communities.

The Albuquerque sessions dealt with the past, present, and future of public folklore. The legacy of public concern by early folklorists was examined along with the impact of the professionalization process and the purported dichotomy between the academic and public realms. Panelists considered advocacy and current methods of representing traditional arts and communities. They examined both culture-specific and comparative approaches for recontextualizing traditions. A culminating session drew together individuals concerned with public folklore from throughout the Society. It considered various dimensions of practice uniting scholarly research and public representations.

Public folklorists' concern about practice corresponds with a recent movement in the social sciences toward what anthropologist George Marcus characterizes as "free play and experimentation in the specific rendering of accounts of social life," marking a shift of concern from "high theoretical discourse" (Clifford and Marcus 1986:166–67). He continues, "The most interesting and provocative theoretical works are precisely those that point to practice." Marcus stresses the growing interest in the ethnographic method across the social sciences and humanities as the way "to evoke and represent diversity in social life—to convey the richness of experience, to probe the meaning of details of everyday life, to remember symbols and associations long forgotten." Elsewhere, James Clifford offers a practitioner's conception of ethnography as a "dialogical enterprise in which both researchers and natives are active creators, or . . . authors of cultural representations" (Clifford 1988:84).

Historically, folklorists have rarely been able to fully articulate theory based upon their practice. Yet folklore practice, the lessons of which prefigure in some measure the conclusions of these critical mavens of postmodern anthropology, has always been central rather than marginal to professional work. And *public* folklore goes a step further in having actually implemented and concretized ethnographically based, dialogically created representations of traditions and communities. We have done this in everything from museum exhibitions, folk festivals, media productions, and training programs for native scholars to the more conventional text-centered scholarly enterprise of publication.

The essays here were written at a time when the terrain of government-based public folklore was shifting. After an initial federal florescence—

marked by the commencement of the Smithsonian Institution's Festival of American Folklife in 1967, the inception of the Folk Arts Program at the National Endowment for the Arts (NEA) in 1974, and the creation in 1976 of the American Folklife Center at the Library of Congress—public folklife programming and expertise became increasingly decentralized as a national infrastructure of folk arts programs in state governments was established. Catalyzed through the grant support and developmental efforts of the NEA Folk Arts Program, the state programs further stimulated local and regional programs in both government and nonprofit organizations.

While federal folklife programs stand at a remove from communities, state and local programs are by their very nature involved with direct constituent relationships. They are more engaged in ongoing dialogues and productions with cultural groups. This has often resulted in a high level of sophistication in creating public representations of folklore. Hopefully, the 1990s will see a new, redefined leadership role in public folklore for the American Folklife Center and the Smithsonian's Office of Folklife Programs, and national initiatives will continue to emerge elsewhere in and beyond the federal government. By 1991 these included an extension of services to the field by the American Folklore Society, expansion of the policy and programming reach of the National Council for the Traditional Arts, and creation of the Fund for Folk Culture.

The writings in *Public Folklore* encompass descriptions and analyses of practice, theoretical perspectives, personal experiences, and historical revisitations of folklore studies, all through the lens of public practice. Four folklorists with long experience in academic and public realms begin the volume with reflections upon the distinctive features of public folklore and its commonalities with other dimensions of folklore practice. Roger Abrahams, Barbara Kirshenblatt-Gimblett, Archie Green, and Bess Lomax Hawes view folklore and folklore studies as essentially public by nature and thereby present primarily unitive views of the field.

Roger D. Abrahams considers commonalities and differences between public and academic practitioners of folklore. He suggests that they differ in their styles of communication, modes of presentation, and audiences. Yet commonalities are found in a shared body of materials, concern for the rights of informants, and the integrity of their cultures. Academic scholarship, like public folklore, is revealed to be subject to employment exigencies, political constraints upon intellectual freedom, and the availability of funding. Abrahams shatters the pretense that academic folklore work has proceeded within a wholly objective, disinterested framework of pure research.

Abrahams celebrates a larger mission for folklorists. In all domains of practice, they should serve as advocates for folk cultures, allied against the forces within modern civilization that devalue the lives of traditional peoples and their practices and "coopt these traditional practices for their own purposes, commercial or otherwise."

The 1988 *Journal of American Folklore* publication of Barbara Kirshenblatt-Gimblett's essay, "Mistaken Dichotomies," originally presented in the aforementioned 1987 AFS practice sessions, sparked a new intensity in public folklore discourse. This oft-cited and controversial article offers a provocative deconstruction of historic differences within the field while seeking to deny a dichotomy between "academic" and "applied" folklore. Yet it has been criticized for using language, perspectives, and examples that reify the dichotomy Kirshenblatt-Gimblett sought to erase. The article was aimed at provoking critical discourse in the field, and her academically centered, dialectical style of writing often appears to show value in seemingly contradictory positions.

Noting the "fundamentally applied character" of folklore studies, Kirshenblatt-Gimblett contends that the folklorist in the academy has a responsibility to provide critical theoretical discourse for and about public folklore practice. However, as many essays in this book show, public practice is not simply guided by academic theory, but actually may generate its own theoretical commentary about practice and representation. There is a historically rich and currently growing body of critical writing about public folklore. This is evidenced in Siporin's bibliographic essay at the end of this volume. In the context of this abundant literature, *Cultural Conservation: The Protection of Cultural Heritage in the United States*, compiled by Ormond H. Loomis for the Library of Congress (1983), critiqued at some length by Kirshenblatt-Gimblett, is a relatively inconsequential, outdated document, never widely embraced or cited by public folklorists.

Kirshenblatt-Gimblett appropriately recognizes the large role of government funding in conditioning the direction of public folklore. However, her characterization of folk arts programs' guidelines as privileging "descent" over "consent" oversimplifies the complex balance struck in supporting community members rather than folk revivalists to practice their arts. In reality, such guidelines are usually quite flexible and reflect prioritization, rather than exclusion. In one example, Kirshenblatt-Gimblett attempts to reinforce her point by constructing an example of a Peking opera apprenticeship grant application purportedly rejected because it involved a student of European descent. While activities involving revivalists have been supported by various folk arts programs, such funding has necessarily not been a priority in the face of the pressing need to sustain and perpetuate traditions within the communities from which they originate.

We find ourselves in disagreement with many other points made in the article, but we appreciate its provocative nature and the new questions it raises. It lays out the grounds of public folklore discourse in four areas: advocacy, representation, art, and cultural critique. We can trace its influence in other essays in this volume and elsewhere that take "Mistaken Dichotomies" as a point of departure.

Archie Green has had a singular influence upon contemporary folklore. The impact of his work is manifest in approaches to ideology, advocacy, and public policy that are now commonplace in the field. In his essay he limns the history of naming our practice, and the title of this volume reflects his conceptualization of the field.

Green describes how public folklore has viewed itself over time. He views Kirshenblatt-Gimblett's and others' use of the term "applied folklore" as symptomatic of the "false dichotomy between pure academicians [who] conduct research" and the "polluting applicators [who] apply their seers' findings." Like Abrahams, he suggests that "the commonality within the discipline of folklore far outweighs the separate settings within which we work."

Bess Lomax Hawes's essay, taken from her American Folklore Society Centennial address, draws upon a life in public folklore, outlining the totality of folklore practice. She considers fieldwork as the key defining feature of the profession. Fieldwork and other forms of research are at the foundation of public presentation (exhibitions, recordings, publications, teaching). Like many other authors in the volume, she views involvements with artists as enduring personal and professional commitments, which cannot be evaded. A deeply ingrained sense of social justice informs her understanding of power relationships to informants, a perspective rooted in a New Deal heritage. Her longstanding calls for "payback" to individuals and communities prefigure current concerns for reciprocity and dialogical engagement with the subjects of research. Speaking to the most prevalent employment situation of contemporary folklorists, Hawes recognizes that administrative skills are essential to our practice.

Reflexive accounts of public folklore practice, often in an experimental mode, constitute the middle section of this book. The writers recount their methods and metaphors of collaboration with traditional artists and communities in producing public representations of culture.

Nicholas R. Spitzer explores characteristics of several genres of folklore representation through personal accounts and analyses of ethnographically based recordings, radio programs, festivals, and concert productions. His essay suggests that our practice is at its best when we engage in dialogues subject to public community scrutiny, an approach that is both personally and socially transformative. He questions the appropriateness of cultural *conservation* as an all-inclusive metaphor for our practice. With its referent to human management of nature, it is ill-suited to the emergent and dialogical characteristics of our work. Spitzer suggests cultural *conversation* as a more apt metaphor for folklorists in that it embraces the realities of culture change and creativity within and between the communities with which we work. However, naturalistic metaphors are pragmatically useful within the larger dialogue, particularly where there is a close interlock of natural and cultural systems.

African American public folklore foregrounds issues of insider and outsider relationships. Outsiders have historically dominated the mediation of this culture's folklore to the public. Gerald L. Davis advocates the development of a truly African American aesthetic in scholarship and media representation—one that responds to a higher emic standard—while acknowledging the potential for conflict between obligations to one's discipline and one's cultural community. Although African American folklore is "ineffable" and "ineluctable" to many outsider scholars, insider folklorists cannot escape the discomfiting gaze of their community as they attempt to use personal knowledge to render the emic integrity of an event. Davis also considers the revelatory and transformative power of media as a research tool and genre of representation. He calls for a visual mode of hard-edged research narrative and reporting through documentary media, questioning the folkloristic validity of cinema verité and belletristic visual narrative.

Robert S. McCarl is also confronted by community scrutiny, here as a cultural outsider and a man working with women in three separate communities. His power to control the content and character of representations of folk practitioners from Indian craftswomen to fire fighters is measured against his accountability to the artists, their communities, and a broader public.

McCarl speaks more unabashedly about "power" than folklorists usually do. Power informs the relationships between public folklorists and their subjects of research and presentation. While power often resides in the hands of the folklorist, the relationships should be dialogical in the mutual shaping of representations. McCarl reflects upon the personally trying and ironic role of public folklorists who may commodify art and objectify artists while attempting to responsibly represent their traditions.

Frank Proschan's narrative about his experiences in assisting an ailing Kmhmu elder and his family is a specific example of public folklore as social intervention. Folklorists have long agonized over how and whether folklorists should intervene. Proschan suggests that appropriate intervention, along with being an ethical and moral imperative, also produces cultural insights and personal satisfactions not otherwise attainable in conventional field research.

Susan Roach examines her role as an agent of change in the work and career of African American walking-stick carver, David Allen. Like Proschan, the personal dimensions of her relationship are inextricably bound to her professional role as a folklorist. Like McCarl, she is concerned that the local, regional, and national visibility that she affords an artist induces changes in the form, style, content, and materials of his work—changes that may seem inconsistent with traditionality. The elevation of Allen's self-esteem and the broadening horizons of his life and economic opportunity seem to allay Roach's fears.

One special occasion in David Allen's public recognition was his participation at the Smithsonian's Festival of American Folklife. For a quarter of a century, this event has been a highly visible public representation of folk artists and cultures. It has hosted thousands of artists over the years for annual audiences of several hundred thousand. The festival occupies a unique place among public folklore events by virtue of its large budget and staff and symbol-laden location on the National Mall. Its modes of presentation of folk artists and its role as a training ground for large numbers of folklorists and community scholars have often been seen as normative. Critical reflection upon the festival in recent years has centered on issues of ideology, authenticity, cultural mediation, and recontextualization.

Richard Kurin, an anthropologist who heads the Smithsonian's Office of Folklife Programs, contrasts the Smithsonian's approach to producing a folk festival with that of the Soviet Union's Cultural Ministry. Kurin characterizes the Soviet International Folklore Festival as highly theatricalized and shaped by state ideology; in contrast, the Festival of American Folklife is seen as presenting ethnographically grounded, interpretively framed, and nonstylized community-based performance. The two festivals are clearly underpinned by national ideologies, although the ideology of the

American festival is elusive and difficult to adduce. Much of the article is about the encounter between two official bureaucratic cultures and how they consciously and unconsciously mediate their representations of folk culture. It is apparent that authenticity has different meanings in Soviet and American societies. For the Soviets, authentic traditions appear to be those that are performed "correctly," that is, in accordance with values of state authorities concerning artistic production.

American public folklorists also struggle with received notions of authenticity. "Authentic" traditions in the United States are often presented in a manner considered to be faithful to their practice within idealized, enclaved folk communities. Yet, the syncretic and emergent qualities of American folk cultures, influenced by complex interethnic relationships and popular culture, are often excluded in public presentation.

Where Kurin considers the mediating role of national institutions as presenters of authentic traditions, Daniel Sheehy focuses on the actual needs of performers in presenting their recontextualized traditions for new audiences. Drawing on examples from his work assisting Latino musicians at performances in staged festival settings, he critically reflects upon both failed and successful collaborations. Folk musicians are often poorly equipped to respond to the expectations and cultural understandings of audiences outside of their own communities. Sheehy contends that folklorists and ethnomusicologists can empower traditional artists to shape the expressive techniques and technical requirements of the proscenium stage to their own culture's aesthetic criteria. But to do this we must understand the conventions of the stage and work knowledgeably with technical specialists in such areas as stage design, lighting, and sound reinforcement. Sheehy calls for cultural specialists to act in a curatorial role by framing performances that interpret traditions and enable artists to present themselves to their best advantage.

The primary employment venue for professional folklorists today is outside of the academy. However, current academic training leaves most folklorists ill-equipped to meet the multiple professional responsibilities and technical skills needed for public folklore practice. We must confront the impact of inadequate academic preparation for public folklore practice. Jim Griffith outlines the academic training and experiential preparation needed for such practice. He suggests that it is essential for the public folklorist to be thoroughly versed in the literature of the discipline and grounded in ethnographic knowledge of the art forms and communities with which he or she works. Griffith introduces the concept of stylistic and repertoire literacy, which entails the ability to make informed aesthetic choices based upon broad experience with traditional art forms. The folklorist must have "heard a lot of talk, listened to a lot of music, looked at a lot of art, and retained what he or she has experienced" to achieve stylistic and repertoire literacy.

Specific technical and administrative skills are also needed by the compleat folklorist. Documentary and presentational arts require mastery of the medium, including competence in operating equipment, or balanced collaboration with other professionals such as audio recordists, sound technicians, videographers, photographers, and exhibit designers. Immersion in the world of administrative work also awaits the newly hired public folklorist. Griffith urges that certain skills be introduced to the public folklore student to prepare him or her for the administrative demands of professional practice. These skills include public speaking and writing, grant writing and evaluation, and communication with varied audiences both inside and outside the workplace. Many public folklorists also shape public policy by virtue of their official capacities in government agencies. It is rather daunting to consider the multiple arenas in which we work and multiple languages needed to negotiate between agencies and communities.

The volume closes with a re-visioning of the history of folklore studies, which foregrounds its public character. While a public dimension marked the discipline even in its prehistory, this aspect had been largely written out of the standard history of folklore studies. With the burgeoning of public folklore activity in the last decade, a new historical consciousness has emerged through which we are rediscovering our lineages in both familiar and unsuspected places. The final four essays provide a rough chronology, opening up the intellectual history of public folklore practice. These articles encompass nineteenth-century literary essayists, world fairs and ethnological exhibitions, the emergence of folklore as an autonomous academic discipline, folklife festivals, and the literature of modern public folklore.

Roger Abrahams turns to the literary and intellectual milieu surrounding the establishment of the American Folklore Society in considering the foundations of public folklore in this country. He reminds us that public folklore includes not only festivals, exhibitions, and media productions of today, but also has historically included essayists, journalists, and social critics. He stresses a common purpose among American folklorists that lies in our active engagement with the traditions of living communities rather than with survivals, and an ongoing commitment to egalitarian ideals. Traditional culture provided an alternative to the social dislocation and deracination engendered by the Industrial Revolution. This intellectual reaction to modernity continues in our increasingly alienated, posttechnological society. As have many of the writers here, Abrahams emphasizes our ongoing commitment to unrepresented people. He notes, "There was from the outset a concern with the ways in which traditional communities might be dignified through receiving ardent notice by folklorists." Abrahams observes that folklore, unlike other disciplines that emerged in the same era, never became well established within the academy. He suggests that this marginal status has both reflected and affected the public character of folklore studies.

Robert Cantwell explores the multiple antecedents of contemporary folk festivals in a historical analysis that traces an arc of nineteenth- and twentieth-century sources. They include the colonialist ideology of world expositions, natural history exhibitions, native poets such as Walt Whitman, minstrelsy, folklore in popular magazines, historical pageants, settlement houses, depression-era federal arts projects, and the folksong revival.

Cantwell's journey through multifarious representations of American folk culture brings him to an analysis of the Smithsonian's Festival of American Folklife. He poses fundamental questions about the festival as a mode of cultural representation and the ideology that informs it. Cantwell explores how and for whom the festival determines the cultures it is to represent. The Smithsonian festival creates a temporary community that attempts to serve as a refuge from divisions of social class and cultural difference. The quest for community is a central if not fully recognized theme in American life. Cantwell shows that this need for community is most acute among the festival's producers, who create this special world and receive as much or more benefit from it as participants and audiences. Yet the festival satisfies this yearning for community in an artificially created context. Cantwell contends that folk festivals should aim toward the restoration of community in an enduring way.

An intellectual history of public folklore can be shaped by a sweeping view of social and artistic movements such as Robert Cantwell offers, as well as the particular focus Robert Baron brings to discourse about public folklore in the early postwar period. Our received idea of the development of folklore studies as an autonomous academic discipline neglects a serious interest in public folklore expressed by scholars at the time. We experience a shock of recognition reading folklorists of four decades ago on such timely issues as revivalism, folk arts in education, the impact of technology upon oral tradition, and if and how folklore should be recontextualized. We hear Stith Thompson questioning whether traditions no longer viable in folk communities should be artificially preserved. Alan Lomax contends that folklorists have a moral imperative to aggressively counter the forces that crowd out and suppress folk traditions.

Baron is one of several contributors in the volume who recast the conflicting views of Richard Dorson and Benjamin Botkin regarding the mission of the folklorist. During the 1950s, Botkin increasingly became a lone voice as public folklore was marginalized from the mainstream of the discipline. Baron points out that the integration of public and academic folklore continues to be a problematic and enduring legacy.

In his survey of the literature of public folklore, Steve Siporin clearly demonstrates a profusion of scholarship. He and other writers in this section belie those who assert that public folklore lacks a critical literature. Siporin demarcates particular areas of intellectual focus, with special attention to the public folklore boom of the last two decades. He reminds us of the historic relationship of public folklore to nationalism and colonialism, and the need to be versed in scholarship about public folklore from other countries. He also notes that the florescence of recent scholarship on material culture can be tied to widespread involvement in exhibitions and documentation of folk art and artists in publicly funded projects.

It is evident from Siporin's bibliographic overview that public folklorists are making an increasingly profound contribution to folklore studies. Public folklore has a surprisingly long history of responding to the deracinating forces of modernity. It offers ethnographically grounded programs that stimulate critical reflection upon issues of representation, ideology, and practice that face the social sciences and humanities today. It is our hope that *Public Folklore* contributes to reinvigorating our own discipline and related fields as well as serving the interests of traditional artists and communities.

REFERENCES

Clifford, James. 1988. *The Predicament of Culture.* Cambridge: Harvard University Press.

Clifford, James, and George E. Marcus. 1986. *Writing Culture.* Berkeley: University of California Press.

Loomis, Ormond H. 1983. *Cultural Conservation: The Protection of Cultural Heritage in the United States.* Washington, D.C.: American Folklife Center, Library of Congress.

McCarl, Robert S. 1985. *The District of Columbia Fire Fighter's Project: A Case Study in Occupational Folklife.* Smithsonian Folklife Studies 4. Washington, D.C.: Smithsonian Institution Press.

Part 1

Reflections and
Directions

The Public, the Folklorist, and the Public Folklorist

ROGER D. ABRAHAMS

How did folklorists arrive at the point at which academic and public folklore came to be distinguished? The question is significant insofar as the distinction is often made qualitatively as well as descriptively. Academic folklorists, from such a bias, have the luxury of dealing with the materials of tradition objectively, dispassionately, even scientifically. By implication, then, those who work directly with the general public debase the work to present it in a manner understandable to an audience that does not share the common culture of the performers. The elitist implications of viewing the problem in this way are obvious enough. The problems are compounded for the academic folklorists and for any other guardians of generalized notions of the authentic when funding resources for public presentation are in the commercial or governmental sectors of the economy.

Public folklorists, from this perspective, are influenced by the politics and economics of necessity. That this begs a number of embarrassing ques-

324. Calavera of Don Quixote

tions is self-evident. For as the Major Domo of Scientific Comparatism of this generation, Alan Dundes, has pointed out in his brilliant "The Fabrication of Fakelore," the primary documents out of which scientific folklorists developed, Grimm's fairy tales and the *Kalevala*, were literary confections developed for both commercial and political purposes (Dundes 1989). Dundes suggests that rather than simply rejecting out of hand the projects of such contaminating forces, it is incumbent on folklorists to study such cultural phenomena ourselves. "Cast not the first stone," he implies.

Further, this move on Dundes's part develops from the increasing recognition by scientifically trained folklorists that folklore as a concept is a complex cultural fiction. An ironic feature of the development of this fiction is that the idea of the *folk* historically arose at that very time in which agricultural peoples left the countryside, forced out by enclosure laws, taken into the armies of empire, or lured by the big city.

Those who maintained the old traditions shared in the simpler and more "natural" and commonsensical, human-scaled endeavor. The founders of the discipline thought of the folk as those who lived close to the soil, or in some other harmonious endeavor arising from the rhythms of the seasons. Arguing in this direction, they were overtly attempting to recover the traditions in which an ancient agricultural set of practices was maintained.

Thus was folklore seen to be situated within a natural landscape, consisting of the embodiments of knowledge derived from the experience of living in a specific place over a period of time. Folklore, thereby, was taken to be an element of the vernacular genius of a locale. Folklorists, from such a perspective, are agents of that special mode of nationalism called "romantic." In this set of notions, vernacular language is regarded as representing the spirit of a place by those operating out of the centers of political control attempting to assert some kind of hegemony. The folk, then, the bearers of the vernacular, are used as a point of "natural" reference. Folklore study begins with collections of materials in the vernacular and a time

Public folklore as a noble quest—at once idealistic and pragmatic. This image of Don Quixote was created by the Mexican artist José Guadalupe Posada in the style of *Día de los muertos* (Day of the Dead) skeleton. Such images often include playful, inversive depictions of historical and political figures.

when vernacularity is used in opposition to the international languages of power (such as Latin), which are not the language of the country dweller, or most urbanites for that matter.

One of the most compelling ironies of folklore study is that the major device against which folklorists have appeared to be reacting, the printing press, is responsible for the very possibility of recognizing the existence of folklore. For the printing press made it possible to conceive of a literature in the vernacular as a set of devices that might be used to bring together a people in the face of the forces of a power-elite that communicated in the international language of Latin. Many of the items earliest committed to script or print are texts of stories, proverbs, and traditional practices of health maintenance, including superstitions. These documents were prepared, to be sure, for those concerned with the failure of memory in the face of the superior capabilities of storage and retrieval of knowledge implicit in the media of script and print. However, the documents came to be employed as a way of knitting together a community that communicated primarily in the vernacular. To be sure, there are major differences between public and academic folklorists, distinctions seen in the strategies each develops to represent client populations and their traditions. Insofar as both academic and public folklorists labor in state or national governmentally sponsored institutions, they operate under similar constraints. To be sure, most public folklorists encounter a kind of programmatic surveillance not experienced by most academics. But there are professional rewards for presentations based on research whether in the form of print or film or museum exhibition, whether one works in the academy or for a public agency. To presume that the basis of such rewards differs in the academy and affects the ways in which the research itself is carried out, is to be naive in the extreme.

Research in any sector emerges from the political concerns of the researcher as they are conditioned by the medium chosen, the audience sought for, and the recognition that those judging will bring their own political, social, and cultural perspective to bear in judging the effectiveness of the presentation. In establishing priorities for areas to be researched, and in developing methods of collecting, the researcher is concerned with the range of possible messages that will finally be conveyed by the report of the work. Folklorists addressing themselves to students and those seeing their clientage in terms of the larger public share a very great deal in terms of professional standards and the intellectual positions from which they instigate their presentations and analyses. Both academic and public folklorists, after all, call for their audiences to recognize the same range of materials, the same needs of the bearers of these traditions, and to fight the same battles vis-à-vis official, institutional, or power-invested purveyors of culture.

The major difference, of course, is that in the academy, the researcher can be assured that those who judge the work will carry many of the same attitudes toward the excesses of the modern world. In this regard, our enemies remain the same—those who would take the folklore away from the folk for their own political or economic gain. This is especially reprehensible, of course, when the evidences of these traditions are employed as means of discriminating against or in some other way coopting the stylized product while disempowering the very bearers of the traditions being presented.

Nevertheless, a distinction continues to be made within the profession between academic and public folklore work. Historically, such differences arose out of the discourse on professionalism as carried out in the last half of the nineteenth century. At that point there was a move on the part of all disciplines to distinguish serious and full-time professional work from that carried out by people of leisure, doing the work for fun—those who came to be called amateurs. Professionalism came to be identified with controlled and reasoned scientific representation.

However, in the twentieth century, science has become more and more identified with the removed precincts of the ivory tower or the research laboratory. Thus, the word "academic" is substituted for "scientific" in many disciplines in addition to folklore, and "applied," "clinical," or "practical" have become the terms by which those schooled in the academy use their training with a public clientele.

The distinction between "pure" and "applied," as between that of scholarly and public presentation of research, is useful only insofar as it recognizes that each client population brings common expectations into the encounter.[1] Those making scholarly arguments tailor their presentations with an assumption of audience knowledge of how these materials were studied in the past and what modes of explanation have been imposed upon them. The public presenter can presume much less about audience knowledge or appropriate modes of presentation. They must develop strategies of presentation by which professional insights are conveyed without recourse to the shorthand communication made possible through the development of professional jargon. Indeed, professional language of all sorts must be questioned before it is employed in public presentations. The distinction between academic (or scholarly) and public presentations designates not the depth or intensity of the research effort but the discourse system used to report the research.

We can point with some pride to the fact that the American folklore movement has progressed beyond the class bias of the study as it was practiced in Europe. The first two generations of American folklorists found a set of traditions that were maintained in the present, in need of quick collection and study. Constance Rourke perhaps said it most simply in her remarkable "A Note on Folklore," written in the late 1920s: "Probably we are still a folk—an imperfectly formed folk—rather than a schooled and civilized people" (Rourke 1942:244).

A half century later, after working in the field and library, Richard M. Dorson made a similar discovery when he found folklore in the cities. He proclaimed a new world of folkloristics, which was to take contemporary life into consideration. Having discovered folklore in the city, in his work in Gary, Indiana, he expounds that American folklorists now found themselves licensed to carry out fieldwork anywhere they chose, not just in some remote village in the highlands or the islands. If he does not go as far as Newell or Rourke in lining whom he would include under the rubric of appropriate people from whom to collect, after all, the wheel, as we all find at some point in our lives, is very difficult to reimagine. Says Dorson: " 'Folk' need not apply exclusively to country folk, but rather signifies anonymous masses of tradition-oriented people." He continues, calling forth a litany of those who have addressed the definitional problem in the remote past: "If for 'popular antiquities' we substitute 'oral culture' or 'traditional culture' or 'unofficial culture' we strike closer to the true concerns of folklorists" (Dorson 1978:23).

Dorson, ever the academic scientist, nevertheless responded deeply to the messages conveyed by his students and colleagues telling him that there remained peoples and experiences "out there in real life" that reflected the continuing life of traditional peoples who had remained underrepresented in both our political and our scholarly lives. To these students, who were answering the social call of the 1960s, studying village folk and bringing them together with other such peoples through comparative academic research was not enough. To those, like Dorson, who feel that power resides in the "pure" search for knowledge, the doubting-Thomas populist in our profession has responded that no knowledge is of value unless it has been tested by experience. The development of public folklorists out of the academic environment represents, then, only the latest compromise reached by the scientists and general public; for in this latest round of discussions, the agencies dealing with the public have called for the kind of professional certification bestowed only by the academy, that is, the Ph.D. or its equivalent.

In addition to locating the work of public-sector folklorists within the historical discourse on American folklore, it seems useful to get beyond the terms of the discourse as it was set out on the one hand by hard-headed academicians like Dorson and his followers, on the other by those of what one might call a "popularist" bent (trying to duck the uncontrollable connotations of both "populist" and "popular"), such as Benjamin Botkin. As more graduates of our folklore programs take employment outside of the academy, the stature of the early folklorists addressing themselves directly to the public has been raised, and conversely, the ivory-tower orientation of the scientific folklorist has come to be judged as naive from a political as well as presentational perspective.

In the process, Ben Botkin has been revealed as a visionary, Dick Dorson as a reactionary (Jackson 1986; Widner 1986). Neither would be comfortable with such a designation, and neither deserves the sobriquets. They shared a vision of finding the richness of American spirit in the lore of the many peoples found here. They went to school, in the main, to the same teachers and called upon similar resources in their studies of American life. Both sought to put their finger on the pulse of America through their researches. Both were essentially administrators and library scholars who occasionally, and not that successfully, made forays into the field.

Dorson and Botkin differed in important respects. Botkin decided to operate outside the university setting. Dorson spent his life solidifying the position of folklore in institutions of higher education in the United States and throughout the world. He equated scholarly technique with scientific accuracy, thereby condemning out of hand most contemporary records of tradition that did not use the apparatus of international folklore scholarship. But he began as an Americanist, and it was only because of his reaction to the cooptation of the folk by one politically doctrinaire group or another that he resorted to the removed scientific apparatus of the historic-geographic distributionalists. Dorson was disquieted and then horrified, as Botkin was not, by the uses made of folk productions by the members of the Popular Front in the 1930s and early 1940s, equating them with the perversions of the German right and the Russian left.

Most important for our present purposes, the way in which Botkin and Dorson limned the field of folklore was a response to the moral imperatives of their time. They were representative folklorists of their era. The opposition between them was an interesting reflection of the moral, social, and especially the political climate of the times in which they worked; it deserves to be understood in these terms.[2]

I dwell on this because the distinction between academic and public-sector folklorists arose from the strange hot- and cold-war politics of culture before and after World War II.[3] By that time, scientific folklore had become equated with the authenticity of traditions. By extension, science and academic status carried with it the power to determine what was truly traditional and what was not. All of this was predicated on some ideal of items of performance being recorded in sufficient numbers of versions that they contained within themselves evidence of requisite oral transmission that authenticity could be presumed.

There were some adequate reasons why a firm distinction between authentic traditions and spurious ones had to be made. Much devastation had been visited on human populations in which national traditions had been implicated in the process by which war and genocide were rationalized. In the late 1940s and throughout the 1950s, the very term "folklore" had come to be regarded as suspect by the American government because it had been contaminated by the agents of nationalism and internationalism who wished to align their political causes with the folk, the people. Folklorists within the academy were tarred with the same brush as those in America who had been attempting to use the traditions of the people as a way of forging an international egalitarian ideology. Moreover, Nazis and Stalinists alike had coopted the idea of folklore for their own perverted ideological purposes. Thus, the uses of folklore for overt political purposes came to be identified, along with all commercial uses of folklore, as producing spurious forms of presentation and celebration: that is, that abomination, "fakelore."

Lest I give the impression that these were more contentious times than our own, there was one factor that brought together everyone in the suspicious 1950s, as it had in the earliest days of the profession: the vitality of the material itself, as it was to be collected. The best way of checking on the authenticity of the lore being presented was to collect and verify the lore with reference to its bearers. This was the science of folklore as it had been envisaged by the designers of the American Folklore Society, and it remains the primary objective in the field to this day. Contention arises more on the form than the content the reports of these collections should take.

By the mid-1950s, the question of authenticity was sufficiently heated because of the political abuses of the materials of tradition that the science of folklore itself demanded the lore be collected by the same people who subjected it to formulation in media of record. This perspective was arrived at by both MacEdward Leach at Pennsylvania and Richard M. Dorson at Indiana. They were not alone, of course. Alan Lomax, for instance, had been engaged in collection as well as analytic and media presentation for nearly twenty years before Dorson and Leach began their own collecting.

But we are in another era now, one in which the idea of disinterested scholarship is no longer much mentioned. For since the 1960s it has become the accepted position that all scholarship arises from the investigator's sociopolitical concerns. From this perspective, the very notion of scholarly distance is itself a political position, one that arises from any vision of a rational (or at least a rationalizable) society that has a heavy investment in mystifying scientific inquiry to obtain professional status for one or another of "the disciplines."

The very idea of a public folklore agenda attacks the necessity for such a set of scholarly presuppositions concerning the primacy of scientific investigation. The public folklore movement recognizes the existence of various publics and their need to obtain cultural equity in a situation in which various sectors of society are contending for scarce resources—resources that are not simply financial. Public folklorists are involved in assisting groups to receive the kind of attention that encourages respectful attention within their own community and beyond—though as some of my colleagues in public folklore point out repeatedly, there is still a bias in the field toward studying groups that have resisted technological advance or who designate themselves as outsiders.

The work of public folklorists, then, is not less objective or scientific than that of academic folklorists. Rather, there is an open admission on the part of all engaged in field collecting that research agendae are dictated by those members of their constituency who seem underrepresented, and therefore disempowered. Fieldwork is carried out with the same sense of need for recognizing that lore should be reported as performed in its "natural context." Increasingly, the key to accurate presentation has resided in the willingness of the folklorist to search out the ways in which the performers themselves (and other members of the performing community) understand and respond to the experience. Folklorist presenters are then charged with explaining the performance from the perspective of the performer and their usual audience.

This intercessory role was taken early in the folksong revival by folklorists such as Alan Lomax, Kenneth Goldstein, D. K. Wilgus, and Ralph Rinzler. They carried out significant fieldwork and brought their best informants onto the concert stages at Newport, the Philadelphia Folk Festival, and by the late 1960s, the Festival of American Folklife at the Smithsonian Institution. They had developed a vision of the possibilities inherent in such public presentations through their earlier work producing commercial phonograph recordings. Indeed, in many ways the work of such folklorist-collector-presenters prefigured the present activities of public folklorists. While the activities of collector-presenters, as well as others who have sought to serve as cultural mediators, needs some celebration, it would not be fitting to represent these endeavors as selfless and magnanimous. For all of us involved have managed interesting and even lucrative careers for ourselves predicated on our presumed "insiders' knowledge" of native traditions.

The primary despoilers of folk culture still are the power brokers who too often forget about life-quality considerations in working out their engineering plans, their business mergers, their multinational takeovers. But the enemies also include those who would coopt these traditional practices for their own purposes, commercial or otherwise. Dorson's blast at fakelorists as those who would pervert the living traditions of others for commercial purposes should include those among us who publish that we may not perish without taking our informants' concerns into consideration in this publication. Our livelihoods are too obviously bound up with discovering and then bringing to public notice the stars of the folk festival and folksong recording industry. We cannot afford to cast stones at the hucksters who convert traditional styles and products into the saleable commodity. We must also continue to make a surveillance of our own more "scientific" practices, attempting to make sure that we aim toward a position of ever-greater cultural equity for all peoples.

NOTES

1. Barbara Kirshenblatt-Gimblett calls attention to this set of distinctions, noting their inappropriateness today (1988 and this volume).

2. See Georges 1989. For commentary on Botkin, see Hirsch 1987.

3. For a fine study of how the Popular Front operated culturally, and in relation to popular uses of folksong, see Lieberman 1989.

REFERENCES

Dorson, Richard M. 1978. "Folklore in the Modern World." In *Folklore and the Modern World*, edited by Richard M. Dorson. The Hague: Mouton.

Dundes, Alan. 1989. "The Fabrication of Fakelore." In *Folklore Matters*, pp. 40–56. Knoxville: University of Tennessee.

Georges, Robert A., ed. 1989. *Richard M. Dorson's Views and Works: An Assessment.* Special issue, *Journal of Folklore Research* 26 (1).

Hirsch, Gerald. 1987. "Folklore in the Making: B. A. Botkin." *Journal of American Folklore* 100 (395): 3–38.

Jackson, Bruce. 1986. "Ben Botkin." *New York Folklore* 12 (3–4): 23–32.

Kirshenblatt-Gimblett, Barbara. 1988. "Mistaken Dichotomies." *Journal of American Folklore* 101: 140–55.

Lieberman, Robbie. 1989. *"My Song Is My Weapon": People's Songs, American Communism, and the Politics of Culture, 1930–1950.* Urbana: University of Illinois Press.

Rourke, Constance. 1942. "A Note on Folklore." In *The Roots of American Culture*, edited by Van Wyck Brooks. New York: Harcourt, Brace and World.

Widner, Ronna Lee. 1986. "Lore for the Folk: Benjamin A. Botkin and the Development of Folklore Scholarship in America." *New York Folklore* 12: 1–22.

Mistaken
Dichotomies

BARBARA
KIRSHENBLATT-GIMBLETT

Even as the American Folklore Society nears its centennial, folklore as an autonomous academic discipline within the American university is less than forty years old. Much of the American debate over "applied folklore" in the period after World War II must therefore be examined in relation to a young academic discipline on the defensive. As Richard M. Dorson fought to establish folklore as an autonomous academic discipline, the discourse on applied folklore entered a new phase, for never before, not even during the activism of the New Deal, did the public sector confront so vociferous an opponent.

Dorson was opposed equally to "popularization," which he saw as largely commercial and exploitative, and to "applied folklore," which he credited with the nobler aim of making the world a better place. For Dorson, popularization produced what he dubbed "fakelore": The hapless consumer was duped into thinking he was getting the genuine folklore article, and folklore as an academic discipline was discredited with each new trea-

Oral Tradition!

CLIFF LANDIS
Sculpture FIRST NEW YORK
MAN SHOW

ALIGATORS DON'T
EAT
POTATO CHIPS.

sury and literary tall tale (Dorson 1971a, 1972). Though applied folklorists were better intended, they were, in Dorson's view, ill-equipped for the task. Further, applied folklore only diverted the professional folklorist from the call of pure scholarship, and the young discipline needed all the talent it could find. In other words, because both popularization and applied folklore blurred the boundaries of pure folklore scholarship and siphoned off intellectual talent, they threatened the fledgling academic discipline.

Ironically, folklore succeeded so well as a discipline that within about twenty years, by the 1970s, the academy had produced more professionals than it could absorb. How, in good faith, could university programs continue to train folklorists who would never work in their profession? As universities began to suffer from the shifting demographics of the 1970s and 1980s, how would these folklore programs stay afloat if they could not compete effectively for students? The tables had turned. The enemy became the solution. Applied folklore was now in the interests of the discipline, rather than in competition with it. The public sector would, and did, absorb the surplus of professional folklorists.

To frame the history of applied folklore in America in the postwar period in this way is not cynical. Rather, it highlights several ironies. First, applied folklore has been instrumental in the academic discipline's consolidation of its own power, initially as a negative raison d'être for the academic discipline, a position for the academy to resist in the struggle for disciplinary self-definition, and later as a way to enlarge the scope of the profession and absorb the surplus of professionals. Second, as folklore was establishing itself in the American university, the American folksong revival was gathering momentum in the coffeehouse, on the concert stage, and in the recording studio. Though maligned as a threat to the academic discipline, the folksong revival created an appetite for formal folklore training: many individuals who would later achieve prominence as academic folklorists began as revivalists (Jackson 1985). Third, even as academic folklore programs depended on the public sector both to recruit students and to absorb graduates, the academy (and I speak here of departments and curricula, not individual folklorists) continued to disassociate itself from applied folklore.

By disassociation, I mean that academic folklore programs have tended

Graffiti in New York City, 1983. Photo by Barbara Kirshenblatt-Gimblett.

to maintain the dichotomy between pure and applied folklore and consistently refused to examine their own essentially and inescapably applied character: the folkloristic enterprise is not and cannot be beyond ideology, national political interests, and economic concerns. Furthermore, while sending their graduates into the applied sector, folklore programs have unwittingly trivialized this arena by treating it as a largely practical, rather than intellectual, undertaking: With recent and important exceptions, folklorists are not being trained specifically for the public sector. By training, I do not mean learning how to write a press release, lobby politicians for money, or run a festival, though these are all essential skills, but rather acquiring a critical knowledge of the history of the field and its essentially applied character.

Nor has the public sector really entered the intellectual life of the discipline, whether as a subject in its own right or as integral to the entire conception and history of the field. Recent reassessments of Benjamin Botkin's career and the growing interest in New Deal folklorists suggest that here, too, there are important exceptions. We have much to learn from European, and particularly, German folklorists, who have lately proposed that *Volkskunde* be turned into an "applied cultural science" (Dow and Lixfeld 1986:2) and are now confronting the painful subject of *Volkskunde* and national socialism (Dow 1987; Gerndt 1987).

The centrality of the issues raised by applied folklore would become clearer if the academic discipline as it is practiced in America would systematically examine the ideological and economic bases of its own practice, as a discourse and as a profession. In an effort to stimulate such examination, the following discussion focuses on four areas of concern: advocacy, representation, art, and critical discourse.

ADVOCACY

Advocacy can distort inquiry, whether in the academy or in the public sector. In campaigning for folklore as a discipline, Dorson discredited popularization and applied folklore and failed to investigate folklore in the public sector as a phenomenon in its own right. An interchange of great potential intellectual interest was thereby reduced to polemic, vituperation, and personal attack. For someone so interested in the relation of American folklore to American history and civilization, an approach like Eric Hobsbawm and Terence Ranger's *Invention of Tradition* (1983), which analyzes the historical formation of "invented" traditions and the role of folklorists in this process, would have carried the debate beyond exposé and defamation to a more reflexive consideration of American folklore as a discipline. Such an approach might have illuminated how the academy claims for itself the authority to represent America to itself "in its most traditionalist form" (Hall 1981:230).

For their part, folklorists working in the public sector are often so overextended and so dependent on fickle government funding that they lose sight of the larger enterprise—the emancipatory potential of folklore as praxis, that is, how what we do as folklorists can be of socially redeeming value in ways that go beyond celebration. Indeed, dependence on government funding shapes the language of advocacy and blunts its critical potential. All the more reason to see such documents as *Cultural Conservation: The Protection of Cultural Heritage in the United States* (Loomis 1983) for what they are—affirmations of heritage.[1] However well intended they may be, documents like this one neither address the root causes of the marginalization of particular groups and cultural practices, nor examine the assumptions and potential consequences of legislation and regulation of cultural practice. These dramatize the need for a critical discourse that is independent of advocacy. The academy could fill that need. Stimulating critical discourse is a vital role for the academy to play. This is the appropriate training for those who would work in the public sector.

REPRESENTATION

Anthropologists speak of their discipline as facing a crisis of representation. Though they locate this crisis in ethnography as a text-making activity, they have extended the discussion to museums, world's fairs, and tourism. Recent expressions of this concern included the Representations Symposium, organized by the Museum of Mankind in London during the spring of 1985; the recent series in Stuttgart of exhibitions and catalogues on the theme, "Exotic Worlds, European Fantasies" (Pollig, Schlichtenmayer, and Baur-Burkarth 1987); and the conference on the poetics and politics of representation in museums convened by the Smithsonian Institution and Rockefeller Foundation in the fall of 1988 (Karp and Lavine 1991).

These programs grow in part out of the work of such scholars as Johannes Fabian (1983), James Clifford and George E. Marcus (1986),

Michel Foucault (1970, 1980), and Pierre Bourdieu (1984). Their publications illuminate the representational practices not only of anthropology, but also, by extension, of folklore—these practices include the denial of coevalness or shared time, the pastoral allegory of cultural loss and folkloristic rescue, the rhetoric of authenticity, the objectification of culture, and the power inherent in the act of representing others.

To paraphrase Castoriadis, folklorists do not discover, they constitute; and the relation of what they constitute to the "real" is not one of verification. In this sense, folklorists, and anthropologists, may be said to "invent" culture (Wagner 1981). Or, as Hermann Bausinger formulates the problem: "Whoever plays 'real folk culture' off against folklorism thereby closes the circle in which folk culture is forced to mutate into folklorism" (1986:114). Distinctions between genuine folklore, on the one hand, and fakelore, revivalism, and folklorism, on the other, are worth reexamining in this light.

Edward Said's notion of orientalism takes this perspective a step further and offers a paradigm for folklore and related disciplines: "Orientalism responded more to the culture that produced it than to its putative object, which was also created by the West. The history of Orientalism has both an internal consistency and a highly articulated set of relationships to the dominant culture surrounding it" (Said 1978:22). These statements remind us that folklorists, like other professionals, are an elite; their knowledge is a source of power; and like orientalism, the study of folklore is "a mode of discourse with supporting institutions, vocabulary [and] scholarship" (Said 1978:2). The academic folklorist generally appears as author, editor, or compiler, holds the copyright, and collects the royalties on folklore collections he or she publishes. In a scathing attack on these practices, Gershon Legman concludes: "And the owners of folklore—God bless us all—now turn out to be the folklorists who collect and print it, generally on government and university grants; but who did not create it, who are as a matter of fact, forbidden by the rules of the game even to try to create it, and who—one ventures to say—bloodywell cannot create it" (1964b:521).

Claims of ownership are also made by political entities. As Kathleen Verdery (1987), Michael Herzfeld (1982), and Benedict Anderson (1983) have shown so vividly, the history of folkloristics and applied folklore cannot be separated from the formation of nationalism as an ideology and the relation of that ideology to the political process of state formation. The history of the discipline of folklore in Europe and America is largely a commentary on the tensions between national identity and state building.

What colonialism is to the history of anthropology, nationalism is to the study of folklore. We have yet to explore what may be called the political economy of the folkloristic sign—that is, how our work in the public sector contributes to the discourse on peoplehood and nationality, recast in the American democratic context as ethnicity, as unity in diversity. The debates on what is American about American folklore and Dorson's contribution to this discourse are worth reviewing in this context.

The many brochures and booklets emanating from the graduate folklore programs and folklife festivals around the country reveal the internal consistency of this discourse, the relationships with supporting institutions (universities, arts councils, crafts associations, museums, historical societies), and the extent to which the folklore enterprise is a product of dominant cultural interests, however enlightened and well-intentioned. The alliance between the institutions of "dominant cultural production" and communities whose endangered heritage we strive to protect is a tricky one. Recent studies that shed light on these alliances include Douglas Cole's *Captured Heritage: The Scramble for Northwest Coast Artifacts* (1985) and Karen Duffek's study of the contemporary revival of Northwest Coast Indian art (1983).

Historians such as Michael Wallace have exposed the ideology of many American history museums, and in so doing reveal that most of them were "constructed by members of dominant classes, and embodied interpretations that supported their sponsors' privileged positions" (Wallace 1981:63). Yet folklorists continue to cite colonial Williamsburg and related projects as exemplary, without consideration of such issues (Loomis 1983:3). This lack of critical perspective is disappointing, though not surprising, considering that we regularly review books, films, and records in the pages of our professional journals, but with the recent exception of the *Journal of American Folklore*, not exhibitions and other public-sector programs.

Following Stuart Hall (1981:234), we might consider the opposition of folklore/not folklore, not as a descriptive problem or matter of coming up with the right inventory of cultural forms, but rather in terms of the "forces and relations which sustain the distinction, the difference" between what counts as a genuine tradition, a revival, fakelore, or elite culture. Hall suggests that the categories tend to remain, though the inventories change, and that institutions such as universities, museums, and arts councils play a crucial role in maintaining the distinctions: "The important fact, then, is not a mere descriptive inventory—which may have the negative effect of freezing popular culture into some timeless descriptive mould—but the relations of power which are constantly punctuating and dividing the domain of culture into its preferred and its residual categories."

In the work of Stuart Hall (1981), Raymond Williams (1977), and other British social theorists, culture is a battlefield where the struggle over meaning and value affects what will count as folklore and what not, what will enter the great tradition and what not: "Educational and cultural institutions, along with the many positive things they do, also help to discipline and police this boundary" (Hall 1981:236). We would do well to examine our role in this disciplining process, and the danger of what Hall calls self-enclosed approaches, which "valuing 'tradition' for its own sake, and treating it in an ahistorical manner, analyze cultural forms as if they contained within themselves from their moment of origin, some fixed and unchanging meaning or value" (1981:237). With this formulation in mind, consider the following statement in *Cultural Conservation*, which I take to be a representative document, since it is a response from the American Folklife Center at the Library of Congress to a request from the Congress:

> The people of the United States benefit from canoe design, lacrosse, and coyote tales; bluegrass music, dinner-on-the-grounds, and clogging; blues music, strip quilts, and cumulative tales. Confucian and Taoist philosophy, ginseng medication, and chow mein; *tamburitza* bands, hewed-log building techniques, and *beseda* costumes; *santos, salsa* music, and buckaroo horse handling and gear. (Loomis 1983:11)

Such lists are essentially definitional exercises—they use what Hayden White (1978) has characterized as the paratactic mode of scholarship. Like the third-person ethnography, lists and collections obscure the hand that shapes the representation. They create the illusion of genuine, which is to say, unmediated, folklore. Dorson's polemic against fakelore might best be seen as a way of claiming for the academy the power to authenticate, to determine what is genuine. The pertinent question becomes: How do some representations become authoritative?

ART

In the sometimes acrimonious debates between folklorists and American folk art historians over the nature of "folk art," struggle for authority focuses around issues of how the material designated "folk art" should be defined, studied, and presented. In recent American folklore theory, particularly in what is known as the performance approach, the discipline has undergone a radical aesthetic recasting, in which folklore is characterized as artistic communication in small groups (Ben-Amos 1972), "artistic action in social life" (Bauman 1977:vii), and aesthetics of everyday life (Kirshenblatt-Gimblett 1983), to cite but three examples. This aestheticizing of the discipline is expressed in the public sector by the term "folk arts," which is emphatically in the plural, to signal a clear separation from "folk art" as defined by American folk art historians. At the same time, folklorists have also stressed the importance of cultural context and indigenous categories and standards, information that is available in abundance, because folklorists generally work with living people. Attention to context and native categories are hallmarks of public-sector folklore projects.

In contrast, American folk art historians have constituted folk art as a branch of art history by redrawing the boundaries of what may be considered art and by referring the new categories of folk art to those of the fine and decorative arts. Defined as having been produced *outside* the academy and art world, folk art is thereby assimilated into both arenas, whether as a subject for study or as a commodity for the art market. Often, little if anything is known about the maker of the object, its function and immediate cultural context. The objects are usually old, the makers long dead. Typically, exhibitions of American folk art feature the autonomous art object, uncluttered by distracting contextual information.

American folk art so defined is thus an aesthetic category deriving not from the objects, their makers, or their consumers, but from the historical avant-garde, who relativized the concept of art by exposing the historical formation and institutional character of the autonomous aesthetic object (Bürger 1984). It is now a commonplace that American folk art was "discovered" and institutionalized as part of the art world by avant-garde artists, dealers, galleries, and modern art museums during the 1920s and 1930s (Rumford 1980; Vlach 1985). What Jean Lipman and Alice Winchester (1974:11) have called "the triumph of a new taste and a new way of seeing" gave us American folk art and signaled that the revolution was not in the objects but in our categories. As Virginia Dominguez (1986:554) has written of ethnological collections, "everything about the collection itself—the way the objects were collected, why they were collected, and how and why they get displayed—points to us." This statement applies equally to folklore and folk art collections.

Many American folk art historians still deny the notion that folk art is an artifact of the discipline and insist instead that folk art is a given in the world. Consider the proposal in the most recent issue of *The Clarion*, a handsome magazine published by the Museum of American Folk Art, that "folk art" serve as an "umbrella concept" for many kinds of objects, because the term would, "over time, allow material to define itself" (Kogan 1987:72), or the statement that "the spirit of folk art . . . makes it resistant to definition and to being put into an academic discipline" (Apfelbaum 1987:31). Such abdications of intellectual responsibility actually leave the task of definition to the market, which misses no opportunity to define and incorporate new categories of saleable items.

Sociologist Howard S. Becker has argued persuasively that the determination of what is art resides not in "the work but in the ability of an art world to accept it and its maker" (1982:227). Paid advertisements in *The Clarion*, which read like a burgeoning lexicon of what may be subsumed under the folk art umbrella, bear out Becker's proposition. Dealers announce "art" (painting, sculpture, and other genres are specified), which they variously describe as folk, primitive, outsider, naive, popular, self-taught, visionary, tramp, country, ethnic, etc. They also offer craft (baskets, pottery, and other types of objects are identified), Americana, antiques, decorative art, eccentric artifacts, relics, and collectibles.

No matter how disinterested the motive, scholarship is implicated in the folk art world by helping to extend the range of what may be studied and acquired, creating the language for talking about the material, authenticating the objects in question, and increasing their commercial value through the very art of documentation. The stakes rise each time objects are exhibited and written about, each time they are acquired or deaccessioned by a museum or prominent private collector and recirculated via the auction house or gallery. As American folk art historians turn increasingly to living folk artists, the commercial exploitation of the artists themselves becomes a very pressing issue and one that folk art scholars have yet to address adequately (Hitt 1987).

Ironically, while both academic and applied folklorists resist the prevailing American folk art paradigm, they too are implicated ineluctably in the folk art world. Folklorists have been instrumental in encouraging arts endowments and councils at the federal and state level to hire folklorists and to establish folk arts divisions and programs. They depend on arts organizations for funding and venues. Consequently, folklorists in the public sector often have to define what they present as art: the NEA Folk Arts Division, for example, explains that "the term *folk arts* refers to the traditional patterned artistic expressions which have developed through time within the many subgroups of our larger society. Folk arts include music, dance, song, poetry, narrative, oratory, handcrafts, and ritual" (Coe 1977:92). While utilizing an enlarged view of folklore as "artistic action in social life" to justify support for a broad range of projects, folklorists use a narrow definition of folk art to reject much that the folk art historians subsume under the "folk art umbrella."

Unlike the classical subjects of art history, much that is called American folk art has historically not been created in the context of an art world, and is appealing for just this reason: such objects seem "to spring out of nowhere" (Becker 1982:264). As a result, what have come to be known as memory paintings, naive art, and outsider art fail to meet the criteria of traditionality that folklorists associate with folklore. They are "too personal." They are not communal enough, as the very choice of terminology suggests—"naive," "self-taught," "outsider." Having invented their own versions of "tradition" and "heritage," folklorists have drawn and policed boundaries that, until recently, have left to the American folk art specialists what folklore as a discipline has not been able to assimilate.

Memory painters, for example, proudly take credit for their personal discovery of a medium and form for recasting their lives: They have forged distinctly individual solutions to common needs. And for reasons that folklorists are at a loss to explain, these individual solutions have a lot in common. Paradoxically, while folklorists have typically studied precisely the kinds of subjects immortalized by the elderly in their memory projects—folkways of a bygone era—folklorists have had difficulty assimilating the memory objects themselves, though this is changing. A pioneering exhibition such as *The Grand Generation: Memory, Mastery, Legacy* (Hufford, Hunt, and Zeitlin 1987) reveals memory projects (not just paintings, but also miniatures and models) to be indigenous modes of life review that reveal much about the social construction of the self through time and the transformation of experience through materials ready to hand. Such insights have the potential to reshape the boundaries not only of the folklore discipline, by creating a theoretical necessity for the inclusion of such objects in the study of folklore, but also of the field of American folk art history, by extending the analysis of such objects beyond strictly aesthetic considerations (Kirshenblatt-Gimblett 1987).

Until this potential is realized, much that has been put forward as folk art by American folk art historians will continue to be rejected by folklorists for not being *folk* and by segments of the art establishment for not being *art*. Falling between the cracks within federal and state arts agencies, where it becomes more difficult to get funding, many American folk art projects will continue to depend for support on a network of collectors and dealers, corporations and business interests. This trend runs against the grain of folklorists who uphold an ideology of resisting commodification and who condemn both elitist appropriations of folk art and irresponsible popularization, on the grounds of exploitation.

In part, the tension between American folk art historians and folklorists may be summed up in the failure of the materials netted under the rubric of folk art to resist commodification, which, of course, is not a failure of the objects but of those who deal with them. In this and other respects, folklorists are also implicated in the modernist project, as characterized by Fredric Jameson: "Modernism conceives of its formal vocation to the resistance to commodity form, *not* to be a commodity, to devise an aesthetic language incapable of offering commodity satisfaction, and resistant to instrumentalization" (Jameson 1981:134–35). While the American folk art field appears to encourage the commercial expansion of the folk art market, folklorists, who are most at home in the nonprofit sector, have resisted this process. Some have gone so far as to define folklore as "noncommercial" (Wilson and Udall 1982:13) and to justify paying little if anything to traditional performers on this ground, a practice Wilson and Udall deplore. Another double bind emerges: Not to pay fair market value is to exploit traditional artists, but to commercialize exchange is to risk the depletion of value.

Consistent with these concerns, folklorists have worked to increase support for folk art*s*, broadly defined, within federal and state funding agencies. Further, they have struggled with the wrenching problem of how to intervene responsibly in the folk art market in order to protect the interests of the artists, a problem the American folk art historians could ignore so long as the artists were dead (Hitt 1987). At the same time, folklorists have often encountered within arts endowments and councils resistance to folklife projects, on the grounds that the material to be presented is not art or does not meet certain aesthetic standards.

Neither the folklorists nor the American folk art historians are in the clear. Both camps, by aestheticizing folklore, are in danger of ignoring that which the establishment does not count as art and will not fund. Both take the risk of depoliticizing the material they study and exhibit by valorizing an aesthetics of marginalization. Willingly or not, both contribute to the rampant commodification of culture.[2] To paraphrase Deborah Silverman, the line between custodians of culture and cultural cannibals is blurred; the museum and the department store become extensions of each other—folk art is produced for a growing and ever more distant market, designs are licensed, and replicas are mass produced. This process may be characterized as the "annexing of museum culture for marketing" (Silverman 1986:19).

CULTURAL CRITIQUE

Is applied folklore in danger of becoming our intellectual midden, basing practice on outmoded concepts? Or will the public sector challenge the received wisdom of the academy? After all, applied folklore is not just a matter of practical, ethical, political, and economic issues (as if this were not enough). Folklore in the public sector also has its own intellectual tradition, the history of which remains to be written. Some important beginnings have been made: David Whisnant's *All That Is Native and Fine* (1983) is exemplary. In a word, applied folklore has the potential to offer a critical perspective on the entire discipline.

As for the academy, will we descent into what German folklorist Dieter Kramer has dubbed the "meaningless administering of a traditional subject without any obligations" (Kramer 1986:42)? Or will we examine our own ideological structures and representational practices? How long will we follow Dorson's lead, with its venerable roots in Enlightenment optimism, that the pursuit of pure knowledge would solve all problems? ("By teaching, studying, collecting, and writing about folklore, the scholarly folklorist is making a noble contribution to man's knowledge of man" [Dorson 1971b:41].) When will we act on Kramer's assertion that "pure science is an alibi for the status quo" (1986:44)?

The history of folklore as a field is inextricably intertwined with nationalism, which is nowhere clearer today than in the public sector, where dependence on government funds has evoked a distinctive nationalistic discourse—unity in diversity—without a critical reconsideration of the phrase. What are the contours of the pluralism and unity we so often assert but seldom explore? Diversity is not a solution to all of our problems: Too often it is a way to mask inequity and conflict and evade more challenging approaches to our material. The public sector has tended to embrace received notions of ethnicity and ethnic group, of heritage and tradition, without considering the historical formation of these notions in the postwar American context.

Even more troubling, a recent critique points out that such ideas privilege descent over consent (Sollers 1986). All the assertions of how diversity protects freedom and choice notwithstanding, there are unexamined assumptions here about heritage as birthright and inheritance. Where do freedom and choice figure? The right to say, "No, I will not claim my heritage."? This was the battle that was fought in America before World War II—the right not to identify or be identified. But, with regard to what one does claim, "descent" still plays a decisive role in our formulations of heritage.

One of the most poignant examples of the problems of descent is a grant proposal to support apprenticeships to a Peking opera master in New York City. By the master's account, the proposal was turned down because the apprentices were of European rather than Chinese descent: During a demonstration of Peking opera that featured his students, the master explained to the audience that he once had two Chinese-American students in his group, but they gave up the training after two years because their parents encouraged them to attend the university and succeed in well-paying professions. The Euro-American students had persisted despite parental objections and at considerable personal sacrifice, and were the only ones willing to make the commitment necessary to master this art. In his view, Euro-Americans would carry the tradition until such time as future generations of Chinese-American youths were willing to take it up again. What he did not say is that students, whatever their origins, are also vital to the survival of the master.

The master's assessment is consistent with the policy of numerous agencies, though these agencies have on occasion funded apprentices whose cultural backgrounds are different from the master's. For example, the guidelines issued by the Folk Arts Program at the National Endowment for the Arts state: "The particular ways these artistic traditions are expressed serve to identify and symbolize the group that *originated* them" (Folk Arts Program Description 1981:1, emphasis mine). The guidelines speak of "sharing the same ethnic heritage," "arts that have endured through several generations," and "authenticity of the practitioners of these arts." The Folk

Arts Program at the New York State Council for the Arts, one of the largest and most innovative such programs at the state level, "strives to sustain traditions as they are rooted in particular traditional communities" (New York State Council for the Arts Program Guidelines 1987:47). NYSCA Folk Arts "stresses support for projects involving individual folk artists whose involvement with a tradition stems from their community membership or direct participation in a specific tradition, as distinguished from revivalists. Revivalists are artists who interpret and revive the traditions for which they are outsiders." The guidelines go on to indicate that "projects which include revivalists as presenters and collaborators with traditional folk artists are, however, eligible for support from the Folk Arts Program," and that revivalists may seek support from other divisions of the council. Examples from many other funding agencies could be cited.

The distinction between traditional and revival performers has long informed public-sector folklore; during the 1930s, for example, Sarah Gertrude Knott distinguished "survival" from "revival" at the National Folk Festivals she organized (Wilson and Udall 1982:7). Because the term "folk" has been used so indiscriminately, some folklorists prefer to speak of "traditional" arts: they argue that "an authentic folk artist seldom uses such a term [folk artist] in describing himself" and note, in contrast, that revivalists use the term "folk" very freely (Wilson and Udall 1982:182). In their handbook for organizing folk festivals, Wilson and Udall offer an elaborate taxonomy of performers on a continuum from the most to the least traditional (1982:20–22). Two decades earlier, Gershon Legman (1964a) had identified the distinguishing characteristics not only of "fake folk-singers," but also of "fake folklorists."

There are no easy answers to how priorities should be set, particularly given that folk arts, as defined here, have only recently achieved recognition as a separate program within funding agencies and competed for limited resources. Such guidelines express the desire to identify and strengthen the work of traditional artists, who struggle, and not always successfully, to keep going in the face of a powerful culture industry, to which revivalists generally have easier access. Such guidelines also express a tension between a proprietary approach to folk traditions (the first priority is to support those to whom the traditions "belong" by right of heritage) and the notion that folk arts belong to everyone. This tension underlies the dual aims of so many folk arts funding programs: namely, to strengthen traditions within a particular community and make them visible beyond that community, a special concern when spending the taxpayer's dollar. The NEA Folk Arts

Program's goals "to help enrich the lives of all Americans by making more visible the sophistication, vivacity, and meaningfulness of our multicultural heritage" (Folk Arts Program Description 81/82 1981:3) has an unintended consequence—funding supports insiders to do and outsiders to watch. Our heritage is "multicultural" only insofar as we are allowed to watch what others do, to consume what others produce.

Other questions pertain to the style and tenor of public-sector folklore. Lobbying for funding contributes to a consensual and celebratory view of folklore, which is intensified by the media we use—festivals, which by their nature are celebratory; museums, which inevitably enshrine and valorize; and mass media, which bring publicity, celebrity, and money. And perhaps most important, our celebrations of heritage have profound implications for the implicit primacy we thereby give to descent, to the inheritance of culture, and to the status quo.

German folklorists know all too well that folkloristics has often been "an applied science in the service of the state" (Dow and Lixfeld 1986:8). And we have seen where arguments based on descent can lead. British social theorists have offered important alternative perspectives on folklore as the site of resistance to the centralization of power, whether in the culture industry or in other institutions. We need to be more aware in our work that the very forces that overpowered traditional cultures return in a new guise to redeem through cultural conservation what was lost through land treaties, slavery, missionizing, gentrification, suburbanization of the rural landscape, assimilatory educational practices, and related forces. Without such consciousness, applied folklore plays into the notion that "folklorism is an aesthetic compensation for economic backwardness" (Jeggle and Korff 1986:136).

Cultural objectification, which is at the heart of what we do, is a complicated process with unpredictable results, one of which is the canonization of particular traditions, individuals, and forms (Handler 1984). There is a reciprocity that must be accounted for: "The observed object changes during and because of observation" (Scharfe 1986:90). Enshrinement, the result of much public-sector work, also changes that which is enshrined. This is what several German folklorists have characterized as the folklorism effect. Here too there is an important cooperative role for the academy in relation to applied folklore—an ethnographic approach to the public sector itself and to the impact of particular projects and activities on those involved.

CONCLUSION

Perhaps the split between theory and practice, the academy and the public sector, is a peculiarly American problem and one not limited to folklore. An American interviewer once asked Umberto Eco how he reconciled his work as a scholar and university professor with his journalistic activities, to which Eco answered:

> This habit is common to all European intellectuals, in Germany, France, Spain, and, naturally, Italy: all countries where a scholar or scientist often feels required to speak out in the papers, to comment, if only from the point of view of his own interests and special field, on events that concern all citizens. And I added, somewhat maliciously, that if there was any problem with this it was not my problem as a European intellectual; it was more a problem of American intellectuals, who live in a country where the division of labor between university professors and militant intellectuals is much more strict than in our countries. (Eco 1986:ix–x)

The time has come for folklorists to reassess their division of labor, to re-examine the split between the academic and applied traditions, and to close it.

NOTES

A shorter form of this article was presented at the forum "Practice—Public Sector Folklore in Retrospect," during the 1987 American Folklore Society meetings in Albuquerque. The forum was part of a series of sessions organized by Robert Baron and Nicholas Spitzer to address the subject of folklore in the public sector. I am indebted to Robert Baron, who over the years has stimulated me to think about many of these issues, and to Edward M. Bruner, Shalom Staub, and Steven Zeitlin for a lively and ongoing dialogue.

1. See also Lauri Honko's reports on the UNESCO Committee of Governmental Experts on the Safeguarding of Folklife during the 1980s in *NIF Newsletter*, published by the Nordic Institute of Folklore in Turku, Finland.

2. One can only hope that lessons will be learned from the commercialization of the South Street Seaport Museum complex in Manhattan. A provocative recent example of highly sophisticated efforts to develop the cultural industry of a city is the Lowell Cultural Plan in Massachusetts, which incorporates "community arts" and "folklife."

REFERENCES

Anderson, Benedict. 1983. *Imagined Communities*. London: Verso.

Apfelbaum, Ben. 1987. "Spirited Debate." *The Clarion* 12 (4):29–31.

Bauman, Richard. 1977. *Verbal Art As Performance*. Rowley, Massachusetts: Newbury House Publishers.

Bausinger, Hermann. 1986. "Toward a Critique of Folklorism Criticism." In Dow and Lixfeld (1986:113–23). Bloomington: Indiana University Press.

Becker, Howard S. 1982. *Art Worlds*. Berkeley: University of California Press.

Ben-Amos, Dan. 1972. "Toward a Definition of Folklore in Context." In *Toward New Perspectives in Folklore*, edited by Americo Paredes and Richard Bauman. Publications of the American Folklore Society, Bibliographic and Special Series, vol. 23, pp. 3–15. Austin: University of Texas Press.

Bourdieu, Pierre. 1984. *Distinction: A Social Critique of the Judgement of Taste*. Translated by Richard Nice. Cambridge: Harvard University Press.

Bürger, Peter. 1984. *Theory of the Avant-Garde*. Translated by Michael Shaw. Minneapolis: University of Minnesota Press.

Clifford, James, and George E. Marcus, eds. 1986. *Writing Culture: The Poetics and Politics of Ethnography*. Berkeley: University of California Press.

Coe, Linda. comp. 1977. *Folklife and the Federal Government: A Guide to Activities, Resources, Funds, and Services*. Washington, D.C.: American Folklife Center.

Cole, Douglas. 1985. *Captured Heritage: The Scramble for Northwest Coast Artifacts*. Seattle: University of Washington Press.

Dominguez, Virginia R. 1986. "The Marketing of Heritage." *American Ethnologist* 13:546–55.

Dorson, Richard M. 1971a. "Fakelore." In *American Folklore and the Historian*, pp. 3–14. Chicago: University of Chicago Press.

———. 1971b. "Applied Folklore." In *Papers on Applied Folklore*, edited by Dick Sweterlitsch, pp. 40–42. *Folklore Forum*, Bibliographic and Special Studies, no. 8.

———. 1972. "The Academic Future of Folklore." In *Folklore: Selected Essays*, pp. 295–304. Bloomington: Indiana University Press.

Dow, James R. 1987. "German *Volkskunde* and National Socialism." *Journal of American Folklore* 100:300–304.

Dow, James R., and Hannjost Lixfeld, eds. 1986. *German Volkskunde: A Decade of Theoretical Confrontation, Debate, and Reorientation (1967–1977)*. Bloomington: Indiana University Press.

Duffek, Karen. 1983. " 'Authenticity' and the Contemporary Northwest Coast Indian Art Market." *BC [British Columbia] Studies* 57:99–111.

Eco, Umberto. 1986. "Preface to the American Edition." In *Travels in Hyperreality: Essays*, translated by William Weaver. San Diego: Harcourt Brace Jovanovich.

Fabian, Johannes. 1983. *Time and the Other: How Anthropology Makes Its Object*. New York: Columbia University Press.

Folk Arts Program Description 81/82. 1981. Washington, D.C.: National Endowment for the Arts.

Foucault, Michel. 1970. *The Order of Things: An Archeology of the Human Sciences.* New York: Random House.

———. 1980. *Power/Knowledge: Selected Interviews and Other Writings.* Edited by Colin Gordon. Translated by Colin Gordon et al. New York: Pantheon Books.

Gerndt, Helde, ed. 1987. *Volkskunde und Nationalsozialismus: Referate und Diskussionen einer Tagung der Deutschen Gesellschaft für Volkskunde.* München: München Vereinigun für Volkskunde.

Hall, Stuart. 1981. "Notes on Deconstructing 'the Popular.' " In *People's History and Socialist Theory,* edited by Raphael Samuel, pp. 227–40. London: Routledge & Kegan Paul.

Handler, Richard. 1984. "On Sociocultural Discontinuity: Nationalism and Objectification in Quebec." *Current Anthropology* 25:55–71.

Herzfeld, Michael. 1982. *Ours Once More: Folklore, Ideology, and the Making of Modern Greece.* Austin: University of Texas Press.

Hitt, Jack. 1987. "The Selling of Howard Finster: When a Naive Folk Artist Becomes the Darling of the Art World. Who Profits?" *Southern Magazine* 2 (2):52–59, 91.

Hobsbawm, Eric, and Terence Ranger, eds. 1983. *The Invention of Tradition.* Cambridge: University of Cambridge Press.

Hufford, Mary, Marjorie Hunt, and Steven Zeitlin. 1987. *The Grand Generation: Memory, Mastery, Legacy.* Washington, D.C.: Smithsonian Institution Traveling Exhibition Service and Office of Folklife Programs, in association with University of Washington Press (Seattle).

Jackson, Bruce. 1985. "The Folksong Revival." *New York Folklore* 11:195–203.

Jameson, Fredric. 1981. "Reification and Utopia in Mass Culture." *Social Text* 1:130–48.

Jeggle, Utz, and Gottfried Koriff. 1986. "On the Development of the Zillertal Regional Character: A Contribution to Cultural Economics." In Dow and Lixfeld (1986:124–39).

Karp, Ivan, and Steven D. Lavine, eds. 1991. *Exhibiting Cultures: The Poetics and Politics of Museum Display.* Washington, D.C.: Smithsonian Institution.

Kirshenblatt-Gimblett, Barbara. 1983. "The Future of Folklore Studies in America: The Urban Frontier." *Folklore Forum* 16:175–234.

———. 1987. "Introduction." In *The Grand Generation: Memory, Mastery, Legacy,* edited by Mary Hufford, Marjorie Hunt, and Steven Zeitlin, pp. 12–15. Washington, D.C., and Seattle: Smithsonian Institution and University of Washington Press.

Kogan, Lee. 1987. Review of Claudine Weatherford. *The Art of Queena Stovall: Images of Country Life. The Clarion* 12 (4):72, 74.

Kramer, Dieter. 1986. "Who Benefits from Folklore?" In Dow and Lixfeld (1986:41–53).

Legman, Gershon. 1964a. Folksongs, Fakelore, and Cash. In *The Horn Book: Studies in Erotic Folklore and Bibliography*, pp. 494–504. New Hyde Park, New York: University Books.

Lipman, Jean, and Alice Winchester. 1974. *The Flowering of American Folk Art: 1776–1876.* New York: Viking Press.

Loomis, Ormond H. 1983. *Cultural Conservation: The Protection of Heritage in the United States.* Washington, D.C.: Library of Congress.

New York State Council for the Arts Program Guidelines: 1987/88. 1987. New York: New York State Council for the Arts.

Pollig, Hermann, Susanne Schlichtenmayer, and Gertrud Baur-Burkarth, eds. 1987. *Exotische Welten, Europäische Phantasien.* Edition Cantz. Stuttgart: Institut für Auslandsbeziehungen and Württembergischer Kunstverein.

Rumford, Beatrix T. 1980. "Uncommon Art of the Common People: A Review of Trends in the Collecting and Exhibiting of Folk Art." In *Perspectives on American Folk Art*, edited by Ian M. G. Quimby and Scott T. Swank, pp. 13–53. New York: Norton.

Said, Edward W. 1978. *Orientalism.* New York: Random House.

Scharfe, Martin. 1986. "Scholarship Visualized: On the Exhibitions at the Ludwig-Uhland-Institut." In Dow and Lixfeld (1986:89–96).

Silverman, Deborah. 1986. *Selling Culture: Bloomingdale's, Diana Vreeland, and the New Aristocracy of Taste in Reagan's America.* New York: Pantheon Books.

Sollers, Werner. 1986. *Beyond Ethnicity: Consent and Descent in American Culture.* New York: Oxford University Press.

Verdery, Kathleen. 1987. Personal communication.

Vlach, John Michael. 1985. "Holger Cahill as Folklorist." *Journal of American Folklore* 98 (388):148–62.

Wagner, Roy. 1981. *The Invention of Culture.* Rev. and exp. ed. Chicago: University of Chicago Press.

Wallace, Michael. 1981. "Visiting the Past: History Museums in the United States." *Radical History Review* 25:63–96.

Whisnant, David. 1983. *All That Is Native and Fine: The Politics of Culture in an Appalachian Region.* Chapel Hill: University of North Carolina Press.

White, Hayden. 1978. *Tropics of Discourse.* Baltimore: Johns Hopkins University Press.

Williams, Raymond. 1977. *Marxism and Literature.* London: Oxford University Press.

Wilson, Joe, and Lee Udall. 1982. *Folk Festivals: A Handbook for Organization and Management.* Knoxville: University of Tennessee Press.

Public Folklore's Name

A Partisan's Notes

ARCHIE GREEN

The days slip into months, the years into decades. No longer do I venture with notebook or tape recorder to snare a song, to track a story. From time to time, young colleagues visit with cassette and camera. They ask variously about lobbying, labor lore, graphic art, discography, or vernacular music. I welcome such queries, but after each session, I find myself concerned with matters of memory and rationalization, hindsight and partisanship. How does one sequence thoughts as words flow endlessly into the little cassette's mechanism?

Writing offers some chance at control—one selects a rhetorical style or seeks a structured pattern. By contrast, I leave taping periods discontented with flamboyant language or dramatic mode. Surely, a paper on the new rubric, "public folklore," presents an opportunity to join recollection and research, to bring together the immediacy of an interviewer's presence and the perspective of time. Here, I gather a few personal impressions of public folklore's naming process, supplementing memory with reading. In this

writing act, the Pequod seems to sail from Nantucket to the San Francisco waterfront. My fellow shipwrights measure the vessel's worth.

During the past decade, the paired terms "public-sector folklore" and "public-sector folklorist" have gained currency as descriptive both of a field of activity and of a professional calling. In the main, these terms have supplanted earlier labels such as "applied folklore" and "applied folklorist." New names point to various public places of work—bureau, museum, park, agency—and to professional jurisdiction.

I do not know who first voiced "public-sector folklore" to categorize employment status or to designate a field of engagement. My memory of this term's probable genesis goes back to the early 1970s, when I had lobbied on Capitol Hill for folklife-preservation legislation. Noting the excitement generated in Washington by the Smithsonian Institution's Festival of American Folklife (initiated in 1967), I observed particularly the response of senators and representatives to folk culture enacted on the Mall.

Even within this staged and decontextualized event, legislators in the roving audience paused at the fiddler's temporary platform, the decoy carver's bench, the quilter's frame. Metaphorically, lawmakers descended from their own grand rostrums to let hoedown, duck decoy, and patched quilt speak to issues of artisanship and pluralism. Literally, I saw legislators and their aides linger on Mall paths while talking to festival participants from our nation's corners.

In exchanges with senators and representatives, I tied folk expressions seen and heard on the Mall to concepts girding the American polity. Essentially, I sought the connection between lawmakers' responsibilities and the life stories of fiddler/carver/quilter. In such conversations, I identified myself as a folklorist, pure and simple—not an applicator, not an ideologue. In short, the separation faded away between classroom teaching, library browsing, hallway buttonholing, and agency planning.

Late in 1974, Roger Abrahams (then chairman of the English Depart-

Scholar and public folklore activist Archie Green led the successful lobbying campaign for the creation of the American Folklife Center in 1976. Green, a former San Francisco shipwright and union shop steward, has published extensively in the areas of occupational traditions, labor history, and folksong. Baton Rouge, 1979. Photo by Nicholas R. Spitzer.

ment, University of Texas) asked me what I might do after the folklife bill passed. Confessing that I had not allowed myself the luxury of looking that far into the future, I replied that I would await the bill's fate. Roger suggested that I come to Austin in the fall as a visiting professor, baiting his proposal with a promise of abundant honky-tonk music. I accepted eagerly.

During spring 1975, Richard Bauman (then head of the UT folklore program) called me by telephone to discuss course offerings: teaching an undergraduate introductory class and one graduate seminar. He asked for thoughts on the latter's content. I could only reply that all my energies had been focused within House and Senate office buildings. Talking to congressional aides had made me conscious of the roots of federal attention to folk culture. Having read accounts of early linguistic documentation of tribal people and of spiritual-song collecting from Civil War freedmen—for which public funds were crucial—I suggested these subjects for the seminar. When Dick asked for a title, I could offer none. My memory indicates that he came up with a happy choice, "Folklore and the Public Sector." I doubt that any one before Bauman had strung these precise terms together into a single phrase.

On the Texas campus, I found the Parlin Hall basement-room seminar most exciting: superior students, lively dialogue, excellent papers. Together, we talked about John Wesley Powell's Bureau of American Ethnology; Robert Winslow Gordon's folksong archive at the Library of Congress; John Lomax's vitality in WPA folk projects; Holger Cahill's path-breaking *Index of American Design*. Students looked into crystal balls: Could they do similar pioneering? In what arena would they serve?

Looking back, I now see that our seminar functioned as a rung in a naming ladder: folklore, public sector, public-sector folklore, public folklore. It is possible that one of the Texas students will recall the precise time and place of name extension from college class offering to a professional and administrative rubric. Until claims to the baptismal act surface, I shall rest with the printed record.

In April 1979, Western Kentucky University folklorists hosted a gathering they called "Conference on Folklore and the Public Sector." Planning had begun in the fall of 1978. By coincidence or design the convenors selected the same title used previously in our Texas seminar. During the late 1970s, Bowling Green teachers had responded to the need to place folklore graduates in "new" positions at the Library of Congress, Smithsonian Institution, and the various state agencies then seeking folk arts specialists.

This early recognition of changing venues within public agencies boded well for our discipline as it faced its enlarged role.

The *Kentucky Folklore Record* (1980) carried fourteen of the conference papers under the title "Folklore and the Public Sector." Drawing upon Alabama experience, Henry Willett defined broadly the mission of state folk programs: education, cultural interpretation, diplomacy. He stressed the opportunity for state folklorists to work collegially with other public servants in a variety of agencies: school, park, community-arts council, agricultural bureau, history commission, educational television. Accepting the challenge of expanding tasks, Willett called upon "the public sector folklorist" to hone skills in self-evaluation.

To my knowledge, Willett first used the rubric "public sector folklorist" in an academic journal. With letters and visits, I have attempted to firm this claim. Previous to the Bowling Green conference, he and a few colleagues had voiced the new term in day-to-day work and correspondence. After the meeting, participants in their respective agencies extended the fresh usage. For example, in a letter to a coworker, Willett penned the abbreviated tag "PSF." On August 7, 1981, Peggy Bulger (at the Florida Folklife Program) wrote to Robert Teske (at the National Endowment for the Arts) requesting grant help for a "Southeastern Regional Conference on Folklore in the Public Sector" (at Atlanta). Bulger concluded her agenda draft by shortening the conference-guiding phrase to "public sector folklorists."

Ormond Loomis indicated that he, Peggy Bulger, Doris Dyen, and other Florida colleagues had turned to the fresh name because the solitary title of "state folklorist" or "folk arts coordinator" did not describe adequately their status. Florida employed more than one state folklorist; the "White Springs crew" did not work within an arts agency. New tags do fill tool chests as old ones lose their edge.

In retrospect, we see that Atlanta participants (including Willett) elevated an initial and internal functional usage to general circulation in governmental circles. The need for a new rubric had unfolded slowly. In 1969, Richard Bauman headed the first Committee on Applied Folklore within the American Folklore Society (AFS). At the 1976 annual meeting, this committee reconstituted itself as the Applied Folklore Section. In 1977, members working in the public sector, and sensitive to negative tones in the term "applied," formed the AFS Public Programs Section. This latter group limped along until 1982, when Suzi Jones, Ormond Loomis, Hank

Willett, Robert McCarl, and Jane Beck pushed and pulled their associates to a stage of regular activity. Beck—accepting the editorship of the section's newsletter—readied her first issue in March 1983.

The *Public Programs Newsletter*, direct in style and open to differences, will prove useful in the years ahead to critics evaluating cultural choices in the United States during the 1980s. The first issue of *PPN* carried a report on the 1982 meeting of its group, as well as the minutes of the Applied Folklore Section. By 1984, this latter group had run out of steam as its members puzzled over the distinctions between applied and public-sector folklore. Put directly, the old term "applied" carried disturbing overtones, while the emerging term, "public-sector," implied fresh challenges.

At this juncture, I address the rubric "applied folklore," a polemical tag with which I have never been comfortable. Avoiding it during my decade of lobbying, I frequently suggested to colleagues that we quietly drop it from our vocabulary. Alert to verbal art and dialectical vagaries within folk societies, we do well to consider self-directed nomenclature—our own signs and signifiers.

Lexicographers have traced the word "apply" back to Chaucer and Wycliffe. As this verb moved from French to English, it meant to fold, to bring into juxtaposition, to contact. By 1656, "apply" had gained an additional contrastive meaning that stood for things apart rather than together: for example, practical use as distinguished from theoretical abstraction. In 1806, we find "applied" modifying learning nouns, as in "applied logic." Since 1806, the adjective has been extended also to science, art, psychology, linguistics, anthropology, and other studies. In 1977, Edward Spicer offered an explanatory paper on applied anthropology in North America, dating its beginnings back to 1917 in Mexico. Margaret Mead, in a parallel paper, reviewed the state of art for applied anthropology.

The *Southern Folklore Quarterly* carried Ben Botkin's "Applied Folklore: Creating Understanding through Folklore" (1953). Identifying himself as an applied folklorist—committed to intercultural education and liberal social action—he traced his new descriptive title back to Ralph Boggs's previous demarcation between scientific and artistic phases in folklore study. Curiously, Botkin did not connect applied folklore to applied anthropology. Over the years, Ellen Stekert, Bruce Jackson, Jerrold Hirsch, and Ronna Lee Widener have contributed fine evaluations of Botkin's achievements. I also knew Ben Botkin, shared many of his values, admired his sensitivity, and welcomed deserved tributes to him. Nevertheless, I did not like his naming venture.

Folklorists are not immune from ritual slaying of elders and subsequent ceremonial acts of reinvestiture. I use this figure deliberately to touch the painful subject of Richard Dorson's vendetta against Botkin. Others have dealt with Dorson's role; here, I examine his long hostility to Botkin's locution, "applied folklore." During 1969, in the *Zeitschrift für Volkskunde*, Dorson looked back at his personal neologism, "fakelore," attributing its origin to a "double shock" response upon viewing Botkin's *A Treasury of American Folklore* (1944).

With the appearance of *A Treasury of New England Folklore* (1944), Dorson threw a few pebbles of "softly expressed criticism" at Botkin's second anthology. Two years later, Dorson abandoned "polite and decorous criticism" in his piece, "Folklore and Fake Lore," for the *American Mercury* (March 1950). His then-new formula served as a brush to tar synthetic writing, popularizations for children, spurious folk heroes, fabricators, amateurs, dilettantes, charlatans, folksong revivalists, off-campus enthusiasts. Closing his 1969 article, Dorson moved from his consideration of popular culture to the political arena. He stated that "the sentimentalizing and prettifying of folklore materials is preferable to the ideological manipulation of folklore, a more insidious kind of fakelore which so far has made little headway in these states" (Dorson 1971:14).

Someday a historian will place Dorson's joined attack on fakelore/applied folklore in large context—personal turmoil, jurisdictional turf battling, consensual rationale for American-Century policy, cold-war passion. At this juncture, I note but three of his statements to elaborate the linkage of fakelore, state ideology, and the application of folkloric findings.

On May 18, 1970, Senator Ralph Yarborough, a Texan populist, called hearings in Washington on then-new folklife legislation. Some twenty witnesses, in and out of the academy, testified in favor of Yarborough's bill. Dorson dissented, charging that folklorists within public agencies would debase the coin of scholarship and lead Americans down the garden path to totalitarianism, left and right. Needless to say, Dorson slowed the folklife bill's passage, but he did not derail it.

In May 1971, Robert Byington convened a meeting at Point Park College, Pittsburgh, to discuss then-current folkloric practices. Among a series of detailed papers, Richard Bauman proposed a Center of Applied Folklore modeled after the Center for Applied Linguistics in Arlington, Virginia. Unfortunately, few of the participants took up the sensible specifics of Bauman's proposal. Instead, they responded to Dorson's spirited attack on the notion of applied folklore itself. Dick Sweterlitsch of Indiana University published the papers in 1971, thus providing documentation of an internal war. In 1989, Byington offered a reflective piece on the Point Park turmoil.

I suspect that in the year after his encounter with Senator Yarborough, Professor Dorson sensed failure in his fight. Essentially, at Pittsburgh he had pulled his colleagues into debate by elaborating his previous lumping together of the acts of popularizing folk material (fakelore), and the activist thrust then gathering momentum within federal agencies (applied folklore). Without reporting Dorson's naming linkage and the force of his attack, one cannot comprehend his pejorative carry-over from popular anthologies to the polity.

Historian John A. Williams's "Radicalism and Professionalism in Folklore Studies: A Comparative Perspective" appeared in 1975. From outside our discipline, Williams viewed AFS differences in terms of dual approaches: comparative/historic-geographic (professional) versus functionalist (radical). Within this schematic formulation, functionalist Botkin encouraged applied folklore, while academician Dorson manned the scholarly barricades. Not all Williams's readers accepted these polarities as descriptive of complex realities within folkloric circles. Nevertheless, his article helped bring to the surface a number of thorny political issues. In the 1930s and 1940s, communists of Stalinist and Popular Front persuasions had turned to American folklore. Williams, energized by New Left perspectives, did not fear to deal with Old Left dogma.

The relationship of dissent to folklore study will continue to catch the attention of historians. We can anticipate that some Red critics, themselves touched by *glasnost*, will revise former rosy views on Popular Front expression. Here, I need only note that Williams, neither glorifying nor vilifying thunder on the left, reinforced attention to Dorson's flaying of applied folklore. In replying to Williams, Dorson drew a line between New Left historians holding "a priori philosophy" and folklorists with an "open mind." Clearly, he saw himself as a value-free scholar untouched by deep ideology, unmarked by loyalty to central tenets in the American state.

Interestingly, at the very time Dorson penned his response to Williams, folklife legislation had marched its course on Capitol Hill. Still dubious about the bill, and anticipating his graduate students' drift to federal agencies, Dorson mounted a final assault on the "activist role we are asked to assume as applied folklorists. . . . Any kook can join the American Folklore Society and publish a book of fakelore and become a spokesman" (Williams 1975:239). In retrospect, it is difficult to comprehend such intensity in welding kooks, fakelorists, and applied folklorists into an invading army threatening the temple. Fifteen years have passed since the Dorson-Williams exchange; the temple stands.

Even as "applied folklore" shakes itself loose from the cloak of fakelore, the former term holds built-in difficulties. Within our discipline, "applied folklore" connotes two constant levels of discourse, the first superior to the second: Pure academicians conduct research; polluting applicators apply their seers' findings. Teachers who gather arcane legends do serious work; public colleagues who assist citizens stranded in society's shallows do trivial work. Such distinctions are not only absurd, but they diminish all. Over the years, I have rejected this false dichotomy. Professors alone do not monopolize the fields of folklore, ethnography, social history, and cultural criticism. College teachers are not immune from values flowing to the campus from large society. Public servants are not immune from the academy's critical thought. The commonality within the discipline of folklore far outweighs the separate settings within which we work.

Richard Dorson used "applied folklore" to stigmatize "enemies," to reduce them to an untouchable caste. Why should we cling to his outdated and demeaning language? I must confess surprise upon reading in the *Journal of American Folklore* Barbara Kirshenblatt-Gimblett's "Mistaken Dichotomies," with its bold precis: "The dichotomy between pure and applied folklore has obscured the ideological, political, and economic basis of folklore as it is studied in the academy and practiced in the public sector." I welcome the phrase "mistaken dichotomies" but am puzzled to know whether Kirshenblatt-Gimblett has discarded the colors of past wars or continues Dorson's stance.

I doubt that the circumstance of varied places of employment obscures the use of conceptual framing tools or dims ability to set experience in large contexts. Further, I question the present-day retention of "pure" and "applied" as modifiers for the discipline folklore. To adhere to this fictive pair is to retreat to fantasyland. In the demon's realm running from Madison Avenue to Gorky Park, "applied folklore" may have covered Paul Bunyan to People's Songs in the 1940s. What earthly hold does this naming construct now have that glues it to public folklore?

Perhaps I am overly sensitive to verbal sticks and stones, but I wonder how anyone, observing solid growth in public folklore, can retain the appellation "applied." The rubric "public-sector folklore" has served for a decade and has come to denominate folk-art exhibitions and craft apprenticeship, as well as the conservation of endangered expression, advocacy of rights for new minorities, exploration of parallels between historical preservation and ethnographic documentation, placement of the concept of cultural equity on political agendas, demystification of national-identity symbols. Concern with such matters in large society has given public folklorists a realistic base upon which to ground theory from all compass points.

During 1983, Hal Cannon wrote, "With the changing times our role as public sector folklorists must continually be reexamined." For a decade, Cannon and his coworkers have not only forged, but also debated and reexamined novel roles. More importantly, they have slowly altered the perceptions of brother and sister cultural documentarians, historical preservationists, and natural conservationists. Among many rewards in public employment, folklorists can be especially proud of bringing respect to their discipline wherever Americans explore nationhood.

We live in a multilinguistic, transregional, ethnically diverse, occupationally segmented society. We honor no singular creed; we shop for alternate faiths; we exploit religious cults; we invest show-business drama with sacred meaning. Revisionism in other countries implies restoring dead leaders to posthumous dignity. American revisionism tends to pull heroes from pedestals, to sweep stars from the skies. At the close of our Revolutionary War, bands played "The World Turned Upside Down." For two centuries we have inverted or recast national tokens. To illustrate: The melting pot has long marked the elimination of difference within a flaming crucible. In current parlance, it has also come to mean cultural diversity and pride in particularity. Given experiences of tension and contradiction, folklorists help decipher codes that both divide and join American communities.

The full study of the growth of public folklore remains untold. Burt Feintuch has made an excellent start in *The Conservation of Culture: Folklorists and the Public Sector* (1988). I select for comment but one of his book's essays which continues to use "applied folklore" as a defining label. Jerrold Hirsch, in "Cultural Pluralism and Applied Folklore: The New Deal Precedent," highlights the work of Ben Botkin and his colleagues. As Hirsch looked back in time, he felt it appropriate to carry on Botkin's coinage. In fact, New Deal folklorists in the 1930s did not use the tag "applied folklore." During 1953 and the years of Senator Joseph McCarthy's inflammatory politics, Botkin's coinage had little chance of acceptance.

Wisely, in his essay's summation, Hirsch pointed away from "applied folklore" to our new term, "public folklore." He noted that "public folk-lorists . . . had to contemplate the relationship between government and culture, and culture and democracy" (Hirsch 1988:64). We can assume that with careful reading we shall find additional early examples of the new us-age, "public folklore."

On November 17–19, 1988, a number of folklorists from Maine to Samoa gathered in San Francisco during a meeting of the National Assem-bly of State Arts Agencies (NASAA). Technically, they formed the Folk Arts Coordinators' Peer Group (we do favor awkward titles). Actually, individu-als came from a variety of agencies beyond arts councils; they represented veterans closing out their careers as well as newcomers fresh from graduate school. I found the wide range of participants and their broad discussions stimulating. Again, I urge others to consult the *Public Programs Newsletter* for reports on problems resolved and unresolved at the San Francisco as-sembly.

During a NASAA discussion period, Robert Cogswell, Tennessee state folklorist, suggested that the time had arrived to drop the word "sector" from our generally accepted group title. He commented strongly that folk-lorists do not need a three-word handle to conduct everyday work. Names function best when they advance discourse, when they cheer travelers on difficult journeys. I have written elsewhere on the tasks facing pioneers in governmental units and need not repeat my sense of their large achieve-ment. I welcomed Cogswell's suggestion at San Francisco of the name "public folklore" and urge its nationwide adoption.

Expanding his remarks at the NASAA gathering, Cogswell wrote:

> To portray the goals of public folklore as subordinate to and somewhat less noble [than academic study], will only undermine our profession as a whole, and do disservice to the people and cultures with which/whom we all work. . . . There is a clear precedent for the term "public folklore." Since 1978, the National Council on Public History has published *The Public Historian.* [Its] articles contain an uncanny series of parallels to issues and opinions for which our discipline has yet to develop appropriate forums and outlets. (Letter to author, April 24, 1989)

No one can predict whether "public folklore" will catch on as a useful rubric, or whether it will be supplanted by an unknown term still on the linguistic horizon. We are better at treating the colloquialisms of others than in creating our own tags. We revel in everyday speech that identifies

shrink, newshawk, sky pilot, disc jockey, headhunter, sea lawyer, anchorman, flack catcher, brainstormer, private eye, starlet. Do not folklorists, pulled to vernacular expression, deserve a distinct label?

I have combined recollection with reading to sketch something of the background for the name "public folklore" and to suggest its virtue over that of "applied folklore." In treating the word "applied," I have neglected "public." Briefly, the latter carries back to the Latin *populus* (the people), and ultimately to the Hellenic *polis* (city state)—a now-imagined organism of civility and homogeneity. We know, of course, of the millennia-long struggle to include Greek and barbarian, man and woman, master and helot within the extended polity. News reports (as I write) from Tibet, Gaza, Afghanistan, Beirut, and Beijing reveal how incomplete is the human endeavor.

We know Robert Redfield's fieldwork in Yucatan, and his term "folk society," a formulation that can be traced in outline to Hesiod's Boeotian poetry. Contemporary folklorists labor to break away from Redfieldian markers of enclavement and tradition. No matter how modern our enterprise, we cannot escape ambiguities embedded in definitions of folk society. After putting aside old norms, we turn back to descriptions of particular people: Hopi, Cajun, mountaineer, boondocker, Holy Roller, Amish, tale teller, balladeer, trickster, quilter, carver, fiddler. No folklorist has the wisdom to study all Americans, to impose totalizing analysis upon a kaleidoscopic citizenry, to compress all who inhabit the United States into a singular mold.

I suspect that "public-sector folklore" made sense in the 1980s because those who voiced it accepted notions of an array of scattered publics. The very word "public" resonates positively: commonweal, general welfare, external service. Public-health nurses guard life; public-interest architects create humane environments. Public folklorists comment upon cultural collision, survival strategy, community vision.

Two recent articles from the Rocky Mountain West by a professor and a public folklorist reveal our discipline's health, and end my report. William "Bert" Wilson chairs the English Department and directs the Folklore Archives at Brigham Young University. In looking back at his study of the *Kalevala*, he describes his discomfort with Finnish nationalistic use of epic poetry. In his early ideological criticism, Wilson's "unstated assumption" told him "that the world is best served when the scholar remains in his study and does not soil his hands . . . with applied folklore or public-sector folklore" (1986:84). (How I wish that old friend Bert would drop the "a" word.)

American Folklore Society members, in their 1971 meeting, had debated the formation of a Center of Applied Folklore. Wilson then voted with the majority against the proposal. Five years later, he took up public folklore tasks by bringing Utah artists and artisans to the Smithsonian's Bicentennial Festival of American Folklife. Subsequently, he served as chair of the National Endowment for the Arts' Folk Arts Panel and in similar capacities back home in Utah. While commuting from Provo to the Potomac, he reflected upon new responsibilities. I need not detail his devoted attention to these duties or his exemplary sense of moral issue. I do refer readers to his sensitive "confession" and "partial repentance" for "soiled hands" in public projects.

Timothy Evans, a graduate from Indiana University, now serves as Wyoming state folklorist. His modest newsletter, *The Hoolihan*, treats cowboy poetry and balladry, the Eastern Shoshone Tribal Council's traditional arts apprenticeship program, the Casper Art Museum's "Keepers of the Earth" exhibit, the Arapaho Language Camp, the Wind River Reservation's "Singing Horse Tours," French-Canadian log barns, and rural country dance string bands. These subjects are not out of the ordinary for state folklorists, coast to coast.

I am struck by the complementarity of Evans's everyday tasks with his *Western Folklore* article, "Folklore as Utopia: English Medievalists and the Ideology of Revivalism" (1988). This ranks among the best in recent considerations of disciplinary history. Evans extends our background to include William Cobbett, Thomas Carlyle, John Ruskin, and William Morris. Not only does he lengthen a time line, but he widens the paradigmatic net that explicates our key ideas. Evans moves readily from British pastoral visions to Wyoming pastures, from distant utopianism to Shoshone tribal members putting their dreams to work.

Evans's insightful essay takes up several of Bert Wilson's existential concerns. I commend their respective observations to those who retain doubts about public folklore's promise. Together, Tim and Bert reinforce my sense of our task's complexity and its unfolding possibilities.

I close these partisan notes knowing that no single individual alone alters language. Clearly, I favor the name "public folklore" and would happily relegate "applied folklore" to history's dustbin. At the same time, in rejecting the binary pair "pure" and "applied," I have not been blind to the reality that some folklorists, wherever they dwell, retain pejorative speech. Both the academy and the bureau can be bastions of privilege; words are weapons. Professors and agency heads alike, at the center of power, enjoy validating the emblematic codes that mark life at society's margins. Individuals within campus and governmental units may feel impelled to obscure tracks—a trait not limited to folklorists.

All public folklorists, beginning as students, train in universities; most colleges exist by virtue of some public taxes. Shared education and common funding should direct us to mutual endeavor. Mystification in nomenclature trails from state capital to college town; metropolis to hamlet. Few folklorists, regardless of training or station, are impervious to the appeal of colorful speech. We shall do well to put our pejorative names aside in favor of ameliorative language.

Most folklorists find themselves far from the seats of semantic and political authority. With few exceptions, we remain conscious of indebtedness to the countless folks from whom we derive kudos. Perhaps our self-chosen professional marginality stems from initial affection for traditional song and story, patched quilt and duck decoy. Does an ancient fiddle tune sustain each new office day? Does a strange incantation doom us to work with hewers and haulers—in Melville's prose, with mariners, renegades, castaways? The Pequod's crew composes a public I have been blessed to serve. Other folklorists have found and will find their publics.

REFERENCES

Beck, Jane, ed. 1983. *Public Programs Newsletter.* Subsequent editors, Steve Siporin (Utah), Steve Ohrn (Iowa). Through 1989, fourteen semiannual issues published.

Botkin, B. A. 1953. "Applied Folklore: Creating Understanding through Folklore." *Southern Folklore Quarterly* 17:199–206.

Bulger, Peggy, ed. 1982. *Report: Southeastern Regional Conference for Public Sector Folklorists, December 11–13, 1981, Atlanta, Georgia.* White Springs, Florida: Florida Folklife Program.

Byington, Robert. 1989. "What Happened to Applied Folklore." In *Time and Temperature,* edited by Charles Camp, pp. 77–79. Washington, D.C.: American Folklore Society.

Cannon, Hal. 1983. "The Role of the Public Sector Folklorist." *Public Programs Newsletter* 1 (2):8–9.

Dorson, Richard M. 1971. "Fakelore." In *American Folklore and the Historian,* edited by Richard M. Dorson, pp. 3–14. Chicago: University of Chicago Press. Reprinted from *Zeitschrift für Volkskunde,* 1969.

Evans, Timothy H. 1988. "Folklore as Utopia: English Medievalists and the Ideology of Revivalism." *Western Folklore* 67:245–68.

Feintuch, Burt, ed. 1988. *The Conservation of Culture: Folklorists and the Public Sector*. Lexington: University Press of Kentucky.

Hirsch, Jerrold. 1988. "Cultural Pluralism and Applied Folklore: The New Deal Precedent." In *The Conservation of Culture: Folklorists and the Public Sector*, edited by Burt Feintuch, pp. 46–67. Lexington: University Press of Kentucky.

Kirshenblatt-Gimblett, Barbara. 1988. "Mistaken Dichotomies." *Journal of American Folklore* 101:140–55.

Loomis, Ormond. 1989. Letter to author, March 17.

Mead, Margaret. 1977. "Applied Anthropology: The State of the Art." In *Perspectives on Anthropology 1976*, edited by Anthony F. C. Wallace and others, pp. 142–61. Washington, D.C.: American Anthropological Association.

Spicer, Edward H. 1977. "Early Applications of Anthropology in North America." In *Perspectives on Anthropology 1976*, edited by Anthony F. C. Wallace and others, pp. 116–41. Washington, D.C.: American Anthropological Association.

Sweterlitsch, Dick, ed. 1971. *Papers on Applied Folklore*. Folklore Forum, Bibliographic and Special Series, no. 8. Bloomington: Indiana University, Folklore Institute.

U.S. Congress. Senate Committee on Labor and Public Welfare. 1970. *American Folklife Foundation Act*. Hearings on S. 1591 before the Subcommittee on Education. 91st Cong., 2d sess.

Willett, Henry. 1980. "Re-thinking the State Folk Arts Program." *Kentucky Folklore Record* 26 (1, 2):12–15.

———. 1989. Letter to author, April 20.

Williams, John A. 1975. "Radicalism and Professionalism in Folklore Studies: A Comparative Perspective." *Journal of the Folklore Institute* 11:211–39.

Wilson, William A. 1986. "Partial Repentance of a Critic: The *Kalevala*, Politics, and the United States." In *Folklife Annual 1986*, edited by Alan Jabbour and James Hardin, pp. 81–90. Washington, D.C.: Library of Congress.

Happy Birthday, Dear American Folklore Society

Reflections on the Work and Mission of Folklorists

BESS LOMAX HAWES

As I have had occasion to remark elsewhere, every dog indeed has his day, and everybody, whether human or institutional, gets a birthday every year. No exceptions are allowed.

And when one hundred birthdays have mounted up, some especial attention must be paid. Just staying intact for that long is an achievement all by itself; getting anything done beyond simple survival is positively commendable. The American Folklore Society has done a good many things during its century of existence. I should like to concentrate my observations here upon its signal achievements in the proliferation of folklorists.

I myself am a folklorist and I was brought up around folklorists and I have been observing them for a good part of the century that we are celebrating this year. The comments that follow, then, are personal and stem from my personal observations, especially from having noted that no two known folklorists—like snowflakes—are alike. Mostly, it seems to me, this chronic variability is due to the fact that most folklorists spend their pro-

fessional lives trying to work out a balance between the several responsibilities that go along with being a folklorist.

In the first place, there is the absolute necessity for fieldwork where one comes to grips with the living data of folklore itself—when, where, with whom, and as it exists. In the second place, there is research, in which one looks for and receives information and interpretations that parallel or contradict or simply vary from one's own observations. In the third place, there is the public presentation of folk materials and the conclusions of one's folkloric studies through printed, filmed, recorded, exhibited, or performed products (of this more later). Fourthly, there is the preservation of the discipline itself through teaching it to others. And finally, whether in government, private employment, or academia, there is office work and administration, where one accomplishes all those things that have to be done in order to get the other parts of the work under way. Every folklorist I have ever known does or has done all of those things in varying proportions. That is what makes us interesting and distinguishes us one from another.

When I look back over my own life, I see that I have done an awful lot of teaching; an awful *awful* lot of administration; a respectable, but not outstanding amount of public presentation; much less research than I should have done; and *far* too little fieldwork. Doing such a little smidge of fieldwork was cowardly of me, but I did have three kids to raise and a lot of other responsibilities. The problem with fieldwork is that not only does it involve you in a very complicated relationship with the particular folk group you are working with (a relationship that will last your lifetime, incidentally), but also that you acquire the responsibility of at least *trying* to figure out what the information you have collected actually means. This is the most difficult, grinding, worrisome, dark journey of the intellect that I have ever undergone, and I can't say I have ever relished it. It is so hard, indeed, that a great many folklorists like me do very little fieldwork, or, if they do, they finesse the thinking part in a number of ways familiar to academics.

Bess Lomax Hawes served as director of the National Endowment for the Arts, Folk Arts Program, from 1977 to 1992. She has also studied and taught about folk music and children's traditions. Photo by A. de Menil.

Fieldwork, however—no matter how grudgingly performed, how brief the encounter—remains the absolute sine qua non of the folklore profession, for it sets the folklorist and the folk into a relationship the exploration of which may take a lifetime. It is never a casual meeting, that first serious discussion between collector and "informant," to use the ugly word that seems the only one we have developed to identify the owners and progenitors of the cultural materials we comment upon.

When I was teaching years ago, I had a student who did an excellent term paper based upon some folk curing beliefs he had collected from an old lady in his neighborhood. At the end of the semester, he voiced a complaint. "You taught me all about how to collect, Mrs. Hawes. What you didn't teach me was how to *stop* collecting. That old lady lives on my block, and every night when I come home, she runs out on the porch and says, 'Hey, boy, I just remembered another one!' I keep trying to explain to her that my project is all finished, but she just won't stop, and I'm starting to go up the alley when I go home just so I won't run into her."

I said, "My dear young man, welcome to the grown-up world. It's a place where real actions have real results, where real people have real feelings as well as real information. And it's a place where old ladies actually think that people who say they are interested in what they know really are interested, and issues like course requirements and semesters and quarters are really irrelevant. You've gotten your A. Now you start to pay back."

And ever after that I used to warn classes: Watch out who you collect from. When you talk with somebody about their folklore, you move quickly and often imperceptibly into a realm of deep intimacy, much deeper—in my experience—than you ever intended to go. And afterwards you find you haven't just collected folklore, you're very apt to have made a new friend with all the responsibilities, as well as the delights, that friendship brings.

The payback. As much as we try to get away from the uncomfortableness of it, the fundamental fact of being a folklorist is that we earn our livings by various manipulations of other people's creative products or information. It just comes with the territory. We are not alone in this, of course. Literary scholars, music critics, and art historians as well depend for their very existence upon the creative productivity of other people.

But folklorists generally confront this problem in particularly unnerving ways. Many of the artists whose works we treat are still alive, for one thing. For another, although there is much current interest in boardroom, corporate, and advertising folklore (basically, the folklore of the affluent), most of the data we enjoy, analyze, comment upon, display, and organize comes from people who are either economically poorer than most academicians or at best less experienced in the ways of "making it" outside their own society. It makes sensitive folklorists worry that they may be exploiting people who are not in a position to protect themselves or who are simply too good-natured to resent the interference.

Those are good worries. I approve of them, although they can become dangerously close to patronizing on the one hand and paralyzing on the other, particularly when one realizes that folklorists, unlike most anthropologists, tend to do their work in their own country, in their own common language. This means that the people you are writing about can read the books you've written; they can look at your films and see how you've transferred their reality to the screen; they can attend concerts and festivals and check up on how performances are miked, what the presenter chooses to remark on, what repertoire is being presented, whose baskets get put into what part of an exhibit case, what the labels say. It's no wonder that many folklorists take refuge in theoretical models. The other is just too hard.

I have come to realize over the years that folklore is an unfinished profession, a profession within which there are still many areas of argument and conflict, a profession within which individuals still have serious choices to make. And just as the individual folklorist is required—by virtue of his membership within the profession—to balance out the conflicting essentials of his work, so too is the discipline of folklore itself.

What this amounts to is that the American Folklore Society, as well as the discipline of folklore, as well as each individual scholar within it, must continually review its degree of conformity with the essential payback requirement. This involves working out and maintaining a particular, but ever-flexible, creative balance between the responsibilities previously mentioned: field activity, scholarly research, the academic classroom, public presentation, and administration. (Assigning equal importance to administration may seem surprising, but if we are not already in a managerial world, we soon will be, and everyone had better learn how to work effectively within it. The administrative skills required to introduce and maintain a folklore curriculum in a university compare very favorably with those necessary to organize a traditional arts festival or regional touring or traditional-artist-in-schools residencies program. The latter activities, indeed, may require even more sophisticated cultural and political deftness.)

Payback, then, functions as an underlying principle, a state of mind, or a state of conscience, perhaps. It has informed the work of folklorists since Bishop Percy; it is not a recent invention. Its operation is especially visible today for the 1990s in the American Folklore Society, where a turn towards public presentation (always the clearest example of payback) has affected both the board and the conduct of the annual meeting.

What is now being termed by some "public-sector folklore" and by others "public folklore" and by others "applied folklore" is not only a very democratic idea and therefore ubiquitous, it is also an idea that has run through American intellectual and political life for a long time. It is an idea that has always been part of the responsibility of the discipline, in greater or lesser extent according to the dictates of the period.

Almost one hundred years ago—to cite the example most familiar to me—John A. Lomax started his work in the Southwest very simply because he thought that the artistic products and the basic points of view of the people who worked the cattle ranges of his day deserved wide attention. He thought everybody ought to know about their contribution and be proud of it. He was strongly influenced by a kind of general grass-roots populist philosophy that was widespread in his younger years, and in spite of various distorting collisions with the fast-changing twentieth century, that particular philosophical grounding never left him.

It was no sudden fascination with modern inventions or the availability of newly sophisticated hardware that led him and my brother Alan to believe that the actual voices, the genuine presences of Americans, should be heard via the use of sound recording techniques and that their actual words should be printed in books. They also maintained that black people in the South and Spanish-speaking people in the Southwest needed some help to get their presence felt too. Later, Alan extended this idea to broadcast—a lovely word, newly coined at that time, which means exactly what it says—those voices across the entire nation through the Columbia Broadcasting System in some of the earliest folk music radio programs of the century. Still later, Alan came to call this procedure "cultural feedback," a term still in active use.

The Lomaxes were not alone, of course. Members of that same intellectual generation like Zora Neale Hurston, Benjamin Botkin, and Charles Seeger felt the same impulses, not only to collect but to broadcast. Their work—along with that of some of the other great collectors of the period (Vance Randolph, Herbert Halpert, George Korson, Frank C. Brown)—was generally supported by the American people, whether through public or private means, because of the general understanding of the time that folklore had somehow to do with common, binding, and healing principles. (This is not a fashionable thing to say now, nor was it then. But even as we contemporary folklorists reject it as too unsophisticated, it remains our fundamental strength.)

We went through a period of neglect of our public responsibilities during the late 1940s and 1950s—a complicated era following World War II when a worldwide thrust towards a particularly specific kind of nationalism took a special turn in the United States with the claim that a broad range of English-language traditional songs were, indeed, a kind of long-lost "national repertoire" of public American song. This movement, sometimes referred to as the folksong revival, occurred on the heels of a shockingly intensive period of postwar political repression—the McCarthy era—and in many ways got much of its emotional force from its attractiveness to the many citizens who opposed the various blacklists and political phobias of the day. Indeed, if we did not have a genuine national repertoire of song before, this era provided us with a rather good one.

From the point of view of the folkloric discipline, however, as early as 1950 a great many prominent folklorists who have been happily pursuing their uncontroversial researches into historical and literary topics found themselves in danger of being pushed to the front lines of what promised to be a pretty public and pretty bloody battle. A number of them, including some quite prominent ones, did not like the prospect at all and left for more academic surroundings as rapidly as possible. It was disappointing, but sadly realistic. The punishments for nonconformity at the time were extreme.

A series of international conferences spearheaded by the Folklore Institute in Bloomington, Indiana, demonstrates how fiercely and distinctly the battle lines were drawn within the discipline.[1] Their reports should be read and reread today for inspiration and perspective. It was a good fight, but in many ways it was lost. For the next twenty years—until the beginning of the 1970s—the folklore world in the United States grew largely silent in terms of its responsibilities for communicating its theories, materials, and principles to the general public or to the specific groups studied by scholars.

It was indeed a long dry spell, but it has been followed, as such periods always have been followed throughout history, by a period of intensive correction. As I have said before, the recent rise of interest within our discipline in the needs and concerns of public folklore was as inevitable as the melting of the glaciers or the intercontinental drift. The payback principle keeps pushing us to correct our imbalances, even if we like them, and even if we would feel much more comfortable to stay skewed.

Today we see fifty of the states and territories of the United States with their own public folklore programs; we see many cities and towns with their own "friendly neighborhood folklorist" or their own especial, properly researched, and proudly presented local cultural event. We see an annual Festival of American Folklife on the National Mall and a round-the-year program emanating from the American Folklife Center at the Library of Congress with its enhanced Archive of Folk Culture. We see the tentative development of regional and other cultural programs that cross state lines, the increased presence of traditional performers in major public media and live presentations, of traditional crafts workers in art museums. One of these days we may have to begin worrying about an overemphasis on public presentation . . . but not yet awhile.

So here we are today, a hundred years after the birth of the American Folklore Society, still arguing, still fussing with each other over how to define folklore, but still knowing all the time just what we're talking about, still balancing on the wobbly old double-decker bus that leans one way now and another way yesterday and will give us a good lurching shake-up tomorrow. What potholes lie in wait? What course-correction failures will cause us to drift off the road? It is pretty clear already, I think, where our next problem areas lie. Maybe, if we start a corrective action soon, we won't lean over too far.

During recent years, it seems to me, a trend has developed of skimping the all-important, baseline, dirt-digging, foundation-laying act of scholarly research into the data of folklore in order to satisfy our concerns with the particular, the individualistic—with things like process and context and methodology and eliciting folk etymologies and biographical data and local histories. You can hardly see the folklore for the trees. Everything seems to be treated as a separate entity and of equal importance with everything else. Everyone is a folk (which of course is true to an extent), and everyone is of equal importance (which of course is also true to an extent), and pretty soon nothing means anything at all.

Folklore has always been in part about pattern. We are not seeing the many thrilling patterns shining through so clearly these days because we have, I believe, been neglecting the need for a solid, underlying knowledge of the data which can clarify how and where in the patterns a particular local tradition fits in. Public folklorists—as well as all other kinds—have to know (or find out) that a fiddle player's tune that he calls "Le Capitaine

Trompeur" is more widely known in mappable regions as "Captain Jinks," and they need to know this for a number of reasons. Scholarly accuracy is one. Copyright and other legal restrictions are another. The possible development of an overview that links this group with another group through time and place is another. Most important of all, in some ways, is the potential empowerment of the individual fiddler who learns that his tradition is of significance not only to himself (he always knew it was pretty special), but to his culture and to its history. The interchanges between folklorist and artist on such issues may seem trivial, but they are the common coin of public folklore. They must be taken very seriously not only by the participants but also by the discipline itself. Most particularly, the information exchanged must be accurate and the most recent available.

I have compressed into the preceding paragraphs a good many warnings and cautionary remarks to my colleagues and my discipline. But birthdays have their commemorative side as well; they can look back and forward as well as up and down. On the occasion of the hundredth anniversary of the founding of the American Folklore Society, let me advise the Society, the discipline of folklore, and every folklorist, including myself, in pretty much the same way:

1. Don't get lazy.
2. Teach as much as you can when you can—*broadcast.*
3. Recognize that the job is as yet unfinished and likely never will be.
4. Get out there and do some good hard fieldwork. That is where all your best ideas and your most important knowledge are waiting for you. If you do your work well, folks will teach you back.

And so—good luck to us all in the century to come . . . and many happy returns!

NOTES

This paper was presented at the 1988 Centennial Meetings of the American Folklore Society. Bess Hawes, director of the National Endowment for the Arts Folk Arts Program since 1976, has written previously on "Happy Birthday" in traditional usage, hence the title of this essay.

1. For coverage of these meetings, see Stith Thompson, *Four Symposia on Folklore,* Indiana University Folklore Series, no. 8 (Bloomington: Indiana University Press, 1953). This period is also reviewed by Robert Baron in this volume.

Part 2

Metaphors and
Methods of Practice

Cultural Conversation

Metaphors and Methods in Public Folklore

NICHOLAS R. SPITZER

I began in-depth folklore fieldwork with Creole zydeco musicians in 1975.[1] Being there in rural French Louisiana, trying to communicate my reasons for being there, caused me to rethink my purposes as a folklorist. I could no longer imagine writing or thinking in accordance with the scientistic formalism then au courant in the field's academic track. Being unwilling to perform in the code of insular scholarship was consistent with my motivation in becoming a folklorist: a desire to experience, understand, and share with others cultural aesthetics beyond those of my rural New England background. I valued my relationships to traditional Creole communities and the individual artists with whom I worked and came to see academic (and later bureaucratic) discourse as secondary to though supportive of those relationships. It was through fieldwork that I fully realized that both the strictures of formal academia and the unexamined romanticism of the outsider were largely irrelevant and sometimes antithetical to the interests of folk artists and their communities.

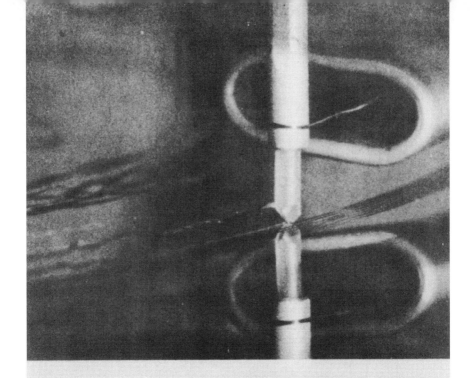

RECORDING IS

LIKE CULTIVATING

Luckily, in my first major project in the field I groped along to follow what I have since come to believe is the central practice of public folklore: using academic and ethnographic research bases to negotiate and create public representations of expressive culture that the core community and broader audiences find useful, edifying, and engaging. In this case the research involved zydeco musicians, and the initial mode of representation was the annotated phonograph record. Zydeco seemed appropriate because it is the most powerful public symbol of the Creole culture—one that they use *themselves* to comment on internal values and aesthetics and their external ethnic boundary relationships to Cajuns and African Americans. As a public performance genre, zydeco moves easily between varied performance contexts, at parties, Mardi Gras, trail rides, church halls, and nightclubs.[2]

These recordings (and later, radio programs, films, and texts) provided representations of Creole culture where relatively little existed. Most zydeco on records was from the more urban rhythm and blues sound; also, far more records of Cajun music—from commercial studio recordings to field recordings—were available. Likewise, most films on French Louisiana were about Cajuns, and much of the writing, scholarly and popular, presented Creole culture inaccurately as a subset or derivative of the Cajun culture.

As I learned from musicians about their lives, ambitions, repertoires, and styles, I realized the value they placed on the tangible results of this project: their music and life stories on a recording. If the project was flawed, in their view, it was because I had no connections to Motown or any other national record company catering to black listeners that fulfilled some of their ideas about success as musicians. Perhaps worse, I was making an LP. They would have preferred 45s for local jukebox play and radio promotion. Most of all, they wanted their *own* 45s, not to be included on anthologies shared with other artists. Yet they tolerated and mostly enjoyed my attentions, respecting my willingness to work with a range of musicians, club owners, and other community leaders in the region. We negoti-

Moses Asch, founder of Folkways Records, gave us an encyclopedic collection of the world's music and other sounds. His earlier record company, Disc Records, used this catalogue cover (juxtaposing the cutting of a recording master against the plowing of a field) in 1947. Courtesy Office of Folklife Programs Archives, Smithsonian Institution.

ated recording logistics, financial terms, and repertoires.

The resulting LPs gave traditional zydeco music some regional and national exposure at a time when few community members thought it had much of a future. The recordings are still found on local record racks and in the heritage sections of school and public libraries in Louisiana—as well as in the now large section reserved for Louisiana music at the national chain store, Tower Records. One LP will soon be reissued on CD. The music has since gone on to gain national popularity in folk festival and rock concert settings in the hands of Grammy Award winners from the late Clifton Chenier to Queen Ida. Creoles created their own Southwest Louisiana Zydeco Festival in 1983, and zydeco has taken its place as an African-French-American contribution in the burgeoning world music scene.

Today I muse over the revival of and recognition for zydeco: the many new directions the music has taken in the hands of young people, many of whom formerly rejected it (some of these innovations opposed by traditionalists); the palpable pride people feel in the music as an expression of their African-French-Creole identity; the anomaly of hearing the music in the background of commercials for hamburgers and Levis. I am glad that my work as a folklorist played a role in bringing some attention to Creole culture through their art. But mainly, I am satisfied with the idea that Creoles themselves have regained a measure of control over the art form and thus have a stronger role in shaping their identity and cultural survival. There is now something of a public dialogue among south Louisiana Creoles about the very nature of "Creoleness" as expressed in music and language, and in social relations to Cajuns and African Americans. And that dialogue—or multilogue—emanates or is stimulated in part from the dialogue of folklorist and community.

METAPHORS AND METHODS OF PRACTICE
AND REPRESENTATION

I believe folklorists are at their best in work that creates such public dialogues about traditional culture within and often beyond a community. Our work—whether supported by public or academic-sector employ—is public by nature, historically and culturally situated, and necessarily responsible to those communities from whom we obtain our information. Acknowledging this will ultimately allow us to produce more conscious, better-realized representations of folklore.[3] Even "pure" researchers, who collect, interpret, and publish folk expression primarily for the apparent increase of knowledge about how systems of aesthetics and meaning are constructed, do not engage their subject entirely free from implicit aspects in their practice. They are themselves part of a political economy of tenure-driven employment that imposes an acceptable format and content for their thoughts, despite protestations of intellectual freedom and autonomy to the contrary. As one patron saint in the high church of critical theory notes:

> The practical privilege in which all scientific activity arises never more subtly governs that activity (insofar as science presupposes not only an epistemological break but also a social separation) than when, unrecognized as privilege, it leads to an implicit theory of practice which is the corollary of neglect of the social conditions in which the science is possible. (Bourdieu 1982:1)

Yet such sentiments are not difficult to propound. Most folklore study is carried out in a relationship that privileges our position by its very nature. Even well-meaning scholarly discourse may be written in a metalanguage of collegial consumption that suggests an unleaped bound between words and action. The difficulty is actually changing in practice the relationship of folklorist to folk, from one of omniscient, scholarly reportage and interpretation to one of cooperation and mutual benefit in the representation of culture.

Rather than indulging primarily in constructing competing interpretive frameworks about traditional expressive culture, folklorists wherever employed should apply their intellectual energy to creating metaphors and methods of public practice in dialogue with members of folk communities. This is not to say that scholarly research should not go forward in library or field. It must continue to serve as a base for representations. However, theoretical activity and library research should serve primarily to enhance linkages between field research and the kinds of representations that reach communities of origin and larger society. Our metaphors, our creative ways of understanding and describing our work with others, should animate the relationship most central to our practice: the informed conjoining of folk aesthetics, expressive patterns, and traditional genres with appropriate modes of representation.

Anthropologist James Fernandez, attempting to provide a critical view of metaphors in expressive culture, suggests that they have "missions"

(1974). This, of course, is his own metaphor. People are the ones with missions. Peoples' missions, from folklorist to folk, are shaped by metaphors available to them and created by them. Victor Turner notes, "Social actions of various kinds acquire form through the metaphors and paradigms in their actors' heads," and "social groups tend to find their openness to the future in the variety of metaphors for what may be the good life" (1974:13, 14). New metaphors for our beliefs in the value of cultural diversity, equity, and continuity will help us better understand, imagine, and explain our work to the many audiences poised to listen.

In reconsidering the mission of folklorists as primarily public practitioners, we must develop a creative repertoire of ideas and actions to extend the reach of traditional cultures through collaborative recontextualization into varied appropriate forms of representation—from film and festival to text and museum exhibit. Such representations should assist traditional communities in recreating their *own* metaphors. One place to begin a quest for metaphors of our practice is in revisioning the occupational structure of our own profession. Like any other group, we need metaphors and other creative devices to expand our sense of possibilities. Let me offer the analogy of medical practice.

In medicine there are doctors who teach and do research in medical schools—not unlike professors in graduate folklore programs, though most folklore graduate students have no regular training analogous to clinical training and certification. There are medical researchers at places such as the National Cancer Institute who are paralleled by folklorists on academic sabbaticals or at special institutes devoted primarily to topical research. There are public health officials, who seem most like state and local folklorists and some federal folklorists. Medical doctors are concerned with public health; and publicly employed folklorists are concerned with "cultural health," existing in an official relation to a polity that supports their place in a bureaucracy. Finally, the most familiar image of the doctor—those in private practice—is probably at first glance the least developed in analogy to folklorists. Yet we do have folklorists who work as consultants, "academic humanists," media producers, museum curators, and occasionally for corporations.

Perhaps the most significant correlate to private medical practice is that all folklorists at one time or another work directly with individuals. Public folklorists with broad social concerns, employed most often in public agencies, experience a cultural cross section of individuals. Thus they must be especially good "general practitioners" in handling a wide range of theoretical issues, genres, ethnic group concerns, ethnography, documentary arts, and communicative abilities.[4] A public folklorist, like a G.P., also practices in full view of communities. More than most medical doctors, our practice is often directly subject to the social and political apparatus of cultural groups, states, or national society as a whole.

Sometimes our work literally takes a social or physical helping or healing role such as doctors may play in assisting people to find their way through the mazes of health and government services.[5] More often it is simply our one-to-one relationships with "informants" that encourage self-confidence in their cultural knowledge and expression in a society whose media, educational systems, and formal institutions have usually invalidated such traditional abilities.

Encounters with individuals are not of course always in the classic folklorist-to-informant relationship. When I served as state folklorist in Louisiana, government workers regularly visited my Baton Rouge office to tell me their life stories, bawdy jokes, and riddles, and occasionally to see if I knew somebody who could uncross voodoo. They also wanted to discuss the scholarly record of their traditions: where the ballad of Black Jack David came from, how Cajuns obtained accordions, why jazz developed in New Orleans. Often they sought a subjective evaluation of their traditions: the "Do we have worthwhile culture?" question. Many such visitors to my office were the first members of their family who had gone to college or obtained white-collar employment, and they sometimes maintained ambivalent relationships to their Cajun, Creole, Isleño Spanish, Anglo-American, African American, or Native American cultural backgrounds. I found myself helping them examine their ambivalence while seeking their help in shaping the message of Louisiana's folklife program.

I also confronted racist and class-bound beliefs within and between groups that I considered barriers to cultural self-esteem and societal well-being. In such discussions a public folklorist can exercise healing powers founded on the respect our discipline has historically had for cultural difference and continuity, as well as the interest we share with a broader public in the meaning of inherited traditions in the modern world.

Ironically, it is primarily we "moderns"—often highly educated, deracinated, lacking community affiliation of the type we study—who may feel most emboldened and "healed" by the traditional knowledge we are privileged to learn, through folk performances we experience, or by the thanks we are given. More literally, my return from near-death of cancer in a Baton Rouge hospital can be ascribed in part to help I gained from a Cajun *traiteur*, black gospel singers, and a Cuban folk Catholic prayer regimen— all found through contact with orderlies, nurse's aides, fellow patients, and neighbors. As an outsider to Louisiana folk cultures without a singular belief system, my belief in the efficacy of many beliefs strengthened me. When I was wheeled from the hospital for the last time, the black woman pushing my chair told me, "We learned to read on two books in my house. It was the Bible and *Gumbo-Ya-Ya* [the Louisiana book of the Federal Writers' Project]. My daddy said those were books about us. And I know you do that kind of work. I'm glad you can get back to it." For public folklore practitioners, where chances for reflective scholarship and time to write are luxuries in short supply, our accomplishments are more often measured in such intangibles as personal appreciation and consciousness-raising at individual and group levels, rather than in the number of books and articles in print or lectures delivered. In our projects, often as not, we surrender or do not seek authorship in what is usually collaborative work.

Practicing folklorists must be equally at ease inside barnyards as bureaucracies, inside church halls as academy walls. In such a multivocal view of the discipline, our own verbal arts are essential to defining the work we do in others' communities. Our purposes must be rendered as eloquently as possible, remembering that as we create our own sense of self, a sense about us is created as well. During fieldwork for the Smithsonian's 1986 Festival of American Folklife program on the state of Tennessee, a mountain musician was told by a friend that the fieldworker (a folklorist) was a doctor. The musician, who knew the fieldworker only as a fellow musician, expressed surprise. His friend explained, "Oh he's not a real doctor, just a goddamn talking doctor!"[6] In the English pidgin of the Daribi people of New Guinea, anthropologists and linguistic missionaries are called *storimasta* (Wagner 1981:18). In rural Louisiana, some years after my initial visit to the household of a zydeco musician and club owner, his wife laughingly confided to me, "You know the first time you came in the door, from the way you looked and talked, I thought you were an encyclopedia salesman."

Reflexive folklorists recognize the importance of their verbal expressive role in culture-brokering between artists, their communities, and larger society. By offering some sense of one's personal otherness and a willingness to converse, the mutuality of accepted difference in the relationship becomes more possible. In practice, our best discussions with people become the dialogic basis for representations of the cultures with which we work.

A young Creole man told me (before we became better acquainted), "It's good you learn to talk with us, dance the zydeco, you know, but do *your* thing, be *yourself.*" My thing was to document the culture, through recordings and photographs and in words. I eased into this activity by assembling a photoboard of kinship. I was promptly hired as a wedding photographer by several Creole families. In bars and pool rooms, kitchens and living rooms, I played back the recordings of zydeco music I had made, hoping to show my sense of mission while getting critical feedback from varied points in the community. I found myself in constant discussion with people about their sense of being Creole and how the music made them feel.

Roy Wagner suggests that the study of culture is itself a cultural act, that our endeavor to know another culture—and efforts of others to know ours—are interrelated acts of cultural invention (1981:9–16). At the beginning of the century, Franz Boas pointed out, "It was only when their relation to our own civilization became the subject of inquiry that the foundations of anthropology were laid" (1904:514). We and our intellectual forebears have all used metaphors and other tropes to explain the interactive and socially situated nature of our work. Such metaphors have helped us in the attempt "to proceed from the known to the unknown" in relationships between ethnographers and others (Nisbet 1969:4). Yet, until recently, our metaphors and epistemologies have not explicitly included the role and relationship of the interpreter, or the fact that interpretations of culture are also an extension of it—whether offered by members of traditional societies or ourselves.

Others' cultures are historically described by folklorists and anthropologists as separate discrete objects through natural metaphorical analogies: cultural "evolution" and social "growth"; a "dying" tradition; cultural diffusion as a "pebble in a pond." Indeed the word "culture" itself is rooted in the Latin *colere,* meaning "to cultivate," later transformed to *cultura* for "a plowed field" in Middle English, and later (and still) associated with "breeding" and being "cultured" or "cultivated"—though it has been transformed and democratized in part by folklorists and anthropologists as something all people possess. More recent descriptive metaphors for culture from folklore study and symbolic anthropology were based on analogies to literature or theatrical performance: culture as text, story, or dramatic action. While these have had some usefulness in expanding our interpretive abilities, surely our responsibilities as folklorists, ethnographers, and anthropologists are not circumscribed as readers, listeners, and audiences that speak only amongst ourselves?

Over two decades ago, Roger Abrahams suggested that what were apparently "simple forms" of folkore are found in complex, socially embedded relationships within and across cultures (1969:104–28). In part he was responding to academics who dismissed folklore as elementary and inconsequential in the world of scholarship, by demonstrating that oral tradition genres possess interior complexities and social and performative kinship to belles lettres and other high art forms in terms of the structure of materials, patterns of performance, and context. Abrahams described a range of genres from the most interactive (conversational forms such as puns, jokes, and proverbs, characterized by the close relation of performer and audience) to the most static and stable (tales, ballads, epics, and other narrative forms, along with material creations).

In retrospect this continuum can be further refined with recent theoretical and ethnographic insights. However, the task of today's practicing folklorists is to describe and act upon a parallel and related continuum of genres of representation. For example, it is something of a truism that certain rituals and other folk genres bounded by age, gender, or religious restrictions cannot easily be included in the more public genres of representation—and often should not be. Scholarly texts, where ethically appropriate, may be a better means for representing such activities. Such texts are static genres with the reading audience at great private remove from both the author and the community represented. In contrast, certain conversational and public play genres, from joke sessions to music events, can be well represented in the media of recordings, radio, and film.

The question to ask about a documentary art form is how effectively is the reconstruction of the material matched to the community aesthetics represented—and in the eyes of what audiences? How well is the boundary between ethnography and art finessed to maximize appropriateness and empowerment as well as inclusion of varied audience sizes and segments (local, regional, national, age, gender, and economic groups)? With such concerns in mind, the contours of several forms of representation of folk traditions (radio programs, festivals, and concert hall performances—all multicultural in content and ostensibly national in audience) are briefly outlined below.

Radio: The Aural Tradition

Mass media representations of folk genres, if made with concern for immediate and community contexts, have the advantage over texts of giving outside audiences a fuller sensory experience of expressive culture in situ. Such documentary forms may have multiple styles and realizations, but they also can involve trade-offs between ethnographic depth, fealty to community sensibilities, and ability to reach broad audiences.

Radio relies upon the field method of audio recording, a relatively inexpensive and unintrusive documentary technology capable of reproducing the verisimilitude of behavior.[7] Audio recording has long been essential to folklorists concerned with individual interviews and oral tradition, although most professionals still do not make broadcast-quality recordings during their fieldwork. Radio is particularly suited as a medium of folk cultural representation because it can extend oral tradition through aural transmission. The finished product can be broadcast back to the homes of featured folk artists and communities.

Perhaps because of the relative ease of production and access, radio programming (like sound recordings) has often been used by communities themselves to link oral and aural traditions. The Grand Ole Opry and King Biscuit Flour Time, countless less widely heard programs, "hillbilly" and "race" phonograph records from the 1920s and earlier ethnic music cylinder recordings all reflect people's interest in hearing their own and related art forms played back through the media. Even today, with the proliferation of community stations, groups as different as Navajos and Cajuns use radio programs to maintain identity through language use or musical programming (Grame 1980). Yet radio, like any other publishing medium, has conventions and constraints built into how it is constructed, edited, produced, distributed, and interpreted. Many of these restrictions, most elaborated in the commercial realm, have acted to standardize, market, and limit traditional expression. However, public radio offers opportunities to folk community members and folklorists to extend and transform tradition.

When I produce Radio Smithsonian programs on folklife, I am bounded by a twenty-eight-minute format, a five-day production schedule, and a gestalt that suggests a style of radio that is neither community oriented nor fully ethnographic. Yet I am able to place folk expression and cultural issues into a series with a regular audience accustomed to the Smithsonian's more generally recognized and legitimated museum work with popular and high culture.[8]

In producing field-recorded features for National Public Radio's (NPR) "All Things Considered," I have had to further restrict my segments to a nine-minute time limitation. Short time frames allow less contextually nuanced representations of traditional culture. Yet they require a command of the complexity of context and content in order to set a priority for what will remain in the piece after extensive editing. For example, ambient sound is used to establish contexts without always explicitly describing them; field interviews are edited into short "bites" that retain coherence and faithfulness to original statements. There is also a tendency to let a part stand for the whole, whereby the personal story of a particular individual is used. In one program, African American sea chanteys were discussed in the words of one chanteyman rather than several practitioners of this song form. Work songs were not treated as a genre, except in broad introductory terms, but instead the focus was on the specific local and individual practice. This need not be a disadvantage, considering that general audiences seem to best grasp issues of diversity and equity through personal accounts. The cultural "story" can flow from the individual account— and hopefully the ethnographic base a folklorist can bring will make this story one that builds on an understanding of the community, the folk artist, the art form, and how it is transformed in representation.

One problematic tendency for folklore radio segments when placed on news programs is that they tend to push the folklorist into the role of omniscient reporter. Too often, sound bites are groomed to their most minimal size and presented as free-floating information devoid of context, with the interlocutor monologically framing each unit from the remote location of the production studio. I try to include selected questions from my field interviews in final radio mixes to remind listeners that what they heard resulted from a conversation with an outsider/folklorist who may have induced a certain direction of response—and, not inconsequentially, to have a voice they can identify with in the dialogue.[9]

Of course the reward for all the negotiation and trade-offs in radio production is airtime for people to be widely heard in their own words and sounds. When a blues lyric about the triumph of John Henry is heard after information about Boris Yeltsin's leadership or American elections, a certain artistic and political parity is symbolically achieved.

Many of the advantages of audio recording for radio can also be linked to production of cassettes, CDs, and LPs. The key difference comes in editing and distribution. Field recordings are usually edited to include only musical performances. Narrative aspects, even from the performer, are

usually limited (unless storytelling is the intended product—not a historically dominant approach). Contextual information, including commentary
of the folk artist and documenter, go into liner notes and cover graphics.
The recording may not be as widely heard as a radio program on a major
network, but it can become a significant artifact of artistic behavior when
placed in the hands of community members—and outsiders—on a more
selective basis than broadcast segments. As such, it provides an enduring
document for artists and communities of their cultural performances.

For example, I recorded nearly seven hours with cowboy singer and
storyteller Brownie Ford at his North Louisiana home. The resulting
CD/cassette offering includes about seventy minutes of music and narrative derived partially from this session, and lengthy notes and photographs
(Spitzer 1990b). In contrast, a nine-minute National Public Radio segment
I did on Ford from the same session includes portions of three of his ballads and about five minutes of him or me speaking. The CD/cassette is
something Ford can sell, promote on local radio, and keep as a personal
representation and archival document. The radio program briefly reached
about three million people nationally. Both audio artifact and broadcast
moment strengthen the traditional artist's position in his community and
encourage status and continuity for his tradition.

Folklife Festivals: From Green Glades to Rust Belts

The primary advantage of folklife festivals as a means of representation in
national settings is that folk artists and community members can present a
range of genres and specialized formats directly to audiences—community
or outsider.[10] Events such as the Smithsonian Institution's Festival of American Folklife require a great deal of prior research and logistic planning that
ultimately will result in an ephemeral product. Thus, long-term impact depends upon much parallel and follow-up work surrounding and after the
event. The brief participation by community members in such national
festivals can be effective if linkages are created to other forms of representation (local festivals, films, radio programs, conferences, publications)
and maintained with the communities represented. Issues to be presented
in the festive context must be targeted carefully to policymakers, institutions, and other groups influential in giving symbolic or concrete support
to communities or art forms represented.

Due to their celebratory, sometimes unfocused, and often multicultural
nature, folk festivals have been called "a low-resolution medium"[11] even by

their most ardent supporters. A critical problem in this regard is how to address general audiences when the festival is far removed from communities represented. Such outsider audiences often expect to experience performances as entertainment, and they are not accustomed to viewing long events and processes that require more than a few minutes or more than general knowledge to understand. Likewise, festivals demand some adaptation and adjustment on the part of performers, who may find it unsatisfying to do short musical sets for wandering crowds of tourists or to explicate revered or complex cultural information to noninitiates.

The Festival of American Folklife has been most effective in those years when—in addition to having an adequate planning and research base—presenters have been carefully trained to provide a frame through verbal introductions, dialogues, and colloquies with performers who can hold a crowd in place and provide a deeper level of understanding. Ideally, presenters—including folklorists and community scholars—are knowledgeable about the repertoires, styles, and cultural and personal histories of performers. Presenters must also be encouraged to learn festival modes of representation and work with participants to locate natural points in performance—tuning up, breaks for costume change or water, momentary pauses between numbers—to creatively interpret what is happening with comments, mini-interviews, or in the case of crafts and foodways, "play-by-play" or "color" commentary, in the metaphors of sports broadcasting.

Community performance genres whose mode is celebratory are often well adapted to representation at such a festival. However, genres such as crafts and occupational skills, not usually conceived natively as performative, must be "made" into performances for festival purposes. This can limit if or how fully such genres or processes are presented. For example, assembly-line work is not usually presented, and the preparation of raw materials for crafts is less often included than the final finishing work. However, audiences can adapt to obvious recontextualization and simplification, thereby leaving with a stronger sense of the aesthetics of work than they previously held.

Just as there are some folklorists and community scholars who become great festival presenters, there are also those participants who are adept at recontextualizing themselves. They have a public repertoire of talk or a genre that easily moves from original contexts to new ones. After observing a few performance workshops on the blues, Piedmont blues guitarist and singer John Cephas started conducting his own on-stage commentaries and interviews with his peers and elders.

One response to the problem of recontextualization at folk festivals is to produce group events within the festival that include a critical mass of individuals from the community represented. In conveying to the public the importance of communities in shaping and creating traditions, this also allows participants to present themselves for audiences approximating or sharing their own cultural understandings. They thus feel less pressure to modify the repertoires, styles, and meanings of what they do. Likewise the burden is taken off the general visitors to appear fully appreciative of something they know little about. Instead, they can watch over the shoulder of the community audience, in the role of the temporary ethnographer, in seeing how the community enacts its traditions for itself in a public space.[12]

When such public space is festivalized, the essence of this symbolic activity is dislocation, according to Brazilian carnival ethnographer Roberto Da Matta (1984:216–25). Normally private things are seen in the street. Likewise, the Smithsonian's Festival of American Folklife has had the potentially powerful role to dislocate or relocate communities on the National Mall in an attempt to frame them with national significance. This widely visible, resource-rich folk festival also has the responsibility of conducting its work in a model manner as regards advance research, cultural representation, participant social and physical comfort, quality archival documentation, and logistical organization. It must select timely, well-focused themes that can play effectively to immediate audiences on the Mall and to those back home as well as to federal officials and the national media.

The emerging critical discourse about public folklore has enhanced evaluation of how well this and other similar events envision, articulate, and attain their goals with some degree of effectiveness (cf. Bauman et al. 1988; Cantwell 1991 and this volume). In recent years, with the decentralization of public folklore programs to state and local levels, the most effective festivals in terms of long-term impact have been those that build on regional or local cultural expression in situ—festivalizing local public space—such as the Cowboy Poetry Gathering in Nevada, the Festival de Musique Acadienne in South Louisiana, and the Banjo Institute in Tennessee (all held in public parks or auditoriums). Content, if not theme, is somewhat self-selected by the location of these events. In these cases, the community audience need not be transported to a far-off festival site, but clearly the festival must appeal to locals to be successful.

Recognizing this trend to local community collaboration and interest in folk festivals, the National Council for the Traditional Arts' (NCTA) National Folk Festival departed the sylvan glens of the National Park Service's Wolf Trap Farm Park in northern Virginia in the early 1980s and now presents itself in such historic former industrial centers as Lowell, Massachusetts, and Johnstown, Pennsylvania. Although the "National" has not had the budget or orientation to experiment as fully with site construction and varieties of signage and interpretation as the Smithsonian, its largely concert-format festivals in grass-roots, Rust Belt locations have been able to build more directly upon concerns about cultural continuity and diversity within working-class communities.[13] Since both Lowell and Johnstown are National Park Service sites, the NCTA has developed fruitful relations with the Park Service and had a major impact on federal cultural policies throughout the park system.[14] The 1990s will be a decisive decade in determining if nationally oriented folk festivals are to retain utility as instruments of public celebration and policy—at a time when the issues of cultural representation are being played out with an inevitably greater sense of connection to communities at local levels.

"How do you get to Carnegie Hall?"[15]

Concert presentations of traditional music at an established classical music venue such as Carnegie Hall raise different questions of recontextualization from those found at folklife festivals. Carnegie's historic use of the label "folk" was largely oriented toward folk revival performers or "art song" interpreters of the musical traditions of other cultures. The performance setting itself is heavily charged in symbolic association with chamber music and symphony orchestras. The hall was designed in the Gilded Age, with proscenium stage, formal fixed seating, and acoustic qualities for the aesthetics of such performances. In serving as an "artistic director" for the Folk Masters series in Carnegie's 1990–91 Centennial Season, I did not have the flexibility of outdoor folk festivals and community-based public events in presenting other than music traditions. The only crafts presented were an Isleño singer's carved duck decoys for use during on-stage interviews, and instruments made by some of the musicians. No labor lore could be presented except that which could serve in a concert setting, such as African American sea chanteys and cowboy poetry. Ritual or sacred traditions were acceptable only if there was music associated with them that could be adapted to stage performance such as black gospel (long adapted within black communities) and Lakota Sioux singing (more rarely on stages). There were no foodways presentations. There were also the limitations of a confined stage space, house and stage management and production protocols unsuited to the performance practices of folk artists, and a portion of the subscribing audience whose primary experience was with classical music.

Yet in selecting performers (and genres) who could transform this space, who could invent folk forms of concertizing, who could shorten their dance tunes and vary their repertoire, ways were found to create events that pleased artists and audiences alike. The Western "high art" concept of musical virtuosity to which Carnegie Hall subscribes in reality varies in meaning and significance from culture to culture. So we had to find particular performers and genres that could play advantageously on the proscenium stage and find concert-hall-defined cultural translations of the concept.

Various American folk guitar (blues, country, Hawaiian) and violin (Cajun, jazz, old-time country, Cape Breton) styles work well in a virtuoso aesthetic context, and thus some evenings were organized by instrument. In contrast, much American Indian music is less focused on musical virtuosity than on "virtuoso knowledge" of ceremonial traditions—the authority of knowledge in practicing tribal traditions. Indian musics are so aesthetically and contextually grounded outside "Western" concert tradition that our program relied upon group variation: Northern Woodland (Mohawk) and Western Plains (Lakota Sioux) ritual song percussion and dance, alongside solo traditions of Comanche flute and Ojibway-French-Irish fiddling. The variation in style in one evening and knowledgeable narrators from each group made for an event that had the audience up and circling the fixed seats in final social dances.

Audiences were informed that in a tradition such as Anglo-American ballad singing, something akin to virtuosity was adroit memory and careful exposition in appropriate style of ancestral stories and events of local history. In African American gospel music, virtuosity could be found in individuals but was considered received from and in service of the Lord. In the case of New Orleans Mardi Gras Indians, virtuosity was located by performers as much in the ability to dazzle with homemade, handmade bead and feather costumes, as in dancing, singing, and drumming in one of the strongest African traditions in the New World.

We decided that the traditions represented should encompass a diversity cognate to New York City cultures, but at the same time bring music not often heard there. A New World theme inclusive of colonial-period Native American, European, an African diaspora peoples, as well as creolization among them, was consonant with these needs—it embraced strong Hispanic Caribbean participation. Acknowledgement of Carnegie Hall's classical-music-driven notion of the individual performer as singular virtuoso artist was satisfied in the "masters" part of the title, "Folk Masters: Traditional Music in the Americas," which also addressed concern for oral-tradition-based performers from the New World.

Part of my job was developing a common understanding with Carnegie staff about the significance and value in their centennial year of such a series, beyond political expediency or exoticism. My primary argument was that Carnegie Hall must stand for and seek musical excellence wherever it resides. For Carnegie's part, encouraged by the New York State Council on the Arts's Folk Arts Program, they accepted the idea of working with a folklorist. Further, given the almost sacred notion of space in this one-hundred-year-old concert shrine on fashionable 57th Street, it seemed clear that association with Carnegie Hall could be a strong validating factor for the artists and traditions represented.

Though most of the series was proposed for the intimate, salon-like (268-seat) Weill Recital Hall, there was some desire at Carnegie Hall to present some shows in the main hall. The problem with the latter venue was that filling the 2,800 seats would raise pressure for ticket sales, thereby skewing the thematic aspects of the program and the kinds of artists and genres that could be included. Although community-based folk music has been presented on a few rare occasions in the main hall in the 1940s and 1950s, by Alan Lomax's 1946 Folksong Jamboree and other earlier events like the 1938 jazz-centered Spirituals to Swing series, I saw a division in the kinds of artists that could be presented in the two Carnegie locations. Widely known and sometimes more commercially styled performers might work well in the main hall, while traditional artists—including those whose personal or artistic style made them suited to a more intimate space—would fit better in Weill. It was also enormously expensive to program in the main hall.

A tactical decision was made to use only the smaller Weill Recital Hall and to put the funds saved into recording the concerts for national broadcast on American Public Radio. The consistency of artists and level of intimacy in performance was preserved, and the audience could be enlarged far beyond whatever the main hall could hold. Contextual and biographical information on the cultures, genres, and performers was represented in a program book and through on-stage interviews with the performers or evocation of field visits. A negotiation between concert hall aesthetics and folk music genres and performance practices was effected.

The concerts sold out quickly, were generally acclaimed in the New York press, and reached nearly two hundred radio stations nationally on American Public Radio. Carnegie Hall had difficulty reconciling its self-image as a preserve of "serious music" and "professional" production protocols with the widely touted success of these folk music concerts and radio programs. They subsequently retreated from similar levels of commitment to research, experimental presentation, national outreach, concerts, and radio broadcasts of folk music. However, many on the Carnegie staff, the folklorist and the artists, left the experience more capable of working with similar elements in future situations—and other concert venues were encouraged to undertake similar projects.

CULTURAL CONSERVATION: PLAYING ON WORDS

All representations of folk art and folklife involve bringing single or multicultural content in varied forms to in-group (community or scholarly), local, regional, national, and/or global audiences. Public folklorists implicitly consider dynamics of the match between folk communities, their expressive contours, and the aesthetics of such representations to audiences, but most explicit comparative discussion on the topic has been conducted informally or in conference settings. The discussion that has taken place is usually under the rubric of "cultural conservation," the metaphor or analogy most often invoked in framing our efforts as public folklorists.[16] Cultural conservation as an idea and activity is still—and will perhaps always be—in formulation. Its meaning varies according to cultures, situations, disciplines, and arenas of involvement. As such the weaknesses and strengths of our work are inevitably engaged and revealed in the process of defining and using this, or any, purportedly all-inclusive term to represent our practice.

When using "cultural conservation" as a descriptive term we must be mindful of its association with naturalistic metaphors such as growth, development, decay, and regeneration, which have historically shaped perceptions of culture and tradition as physically bounded, atomistic, and subject generally to the laws of nature. Further, cultural conservation is intellectually and ethically problematic as a single organizing metaphor for our work with traditional societies in that the implicit comparison is of cultures, traditions, communities, and artists to natural entities subject to similar stewardship and conservation by apparently higher levels of human authority. Of course folklorists would not consciously acknowledge or advocate such a vantage point, but cultural conservation's metaphorical referent can imply limitations upon our understanding of and collaborative action with communities on issues of cultural continuity, equity, and diversity.

Does cultural conservation orient us to a primarily pastoral, bucolic, and uncritical view of culture? Does cultural conservation suggest that we see ethnic groups as somehow always reviving certain accepted cultural traits and bounded not just from mainstream society, but also from other groups? Could cultural conservation suggest restrictions on cultural change that might be beneficial to a social order? Certainly most ecological conservation strategies do account for dynamic change in natural communities. But can anything even in a dynamic natural model prepare us for the historic and current social realities of contact between cultures, conflict, colonialism, and creative adaptation through a process such as cultural creolization?

At best, perhaps, cultural conservation cannot be taken as a metaphor for the literal "saving" or "conserving" of a specific culture from "death" or diminution, but as a metonym indicating the pragmatic alliance with individuals and in communities where the link of balance and continuity in natural and cultural forces is especially in need of articulation. Cultural conservation may strategically provide folklorists some commonality of purpose with activist scientists and citizens from the natural conservation movement. It also infuses human and cultural concerns into environmental study and planning, which is all too often acultural or conceives of human beings only as despoilers antagonistic to nature, not cohabitants and a part of nature. The combined work of environmental scientists and cultural specialists within a broader humanistic framework of natural conservation, linked to cultural continuity and creativity, potentially offers a significant theoretical position and data base from which to shepherd natural and cultural diversity. As such, cultural conservation is acceptable as a rubric for action as long as it is applied with careful reflection upon who and what are involved in the conserving of culture, and how it is achieved.

A more elusive issue is the convenience with which cultural conservation and related terms ("cultural preservation") can fall into a facile bureaucratic rhetoric that provides a monologic cloak of political correctness for inaction or ineffective action. This concern appears to motivate David Whisnant's critique of Hunt and Seitel's description of cultural conservation as possible without dismantling larger economic and social systems (Whisnant 1988:236; Hunt and Seitel 1985:38–39). Most public folklorists' work actually falls in the tough negotiating space between such idealistic rhetorical calls for overhaul of how world economy and society affect local cultures, and the more polite, politically acceptable, official language of cultural conservation. At our best, we occupy the difficult but fulfilling terrain where the pragmatic realities of class and power faced by folk community members and public folklorists alike result in our most tangible successes—and compromises—in the pursuit of continuity and equity for diverse cultures. Our work should be at neither theoretical nor bureaucratic remove from real communities, though to be effective, it must engage both the insights of theory and the power of institutions.

One can agree that for too long we have been reifying naturalistic metaphors in describing culture but at the same time should reject blanket characterizations that "attempts at cultural preservation inevitably alter, reconstruct, or invent the traditions that they are intended to fix" (Handler and Linnikin 1984:288). There is no dispute that traditions are cultural inventions and inherited re-creations to begin with—though that does not deny their meaning and significance to groups. Handler and Linnikin misconstrue the "preservation" metaphor as representing the totality of cultural conservation activity when they are implying a segment of the specific orientation of *historic* preservation devoted to bricks, mortar, paint, and physical renovation. "Fix" is also an inappropriate descriptive metaphor since its use implies a broken machine, material in need of repair, or making something permanent. Many public folklorists, even those acting in the rhetoric of "preservation" or focusing on the significance of landscapes, are attempting neither repair nor re-creation of an imagined pure form. Rather our mode is collaborative in representing culture under new and current conditions. We assume that performances and meanings will inevitably be altered in representation and do not presume picture-perfect reframing of some isolated, inviolate cultural expression or community. To suggest otherwise is to be uninformed about most professional public folklore practice. Dell Hymes summarizes the situated, pragmatic, and aesthetic view of our work: "Much 'applied folklore' is genuinely part of the tradition with which it deals, a part of their adaptation to new conditions of performance" (1975:355). The symbolically constructed interpretation and representation of tradition must reinvent the original invention with "fidelity, insight, and taste" (1975:356).

And lest we be too quick to discard the organic and natural metaphors of earlier anthropology and folklore practice, many people with whom we work use such metaphors themselves to describe the importance of their "roots." From the account of *The Golden Bough* to the tale of the "Golden Goose," from plant and animal clan totems to family trees and the Tigers of Detroit, human analogy to and association with nature is thoroughly part of all peoples' expressive culture. In *talking with* tradition bearers we accept and use metaphors of mutual understanding and action—even naturalistic ones. Theoretical or pragmatic policy concerns aside, our need to be plain spoken with people about "preserving the roots" means that we have to remain open to all metaphors that succeed in redirecting the educational, political, economic, and media systems and policies that reduce cultural diversity, continuity, and creativity.

In our own community of folklore professionals, we are moved when Alan Lomax speaks of "cultural pollution" from mass-market media into that "big river of oral tradition" (1975), or by Moses Asch's idea that "Recording Is Like Cultivating" (1947). The latter phrase suggests the value of his work in recording and distributing an encyclopedia of the world's expressive sounds. To me, sowing the seeds of musical performances in the vinyl furrows of LPs or the digital fields of CDs is a way of documentary cultivation as a practicing folklorist. Such natural metaphors help us consider the pursuit and encouragement of oral literacy for all, in an age of information overload that encompasses aspects of both premodernity and postmodernity in its de-emphasis of the written word.

As one example of a locally appropriate and effective use of cultural conservation as a natural metaphor for social action, New Orleans documentary photographer Michael Smith has invoked the image of "cultural wetlands" to describe urban African American neighborhoods where traditions of street parade, music, and carnival flourish (1983:27). This usage resonates well with Louisiana policymakers who have had to deal with erosion and pollution of the Louisiana coastline and Mississippi River estuary, and concomitant threats to seafood supply and drinking water. For urban neighborhood people, the particular analogy of cultural production to a source of sustenance and pleasure (crabs, oysters, shrimp) is seen positively. The metaphor does not dwell on nature for its own sake. It does not analogize control of the "Wild Kingdom" by outsiders wanting to experience a rare bird or camp overnight; instead, it asserts the value and fecundity of the rural regional wetlands and by association the urban traditions as essential for life itself in the city's neighborhoods.

I sometimes think that all people are folklorists of sorts (perhaps one reason the term is widely, loosely, and sometimes maddeningly applied by nonprofessionals) in the sense that we all consciously or unconsciously assess our relationships to cultural tradition through the metaphors we inherit or create. As professional public folklorists, the work we should train for is literally communication rather than conservation. We must strive for eloquence in speaking with individuals and groups about their traditions. In this view, perhaps cultural *conversation* is a stronger universal metaphor for our public practice than *conservation*. In representing ourselves to communities through talk, we learn their meanings and they ours. We negotiate mutual representations in museums or in the media, on the festival stage or in the text. These exhibits, programs, and publications can reach nations, regions, and states of talkers while they feed back into the source communities with new ideas, techniques, and models for the future of tradition—constituting a vocabulary with which those talkers can speak for themselves.

Conversational genres have an emergent, problem-oriented quality and flexibility that I associate with the manner in which our practice should proceed: Public folklorists must have a wide range of languages and tropes available for use—on the bayou or on the radio, at private university or in government service—to describe and understand our varied and evolving missions. Like medical doctors serving communities, we must be comfortable with a diverse mix of people, venues, specialties, methods, and problems of professional practice. We still need to elaborate upon and make explicit the theories and methods of our practice—a job that will require cooperation of folklorists from all sectors of employ for a long time.

Yet the most hopeful association of the medical metaphor lies not in expanding the means and bounds of our professional practice, but in analogy to human health and well-being. Good health, the prevention of illness, and the process of healing are all the final responsibility not of doctors but instead of people as social and natural beings. Cultural survival and continuity will ultimately turn on the work of communities, community scholars, and traditional artists, not folklorists. But folklorists can be catalysts with metaphors, methods, theories, and acts that help to achieve a cultural equity that enriches us all.

NOTES

An earlier version of this paper was presented in October 1987 at the "Practice" sessions during the meetings of the American Folklore Society. I am indebted to Frank Proschan, Robert Baron, and Susan Levitas for their comments, and to Roger Abrahams, Dick Bauman, and

Bess Hawes for their longstanding dialogues with me about folklore in public places. Special thanks go to Archie Green, without whom this essay and book would not have been possible.

1. My initial contacts in the area began in 1974 with follow-up work for the Smithsonian's Festival of American Folklife in 1975. In 1976 I spent six months involved in fieldwork with the support of the National Endowment for the Arts, Folk Arts Program. This was followed by frequent visits to Creole communities for weekends, holidays, family reunions, *boucheries*, Mardi Gras runs, dances, and funerals, among other occasions. After moving to Louisiana to work for the state in 1978, I continued regular visits and fieldwork up until 1985. This work is summarized in *Zydeco and Mardi Gras: Creole Identity and Performance Genres in Rural French Louisiana* (Spitzer 1986). In addition to the above-noted agencies, I thank the University of Texas, the Wenner-Gren Foundation, the Louisiana Division of the Arts, and the National Park Service for their support of my research and productions.

2. The recordings that resulted were *La-La: Louisiana Black French Music* (1977) and *Zodico: Louisiana Creole Music* (1978), and later the film *Zydeco: Creole Music and Culture in Rural Louisiana* (1984).

3. I have further elaborated on this point in my paper "Folklore's Public Nature," delivered at the 1989 meetings of the American Folklore Society in Philadelphia.

4. Robert Baron's essay in this volume elaborates on the theme of folklore as a practicing profession. He notes the inability of the discipline to fully integrate public practitioners.

5. See for example Frank Proschan's work with an ailing Kmhmu elder, in this volume.

6. I was serving as "curator" of this festival program. This story was related to me by Joe Wilson.

7. Photography has many of the advantages of audio recording as to logistics, cost, low intrusion, and particularly, its single-sense dimension. Of course it does not reproduce continuous active behavior except in sequence stills and is less well served in broadcast than exhibit and publication. However, it is excellent as an archival medium, and like audio—since it exists in one sensory dimension—it allows the audience to engage imaginatively with its representations. For more examples and elaborated discussion see "Cultural Conservation and the Tradition of Media Documentation" (Spitzer 1988).

8. Radio Smithsonian was a magazine-format program broadcast to roughly one hundred stations. It ceased to exist at the end of 1990. Programs I produced during its tenure included "Music and Cultures of Senegal," "Looking for New England" (1990), "New York City Taxi Drivers' Lore," "*A la mode chez nous*: French Folk Culture in North America" (1989), "Visions of Folkways Records," "Back in the USSR: US/Soviet Cultural Exchange" (1988), "America's Many Voices: The Cultural Conservation of Linguistic Diversity," "From Homeland to New Home: The Culture of Migration," "World Music in the American Capital," "Folkways Records" (1987), and "Blacks, Whites and Blues: Cultural Crossover in American Folk Music" (1986).

9. Recent NPR segments have included five pieces for Black History Month in 1990 on Mardi Gras Indians, sea chanteymen, gospel brass bands, zydeco music, and Piedmont blues, as well as segments on cowboy singers and an Anglo guitar maker.

10. Material here is drawn from my text for the 1987 Festival of American Folklife's "Presenter's Guide" of the Smithsonian Institution's Office of Folklife Programs. For a historical overview of folk festival representations, see Robert Cantwell's essay, and for a current depiction of a Festival of American Folklife program see Richard Kurin's essay, both in this volume.

11. Personal communication with Robert Byington, former deputy director, Festival of American Folklife, Smithsonian Institution.

12. Frank Proschan, working with national networks of Laotians, was able to bring significant cognate local community members to the Festival of American Folklife in 1987. Also, see Richard Kurin's discussion of Italian and Soviet participants at the 1988 Festival of American Folklife in this volume.

13. Estimated audience size of the two major folk festivals varies. The Smithsonian's Office of Folklife Programs has projected attendance on the Mall from one to one and a half million in its promotional literature. The National Park Service (NPS) estimates a more conservative 151,000 over the eight-day event in 1991 (Mall Operations Office of NPS). The last National Folk Festival in Lowell, Massachusetts, drew 186,000 people over three days (NPS and Lowell Police Department).

14. For discussion of the National Folk Festival and the related touring projects of the National Council for the Traditional Arts, see program book, *50th National Folk Festival* (1988); *Masters of the Folk Violin* (1989); and *Masters of the Steel String Guitar* (1990). Also useful is Joe Wilson and Lee Udall's *Folk Festivals: A Handbook for Organization and Management* (1982).

15. The answer to the question, asked naively of a New York taxi driver, is "practice, practice, practice!" The discussion that follows is drawn in part from my essays in the Carnegie Hall program book, *Folk Masters: Traditional Music in the Americas* (Spitzer 1990a).

16. Cultural conservation framed various efforts of two of three federal folk culture programs in the 1980s. The Library of Congress's American Folklife Center has perhaps been the most consistent public advocate of this term through *Cultural Conservation* (1983) and a variety of field projects and meetings, including its 1990 Cultural Conservation Conference. The Smithsonian's Office of Folklife Programs's primary statement on cultural conservation is found in the 1985 *Festival of American Folklife Program Book*. More complete scholarly coverage of activity embraced by the term is found in *The Conservation of Culture* (Feintuch 1988).

REFERENCES

Abrahams, Roger D. 1969. "The Complex Relations of Simple Forms." *Genre* 2 (June): 104–28.

Asch, Moses. 1947. *Disc Records Catalog.* New York.

Bauman, Richard, Inta Gale Carpenter, Richard Anderson, Garry Barrow, Patricia Sawin, William Wheeler, and Jongsung Yang. 1988. *The 1987 Festival of American Folklife: An Ethnography of Participant Experience.* Bloomington: The Folklore Institute, Indiana University.

Boas, Franz. 1904. "The History of Anthropology." *Science* 20: 513–24.

Bourdieu, Pierre. 1982. *Outline of a Theory of Practice.* Cambridge: Cambridge University Press.

Cantwell, Robert. 1991. "Conjuring Culture: Ideology and Magic in the Festival of American Folklife." *Journal of American Folklore* 104 (412): 148–63.

Da Matta, Roberto. 1984. "Carnival in Multiple Planes." In *Rite, Drama, Festival, Spectacle: Rehearsals toward a Theory of Cultural Performance,* edited by John MacAloon, pp. 208–40. Philadelphia: Institute for the Study of Human Issues.

Feintuch, Burt, ed. 1988. *The Conservation of Culture: Folklorists and the Public Sector.* Lexington: University Press of Kentucky.

Fernandez, James W. 1974. "The Mission of Metaphor in Expressive Culture." *Current Anthropology* 15 (2): 119–45.

———. 1977. "The Performance of Ritual Metaphors." In *The Social Use of Metaphor,* edited by Christopher Crocker and J. David Sapir, pp. 100–131. Philadelphia: University of Pennsylvania Press.

Grame, Theodore C. 1980. *Ethnic Broadcasting in the United States.* Washington, D.C.: American Folklife Center, Library of Congress.

Handler, Richard, and Jocelyn Linnikin. 1984. "Tradition, Genuine or Spurious." *Journal of American Folklore* 97 (385): 273–90.

Hobsbawm, Eric, and Terence Ranger, eds. 1983. *The Invention of Tradition.* New York: Cambridge University Press.

Hunt, Marjorie, and Peter Seitel. 1985. "Cultural Conservation." In *Festival of American Folklife Program Book.* Washington, D.C.: Smithsonian Institution.

Hymes, Dell. 1975. "Folklore's Nature and the Sun's Myth." *Journal of American Folklore* 88 (350): 345–69.

Library of Congress. 1983. *Cultural Conservation: The Protection of the Cultural Heritage of the United States.* Washington, D.C.: American Folklife Center, Library of Congress.

———. 1991. "Cultural Conservation Conference." *American Folklife Center Newsletter* 12 (3/4).

Lomax, Alan. 1975. "Letter to James Morris." Folklife Archives, Office of Folklife Programs, Smithsonian Institution.

———. 1977. "An Appeal for Cultural Equity." *Journal of Communications* 27 (2): 125–38.

National Council for the Traditional Arts. 1988. *50th National Folk Festival.* Washington, D.C.

———. 1989. *Masters of the Folk Violin.* Washington, D.C.

———. 1990. *Masters of the Steel String Guitar.* Washington, D.C.

Nisbet, R. 1969. *Social Change and History.* New York: Oxford University Press.

Smith, Michael P. 1983. *Spirit World: Pattern in the Expressive Folk Culture of Afro-American New Orleans.* New Orleans: Louisiana State Museum.

Spitzer, Nicholas R. 1977. *La-La: Louisiana Black French Music.* Maison de Soul LP 1004.

———. 1978. *Zodico: Louisiana Creole Music.* Rounder LP 6009.

———. 1984. *Zydeco: Creole Music and Culture in Rural Louisiana.* Fifty-six-minute ethnographic music video. New Orleans: Center for Gulf South History and Culture.

———. 1986. "Zydeco and Mardi Gras: Creole Identity and Performance Genres in Rural French Louisiana." Ph.D. diss., University of Texas, Austin.

———. 1988. "Cultural Conservation and the Tradition of Media Documentation." In *Festival of American Folklife Program Book.* Washington, D.C.: Smithsonian Institution.

———. 1990a. *Folk Masters: Traditional Music in the Americas.* New York: Carnegie Hall Corporation.

———. 1990b. *Brownie Ford: Stories from Mountains, Swamps and Honky-Tonks.* Flying Fish CD FF 70559.

———. n.d. *Presenter's Guide: 1987 Festival of American Folklife Programs.* Washington, D.C.: Office of Folklife Programs, Smithsonian Institution.

Turner, Victor. 1974. *Dramas, Fields and Metaphors.* Ithaca: Cornell University Press.

Wagner, Roy. 1981. *The Invention of Culture.* Chicago: University of Chicago Press.

Whisnant, David E. 1988. "Public Sector Folklore As Intervention." In *The Conservation of Culture: Folklorists and the Public Sector,* edited by Burt Feintuch, pp. 233–47. Lexington: University Press of Kentucky.

Wilson, Joe, and Lee Udall. 1982. *Folk Festivals: A Handbook for Organization and Management.* Knoxville: University of Kentucky Press.

"So Correct for the Photograph"

"Fixing" the Ineffable, Ineluctable African American

GERALD L. DAVIS

I n "A Photograph: Lovers in Motion," a play in a collection of theater pieces by African American poet Ntozake Shange, the character Sean David boasts:

i realize yr not accustomed to the visions of a man of color who has a gift/ but fear not/ i'll give it to ya a lil at a time. i am only beginning to startle/ to mesmerize & reverse the reality of all who can see. i gotta thing bout niggahs/ my folks/ that just wont stop/ & we are so correct for the photograph/ we profile all the time/ styling/ giving angle & pattern/ shadows & still-life. if somebody sides me cd see the line in niggahs/ the texture of our lives/ they wda done it/ but since nobody has stepped forward/ here i am. yes. (Shange 1981:92)

I have long respected Shange's wordsmithing. The statement above both exemplifies the dynamism of her ear and craft and symbolizes my concern for an emic perspective in the use of media imaging technology for inter-

pretations of African American expressive performance. Shange offers to African Americans especially, and to those non–African Americans responsive to such matters, an articulated, rationalizing aesthetic canon to guide the representation of expressive aspects of the cultures of African peoples through media technology. "i gotta thing bout niggahs/ my folks/ that just wont stop/ & we are so correct for the photograph/ we profile all the time/ styling/ giving angle & pattern/ shadows & still-life."

Shange's use of the photographic process as a metaphoric frame for her elegant cultural aesthetic also permits her to target the inability of cultural researchers, folklorists included, to successfully "fix" African American expressive invention. Shange is quite explicit on this point. "if somebody sides me cd see the line in niggahs/ the texture of our lives/ they wd done it/ but since nobody has stepped forward/ here I am."

Whether or not one agrees with Shange's polemic, the products of African American informal expressive genius have had a seminal influence on American cultural life far in excess of the percentage of African Americans in the national population. Additionally, the study of Black folk has been invaluable to American scholars and crucial to the advancement of American social science and humanities. Interpretations of the expressive ways of Black folk in print and moving image media have resulted in handsome academic fortunes for some scholars and have powerfully affected American social "scientific" and humanistic thought. And yet, for all of that, the expressive ways of African Americans remain largely ineffable and ineluctable, and African Americans continue to be uniquely invisible and ubiquitous in the context of the American polity. "& we are so correct for the photograph/ we profile all the time/ styling/ giving angle & pattern/ shadows & still-life."

In his frequently referenced history of African Americans in United States films, *Toms, Coons, Mulattoes, Mammies, and Bucks*, Donald Bogle explains how it is that few Americans are without a functional stereotypic image of the African American (1973). Bogle argues that the five principal categories for the presentation and representation of African Americans in

Jessie Lee Smith (left) of Tifton, Georgia, converses with folklorist Beverly Robinson. Photo by Carl Fleischchhauer, courtesy American Folklife Center, Library of Congress.

theatrical (and "documentary") film he identifies are viscious Hollywood caricatures promulgated on the scholarly works of academics and literary popularizers from America's neointellectual antiquity. And because of the power of the Hollywood cinema and American television to mold perceptions, Bogle asserts that most Americans accept those insidious caricatures as the facts of African American life and personality.

And there is a darker realization in the shadows of Bogle's commentary. Disconcertingly large numbers of African Americans have also come to accept those fictionalized images as legitimate representations of African American contemporary social pattern and custom. Academic and commercial inventions have become, seemingly, our cultural orthodoxies. If African Americans are familiar strangers to Americans, we have also estranged ourselves from those powerful nurturing mechanisms that have guided Black folk through the socially dissembling seas of historical slavery and contemporary "invisibility," to borrow a concept from Du Bois (see especially 1903, 1924, 1940), Ellison (1952, 1964), and others who have represented well the particular conundrum of being socially and culturally African *and* politically American. But the elemental stuff of tradition has not disappeared from the lives of Black peoples. It has, rather, been layered over, become more deeply imbedded, more fully absorbed into the expressive systems and aesthetic presentations that keep people of the African diaspora distinct and dynamic.

I am an American folklorist concerned to examine cultural performance and represent the terms of what I discover in sanctioned scholarly formats. And I am an African American folklorist who believes passionately that the cultural systems of African American people are largely unexplored regions and that African Americans ought to be charting the truest course through this relatively unpathed terrain. The point at which the two most significant elements of my folklorist persona connect is also the point of my greatest personal discomfort. As an American folklorist I have chosen to be obligated to my discipline to increase knowledge and further enhance available scholarship; as an African American *and* folklorist I have elected to further enrich my own self-knowledge, and in a companion study, represent part of what I grow to understand in emic terms developing from and appropriate to African American people. How else can I and those of my African American and partisan non–African American colleagues who share my sense of mission meet Shange's challenge to "see the line in niggahs/ the texture of our lives/ [and] startle. . . . mesmerize & reverse the reality of all who can see?"

This seemingly self-serving and "regrettable" political orientation will profoundly disturb some of my non–African American colleagues who are justly proud of the activist nature of much of American folklore scholarship, particularly that considerable segment of the scholarship that centers on "underrepresented" communities. In spite of the fact that African American traditional ways surrounded me much of my life, I was drawn to the academic study of folklore through published reports of the appropriation of traditional culture forms to the contemporary political process by modern African political leaders and mainland Chinese intellectuals and politicans, and through my work in Tanzanian community development and national culture. I took myself quite seriously in the late 1960s, when I presented myself first to Alan Dundes and two years later to Kenneth Goldstein with a respectable Afro, dressed in a dashiki, having somewhere on my person a copy of *Quotations from Chairman Mao Tse-Tung* (a small-format, red-vinyl-covered volume known popularly as "The Red Book"), fully versed in neorevolutionary rhetoric.

In those days, my study of folklore had a tightly focused pragmatic purpose, the utilization of the workings of tradition as a positive intervention to aid the politicization of African peoples. My good friends at Berkeley, Alan Fong and Carlos Aarce, thought of folklore similarly with respect to their own communities in the context of what we regarded as a brutally unyielding, Anglofied, hegemonic America. And I suspect several of my African American folklorist colleagues came to our study similarly purposed. We knew little of the romance of the folk articulated with such unnerving good intention by so many of our fellow students; we were about a serious business—LIBERATION.

In the first instance, we young and very passionate activists understood liberation as an absolute necessity, and we spoke easily of "colonizers," "the people," "the masses," and the most imperfectly understood of our political buzzwords, "THE power structure." We meant that African Americans "by any means necessary," to quote Malcolm X out of context, had to wrest from those who were accustomed to making such decisions the power to control the destinies of our communities and lives. We were also convinced that bourgeois sentimentalities were inappropriate to our high cause. And therein, of course, lies a fundamental contradiction. As in China and many parts of Africa, many of the leaders of the several African American political organizations of the 1960s were either the sons and daughters of privilege or of families fully conversant with the values of middle-class life. Few in the leadership were able to successfully set aside those thoroughly inculcated values, which ultimately prevented the exploitation of a genuine dis-affection with the American Promise sufficient to fuel a long-term assault on the massively interlocked systems of discrimination by race in America.

The affect of costume and the pretensions of political posturing are less pronounced now, but the sense of high purpose remains. And I think it is a sense of purpose shared by all of us who find immense satisfaction working wholly or in significant part in communities to which we are somehow na-tive or "insider" by virtue of race, ethnicity, gender, sexual orientation, physical disability, regional affinity, or religion. While all of us perform well in a variety of professional contexts, our handle on method, practice, and theory-making, the "doing" of scholarship and the foundation of ad-vocacy public-sector work, will likely reflect our enlived sensitivities, sensi-bilities, and commitments to our native communities. Contemporary American folklore scholarship is certainly richer for these perspectives, and the practice of public folklorists contributes rather handsomely to the maintenance and development of these perspectives, which frankly cham-pion informed, if generic, emic perspectives. "i gotta thing about . . . my folks/ that just wont stop/."

Part of the process of deepening one's native or insider sensibilities—one is not genetically disposed to deep cultural knowledge—is the sharp-ening of one's "cultural eye," of knowing intimately and intuitively the di-mensions and varieties of an observed expressive event. While I no longer believe that only natives can and ought to conduct research in their own communities—how many times have I had cause to marvel at excellent ex-aminations of aspects of African American expressive culture by "out-siders," and quite wonderful examinations of non–African American mate-rials by African Americans?—I do passionately believe that folklorists doing work in communities of which they are part ought to produce a dif-ferent, richer, and more insightful analytic product than an outsider might produce. If not, then the business of "insider/outsider" as a set of her-meneutic principles is a facile, specious construct. Further, it is the native or insider's responsibility to define and illustrate the emic, interior nature of a selected expressive event so that the terms and the event are recogniz-able to an acceptable proportion of an "owning" community, even if such an identification opposes customary folklore or folkloric practice and the-ory. But even for the informed insider, the business of "knowing" is a dy-namic, accretive process.

Fine-focusing one's "cultural eye" is as much a matter of frankly parti-san allegiance, idiosyncrasy, and temperament as it is the artful application of established theory sets. (I have always been fascinated by the critical role of idiosyncrasy in the production of especially interesting research products.) "i gotta thing bout niggahs/ my folks/ that just wont stop/ & we are so correct for the photograph/." Apparent in print representations of cultural events, the point is axiomatic in the production of media representations of expressive cultural systems. Some folklorist-media producers simply "see" better than others or have a more refined and sophisticated cultural eye (perhaps because of partisan allegiance, idiosyncrasy, or temperament). The insider folklorist-producer ought always to have a head start in these matters, and therefore should produce a more densely analytic media product than the outsider. If the insider's cultural eye is well-focused, and assuming even a rudimentary understanding of the nuts and bolts of media production, the manipulation of media technology to serve the producer's emic purpose ought to result in an especially luminous, articulate representation of a recorded event. Ideally. Unfortunately, few of us, insiders or outsiders, are that articulate in the expressive ways of our communities or the communities we select to examine. So the folkloristic enterprise provides a sanctioned framework for examinations that are, oftentimes, peculiarly personal. While this is part and parcel of the enigma of the doing of folklore it also permits the visiting of racist and sexist views in the scholarship as well.

Some of my good friends wonder at my intense observation of the ways some Black men strut, display, and proclaim their male "stuff" and sculpture their hair, and my fascination with the pseudo-feminine, *seemingly* contradictory behaviors of other sets of Black men. My former wife did not share my peculiar habit of sitting at the windows of our third-floor West Philadelphia apartment on spring Sunday mornings to watch African American church matrons enter the Baptist church across the street with their sometimes wondrous millinery creations perched with queenly security on their heads. And my African American undergraduate students, who are used to my perambulations around campus, make me the butt of friendly, I hope, jibes as I try to hide my not-inconsequential self at the midnight hour on late spring nights among the masses of Black folk assembled to watch the pledge line of some fraternity or sorority step in one of our college halls.

This too is part of the doing of folklore. We folklorists are forever mingling and watching and notetaking in genuine attempts to understand the essential nature of expressive events linked to tradition. But unlike my Catholic friends, who are required, as a testament of Faith, to accept the

Mysteries, I am energized by what are frequently represented as the imponderables of African and African American expressive invention. The enriching of the field and depth of vision of my cultural eye in African American expressive systems is as much a matter of a deliberate and disciplined native son tutorial as it is a dedicated quest to understanding and appreciating my own varied elements, although in larger contexts than the individual. When I watch and think deeply about African American expressive acts, I am simultaneously wondering how best to represent and *interpret* what absorbs my interest in terms and modes acceptable to African Americans *and* to the scholarly discipline of folkloristics.

"/ & we are so correct for the photograph/ we profile all the time/ styling/ giving angle & pattern/." Trying to get a handle on the *visual* headcovering aesthetic of Black women in Africa, African America, and the African Caribbean testifies as much to my strong belief in the diaspora as a heuristic construct for interpreting much of African American expressive invention as it does to my larger, shared fascination for the powerful dynamic of hair-lore in African diaspora everyday life. Glorying in the complex and varied postures of African American males also has a didactic purpose; an entire American polity seems dedicated to murderously ripping what is distinctly his from the African American male, and yet he continues to survive and invent new and potently distinct presentations and performances. (And on the point of my fascination with the varieties of African American maleness, Lord I love to hear quintessentially macho, strapping males caution their less worldly cut-buddies not to "fuck with those faggots, they'll kick your ass!") On the business of gender-segregated African American greek-letter organizations, I am compelled by the density of the *very visual,* layered encoding of emblematic icons—costume, paraphernalia, patterned movement, and structured narrative—symbolic of and related to deeper varieties of esoteric knowledge held in some "secret" community organizations and historically African societies and designed to guide exemplary public behavior and sanctioned community roles. (In this case the historic ideal is probably more attractive and noble than the contemporary manifestation, regrettably.)

"if somebody sides me cd see the line in niggahs/ the texture of our lives/ they wda done it/ but since nobody has stepped forward/ here i am. yes." As Shange requires, I revel in the expressive stuff of Black folk; so watching closely the things groups of Black folk do is usually a joy and is always interesting. But the obligation to represent the product of that observation in a legitimately emic media format is made more difficult by my inclination in the direction of simplified or romanticized imaging. "gotta thing bout . . . my folks/ that just wont stop/." I suppose it is a consolation of some minor sort that this business of accurately representing the emic integrity of an expressive event in media is as elusive for those of us who are insiders as it is for our outsider colleagues. In the African American circumstance, we must not allow ourselves to be held guilty of the caricatures of Black folk Alan Lomax so pointedly criticized in the work of some outsiders. But we may have to bear some culpability for the perpetuation of those caricatures in the representational media. As African American folklorists—vested interest specialists in discerning and representing in academic modes the expressive knowledge systems of African peoples—we have, at times, unwisely used the museum or gallery exhibition, videotape, photographs, and film to extend the same mawkishly sentimental, remarkably uncomplicated, and largely ill-examined notions of Black folk art, aesthetic, and life held by uninformed "outsider" colleagues.

Let me push this admittedly singular view a bit further. I passionately believe that African American folklorists ought to be the cutting edge, the avant garde in the development of an authentic African American folkloristic body of materials. But as we presently stand I think we are guilty of a sort of gentle sophism. We are folklorists, and justly proud of that earned distinction. But our work is too rarely folkloristic, especially when we turn our energies and talents to the media representations of African American folklore and folklife. Ultimately, our reluctance to aggressively manipulate the images entrusted to us to illustrate a rigorously developed theoretical or conceptual position, anchored in a well-defined African American emic value, will put us in the unenviable posture of the misguided African American minstrel who naively mimicked White folk badly mimicking Black folk satirically parodying plantation manners. Put another way, we are not required to follow the uncertain lead of many of our colleagues in using imaging media as a kind of belletristic visual narrative rather than as a visual mode of hard-edged research analysis and reporting (though I hope our focus will always remain "soft" and true). As African American folklorists we can discharge our various and sometimes conflicting obligations to the discipline, social advocacy, and our communities by clearly and exhaustively examining the complex performance and expressive systems of African peoples in ways we deem valuable and purposeful. And certainly we should only use existing models if they make sense to our steeled purposes.[1] "i am only beginning to startle/ to mesmerize & reverse the reality of all who can see [because] i gotta thing about . . . my folks/ that just wont stop/ & we are so correct for the photograph/."

In the body of film work on African American folk, one of the most curious segments occurs in Les Blank's *The Blues Accordin' to Lightnin' Hopkins.*[2] At one point in the film, Hopkins and an Anglo male member of Blank's crew are sitting on a porch eating watermelon. Before they begin eating, Hopkins offers the man a fork. In the film there is no indication that the Anglo male either understands or appreciates the humorous jibe to which he has been subjected. While it would be ridiculous to expect the folklorist-filmmaker-producer to isolate and offer an explication for each discrete unit of meaning in a production, the tunnel vision that resulted in blind-spotting significant bits of information in the Hopkins film is endemic to an anemic, narrowed field of vision too frequently employed in media examinations of African American materials.

African American "watermelon lore" is pretty standard fare to anyone reasonably familiar with African American images. Fortunately, most informed outsiders are appropriately cautious when approaching the topic or in a circumstance in which watermelon figures. But in all-Black social contexts, folk will break into peals of good-natured laughter at watermelon jokes or at some unfortunate "cousin" who brings to mind old and unflattering images while "scarfin'" on some good, red, sweet watermelon meat. Granted the muted self-deprecation that oftentimes attends these riotous moments, watermelon eating in African American contexts can be a heavily coded event.

When one Black person offers another Black person a fork with which to eat watermelon, the person proffering the fork is signaling that the one to whom the fork is offered has moved to the margins of deep Culture, that the person has been somehow compromised. The perceived movement away may have been through education or migration from a rural to an urban area or as a result of some other change in status. Mark that the perception may not necessarily be a negation of the fork-receiver's achievement, there may be genuine recognition of and pride in the fork-receiver's elevation. But the fork, in the highly social context of buddies chompin' down on some watermelon, becomes a weapon of satire and is emblematic of the pretensions of "high" (read Europeanized) folk. As such, the fork also becomes a wonderful structural key, anchored in African American folk thought and humor, to a variety of internally appreciated social-context judgements. In this hypothetical situation, the African American folk-

receiver is being obliquely or directly reminded not to forget his or her cultural foundations.

One of Blank's intentions in the Hopkins film is to show the bluesman in several "natural" contexts—a rural dance, picking with some buddies on a store porch, and on his own porch. And with each new segment, the viewer's sense of Lightnin' Hopkins's community life deepens. But I'm not sure whether the viewer has any enhanced sense of the historically long tradition Hopkins represents (an important, necessary context), or of the griot/commentator-observer/aesthetician/innovator/composer/gender-bearer/dynamic "man-of-words"[3] nature of the bluesman, or of the fiercely bigoted, paternalistic world the bluesman frequently confronts when he leaves his community to do a gig. It's my contention, and I think this goes to the heart of this "insider/outsider" paradigm, that when Hopkins offered the fork to the Anglo male with which to eat his watermelon, he was rendering a metafolkloric observation on the dynamic of the personalities and the circumstances of the filming event. Whether out of respect, or affection, or a wry sense of humor, the point was clearly made. The young Anglo male was an outsider. As such, he was probably shielded from critical bits of valuable information.

I do not believe that African American expressive performance responds solely to or can only be understood in the context of a racist America. But if the point of *folkloric* filmmaking (or videography) is to illustrate significant elements of expressive, aesthetic performance in contexts a mature community recognizes and values as "traditional," the astute folklorist-filmmaker-producer will carefully construct her or his product to recognize the integrity of the community values underlying the expressive act. Ironically, the outsider folklorist-filmmaker can get away with artfully or even badly produced formula portraiture or static representations of crafting systems, especially if the filmmaker is working in communities to which he or she is not native. The insider folklorist-filmmaker, however, must evince a higher standard and should always work to respectfully represent or interpret the materials of his or her community.

If the insider/native folklorist-filmmaker (or videographer) is going "to startle/ to mesmerize & reverse the reality of all who can see," she or he is going to have to move beyond the standard visual conventions of the documentary *style* known commonly as cinema verité. The promise of cinema verité, the "method" most film and video documentarians have embraced, is unstructured or spontaneous realism. In this sense the precepts of "verité" filmmaking as a visual mode for *authentically* documenting and interpreting traditional or tradition-linked cultural events are fictive. The nature of media production is the manipulation of images. At every step in the media production process, creative decisions are made that reflect the informed idiosyncratic cultural eye of the person behind the eyepiece or the editor or the producer. Ideally, the insider with the truer cultural eye will produce the media analysis of an expressive cultural event closer to the way the event is understood, experienced, and symbolized in situ.

To accomplish that task fully, the native folklorist-filmmaker cannot restrict herself or himself to the existing conventions of media documentation. Dan Sheehy, in another article in this volume, suggests that presenters of folk performers should learn from choreographers, theatrical producers, and others who have spent their professional lives bending performing spaces to suit the needs of performers, without compromise to the integrity of the performer or his material. Similarly, folklorist-filmmakers ought to range far and wide to discover and articulate inventive techniques for enhancing the quality of the representation of the people with whom we work and those products they create guided by a traditional aesthetic.

Hopi filmmaker Victor Masayesva has successfully experimented with animation to represent those aspects of Hopi religious life forbidden to the eyes of the uninitiated. Combined with live footage and a pacing (timing) that reflects the Hopi respect for time in nature and the universe, Masayesva's work has met with the enthusiastic approval of Hopi priests and Hopi audiences. African American folklorist Adrienne Seward is hard at work on an examination of the film oeuvre of Spencer Williams (the original African American Andy of Amos and Andy), which is rich with visual translations of African American folk materials in terms easily recognizable by the masses of those African Americans familiar with traditional materials. And several years ago, I attempted a conceptual riff on an experiment in "concurrent theater" conceived and mounted by sculptor Benjimano Buffano (his elegant stainless steel sculpture greets anyone approaching San Francisco International Airport) in which he used multiple playing areas in a theater to isolate layers of an event (coordinated through dialogue, lighting, etc.). I ventured that since African American folk are accustomed to handling a variety of visual stimuli simultaneously, six forward-positioned viewing screens with each screen handling an element of an event would multiply the quality and the quantity of the data one could offer African American audiences. The idea still intrigues me, as an intellectual notion, because I think we habitually deny to audiences a sort of informed stimulation appropriate to their capacities. And certainly we ought to look more closely at the theatrical film constructions of Melvin Van Peebles and Spike Lee to have a clearer idea of the importance of community style, point of view, shooting angles, and teasing the equivalent of visual–one-liners from narrative events to achieve an insider/native perspective. "gotta thing bout niggahs/ my folks/ that just wont stop/ & we are so correct for the photograph/."

In any event, as African American folklorists (or as insiders), we need to keep in mind Shange's prescription for a closer identification in visual media of community-sanctioned invention and performance. And we ought to do a little more with risk-taking; we are under no mandate to be methodologically conservative. Black folk are certainly "so correct for the photograph/ we profile all the time/ styling/ giving angle & pattern/ shadows & still-life." Guided by this prescription, we can explore all manner of African American folklore and folklife, so long as it is "correct for the photograph," and remembering that not everything Black folks do requires visual representation. As we try to understand what it is we are seeing when we watch African American performance, and as we very self-consciously identify and build media models for the representation and interpretation of what it is we are watching, we cannot fail to do honor to Shange's canon and render the expressive ways of Black folk less ineluctable and ineffable . . . to Black folk, and to others.

> i am only beginning to startle/ to mesmerize & reverse the reality of all who can see. i gotta thing bout niggahs/ my folks/ that just wont stop/ & we are so correct for the photograph/ we profile all the time/ styling/ giving angle & pattern/ shadows & still-life. if somebody sides [us] cd see the line in niggahs/ the texture of our lives/ they wda done it/ but since nobody has stepped forward/ here [we are]. yes.

NOTES

A shorter version of this paper was prepared for a forum convened by Diana N'Diaye at the 1987 Annual Meeting of the American Folklore Society entitled "African-American Folklorists in the Public Sector: Issues & Perspectives." The original version was intended as a contribution to a dialogue between African American folklorists, principally; this expanded version retains the original focus and intent and, additionally, wants to speak to the issue of insider representation of community expressive events and values through media.

1. In the foreword to *Three Pieces*, Shange advises, "We are compelled to examine these giants [African American musicians, singers, and dancers] in order to give ourselves what we think they gave the worlds they lived in/ which is an independently created afro-american aesthetic" (Shange 1981: ix).

2. Les Blank, *The Blues Accordin' to Lightnin' Hopkins*. 16 mm, 31 minutes, 1969. Distributed by Flower Films, El Cerrito, California.

3. This conceptualization is attributable to Roger D. Abrahams and is articulated in several of his publications, especially "The Training of the Man of Words in Talking Sweet," *Language and Society* 1, no. 1 (1972): 15–29.

REFERENCES

Bogle, Donald. 1973. *Toms, Coons, Mulattoes, Mammies, and Bucks*. New York: Viking.
Du Bois, William Edward Burghardt. 1903. *The Souls of Black Folk*. Chicago: A. C. McClurg; New York: Johnson Reprint, 1968.
———. 1924. *The Gift of Black Folk: The Negroes in the Making of America*. Boston: Stratford; New York: Johnson Reprint, 1968.
———. 1940. *Dusk of Dawn: An Essay toward an Autobiography of a Race Concept*. New York: Harcourt, Brace.
Ellison, Ralph. 1952. *Invisible Man*. New York: Random House.
———. 1964. *Shadow and Act*. New York: Random House.
Mao Tse-Tung. 1966. *Quotations from Chairman Mao Tse-Tung*. Peking: Foreign Language Press.
Shange, Ntozake. 1981. "A Photograph: Lovers in Motion." In *Three Pieces*. New York: St. Martins Press.

Public Folklore

A Glimpse of the Pattern
That Connects

ROBERT S. McCARL

In spite of the increase in public folklore jobs, there are few theoretical discussions of the assumptions that lie behind this important aspect of cultural work.[1] The discussion that follows addresses this oversight by reaching out to a view of public folklore as it is actually carried out. I find that the insights of Gregory Bateson provide a useful framework in which to place this discussion, particularly his notion of the "pattern that connects" (Bateson 1979:13–15). I take Bateson's pattern to include all living things that have developed time-tested abilities to respond to and comment upon a changing environment. Rather than suggesting a deterministic fit between an individual and his or her ecosystem, Bateson's concept of the pattern that connects suggests that the variety of adaptations may cause organisms to collectively forget the balance between adaptation and change necessary for group survival. My thesis here is that certain individuals (often the raconteurs we work with as public folklorists) take it upon themselves to remind members of their culture of this deeper, life-sustaining level of meaning.[2]

I began the "research" for this paper as an associate professor, and I write now from the perspective of a public folklorist. It is important, I think, to briefly discuss my reasons for leaving an academic position to direct a state folk arts program. I received tenure in the Anthropology Department at the University of South Carolina in 1986. Having completed a dissertation on fire fighters, I was intrigued with the opportunity to build a public-sector master's program at Carolina parallel to the existing program in public-sector archaeology. After six years of administrative and departmental equivocation, however, I began to seriously look for work in the West, where I had grown up and where (under Barre Toelken) I was first introduced to the concepts and promise of folklore as both a discipline and an ethical point of view.

It is neither useful or tactful to explore all of the many reasons for my decision to leave academia, but I do think it is important to touch on a few key considerations that affected my move. First, I have always considered work in folklore as having public or community value. In my master's work with the descendants of a German communitarian sect in Aurora, Oregon; my small town cultural work as a part of the University of Oregon's rural humanities forum; my fire fighters research and my work with members of the Brown Lung Association in South Carolina, I have done my fieldwork in full view of a community and attempted to present it in such a way that they can utilize my perceptions as they see fit. As I prepared my tenure and promotion file I realized that although the department had recognized service as equal in importance to publication, that in no way guaranteed that the university administration would agree. Ironically, I found myself emphasizing and stressing my publications record and minimizing my service even though that aspect of my work had brought me into the university in the first place.

Secondly, my teaching became increasingly mechanical and structured. When I began teaching I relied on the currency of my knowledge in the field to carry lectures, select books, and plan courses. As the years marched on, I relied heavily on those earlier notes and found it difficult to find the

Eva Castellañoz, Mexican American *corona* maker, arranges individual flowers to begin making a *corona* for a *quinceañera*. Nyssa, Oregon, 1987. Photo by Jan Boles.

time to keep up with the reading and be creative about my teaching. I found the students (for the most part) uninterested, bored, and boring, and my courses began to resemble high school classes with nightly home-work assignments, multiple exams, and highly structured syllabi. The longer I stayed in academia, the less creative and enthusiastic I grew toward my pedagogical responsibilities.

I began to realize that there was little future for me in the occupational culture of academia. I was a beneficiary of the 1960s salad days of college admissions—a low C high school student from a working-class back-ground who squeaked into the system. Once I received a doctorate and be-gan to teach in an academic department, my background increasingly alienated me from the elitism and pedigreed hierarchies of the academic world. I could choose to stay in my secure tenured position, publish my ar-ticles, and fight for research grants, or I could realize the futility and lack of challenge (for me) in that world and go home to work in a position and a part of the country that could use my skills. It really wasn't much of a choice. Looking back on that decision after five years, I find increasing justification for my disillusionment. I continue to teach night courses at Boise State University and give lectures throughout the region to college students. I am amazed at the ennui, cynicism, and lack of commitment (among faculty and students) on most college campuses. The public sphere has its problems, but I am pleased to be dealing with various constituencies on a more direct, community level.

Which brings me to one of the key differences between my experiences as an academic and my work in a state agency: immediate accountability. When I wrote papers, taught classes, served on committees, and developed curricula in the university, I was a state employee second and a university faculty member first. This distinction extends beyond parking and library privileges to a lifetime of deferred accountability; that is, the state legisla-ture could fix my salary and affect the physical space in which I worked, but I was accountable in my research only to other academics. At the Arts Commission this accountability extends less directly to the legislature, but more immediately to the various ethnic and cultural groups with which I work. And within those groups, key individuals monitor, question, and cri-tique my fieldwork and my choices every step of the way. There is no lag between presentation of my ideas and the community's response. As my relationship with these groups continues, that evaluative loop pulls tighter and tighter.

TIME AND SPACE: THE CORONAS OF EVA CASTELLAÑOZ

One of the first people I met when I took the folk arts coordinator's position in Idaho was Eva Castellañoz. Eva is a *corona* maker from the border area of western Idaho and eastern Oregon outside of Nyssa, Oregon. I met her four years ago when folklorists Steve Siporin and Alicia Gonzalez worked with Eva on a slide/tape program that eventually led to her nomination for and receipt of a National Heritage Award in 1988. Eva is at the center of a number of women's traditional activities including the *quinceañera*—the celebration of a young Mexican girl's rite of passage into womanhood. Eva is a remarkable person whose energy and commitment to Mexican American tradition is both profound and celebratory. She taught herself, after watching flower vendors in Mexico City, how to make wax and paper bouquets and *coronas*, or crowns, and she has been making these ritual items for quinceñeras and brides for over a decade (Gonzalez 1987).

As a raconteur who interprets the subtleties of a ritual tradition stretching back to its Pre-Columbian origins, Eva pays a price. Throughout our continuing collaboration, she remarked that "people in Nyssa think I am crazy to spend so much time making flowers" (Gonzalez 1987:3). She also maintained that it is important to understand how flowers, coronas, and bouquets "hablan" (speak) during a particular ceremony. Eva is a folk artist pursuing a traditional art form in a large, dispersed Mexican community comprised primarily of migrant laborers and their families. Yet she is also much more than that. In a cultural milieu dominated by the Catholic church and the uncertainties of agricultural employment in Oregon's Jordan Valley, her wax and paper creations represent the strength of women and the *comadre* system that support this craft. To her nine children and her grandchildren, she maintains the stability of a traditional Mexican American household in a community consistently confronting negative ethnic stereotypes and a self-conscious denial of traditional cultural practices. Eva's coronas provide a focus for not only her creative needs, but as importantly, they provide her with an opportunity to link the ethnic past with the pluralistic present using her craft as a self-conscious, pedagogical device.

Eva is an optimist. Her father's migration from Juanauato to Pharr to Nyssa provided the family, and particularly Eva, with a goal: to settle in a Mexican American community in the United States and raise her family. Having achieved that goal, she has consistently linked her belief in the future with her adherence to the traditions of the past. She says,

> We should feel proud of the traditions we have that are beautiful and speak. They don't just exist—they have meaning. They say something and we need for people to be educated about what they are saying. When they come to me, I ask them, "Do you know what they are saying? I'm going to tell you so that you will know." And they like that I tell them. . . . Even though I am here in Nyssa, I am Mexican. One can't forget things because they are far away. We don't stop being what we are just because we are here. And we can't leave behind what is good. We can leave behind everything that is bad, but what is beautiful, no. (Gonzalez 1987:5)

It is this ability to use her art to pull together a number of temporal, personal, spatial, and political dimensions of her life and that of her comadres that makes Eva a remarkable person. Presenting Eva to outsiders as a representative of her culture, however, invites Americo Paredes's warning to Anglo ethnographers not to impose upon Chicanos or other minorities our implicit assumptions about their culture (Paredes 1977:2–3, 19–24). This presentation of a folk artist as stellar performer and ethnic "other" also anticipates more recent discussions by Michael M. J. Fischer regarding the complexity of ethnicity itself as a paradox: "Ethnicity is something that is reinvented and reinterpreted with each generation by each individual. . . . Ethnicity is not something that is just passed on from generation to generation, . . . it is dynamic. . . . [It] . . . emerges in full—often liberating— flower only through struggle" (Fischer 1986:195). Fischer's discussion of ethnicity and ethnic expression provides a useful approach to Eva's work in that her coronas are based on traditional Mexican designs and ritual uses, while they provide a measure of personal stability (both economic and cultural) in a rapidly changing sociopolitical environment. As Fischer states, "Whereas the search for coherence is grounded in a connection to the past, the meaning abstracted from that past, an important criteria of coherence, is an ethic workable for the future" (Fischer 1986:196).

For Eva, the making of coronas provides her with an opportunity and an obligation to pass her ethics and strengths on to the next generation of Mexican women. She says, "Some girls come to me because they want what other brides or quinceañeras wore. But I tell them no. You should use these for their significance in your life . . . each of the items (azahares [blossoms], coronas, lazos [lassos], and the arras [chests]), 'hablan' or speak" (Gonzalez 1987:4).

The making of coronas as a part of the quinceañera ceremony represents only a portion of a much larger cultural complex. The rights of women in Mexican American culture dominated by patriarchy and the Catholic church are explicitly addressed in the rite of passage and Eva's role in the ritual activity. The quinceañera is a secular coming of age ceremony that begins in the church but ends in the school gymnasium. It celebrates not only sexual maturation, but also the distribution of scarce material goods in an economically depressed, migrant community. Perhaps most importantly, it provides young people in Nyssa and throughout the valley with a mixture of American and Mexican secular and religious objects (cars, religious artifacts, coronas, American rock and roll) and places these items under their control. Eva choreographs, creates, and encourages a liminal context within which all of these elements transcend her individual control and pass through the collective will of her comadres to impart the strength and beauty (Bateson's "pattern that connects") of becoming a Mexican American woman today. Eva engages the young people in Nyssa in a dialogue with both their individual ethnic identities and their adult roles in a multilingual and multicultural world. By participating in that discourse, young people either begin to respond to the pattern, strength, and grace that Eva presents through her art, or they do not. As an artist she can only impart that message to those who are open to it, be they Mexican, young, male, female, or Anglo.

As a folklorist who has assisted Eva in drawing national attention to her art and community, I now have to accept the responsibility for assisting her in creating new economic and educational options in her life and work. The Hispanic and Mexican American leadership in Oregon and Idaho is intrigued by Eva's notoriety, and they have only recently accepted her into any decision-making role with regard to cultural programming. As one leader put it, "We aren't sure that the corona and the quinceañera are the image of the Mexican American people we want to project. It might be too stereotypical, too mestizo." The Idaho school system readily accepts our slide/tapes of Eva for viewing in the classroom, but our offers for demonstrations and residencies have only recently been approved on an experimental basis. And finally, Eva's coronas have been sought by collectors from the Southwest and the Los Angeles area. Although there are many corona makers and bridal houses throughout the region, Eva's flowers are particularly beautiful, and custom made to each woman. This additional source of income carries with it, however, a market exchange that lies outside of the previous comadre network of balanced reciprocity (Polanyi 1968:122–25).

Having commodified Eva's art in an attempt to communicate the cultural values and context that created it, I now must find ways to assist her in negotiating these new demands in the most positive manner. Which brings me back to the notions of time and space. The use of these ritual traditions by Eva and the other Mexican people in Nyssa is a modern manifestation of a cultural tradition that extends back to the early cultures of Meso-America. Like all folklore forms, these expressive media have existed because they provide a type of interaction and exchange that communicate important information within this culture. At the same time, the distribution of these traditions throughout the globe creates a truly dispersed and extremely complex multiplicity of contexts within which the traditions operate spatially. For me to truly collaborate with Eva I must first determine her priorities and understand the ways in which symbols of the past are being used to anticipate the future. To alter that function, to turn the corona into a product, or Eva into a "folk performer," without a physical or temporal context that she has chosen and is comfortable in, is to simply reinforce her objectification in the wider community.

Returning to Bateson's framework, Eva's coronas provide a pattern of grace or beauty that connects Pre-Columbian ritual and material culture to contemporary personal, female, and Mexican American cultural politics in Nyssa, Oregon. As a public folklorist it is my job to understand that pattern and respond to it as both an individual and a cultural worker. I cannot and should not attempt to empirically document and interpret Eva to outsiders since this violates her individuality by making her a "representative" performer, and it assumes that I can identify and present her struggle adequately. I cannot. What I can do is provide opportunities (create new times and places) within which Eva can reach out and grasp a pattern from the past that provides a contemporary "coherence . . . an ethic workable for the future" (Fischer 1986:196). Neither Eva nor I can articulate the patterns as we see them individually, but together we can develop a shared approximation or paired image (hers female and Mexicano, mine male and Anglo) that works for both of us.

The key consideration is that as an artist and an individual Mexican American woman, Eva has chosen the solitary task of both traditional corona-making and the maintenance of the traditional Mexican customs and rituals that surround that complex. She has consciously made that choice in her own life, even when large numbers of her peers are leaving these traditions as quickly as possible to accelerate their assimilation into Anglo society. Eva's perception of a "pattern that connects" allows her to see power and beauty in everyone and everything, whether it is quinceañeras or flowers:

Even though a lot people don't think so, I believe that the flowers have their own personality. For me they do, because I work with them and I see that some flowers let their little petals bend, others don't. Some flowers will take the wax, but this one didn't. So I think that they have their own mind and I respect each one. No two are exactly alike. . . . A rose is a rose, and it's a rose. And it won't look like a carnation because, it is not. Even if I want it to. . . . It's a real pity, that a simple paper can be transformed. . . . *y nosotros seguimos los mismos* . . . and we continue the same . . . and we're people. We're alive. (Gonzalez 1987:3,5)

It is this linkage of traditional forms of communication with contemporary social, cultural, and biological needs (the pattern that connects), which illustrates not only Eva's power and strength within her own community, but as I will later demonstrate, also provides the cultural worker with an opportunity to assist her and other tradition bearers to express themselves in a voice that we do not confuse with our own or otherwise freeze in yet another empirical tableau.

Eva's life and her work are in a constant state of transition from the nomadic subculture of the *campesino* to the more heterogeneous, working-class life of the sedentary agricultural worker in Nyssa. Yet behind this transition lies a cultural model—a way of perceiving and living in relationship to a much more fundamental cycle (birth-maturity-conception-death) that is at once personal, social, and biological. I can assist Eva only so long as I remain personally aware of this underlying linkage of her present struggle with that cycle. Eva's "pattern that connects" is not reducible to any single depiction or presentation, it is not a model or an abstraction of ethnicity. Her gift is an ability to see connectedness between what goes on today with a future that is personally and culturally balanced. As an artist she creates rhythm out of the cacophony of everyday life.

THE CONTEXT OF CRAFT: MINNIE DICK'S BASKETS

Steve Siporin began and I have continued a Native American apprenticeship program in the traditional arts. In Idaho, representatives from each of the five tribes sit on a panel that grants modest awards to a master craftsperson to teach an interested apprentice an endangered art, craft, or other traditional activity. We have supported Kootenai canoe building, the construction and use of a traditional Lemhi saddle, the making of a Nez

Perce drum from the killing of the elk to the teaching of the songs, and recently a Shoshone project teaching the harvesting and construction techniques of making a pine nut winnowing basket. My job is to locate the master craftsman, document the craft or skill, and then work with the apprentice to submit the application. The decision to fund or not fund the apprenticeship lies with the panel.

I concentrate here on the winnowing baskets made by Minnie Dick, from the Duck Valley reservation, which is located on the Idaho-Nevada border. Mrs. Dick is a ninety-year-old Shoshone woman recognized by both Paiute and Shoshone people as one of the last basketmakers still making willow baskets in the traditional manner.

Minnie stipulated to me upon agreeing to do the apprenticeship that she did not want to teach one person alone. She knew that there were many women (Shoshone and Paiute) at Duck Valley who wanted to learn how to make baskets. She also made it clear that she did not want to teach younger people, because, she said, "Young people don't want to do the work, they won't keep coming to class." In cooperation with the former tribal chair, Whitney McKinney, and his wife, Ivora, I therefore contacted a number of women elders through the tribal senior center. An announcement written by Ivora named the place and date of Minnie's "class" in the basement of the center, and it clearly stated that the instruction was designed to teach "basketmaking" to grandparents only. This cover term for all forms of traditional willow work would soon teach me a few things about the cultural and economic context of traditional arts, at least on this reservation.

The day of the first class, we arrived at the senior center, and Minnie was warmly greeted by her peers, many of whom had not seen her for over a decade, since she went to live with her son in Lee, Nevada. I left Minnie with her class of eight students and made the three-hour drive back to my office in Boise. When I walked in the door I had a message to call Ivora at the senior center in Duck Valley. I made the call and was informed by Ivora that Minnie was not teaching the making of a winnowing basket, but was instead beginning the class with instruction in the making of willow sun shades for baby boards, or as they are called in the area, baby baskets. I spoke to Minnie on the phone and immediately recognized that she was very uncomfortable with the arrangement. The drive back to Duck Valley seemed longer this time.

I learned that night that the eight women who signed up for the class could not have cared less what any outsider wanted to have happen in the course. They all knew that finely made sun shades on willow baby baskets made them attractive to modern Indian mothers and commanded an extra fifty or sixty dollars for the overall price when sold to outsiders. The making of baby baskets was what they wanted Minnie to teach. When Minnie tried to insist on teaching the winnowing basket, the women told her that few people harvest nuts anymore and that it was a waste of time to learn how to make those things. The following morning Whitney (armed with numerous examples of winnowing, carrying, and small jewelry baskets made by his grandmother) and I met with the class.

The basic issue was that the women in the class recognized the economic and personal feasibility of learning to make baby baskets and shades, while the winnowing baskets had no known use to anyone except a few elders who still harvested nuts. Whitney pointed out that just about everybody makes the baby baskets, while we could find no one who could make the winnowing type. Minnie said nothing. She just sat there splitting willows and working on a winnowing frame. The class eventually accepted a compromise. Minnie would teach both types of basketmaking, but the primary emphasis in the class would be on the winnowing form. Once the women had learned how to harvest, split, and weave that form, Minnie would move on to the shades for the baby boards. That is the way it worked, and after four weeks of instruction, the women successfully learned how to make both types.

In addition to drawing into question the efficacy of government programs designed to preserve Native American crafts through artificial stimulation, this example also raises some important considerations of context and my interpretation of the concept. Since the mid-1960s, context to folklorists has meant "narrowing the perspective of sociolinguistics somewhat, focusing not on the entire network of culturally defined communicative events, but upon those situations in which the relationship of performance obtains between speakers and listeners" (Ben Amos and Goldstein 1974:4). The ethnography-of-speaking approach provided a tremendous and long-overdue interest by folklorists in the actual processes and interactions of performer and audience, which continues to influence the field (Paredes and Bauman 1972). Yet our desire to generate microanalyses and empirical documentation of specific events has moved us perhaps too far beyond Malinowski's original distinction between the general context of the culture and situational context of the performed cultural practice (Malinowski [1935] 1965:22). It is to this original dichotomy that I would like to return the discussion of Minnie's basketmaking because it is only through an expansion of this notion of context that we can truly understand the broader "pattern that connects" her work to broader global contexts.

The historical reliance of the Great Basin people on the pine nut as a primary protein source no longer exists (McKinney 1983:7–9). Yet the annual migration to the Sierras by small groups of senior pine nut harvesters perpetuate the customs, rituals, and material culture of the pine nut complex at least among the oldest generation of the western Shoshone and the northern Paiute people. In addition to this historical context, the subsistence economy of most seniors on the reservation demands that they exchange traditional craft objects from beadwork to quillwork and baby baskets, either for money, through the gift shop in the rec hall or the motel; or to people in the area who can supply them with game, food, or wood, not available as part of the ever-diminishing supply of BIA or social security support. Taken in its entirety, these considerations and expectations comprise the cultural context within which any individual performance must be placed.

Basketmaking continues to be an economic activity with specialists such as those documented by Margaret Wheat commanding significant amounts of trade items and money in exchange for their wares (Wheat 1967:1–7). This is a practice that apparently extends well into the precontact period. Minnie's agreement to teach basketmaking simply reinforced an existing need in the minds of her peers. The baby basket is a viable product both in the family and outside of the culture for Anglo collectors, so it is to that product that the attention turns. Perhaps we should add to Malinowski's cultural and situational context a third consideration for a macroeconomic context when we turn our attention to the documentation and presentation of the traditional arts for specific organizational goals of our own. My relationship to Minnie and her work shifts from the balanced reciprocity of her previous mode of production to a more negative reciprocal relationship between buyer and seller. In causing this shift, I must ask myself how it is possible to keep Minnie's needs in line with the professional needs my intervention as a public folklorist (government official) represents. This is a crucial question, as James Clifford states: "Once 'informants' begin to be considered co-authors and the ethnographer as scribe and archivist as well as interpreting observer, we can ask new, critical questions of all ethnographies [and other cultural work]. However monological, dialogical or polyphonic their form, they are hierarchical arrangements of discourse" (Clifford 1986:17).

Just as I discussed the need to be sensitive to notions of cultural, personal, and collective time and space in order that we not turn a cultural practice into a bureaucratic or ethnographic distortion, we must also adjust our limited notion of context. The context of Minnie's basketmaking extends beyond the past into the future as the economic activities on the reservation react to and influence a global, not just a personal or even tribal economy. In spite of my personal or professional notions of traditional craft, the women taking Minnie's basketmaking course see that activity in economic terms that extend well beyond family to include consumers on and off of the reservation. As coparticipants and voices in the exchange of ideas and the brokerage of knowledge and power brought to the surface through my intervention, I have precipitated a dialogue about a multiplicity of contexts, which may or may not prove acceptable to an individual basketmaker. The important thing for me to keep in mind in this basketmaking discourse is that my voice is simply that of participant, not the leader of the discussion.

It is also important to keep in mind that the reservation exists as a unique cultural entity within even broader, global contexts. The current tribal chair at Duck Valley, James Paiva, is engaged in a historic water rights adjudication that will affect the members of this culture for generations. Rights to reservation water eventually draining into the Snake and Columbia systems provides potential income and security or the loss of same that will have a significant impact on Minnie's children and grandchildren. The complexities of making a baby or winnowing basket reveal choices between various forms of generalized, balanced, and negative economic options that must be understood in their sometimes contradictory complexity. My preference for the "organized" revival of a traditional art must be countered with a more realistic (insider's) appraisal of how that revival may affect the lives, fortunes, and values of the Shoshone-Paiute people, not as I might like it to be, but as they understand the realities of the various economic contexts in which they individually and collectively live.

Returning to Bateson's approach, Minnie's ability to see the pattern that connects is tangibly realized in the winnowing basket itself. As a utilitarian object it returns the user to a way of life and a technical interaction with the natural cycle that lies at the heart of the sacred/secular pine nut complex. As an object of individual artistry it connects the maker to the pattern of symmetry and beauty that can only be realized through a submersion of the artist in the unconscious acceptance and elaboration of basketmaking techniques from harvest to use. And finally, to the elder women who participated in the class, the basketmaking instruction inverts the natural process of supply and demand by creating a new, artificial context for a traditional form on the verge of obsolescence. My job is to attempt to understand all of these contexts and not violate any one of them in my zeal to create a successful folk arts program measured only by Anglo standards.

Equally as important, a reification of Minnie's basketmaking or a romanticization of her role as an isolated native performer could also result in a denial of the very economic contexts Minnie and her peers require to survive in a subsistence economy. Once a cultural process is set in motion (be it a natural or artificial revival, innovation, or evolution) it seeks its own striving for grace and balance within a personal, local, and global context that extends well beyond any single individual's perception or control. Minnie's choices as a person and an elder demand respect, while her choices as an artist and a teacher demand encouragement and support shorn of romanticization and objectification. As a collaborator and public advocate, my job is to perceive these different levels and patterns while tempering the impact of my will or world view upon them.

The pattern that Minnie articulates in her basketmaking extends beyond the creation of a utilitarian art object to address a personal need. Minnie returned to Duck Valley to renew friendships and strengthen family ties while also sharing knowledge about basketmaking. Her presence in the small reservation community of Owyhee as a traditional elder who is willing to share and talk about the old ways to children and grandparents extends the context of women's knowledge and power to the time before European contact. Each individual in the Duck Valley community must come to terms with the impact of the traditional ways on their increasingly Anglicized lives. Minnie's confidence and ability states in a clear and powerful manner what the loss of that pattern will mean to Duck Valley people.

CONTEXT AND POWER: FIRE FIGHTER BEA RUDDER

My initial field experience with the District of Columbia fire fighters began in December of 1979 and ran until March of 1980, when I produced "Good Fire/Bad Night," an ethnographic sketch of the culture as I had found it (McCarl 1980). I have written elsewhere about the positive and negative results of this process, but it is important here to point out that the original booklet (we printed two thousand copies for the fire fighters themselves) became a cultural document designed to elicit a response from the fire fighters (McCarl 1985:21–22). It never created any formal discussion, but it has been read and discussed informally by most of the fire fighters in the city. In 1984, Smithsonian Institution Press republished the original sketch with an accompanying bibliography and a theoretical section laying out the academic rationale for my approach (McCarl 1984). And last year, after being away from active fieldwork in the department for a number of years, I was asked to do a film that would supplement the Smithsonian monograph. At first I refused because of my commitment to projects in Idaho and my feeling that I was becoming stereotyped as a male folklorist who could only work in male-dominated occupational cultures. Rethinking that position, however, and talking it over with a few friends still in the department, I realized that I had the opportunity to experience cultural change over an almost fifteen-year period, and that the role of women in that culture could provide me with an opportunity to expand my theoretical perspective and grow as a public-sector folklorist. I decided to go ahead with the film, and we have been shooting in Washington for the past two years.

This interview with Bea Rudder illustrates the achievements of women in the fire service in the last decade. Bea was the first woman fire fighter in Washington, D.C., and she was suing the city and the department for admission into the fire fighting division in 1979–80, when I was completing my initial research. At that time she graciously agreed to an interview, even though I was working through the white-controlled union, and her lawyers strongly advised her against it. One of the narratives I collected from Bea contrasts sharply with the confidence and expertise we shot during the shooting of the film, and I would like to share both stories. In 1979 I was asking Bea what it was like being the first woman fire fighter in Washington. She replied as follows:

> I think that the only way they would feel that you are a great fire fighter is if you go in and single-handedly brought out ten people at one time and lost both arms and legs—then they'd talk about it. But if you go, just go in and do your job, just like they're going in and doing their job, then that's not good enough for them, you gotta be great. And of course they pat each other on the back all of the time. Build up each other's egos. First time we had a fire, and it took a few fires for them to find out that I could carry my weight, for them to at least settle down a little bit. While at first a lot of them just ignored me as if I wasn't here, and I know it was because they didn't know what to say to me: "What on earth am I going to say to this woman?" So they just chose to pretend I wasn't here. But they settled down a little bit and I

think that when they found out that they won't die because of me, you know, and that it doesn't make that much difference that I'm a woman, you know, the company's still run the same. . . . We've had a couple of second alarms. We had a fire at the GSA building, that was a second alarm . . . it was a lot of people rushing and shoving, that's the main thing I can remember. I hadn't been in the company that long. This is not something, fire fighting is not something that you can walk into the firehouse today, and tomorrow you say you like it. (Fire Fighter's Project, recorded on September 20, 1979, tape 1, p. 1)

In the monograph and in later papers and articles, I have used this narrative and others like it from women fire fighters to discuss the lack of a female fire-fighting tradition. I pointed out the incredible pressures on women who were denied access to the informal body of working knowledge necessary to perform the requisite skills of fire fighting, while they were continually being judged by men as if they had access to this occupational folklore. Ten years later, however, the strength and achievements of women in the work culture has forced me to rethink my previous characterizations. Compare that narrative with the following transcript taken from the film in progress:

McCarl: Maybe you could talk a little about your experiences at 16 Truck . . . ?
Rudder: I couldn't wait to become an officer. . . . During my probation year, I wanted to become an officer right away—couldn't wait. And it wasn't because of the officer that I had, although he was part of the reason. But as I was detailed around during that year, I met some very fine people that truly impressed me with their leadership qualities and their ability to take four men and have them working together—actually working like a machine on the fire ground. It's . . . like poetry. And I really wanted to do that. Not only that, but I wanted to have the responsibility of having a rookie and impart to that rookie some of the knowledge that I had learned.
  So I was detailed to Truck 16, yes. And it was the first time I was assigned to a truck company. Previously I was assigned to engine companies and the squad. Um . . . I was apprehensive. I had heard from my friends that there were a lot of men out there who were going to raise hell and refuse to work with a woman fire fighter. . . . Maybe their mother told them never to be bossed by a woman. Anyway—that may be cruel. I liked the responsibility of being an officer and being the one having to make the decisions. While I was assigned to Truck 16, I was assigned . . . worked with two rookies. The last rookie I worked with was exceptional. I truly enjoyed working with him and

telling him about my experiences. And actually seeing what I told him work on the fire ground. It's passing something on. He may forget my name, but he'll tie a knot a certain way that will help him one day and that is very gratifying. (District of Columbia Fire Fighter's Film, recorded on November 19, 1987)

In the preceding material, Bea is speaking as a sergeant in the department who has directed men on the fire ground as an officer. Her achievements in this highly competitive and demanding trade are attributable to her personal strength and courage, her honest appraisal of her abilities, and the respect she has earned as a fire fighter first and a woman second. Her power is a personal power, which informs and underscores her daily actions. There is still no collective, female fire-fighting tradition, but that has not kept Bea and the other twenty women in the department from learning the techniques of the culture and changing the ethos of the trade in the process.

I cite the preceding example in some detail because it reveals the importance of power and opposition within culture, and perhaps more importantly for this discussion, it has provided me with the means to mature in my effectiveness as a folklorist. Having been a student of the ethnography of speaking approach, and an early convert to Roger Abrahams's notion of the rhetorical power of folklore as a means through which "social misalignment must be confronted," the oppositional function of women's narratives in fire fighting fit neatly with my overall, normative view of the culture (Abrahams 1972:29). Yet a reappraisal of that perspective reveals that I was approaching women's fire-fighting tradition as a cultural monolith and empirical whole, when in reality it exists in a dialectic tension between personal power and male hegemony. Bea succeeds because she is tough and resourceful, but she also knows that there is informal knowledge that she needs to survive. Characterizing this in more Marxist terms, she acknowledges the differences between the forces of production (the techniques of work) and the relations of production (the social arrangements of the workplace) (Marx [1904] 1972:161–62; Heilbronner 1980:64–65; Burawoy 1979:16). Having understood the difference between the two, her social success is in part a measure of her ability to both physically and rhetorically move into the culture (Fernandez 1971:39–40). Bea's occupational narratives are not detailed technique descriptions like those of men, nor are they lists of complaints about the harassment she has experienced. They represent emergent tradition that mixes technical expertise with social concern in a way that continually reinforces her position as a fire fighter who is female. The folklore being expressed here is powerful and oppositional because it internalizes and changes fire-fighting culture while it transforms it.

This latter point leads to an examination of Bea's power as an individual within a hierarchy of power and an emerging discourse about her strivings toward a pattern that connects. This pattern is linked to the synchronization of Bea's (and other women's) entry into an occupation that is undergoing rapid technological and social transition within the city. We see in her stories and her life an ability to anticipate and express her changing role while she recognizes the inability of male fire fighters to come to terms with her. As Edward W. Soja points out in *Postmodern Geographies*, Foucault's notion of the "heterotopia" may provide a useful framework for this phenomenon. Citing Foucault, Soja describes heterotopia as "another space . . . actually lived and socially created spatiality, concrete and abstract at the same time, the habitus of social practices. It is a space rarely seen for it has been obscured by a bifocal vision that traditionally views space as either a mental construct or a physical form—a dual illusion" (Soja 1989:17–18).

The fire department and the city Bea inhabits is parallel to, but different from, the fire department inhabited by a second- or third-generation male fire fighter. Just as subways, high-rise buildings, and the proliferation of hazardous chemicals in our environment have necessitated changes in the techniques of fire fighting generally (the forces of production), Bea's movement up the command structure of the fire department provides her with an opportunity to see a pattern in her life and work beyond the historical and contextual constraints of her experience. The space that Bea has created for herself within the heterotopia of Washington, D.C., is both physical and mental, fixed and mutable. It transforms and is transformed by the male culture, but (like that of Eva and Minnie) responds to a level of meaning only partially visible to other participants in the struggle.

CONCLUSIONS

In the preceding sections, I have attempted to depict my interactions with a number of women artists and workers whom I have met and collaborated with as a public folklorist. Having posited (or more accurately, restated) a general theoretical model taken primarily from Gregory Bateson, I must also maintain a cautious skepticism toward any abstract model of social interaction of any generalizations taken from such a model. We live in an era when E. P. Thompson's *The Poverty of Theory* and Michel Foucault's *The Order of Things* and *The Archeology of Knowledge* call into question the lineality and narrowness of academic models and Western humanism. Yet if we are (as Stuart Hill asserts), "inaugurat[ing] the retreat from theoreticism" in this critical rereading of empiricism, then let's do so pragmatically. Folklore, as guilty as any field of romanticism and the comforting ideals of empiricism, has not yet developed a more dialectical or dialogical approach that has a strong following in the discipline. It is only, perhaps, through the unique network of public folklorists, who are not bound by the strictures of academic life or by its "tenure patterns, canons, . . . [or] the influence of disciplinary authorities," which shape academic discourse, that a truly reflexive, polyphonic approach to the study of expressive culture will emerge (Clifford 1986:21).[3] Academically trained, yet situated much more closely to the communities with which we work, we will be tested in our effort to discern "the pattern that connects" by our daily ability to link our professional skills to the transcendent struggles of people like Eva, Minnie, and Bea.

Finally, in examining the nature of grace (he also refers to this concept as psychic integration) as a useful metaphor, Bateson writes, "Each culture has its characteristic species of grace toward which its artists strive, and its own species of failure" (Bateson 1972:129). He goes on to point out in *Steps to an Ecology of Mind* that all systems of communication are hierarchical, with levels of conformity and nonconformity to the conventions of this striving. Most importantly, he suggests that human groups have the capacity to shift from what he calls complementary relationships (in which the patterns at one end of the relationship are different, but fit in with the patterns at the other end) to symmetrical relationships, in which people respond to what others are doing by themselves doing something similar (Bateson 1972:97).[4] As folklorists, we do not have to create or stimulate cultural pattern or value (in fact we should not consider this a positive goal of our work). On the contrary, we should seek to discover practitioners and cultural insiders who perceive and can articulate a pattern and assist them in making their point of view overt. I am not suggesting that we abandon the rigor and importance of the ethnographic process (taxonomy, documentation, contextualization, literature review, insider review, etc.), but that we make explicit our reliance upon key insiders who perceive and can articulate patterns that are invisible and quite possibly unknowable to outsiders.

Perhaps the most significant aspect of Bateson's concept of grace within hierarchies of communications is his expansion of our notion of context to a global, ecological plane. Within this macroenvironment, the personal/interpersonal and infra/superstructural contexts that have preoccupied the study of folklore can give way to more realistic theoretical and political frameworks. If we combine Bateson's ecological model with a healthy skepticism toward the empirical "data" we collect by admitting the "cracks and planes of fracture" in our own strivings, we may be approaching a model of cultural work that is both situationally and universally pragmatic.

Folklorists appreciate and attempt to understand stories. Whether we accept or reject Bateson's universal and pan-species definition of stories, we might admit that stories as artistic constructs provide us with a glimpse of the "grace" that Bateson describes. In my dealings with Eva, Minnie, and Bea as a folklorist, I recognize their commitment and response to a force that I am only dimly aware of. The changing of seasons and the maturation of a young Mexican American woman; the perfect few weeks in the fall when the willow on the creek bottoms is just right for splitting; and the onslaught of the rugged winter and Christmas season in Washington's ghettos, when families and children burn to death trying to stay warm in cardboard boxes or shooting galleries in Anacostia—these are all responses (stories) resulting from human interaction with a changing, but cyclical environment. Yet there is never a perfect "fit" between cultural expectation and environmental context, and it is into these cleavages that artists like Eva, Minnie, and Bea are drawn. Michel de Certeau suggests that it is within these inconsistent, "delinquent," and idiosyncratic contexts that true cultural opposition and human change takes place (de Certeau 1988:130). We might view the flowers made by Eva as a direct challenge to the patriarchy of the Mass and the hegemony of male, Mexicano culture; the baskets taught by Minnie as a refusal to mimic transgenerational education when succeeding generations have no time for or interest in the old ways; and the actions of Bea as an individual triumph of will over formal and informal relations of production that are committed to sacrificing individual will to collective, political, or economic goals. In the abstract, we can have it both ways—their art can be seen as both empirical and dialectical perspectives. Yet as people, these three women resist and defy our classifications.

Minnie, Eva, and Bea are the voices for those changes and the human perspectives that they empower. I cannot and should not presume to speak for them. As a professional public folklorist, however, I can offer them brief windows of opportunity to make their insights into the pattern that connects known to outsiders; and (imperfect as that may be) in so doing, share just a glimpse into that broader, global dance of interconnecting parts that lies behind our perceptions. As Clifford Geertz states, we must seek art and its practitioners not in isolation or in an abstraction, but "in their natural habitat—the common world in which men [and women] look, name, listen and make" (Geertz 1983:119). Our job is not to make the artist and her art understandable through simplification, it is to acknowledge the complexity, confusion, and discontinuity of cultural action and respond to that pattern as honestly and openly as our personal ideology will allow.

NOTES

This article is a revision of a paper delivered at the American Folklore Society meeting in Alburquerque, New Mexico, October 1987. The session was titled "Mixed Metaphors: Enculturation within/Education between Cultures," cochaired by E. Richard Hart and me. I would like to thank E. Richard Hart, Charles M. Carillo, Calbert Seciwa, Whitney McKinney, Steve Siporin, Archie Green, and Shelley McCarl for critical comments and suggestions. Any errors or omissions are, of course, my own.

Field recordings cited in this article refer to interviews conducted as a part of this study. The funding for this project was provided in part by the National Endowment for the Arts, Folk Arts Program; the Washington, D.C., Labor Council; and Local 36 of the District of Columbia Fire Fighters Association.

1. A notable exception can be found in Feintuch 1988. Also see Whisnant 1983 for a more in-depth analysis of the virtually unexamined political context of folklore theory.

2. Folklorists have long been interested in the relationship between both the classificatory and (more recently) the ecological models generated in biology and the physical sciences. Stith Thompson ([1964] 1977:413–14) explicitly links folktale classifications and scholarship to nineteenth-century floral and faunal taxonomies; Carl Wilhelm von Sydow's Darwinian approach to the adaptation and growth of folklore forms extends this affinity (von Sydow [1948] 1865); Barre Toelken attempted to apply the biological paradigm to a more processual approach to folklore study (1967); and Victor Turner suggested (1974) that this relationship was both fruitful and largely unexplored (1974). The cultural evolutionary and ecological model is most thoroughly presented in the works of Julian Steward (1955) and Leslie White (1959). A discussion of the ecological and sociobiological contributions and challenges to the study of culture can be found in Harris 1968. Possibly the American emphasis upon orally transmitted forms of folklore to the exclusion of more wholistic or materialistic studies (until recently) has mitigated the strength of a more ecological approach to the relationship between folklore

and the global environment. See Schlereth (1984:32–75) for a more thorough discussion of the development of materialist studies in a broader theoretical and ecological context.

3. A useful critique of folklore scholarship from a Western Marxist perspective can be found in Limon 1983. Also see Williams 1975 for a broader, historical discussion of radicalism and professionalism in folklore, as well as Dorson's reply (1975). A more reflexive approach to folklore can be found in Portelli 1988. Richard Lee in his work with the !Kung provides a specific linkage of a more Marxist approach to culture with the type of open-ended systems theory suggested by Bateson. Citing the work of Maurice Godelier, he states:

> Godelier, for example, has drawn attention to important correspondence between the Marxist concept of contradictions and systems theory's notion of feedback: "In order to explicate the dynamic of systems and their history, it is necessary to develop the notion of contradiction. . . . Cybernetics, in showing how systems can be regulated by feedback, has posed in new terms the problem of the existence of contradictions in physical and social systems. The mechanisms of feedback ensure a system's relative independence by relating the internal variation of its components to the external conditions of its functioning. . . . The condition under which a system can reproduce itself is thus not an absence of contradictions, but rather one in which contradictions are regulated and to this regulation maintains a provisional unity." (Godelier 1974:55, cited in Lee 1979:5)

One of the best ways to understand how a system works is to watch it undergoing transformation (Lee 1979:5). Godelier's "provisional unity" parallels Bateson's more felicitous notion of the pattern that connects. Both Lee and Godelier's concentration on the structural core of a culture (the biological and technological base) from which the division of labor and other infrastructural and superstructural elements of culture emanate is a more cultural materialistic and empirical linkage of biology and human behavior that I am suggesting here.

4. The classical dichotomy of social organization provided by Bateson parallels previous models suggested by social theorists from Weber (*Gemeinschaft/Gesellschaft*) to Durkheim (mechanical and organic solidarity). What is significant about Bateson's dichotomy is not its originality, but his perception that human groups (like other living organisms) can evolve. Like Bateson, I think that this evolution can be both graceful and in concert with the desire of groups and individuals to alter their social interaction.

REFERENCES

Abrahams, Roger D. 1972. "Personal Power and Social Restraint in the Definition of Folklore." In *Toward New Perspectives in Folklore*, edited by Americo Paredes and Richard Bauman, pp. 16–30. Austin: University of Texas Press.

Bateson, Gregory. [1936] 1958. *Naven: A Survey of the Problems Suggested by a Composite Picture of the Culture of a New Guinea Tribe Drawn from Three Points of View*. 2d ed. Stanford: Stanford University Press.

————. 1972. *Steps to an Ecology of Mind.* New York: Chandler.

————. 1979. *Mind and Body: A Necessary Unity.* New York: E. P. Dutton.

Ben-Amos, Dan, and Kenneth S. Goldstein. 1974. "Introduction." In *Folklore, Performance and Communication,* edited by Dan Ben-Amos and Kenneth S. Goldstein, pp. 4–7. The Hague: Mouton.

Burawoy, Michael. 1979. *Manufacturing Consent: Changes in the Labor Process under Monopoly Capitalism.* Chicago: University of Chicago Press.

Clifford, James. 1986. "Introduction." In *Writing Culture: The Poetics and Politics of Ethnography,* edited by James Clifford and George Marcus, pp. 1–27. Berkeley: University of California Press.

de Certeau, Michel. 1988. *The Practice of Everyday Life.* Berkeley and Los Angeles: University of California Press.

Dorson, Richard M. 1975. "Comments on John A. Williams, Radicalism and Professionalism in Folklore Studies: A Comparative Perspective." *Journal of the Folklore Institute* 11:238–39.

Feintuch, Burt, ed. 1988. *The Conservation of Culture: Folklorists and the Public Sector.* Lexington: University Press of Kentucky.

Fernandez, James W. 1971. "Persuasions and Performances: Of the Beast in Every Body . . . and the Metaphors of Everyman." In *Myth, Symbol and Culture,* edited by Clifford Geertz, pp. 39–61. New York: W. W. Norton.

Fischer, Michael M. J. 1986. Ethnicity and the Post-Modern Arts of Memory. In *Writing Culture: The Poetics and Politics of Ethnography,* edited by James Clifford and George Marcus, pp. 194–234. Berkeley: University of California Press.

Foucault, Michel. 1970. *The Order of Things: An Archeology of the Human Sciences.* New York: Pantheon.

————.1972. *The Archeology of Knowledge and the Discourse on Language.* Translated by Alan Sheridan. New York: Tavistock.

Geertz, Clifford. 1983. "Art As a Cultural System." In his *Local Knowledge.* New York: Basic Books.

Godelier, Maurice. 1974 (cited in Lee 1979:499). "Considerations theoriques et critiques des rapports eutre homme et son environment." *Information and Social Sciences* 13:31–60.

————. 1977. *Perspectives in Marxist Anthropology.* Cambridge: Cambridge University Press.

Gonzalez, Alicia M. Eva Castellañoz. *Corona Maker: Mexican-American Ceremonial Traditions.* 1987. 150 slides, tape program, and accompanying script, 15 minutes. Translated by Mary MacGregor-Villarreal. Produced by Steve Siporin and Robert McCarl. Idaho Commission on the Arts, 304 W. State, Boise, Idaho 83720.

Harris, Marvin. 1968. *The Rise of Anthropological Theory.* New York: Crowell.

————. 1979. *Cultural Materialism: The Struggle for a Science of Culture.* New York: Random House.

Heilbronner, Robert L. 1980. *Marxism: For and Against.* New York: W. W. Norton.

Lee, Richard B. 1979. *The !Kung San: Men, Women and Work in a Foraging Society.* Cambridge: Cambridge University Press.

Limon, Jose. 1983. "Western Marxism and Folklore: A Critical Introduction." *Journal of American Folklore* 96:34–53.

Malinowski, Bronislaw. [1935] 1965. *Coral Gardens and Their Magic: The Language of Magic and Gardening.* 2 vols. Bloomington: Indiana University Press.

Marx, Karl. [1904] 1972. Preface to *A Contribution to the Critique of Political Economy.* In *Karl Marx: The Essential Writings,* edited by Frederick L. Bender, pp. 161–63. New York: Harper and Row.

McCarl, Robert S. 1980. "Good Fire/Bad Night: A Cultural Sketch of the District of Columbia Fire Fighters As Seen through Their Occupational Folklife." Washington, D.C.: District of Columbia Fire Fighters Association, Local 36.

———. 1984. *The District of Columbia Fire Fighter's Project: A Case Study in Occupational Folklife.* Smithsonian Folklife Studies, no. 7. Washington, D.C.: Smithsonian Institution Press.

———. 1985. "Fire and Dust: Ethnography at Work in Communities." *Practicing Anthropology* 1 and 2:21–22.

McKinney, Whitney. 1983. *A History of the Shoshone-Paiutes of the Duck Valley Indian Reservation.* Owyhee, Nevada: Duck Valley Shoshone-Paiute Tribal Council and the Institute of the American West.

Paredes, Americo. 1977. "On Ethnographic Work among Minority Groups: A Folklorist's Perspective. In *New Directions in Chicano Scholarship,* edited by Ricardo Romo and Raymund Paredes, pp. 1–32. Monograph No. 1. Santa Barbara, California: Center for Chicano Studies.

Paredes, Americo, and Richard Bauman, eds. 1972. *Towards New Perspectives in Folklore.* Austin: University of Texas Press

Polanyi, Karl J. 1968. "The Economy As Instituted Process. In *Economic Anthropology: Readings in Theory and Analysis,* edited by E. E. LeClair and H. K. Schneider, pp. 122–43. New York: Holt, Rinehart and Winston.

Portelli, Sandro. 1988. "Research As an Experiment in Equality. *New York Folklore Quarterly* 14:45–59.

Schlereth, Thomas J. 1982. "Material Culture Studies in America: 1876–1976. In *Material Culture Studies in America,* edited by Thomas J. Schlereth, pp. 1–78. Nashville: American Association of State and Local History.

Soja, Edward W. 1989. *Postmodern Geographies: The Reassertion of Space in Critical Social Theory.* New York: Verso.

Steward, Julian H. 1955. *Theory of Culture Change.* Urbana: University of Illinois Press.

Thompson, E. P. 1978. *The Poverty of Theory.* London: Merlin.

Thompson, Stith. [1946] 1977. *The Folktale.* Berkeley: University of California Press.

Toelken, J. Barre. 1969. "A Descriptive Nomenclature for the Study of Folklore. Part 1: The Process of Tradition." *Western Folklore* 28:91–101.

Von Sydow, Carl Wilhelm. [1948] 1965. "Folktale Studies and Philology: Some Points of View." In *The Study of Folklore*, edited by Alan Dundes. Englewood Cliffs, New Jersey: Prentice Hall.

Turner, Victor. 1967. *The Forest of Symbols: Aspects of Ndembu Ritual.* Ithaca, New York: Cornell University Press.

———. 1974. *Dramas, Fields and Metaphors: Symbolic Action in Human Society,* pp. 14–15, 28–33. Ithaca, New York: Cornell University Press.

Wheat, Margaret M. 1967. *Survival Arts of the Primitive Paiutes.* Reno: University of Nevada Press.

Whisnant, David E. 1983. *All That Is Native and Fine: The Politics of Culture in an American Region.* Chapel Hill: University of North Carolina Press.

White, Leslie A. 1959. *The Evolution of Culture: The Development of Civilization to the Fall of Rome.* New York: McGraw Hill.

Williams, John A. 1975. "Radicalism and Professionalism in Folklore Studies: A Comparative Perspective." *Journal of American Folklore* 11:211–38.

Wilson, E. O. 1975. *Sociobiology: The New Synthesis.* Cambridge: Harvard University Press.

Field Work and Social Work

Folklore as Helping Profession

FRANK PROSCHAN

olklorists have traditionally been concerned with folklore of two primary kinds; on the one hand are leisure-time activities such as music, song, tale or ritual, festival, and prayer. On the other hand are subsistence-related activities such as crafts, folk agriculture, folk housing, occupational traditions, and foodways. These realms of human activity and artistic creativity by no means exhaust the scope of folklorists' curiosity in the 1990s, but it is unarguable that they have long dominated the professional interest of folklorists. This preoccupation with a relatively small domain of human cultural activity has increasingly been challenged by innovative examinations of other realms of creativity and (especially within public folklore) by new ways of comprehending and presenting even familiar forms.

The dichotomy between performance forms and material culture—here presented simply for its heuristic value—maintains its tenacious hold on our scholarly activity. Today, for example, this division is reflected prag-

matically in a division of scholarly labor in which material culture studies offer the last retreat for the defenders of male privilege,[1] who implicitly denigrate performance studies as womanly work. (Compare the historical peripheralization of folklore as a whole during the 1930s–1950s, as scientistic social anthropology gained dominance over cultural anthropology, and collecting of myths and folktales was consigned to women and unimaginative "research workers whose only bent is painstakingly to follow direction," in Mead's classic formulation [1949:296].)

Our conception of how to approach folklore research—and particularly fieldwork—are shaped in large part by a pastoralism that continues to have a pervasive influence on our practice, even as folklorists increasingly turn their attention to urban settings or electronically mediated communications. We are inclined to idealize a vital, vibrant folk community as one somehow bounded if not set apart, where the natural environment, social context, and economic base remain more or less continuous with those in which the folk traditions evolved over time. Even when we study transient traditions or temporary communities, we typically invoke values of continuity in time and space, and solidarity and consensus in social relations.[2] In a pastoral, idealized "traditional community" setting, a folklorist may have relatively easy access to folk performances and informants. In such traditional communities (some of which do, indeed, exist), time-tested balances prevail between work and play, between artist and audience, between product and resource, between act and consequence. Folk traditions persist in such communities in large part because they provide preexistent solutions that can be applied to recurrent problems, and artistic shape in which to render continuing experience. And so, for a student of tradition as for the community members, there is a predictability about life and work and a realistic expectation that certain traditions can be observed, documented, collected, and presented.

That these are almost truisms does not necessarily diminish their truth. And the fact that many traditional communities do not present a situation of pastoral harmony does not in any way deny that many communities do,

Ta' Yong Prachitham officiates at a ceremony for Kmhmu friends in Stockton, California. Photo by Frank Proschan, courtesy Office of Folklife Programs Archives, Smithsonian Institution.

and that we can continue to learn much by examining the artistic creativity that flourishes in those circumstances. However, folklorists have increasingly in recent decades broadened their purview to consider settings of social conflict and contestation, transformation and innovation, stress and dysfunction. Often such considerations center on new forms evolved or innovated as cultural expressions opposed to the domination of larger culture; less often do they examine how ancient traditions persevere as quiet acts of resistance. Even less frequently do folklorists consider how certain traditions are lost or abandoned in the face of sociocultural transformations. Maintaining and practicing many folk traditions may be matters of low priority, for example, to members of a community beset by massive social change, economic pressures, and cultural—or, indeed, geographical—dislocations. The community's priorities will not always coincide with those of the scholar, whose questions about old songs or the best storyteller usually do little to ensure there is food on the table or a place to sleep for anyone other than the questioner (grantee, contractor, public employee).

This recently expanding field of study (accessible to public folklorists and academics alike) often has practical consequences for the way we approach our work. A folklorist working with a community in turmoil will likely have a more difficult time observing and documenting traditional practices than one working in a situation of lesser change. For many folklorists, this argues in favor of finding another research situation—one more congenial and harmonious, and presumably more fruitful than a community in turmoil. And whether we are public folklorists undertaking short-term research leading to an imminent event or product, or academic folklorists limited by the term of a fellowship or the length of a summer break, deadlines and time limitations often figure into our selection of research communities and sites. But when we gravitate toward the pastoral and avoid situations of social upheaval, we give up unique opportunities for productive folklore research.

When the problems a community faces are not familiar recurrent ones but new ones, formerly inconceivable, can traditional solutions suffice? When the daily experiences of one's life make little sense in relation to past experiences, how can they be molded into traditional artistic shape? For those whose work week never ends, what happens to "weekend traditions" (to borrow a phrase from Roger Abrahams)? And how do traditions persevere when artist and audience are separated by miles or oceans, when natural resources are unavailable and vital objects cannot be produced, when acts of nature and of people no longer have the consequences they have always had before? And where, in all of this, stands the folklorist?

In attempting to explore these questions, I draw on a decade of collaborative work with Southeast Asian refugees in the U.S., work that has included conventional folklore research and documentation as well as fifteen months directing a multiethnic social service agency, the Refugee Resource Center, operated by the Lao Khmu Association in Stockton, California. That work has resulted at various times in the driest of academic discourses, in popular publications and presentations, in multisensory public spectacles, in legal pleadings and representations, and in lives saved, disasters prevented, and shattered psyches restored. The former are well within the familiar territory of folklorists, the latter, less so—or at least, less often acknowledged to be part of our public and professional responsibilities. Yet within our own heritage as folklorists stand numerous predecessors whose work combined research and advocacy, observation and intervention, scholarship and partisanship. Some of those pioneers were social workers or educators engaged by necessity or affinity in public folklore and applied cultural work, such as Jane Addams, Myles Horton, or Eliot Wigginton. Others were folklorists—too numerous to name—whose personal involvements with informants or whole communities transcended the strictures of scientific objectivity and developed into relations of mutual respect and interdependence.

Yet while those approaching folklore and cultural work from the perspective of social work are unembarrassed by their involvement with folklore, those of us approaching social work from the perspective of folklore have not always had the same self-confidence. Those folklorists trained as anthropologists have been threatened by their teachers with the bugaboo of "going native," while those with a scientistic bent fear contamination of their data. Moreover, we have all seen the process of historical revisionism in which the well-motivated, honest, humane, and compassionate involvement of folklorist with folk artist is condemned self-righteously by later generations as patronizing, exploitive, and corrupt. Thus in luxurious hindsight we caricature do-gooding settlement school workers and lampoon Elsie Clews Parsons on her yacht, belittling their substantial accomplishments, both intellectual and practical. Alan Lomax's financial relationships with bluesmen are exaggerated by some to the swindles of an Ivan Boesky or Robert Vesco; the historical context of those relations is ignored, and the mutually beneficial results of the research relationships (friendships) are diminished or denied. To be sure, careful scholars are increasingly moving beyond caricature to history, but they face resistance from those who have heard the gossip and do not want to be confused by the facts.

It is time, I believe, for folklorists to assert unabashedly two truths, the veracity of which I will support through an extended example drawn from my recent work with Kmhmu refugees from Laos. My first claim is that the social functions and deepest meanings of folk traditions are often displayed most clearly and compellingly at times of social stress. They are revealed especially to those whose relations with folk communities and their members are intimate, personal, pragmatic, and involved. Indeed, this is even more so the case for folk communities beset by the kind of pervasive social and cultural disruption I mentioned before. The second truth is that folklorists, by virtue of our broad interdisciplinary training and indeed because of the very nature of the expressive phenomena we study, possess unique abilities to intercede humanely in social and personal crises and to mitigate the harmful consequences of social disruption—abilities that impose upon us attendant responsibilities.

In support of these assertions, let us consider events surrounding a severe stroke suffered by one man I have known since 1982. At that time, I began long-term research and documentation among the three thousand Kmhmu highlanders who have come to the United States as refugees from their homeland in northern Laos (Proschan 1989). The indigenous people of Laos have resettled in a half-dozen U.S. cities, primarily on the West Coast. Ta' Yong was universally acknowledged within the Kmhmu community in Stockton, California, as a storyteller of unequaled brilliance. Prior to his conversion to Catholicism in a Thai refugee camp, he had been a practitioner of healing arts and a ritual specialist with deep knowledge of Kmhmu tradition. He was clearly an authority whose knowledge was crucial to the success of a documentation project on Kmhmu verbal arts that I undertook in 1984 and 1985, in collaboration with two Kmhmu community scholars, Khammeung Manokoune and Rene Seu.[3]

However, whenever I and my Kmhmu research collaborators tried to arrange to record interviews and storytelling performances, Ta' Yong claimed problems with his back, or his sore gums, or his schedule. In fact, as I learned only after months of disappointment, his reluctance to be interviewed had its real basis in issues of émigré politics, family feuds, and differences of dialect, region, and religion. Because my collaborators and I had come to be associated with one politically aligned faction of the community (through a number of circumstances too Byzantine even to summarize), Ta' Yong heeded the counsel of his faction's leaders and declined to cooperate in the research. The nature of the factionalism within the community was such that I was in a no-win situation—my genuine but unsuccessful efforts to record Ta' Yong went unacknowledged, and I was perceived instead as neglecting and ignoring him, contributing in circular fashion to a hardening of factional lines.

What I have been able to present succinctly here in fact took me months to understand. But as the dimensions of the community's factionalism and the intricacies of familial, regional, religious, and historical relations and differences became clearer, my understanding of the place of traditional knowledge and practice in the community was enriched many fold. The previously mysterious social dynamics of one particular ceremony I had documented, for example, could only be understood in the light of this deeper knowledge. One weekend, an elder of the faction with whom I worked most closely sponsored a wrist-tying ceremony for his wife. In California, in the absence of the traditional religious specialists who would have led a ceremony in the Kmhmu homeland, a knowledgeable elder would typically be asked to officiate. Ta' Yong and his next-door neighbor (also an elder) both seemed to be leading this particular ceremony, sometimes pausing to discuss what should be done or what should follow—not a particularly striking occurrence, since most Kmhmu ceremonies I attended involved consultation and negotiation over the sequence and content of ritual actions. What I found out only a good deal later was that the two elders were aggressively competing for authority over the ceremony, each seeking to officiate in an attempt to demonstrate his greater claim to traditional knowledge and ritual power. I had mistaken their competition for collaboration!

At the same time, both elders and a third guest who attended were members of the faction that was usually aligned against the man in whose home the ceremony took place. Ta' Yong and his neighbor were, as elders, in a certain sense above politics, and I could easily understand why they would be asked (and how they could agree) to lead the ceremony—they had the knowledge that was needed, and an invitation to officiate honored them as their presence honored the hosts. But the younger man was a prominent partisan leader of the opposing faction, one who had previously spoken to me of his host in very negative terms. When I later asked why he had been invited in light of his well-known hostility to the host's faction, I was astonished to learn that he was the brother of the hostess being honored by the ceremony—the chilled and distant relations between them had made it inconceivable to me that they were indeed brother and sister!

The community-wide deference accorded to Ta' Yong and the respect in which he was held, even by members of other factions, revealed a shared appreciation of Kmhmu tradition and a shared consensus about who possessed authoritative knowledge—a consensus that transcended petty differences. Even if people disagreed about almost everything they could find to disagree about, they nevertheless shared a concern for cultural conservation and a respect for the knowledge of elders. That broad consensus also aided my research by offering ongoing confirmation of emerging understandings and conclusions. Despite my continuing frustration that my collecting agenda was hindered by the stubborn obstinance of Ta' Yong and his friends, that same behavior, once understood, elucidated so much of what I had already documented. His absence on this occasion, or his participation on that occasion, which ceremonies he officiated and which ceremonies he merely attended, who substituted when he was absent and who deferred when he was present—all took on new and complex dimensions of meaning in the light of my emerging knowledge of social relations. Not only his actions but also those of others helped me in my research: the patient efforts of the opposing faction's leaders to keep channels of communication open and to tolerate slights and annoyances offered an example that I could only attempt to emulate.

That knowledge and understanding emerged slowly, as I have said, and only through long and intensive involvement with the community in activities and efforts that were often remote from those conventionally part of folklore research. One clue might come with helping someone fill out a Social Security form, when they report coming to me after so-and-so from such-and-such faction refused to offer help. Another clue might surface during planning for a fund-raising party, when the subtle diplomacy of who asks whom to do what is decided. A third clue would be revealed when I helped someone register a discrimination complaint at the local community college. And a fourth might come when I helped someone sign up for a garden plot at the community gardens. This then was the situation in June 1986, with my gaining increasing understanding of how Ta' Yong's knowledge of Kmhmu traditions fit into the community in which it was displayed and performed, and sharpening my comprehension of the social functions and the deepest meanings of those traditions themselves.

My frustration at the obstacles inhibiting Ta' Yong's cooperation in the research were in some small part balanced by those unforeseen benefits. Yes, I had not yet had the chance to record more than a few stories from Ta'

Yong, but as my understanding of the community, its traditions, and its social relations deepened, and as my opportunities to provide immediate practical benefits to Ta' Yong and his friends continued, the possibility that he would cooperate began to develop. Unfortunately, my frustration was replaced not by success but by eternal regret, as the news came that Ta' Yong had suffered a severe stroke that left him paralyzed, almost blind, and initially unable to speak. Yet even that disaster and its aftermath provided me with deeper understanding of Kmhmu tradition and society.

The crisis revealed that while factionalism was deep and pervasive within the community, realignments and reconciliations could occur instantaneously. For, at the time of his greatest need, Ta' Yong received little help from the members of his own faction except for a few members of his closest family. One of the group's leaders, a professional public health worker, didn't even bother to come to the hospital. That same leader's sister, a nurse, was no more helpful than he (both were the children of Ta' Yong's next-door neighbor, the friendly competitor we met above). Ta' Yong's own daughter, employed as a nurse's aide in a hospital almost within sight of her father's home, refused to assist him. Indeed, I and others outside Ta' Yong's group were the ones who stepped in to help him and his family during the crisis, especially two Kmhmu who worked with me in the social service agency.

The crisis also revealed to me traditional beliefs and ways of thinking that would otherwise never have surfaced. Ta' Yong's next-door neighbor, theretofore a member of the same faction and with seemingly shared sentiments and affinities, was accused by Ta' Yong's family of causing the stoke through magic. The two had a friendly rivalry of long-standing (ultimately evident even to a naive folklorist) as to who was most knowledgeable about Kmhmu tradition, competing (as we saw above) to officiate at ceremonies and vying for respect in the community. The neighbor-rival was from a different region of Laos than the largest part of the community and from an elite Kmhmu subgroup; he had a certain right by virtue of his cultural heritage and social status to lay claim to superior knowledge. Yet that same exotic background meant he was viewed with some suspicion by others. The fact that the neighbor's children (the public health worker and nurse) offered no help at a time of great crisis was taken as confirmations of their father's devious intent: Not only did he bewitch Ta' Yong, but he also forestalled his children's assistance.

The allegations of witchcraft were surprising to me—not because they weren't to be expected as tradition-based explanations for the mysterious ailment that is a stroke, but because whenever I asked (as a researcher) about spirit beliefs and magic I was told that they had been abandoned. The quiet fervor with which Ta' Yong's family repeated their accusations against his rival provided a striking contrast to the pious avowals I had always heard before—on the part of Ta' Yong, his neighbor, and the community in general—that following their conversion to Catholicism nobody believed in the spirits anymore. The continued vitality of the traditional belief system and the widespread adherence to those beliefs became apparent at the moment of crisis, contradicting the otherwise consistent testimony and public ideology that they were things of the past.

I could not have learned any of this if I had declined to involve myself in mundane pragmatic matters such as making hospital arrangements, providing chauffeur service, or buying pharmaceutical supplies for fear that such involvement would compromise my scholarly objectivity. Indeed, such disinvolvement would instead have perpetuated my ignorance and guaranteed my continued gullibility. Maintaining a hermetic barrier against the community would have had substantial consequences for my knowledge of Kmhmu culture, but even more serious ones for Ta' Yong himself, as we shall now consider. Here I return to my second assertion: that folklorists have unique skills and abilities to intercede humanely in social and personal crises and to mitigate their harmful consequences. We are sensitized, through our training and experience, to matters of interpersonal and interethnic communication to which most people are oblivious. And we are aware of cultural and social traditions and their variability to a greater extent than most people. Remarkably, it is often professionals whose daily work brings them into contact with a multicultural clientele who are least aware of such cultural and communicative diversity. Police officers, teachers, welfare caseworkers, or medical workers often persevere in an eternally reinforcing mind-set that their methods are universally effective without regard to cultural difference, precisely because the people they serve are often so needy that they are willing to tolerate inhumane or insensitive treatment without complaint.

Thus, to take one example, when a hospital staff is eager to dump a Medicare patient out their doors to save money, a folklorist's intervention can be critical. In the present case, the hospital staff was convinced that Ta' Yong's wife and family were incompetent to take care of him. After all, the staff explained to me in as many words, the family couldn't even speak English. The wife and family might not have understood much English, but they understand quite perceptively the arrogant contempt the hospital staff was expressing. Despite their own desire to bring Ta' Yong home, their response to the staff's arrogance was to exhibit uncertainty and fear: Here they were being told in unmistakable terms by persons in authority that they were too stupid to take care of Ta' Yong. Knowing little about his medical needs and their caretaking responsibilities, and nothing about the home health care assistance guaranteed them by law, the wife and family were understandably frightened of taking on his care, and they accepted the staff's judgment that they were incompetent to do so.

The staff made no real effort to explain to the family what would be involved in caring for Ta' Yong at home and reached the foregone conclusion that he could not be trusted to the family's care. The hospital staff insisted that he be warehoused at a nursing home and that the decision be made immediately, almost without regard to the family's concerns and wishes and completely without regard to the style and tempo of decision-making within Kmhmu culture. It was clear to me, if not to Ta' Yong's family, that the hospital staffer dominating the discussion was neither the doctor nor the social worker, but the billing clerk, counting minutes and dollars flying by while we dillydallied. At that point, the culturally sensitive intervention of a folklorist became critical.

From my knowledge of Kmhmu culture and social structure (and of the medical nature of strokes), I knew that if Ta' Yong were to enter a nursing home at that time, it would mean his imminent death. Still disoriented mentally from the stroke, depressed by its effects, frightened by his future prospects, with limited ability to see what was around him, and with his speech still impaired by paralysis, Ta' Yong would face grim prospects in a nursing home. We know that many illnesses and afflictions combine somatic and psychological causes and influences; in many cases (and particularly for a stoke) physical recovery is dependent in large part on one's mental health. There was no chance that Ta' Yong could receive the attention, care, and psychological support in a nursing home that would permit him some degree of recovery. I also knew that the Kmhmu traditionally took good and attentive care of community members with disabilities, that family members and neighbors had a duty and obligation to take care of the needy—a duty Ta' Yong's extended family was willing to accept (excepting his negligent daughter.)

On the other hand, I had seen, for Kmhmu whose affliction was intransigent, for those whose time had come to die, community members would not attempt to rally them with false encouragement or Pollyannish denial. People as old as Ta' Yong, once afflicted with a life-threatening disease, might simply accept their imminent death and do little to forestall it. Clearly if Ta' Yong were dumped in a nursing home, defined by medical authorities as having intractable and irresolvable problems, family and community would likely withdraw their attentions, and the hospital staff's judgment would be confirmed.

Weighing the possibilities with the Kmhmu colleagues working with me in the social service agency, we agreed that the prospect that seemed to offer the greatest hope for Ta' Yong's future health and happiness was to bring him home. For such an effort to succeed, however, we needed to fight the hospital first to gain some time—both to make the logistical arrangements and, more importantly, to submit the proposed course of action to a communal decision-making process. Logistics included initiating Medicare applications, Social Security arrangements, In-Home Supportive Services applications, renting a bed and a wheelchair, purchasing needed supplies and palatable food. The communal decision-making process was more delicate, bound up together with the factionalism I have discussed and complicated further by the intricacies of Ta' Yong's family situation, his daughter's disinterest, and his neighbor's purported witchcraft. Sensitive to those complications, I could submit the course of action that my colleagues and I had agreed was most promising to the assembled neighbors and relatives. In traditional fashion, questions were raised, reservations and fears voiced, opinions offered, grudges confirmed, complaints listed, alternatives evaluated, and informal consensus reached—Ta' Yong would come home.

Ultimately, there was no fairy-tale happy ending to the story. The stroke was of such severity that Ta' Yong regained little mobility and only partial sight. His speech, however, improved substantially, and he was soon able to eat, feed himself, and attend to his own hygiene. But after a few months, the promises of relatives and friends to assist with Ta' Yong's care were slowly forgotten, and the burden of taking care of him devolved onto his wife—herself also old, with limited English, and insufficient strength to lift him unassisted. She decided that she could not continue to care for Ta' Yong at home and would not be able to handle any emergency that might arise, and she felt that a nursing home was now needed. But now, there was time to locate a nursing home relatively close to her home, where she could visit every few days. Ta' Yong's post-stroke depression had lifted as he regained some of his faculties, and he could participate in the decision where he would stay (and he could now articulate speech well enough to get by in the monolingual English-language nursing home environment). A nursing home was no longer the death sentence it would have been if it had come immediately after his hospitalization. In the time since this paper was first presented at the 1987 meetings of the American Folklore Society, Ta' Yong and his wife decided that the Baptist nursing home was mistreating him because he was Catholic, and he returned home for the second time. After several months, however, the long-term debilitating effects of the stroke took their toll and he died—four years later than would likely have been the case if he had gone directly from hospital to nursing home immediately after his stroke.

More examples could be provided from my work with Southeast Asian refugees of how the cultural sensitivity and professional skills we develop as folklorists can be of service to the communities we work with. I have applied the techniques of discourse analysis and the insights of performance theory to explicate a transcript of a welfare hearing and demonstrate that the claimant was denied due process. I have used interviewing skills and interpretative procedures originally developed to elicit folklore data to assist people to prepare affidavits for immigration and other agencies. Other colleagues have used Cambodian youth dance performances to defuse gang rivalries or have employed inscribed bones traditionally used as record-keeping devices by the Hmong to establish someone's age and their eligibility for Social Security benefits. In each case, the skills and sensitivities of a humanist researcher were crucial in addressing the real-life problems of people who would otherwise have few advocates.

In presenting this extended example and mentioning these others, I have not intended to offer my own experience as uniquely virtuous or as the only responsible way of approaching folklore research in today's world. It is, rather, typical of the way that many folklorists—especially those in public-sector employment—relate our own research and scholarly agendas to the multiple agendas of the communities with which we collaborate. What is perhaps atypical is my unabashed acknowledgment that this is part of my work and my self-identification as a folklorist. Working with an ethnic group whose heritage had been one of inferior status and disenfranchisement within their homeland, I soon came to understand that a sense of *noblesse oblige* is not necessarily limited to those on whom fortune has smiled. The Kmhmu have a strongly ingrained tradition that I call *l'oblige des pauvres:* I may have little, but what I have is at your service. To refuse to provide help to someone in need is to jeopardize one's membership within the community. Let us establish within the community of folklorists that same tradition of service and responsibility.

NOTES

This article is dedicated to Ta' Yong Prachitham, 1911–1990.

1. Compare Michael Ann Williams's discussion of the "man's world" of folk architecture studies (1990).

2. Barbara Kirshenblatt-Gimblett, referring to the work of Werner Sollers, speaks of how received notions of folklore and ethnicity "privilege descent over consent" (1988:149 and this volume). More often, our notions of traditional communities privilege assent over dissent.

3. This extended collaborative research was supported by the Indochina Studies Program of the Social Science Research Council and American Council of Learned Societies. Additional support over the years has come from the University of Texas at Austin, the Smithsonian Institution Office of Folklife Programs, National Endowment for the Arts Folk Arts Program, National Endowment for the Humanities, Asian Cultural Council, and Lao Khmu Association. Recordings prepared as part of this research are archived at the Library of Congress (with the Indochina Studies Program collection) and the Smithsonian's Folklife Archives.

REFERENCES

Kirshenblatt-Gimblett, Barbara. 1988. "Mistaken Dichotomies." *Journal of American Folklore* 101:140–55.

Mead, Margaret. 1949. Methodological introduction. In *The Mountain Arapesh: The Record of Unabelin with Rorschach Analyses. Anthropological Papers of the American Museum of Natural History* 41 (3): 293–302.

Proschan, Frank. 1989. "Kmhmu Verbal Art in America: The Poetics of Kmhmu Verse." Ph.D. diss., University of Texas, Austin.

Williams, Michael Ann. 1990. " 'Come on inside': The Role of Gender in Folk Architecture Fieldwork." *Southern Folklore* 47 (1): 45–50.

The Journey of
David Allen,
Cane Carver

Transformations through
Public Folklore

SUSAN ROACH

The effects of public folklife presentations on folk artists and their art have concerned numerous folklorists (Degh 1969; Carey 1976; Camp and Lloyd 1980). Georges and Jones (1980:151–52) cite several examples of folk artists, such as Huddie Ledbetter ("Leadbelly"): Alex Kellam, Maryland fisherman and storyteller; and Zsuzsuanna Palko, Hungarian storyteller, who have received public acclaim through folklorists' presentation of their work. Other folklorists have voiced concern that the cultural intervention brought about through public folklore may undermine the authenticity of the folk tradition (Staub 1988; Joyce 1986a). In calling attention to the effects of such cultural intervention by public-sector folklorists, Staub (1988:166) asks, "Do we know whether folklorists are truly preserving traditions or serving as the unwitting agents of change to the very things the field seeks to conserve?" To deal with this question, Staub further suggests that folklorists engage in "serious self-scrutiny and ongoing self-conscious practice" and "confront the problems

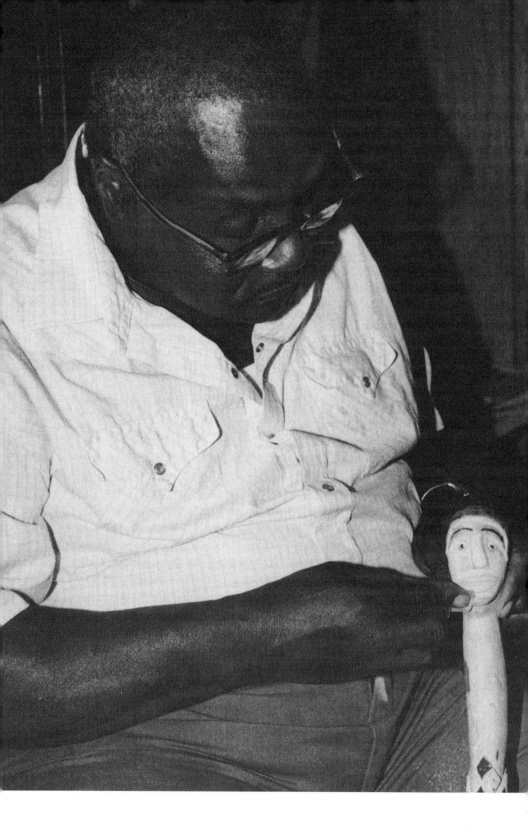

of our terminology and our invention of categories external to the communities that we serve (1988:169). Not only do we need to take note of our own intervention, I propose that we also need to carefully follow up presentations to note how the folk artists and their works are affected by this cultural intervention.

Such follow-up may be difficult, for often public folklore projects involve contract workers from outside the region. When the project is complete, the folklorists move on with no opportunity to measure the long-term effects of programming. Having been a free-lance public folklorist living in North Louisiana for a number of years, I have been able to work with several folk artists here over a longer period of time than is usually allowed the contract fieldworker. During these years, my folklore work included short-term contracts for the Louisiana Folklife Program (usually involving state folklife festival fieldwork and public presentations) and longer-term folklife grant projects (involving fieldwork resulting in regional festivals and/or exhibitions and publications). Additionally, as a consultant on the Louisiana Folklife Festival Board since 1985, I made recommendations for folk artists and special events for festival presentation. Given these years in one location and the fact that I often dealt with some artists repeatedly, I have had the opportunity for extended observation of the effects of public folklore presentations on these artists.

One artist I have documented with taped interviews and photographs from 1979 to 1990 is David Allen, an African American walking stick carver. While I initially documented his work in the course of field research for festivals and exhibitions, I became intrigued with him and his canes and their evolution and took every opportunity over the years to visit him and his wife, a quilter whom I was also interviewing for my dissertation fieldwork. Because of these visits and our working together at various festivals, we became good friends and frequently discussed our festival experiences. During these years I watched David Allen journey from relative obscurity in rural North Louisiana to his "discovery" and subsequent presentations in local, regional, and national public folklife events and the media. Allen's journey provides an example of the continuity and transformations in an

David Allen, a wood carver from Homer, Louisiana, sands the face on one of his walking sticks. Photo by Susan Roach.

artist's work, life, and world view wrought by his experience with public folklore.

PUBLIC FOLKLORE CONTEXT

Often, folklore research done for the purpose of staging folklife festivals precipitates many folk artists' discovery, and this was true in David Allen's case as well. A North Louisiana folk festival directed by the Reverend Frederick Douglass Kirkpatrick, Jr., and supported by funding from the Louisiana Folklife Program and the National Endowment for the Arts occasioned Allen's initial experience in public folklore. Because of his background, Reverend Kirkpatrick's direction of this project made it somewhat atypical; nevertheless, the festival fieldwork provided me an excellent entrée into the rural black community. A native of North Louisiana, Reverend Kirkpatick had attended Grambling State University, taught physical education in public school, and eventually joined the Southern Christian Leadership Conference and the civil rights movement. He moved to New York, where he preached and performed folk and protest songs. While performing in New York, he met Bess Lomax Hawes, who later encouraged him to apply for a grant to organize a festival to promote folk culture in his home state so that he could return there.

Kirkpatrick's approach to folk festivals was an aggregation of his traditional African American background, his social activism, and his work with artists such as Peter Seeger in the 1960s folk music revival. With his upbringing as the son of a Baptist folk preacher, Kirkpatrick believed strongly in the strength of a traditional country life-style, emphasizing achieving independence through traditional subsistence skills such as farming, carpentry, and sewing. He was not so much concerned about preserving tradition per se as he was about using traditional skills to make productive members of society. He saw folk craft as a means for young blacks to develop a saleable skill that would keep them out of trouble in the cities and off welfare rolls. In his statement at a Senate subcommittee hearing advocating passage of an American Folklife Foundation bill, Kirkpatrick illustrated his beliefs in stating why he thought bill S.1591 should be passed:

> It [the bill] is what fertilizer is to a turnip patch. It would mean life, growth, push, and a renewal of our base and a resurrection of a life that had been

almost destroyed. . . . This bill would serve as a catalyst in starting a drive to put some humanity back into the society, some love, and some cooperation which Dr. King talked about so diligently before he was killed. . . . We need cities today that appreciate all human arts and crafts. . . . As a lover of humanity and a victim of unrecognized culture, I ask your support of this bill because everybody's got a right to live. (Kirkpatrick 1970:55–57)

Kirkpatrick brought this philosophy back with him to North Louisiana when he returned for the folk festival project with state and national grants. Since Kirkpatrick had no folklife programming experience or academic training, the funding agencies advised him to obtain a folklorist for the project. Thus upon the referral of Nick Spitzer, then Louisiana state folklorist, Kirkpatrick hired me, fresh out of graduate school. Although he had been away from his native Claiborne Parish for many years, Kirkpatrick already had many community contacts ranging from folksingers to housewives making popular crafts such as flowers from egg cartons. Among these contacts was David Allen's daughter-in-law, who told Kirkpatrick about her father-in-law's wood carving and her mother-in-law's quilting. Thus, upon her referral, Kirpatrick and I first met David Allen and his wife, Rosie Lee Allen, who welcomed us warmly into their home.

ARTIST'S BACKGROUND AND ART FORM

Upon interviewing David Allen, I found that his experience with walking-stick carving did not neatly fit my academic definition of folk art as those traditional art forms passed on through informal learning in a community context (see Glassie 1972). Partially included by this definition, Allen's work came out of a traditional southern pastime craft—whittling or wood carving; however, having never seen carved walking sticks, Allen originated his own forms and technique development. This seemingly independent creation of forms with analogues to work done by other African Americans and Africans (Vlach 1978:41) is found in other carvers such as David Philpot, Henry Gudgell (Perry 1989:42), and Sultan Rogers (Ferris 1989:80). Although Allen does not remember seeing any carved walking sticks during his youth, he does note that in his community, sticks were commonly cut and used in walking, especially at night, as an aid for sure footing and a weapon for warding off dogs and other potential attackers.

Allen did have a history of woodworking experience in his family, and in his rural community, whittling was a traditional pastime. His father, a farmer in Claiborne Parish, made white-oak baskets and hickory ax handles, and passed on his expertise with wood to his son. Thus, Allen's walking-stick carving emerged as an extension of this background.

Born in Claiborne Parish, Louisiana, in 1925, David Allen began whittling toys as a boy. His first tries at whittling were accomplished with a pocketknife, which he had found under the house. He had to keep the knife hidden and work on the sly because he was considered too young to be playing with knives. He began whittling on sticks and twigs and learned to make simple toys such as slingshots and, later, objects such as shoeshine boxes. David Allen's idea to carve walking sticks came to him rather unintentionally about the age of fifteen. He describes making his first stick: "One day I was walking down the road. I cut a little gum stick down and was walking with it. I sat down under a shade tree and started trimming on the thing, and the more I trimmed, the more I liked it" (Allen 1981). The carving he had done was incised into the bark only, which unfortunately popped off as the wood began to dry, leaving the wood underneath with no carved design on it.

Mr. Allen forgot about the carved stick for years, busy with his various jobs as porter, grocery boy, carpenter, logger, plumber, and with raising his and his wife's six boys. When he became disabled with a heart condition and cataracts in the 1960s, he took up carving again. He began again on a fishing trip when he saw some hickory saplings, tempting him to try carving another stick. The hickory retained its bark when it dried, making it a better medium for his incised carving. After carving several sticks in this manner, he began stripping away the bark and carving the underlying wood itself.

Through the years as he worked, he developed his techniques and a repertoire of motifs, many of which he still uses. His 1979 canes show his improvisations on the carved shaft with a variety of complex spirals, stripes, diamonds, and floral designs—the latter he calls four-leaf clovers, which he believes bring good luck. The motifs appearing on the early cane handles include the heads of men and animals such as snakes, prominent in his traditional background, along with elements of popular culture, including cartoon characters such as Snoopy, the Pink Panther, and spacemen. Colored glass stones and beads from his wife's costume jewelry accent features on his figures. Dark colors achieved through burning the wood with a propane torch contrast sharply with the natural wood color and highlight his designs. His early tools included a hatchet, hacksaw, pocketknife, wood rasp, glass, and sandpaper.

From the start, Allen's techniques, designs, and the carved cane itself were self-devised. As he puts it:

> I don't have no plans and nobody sent me no ideas. All this come up in my mind. I see what I want when I start. . . . I don't have to see something to do it. I just do it. It just come to me. If I see something I want to do, I can do that something. It's in my head. I can just think what I want to do and do it. Everything's just easy for me to do. I wasn't trained to it. Something just comes to me and I do it. (Allen 1981)

He digs around the root of the sapling to see what designs the root brings to his mind, believing that he must "see" the design in his mind in the particular piece of wood before he cuts it: "I can see it pre-finished or finished when I'm digging it up" (Allen 1979). In this respect, his work is visionary (see Naisse 1987); that is, he imagines or "sees" his designs in the raw medium. Echoing the creative processes of other African American artists, his ideas, rather than being handed down to him from another wood carver, come to him in visionary flashes or sometimes in dreams.

PUBLIC PRESENTATIONS

With this traditional background, the highly creative visionary carvings, and his ability to talk about his work, Allen was a choice artist for a variety of public folklore formats. Of those formats listed by Staub (1988:167–68), Allen participated in festivals, exhibitions, demonstrations, workshops, apprenticeships, and television from 1979 to 1990. Mr. Allen's first such event was a small community festival in Homer, Louisiana, in 1979. Allen demonstrated his carving through the day and was briefly presented by Reverend Kirkpatrick on a small stage set up under the trees. Kirpatrick lauded Allen's work, especially his "creative imagination." Allen then talked for five minutes on how he made his canes. There was a small turnout of community members, and Allen did not receive much attention at the time. He had been scheduled to participate in a sister festival held the next weekend in Grambling; however, he missed the bus that was transporting the Homer-area artists. With this disappointment, Allen's first festival experience ended up with no great repercussions or recognition except for a publicity photograph in a Ruston newspaper.

Even so, during the next years, his pubic folklore opportunities multiplied. In 1980, upon my recommendation, Mr. and Mrs. Allen participated in the Natchitoches Folk Festival, a large regional Louisiana festival. Since the crafts director of that festival, H. F. Gregory, was curating a folk craft exhibition the next year, Allen's work was also included in a folk craft exhibition and catalogue, *Doing It Right and Passing It On* (Gregory 1981), produced by the Alexandria Museum in central Louisiana. Upon reflection, Allen sees this publication as a significant event, which caused his popularity to grow: "After I met you all [folklorists] and I got published, they went wild" (Allen 1987). Subsequently and often on my recommendation, he was invited to attend many other festivals such as the New Orleans Jazz and Heritage Festival, the Red River Revel in Shreveport, the Louisiana World Exposition in New Orleans, and the Louisiana Folklife Festival in Baton Rouge. In late 1980, I also recommended him as a featured artist on "Louisiana Alive," a television production of Louisiana Public Broadcasting; I also accompanied the television crew to his home and conducted the interview.

In all of his festival appearances, he was accompanied by his wife, who was usually contracted to demonstrate quiltmaking. To this day Mr. Allen will still not participate in a festival unless his wife is also invited. He was also invited to participate in other regional craft and harvest festivals where he would have to pay a fee to rent a booth. He refused such offers. His refusal to purchase booth space in popular festivals may be attributed to the fact that he had become accustomed to the honor of being paid to demonstrate and sell his work at academic and government-sponsored folk festivals.

However, several times upon my personal invitation, the Allens have traveled to nearby Ruston to participate in special events featuring artists' exhibitions/demonstrations with no booth fee or sales commission charged; their participation seemed tied to my involvement in the project. Likewise, in 1988, when I was contracted by the state to help folk artists apply to participate in the Louisiana Crafts Program, a state-government marketing project, the Allens gladly consented to participate. Later that year because of my invitation and involvement in a similar local project, he put a few canes in a new regional consignment gallery featuring folk and fine arts.

With all this varied public folklore experience, the high points for Allen were in 1981, and again in 1985, when he was invited to the Festival of American Folklife in Washington, D.C., upon my referral. His participation in the national festival finally merited him much-wanted attention from his hometown newspaper, the *Guardian Journal.*

Before this time and afterwards, he had received wide media coverage. He already had been featured in a number of other Louisiana papers in Natchitoches and Baton Rouge, as well as Natchez, Mississippi, and felt neglected by his home town. Later, full-length feature articles in other regional papers focused on his national appearance with such headlines as "David Allen's Walking Sticks: Smithsonian Institution has taken a fancy to them" (*Shreveport Times,* June 26, 1983) and "David Allen—The Cane Carving Philosopher Who Has Carved His Way into the White House" (*Louisiana Country,* May 1984). As a result of his participation in the Louisiana Crafts Program, he was one of the selected folk artists featured with a full-page color photograph in a crafts program article for an airline magazine (Sandmel 1990:44). Allen's carving, his success, and his easy-going philosophical conversational style, no doubt, made him an ideal feature subject, and these features brought him more customers for his canes. People sought his canes at his home, through the mail, and by phone—all of which worried me greatly. However, each time I asked Mr. Allen if he were bothered by all the attention and interruptions, he insisted that he loved it.

EFFECTS OF PUBLIC PRESENTATION

The commodification of Allen's work through media attention and local and national appearances, all of which stem from my initial fieldwork has effected changes in the artist and his work—consequences potentially raising numerous issues among folklorists. Perhaps paramount is the issue of authenticity. Staub outlines this concern using examples of a Mexican wood carver's altering a mask design to facilitate nontraditional display and a German gypsy basketmaker's modifying his traditional baskets for craft fair consumption (Staub 1988:166, 170). In order to determine the effect of such intervention on the authenticity of the craft, we must look at the history of the craft, the process, the materials, and the artist's and community's response to changes.

Related to authenticity is the issue of marketing. The pervasiveness of the influence of customer demand in marketing traditional art has been noted by Joyce: "In our relatively brief American history, individual purchasers have always made their wants known to artists, who were, in turn, anxious to please. Customer demand has thus influenced the design, materials, and techniques for making practically every traditional object in this country" (Joyce 1986a:238).

Graburn in his *Ethnic and Tourist Arts* attributes such change in what he terms "fourth world traditional art" to two major sets of forces at work: material and technical opportunities and cultural and formal influences: "More important than the availability of new materials and techniques is the advent of new ideas and tastes. Contacts with foreign peoples, education, literacy, travel and modern media so broaden the ideas and experiences of Fourth World peoples that they may want to change, break away from or enlarge upon their previously limited traditions" (Graburn 1976:12). According to Graburn, "fourth world" is a "collective name for all the aboriginal or native peoples whose lands fall within the national boundaries and techno-bureaucratic administrations of the countries of the First, Second, and Third Worlds" (1976:1). In Graburn's model, then, David Allen, a native southern African American and therefore a minority, may be termed a "fourth-world" member whose art has given him contacts that have broadened his awareness and produced cultural, formal, material, and technical change in his work.

Expanded Awareness of Cultural and Artistic Value of Work

Perhaps the most important cultural influence of Allen's first visit to the 1981 Festival of American Folklife in Washington was the development of his consciousness of the connection of his work to the African tradition. While I had noticed similarities in his work to that of other wood carvers in the United States and Africa, I had not mentioned this to him, even though I wanted to, since I did not want to intervene more than I already had. However, in Washington, when a festival worker showed him African carvings, Allen learned that his canes had much in common with those of Africans and other African Americans. He told me about this in the following personal narrative:

> I tell you what I did find out, and the people at the Smithsonian was surprised. They got some African carving there, and uh, and they wanted to know if I ever been to Africa and seen any work, and I told them, "Naw," and they went and got a book and some of the work and some of it they had; if I hadn't known I didn't do it, I'd a swore I had done it—the same identical

thing. And they got the book on it, showing it to me and got some of the work in there right across the street from me [National Museum of Natural History] and showed it to me, and it was almost identical, and they wanted to know if I'd ever seen it and I said "Naw." They wanted to know where did I get the idea. I said I guess . . . some of my peoples brought it over. (Allen 1981)

Indeed, Allen's carving shows great similarities to African American and African walking sticks and staffs such as those included in the Cleveland exhibition and catalogue, *The Afro-American Tradition in Decorative Arts* (Vlach 1978:27–43). African American walking sticks documented there exhibit reptile motifs, human figures, and striking geometric designs. Aesthetic continuities between the African American carvers include improvisation, highly polished finishes, symmetrical postures of sculpted figures, human figure finials, geometric incisions, serpentine fluting, and coiled snakes (Vlach 1978:41–42)—all of which appear in Allen's work before his trip to Washington.

Reflecting this thrill at his discovery of the similarities between his sticks and those from his ancestors' native land, Allen gave his art form a new name, "Africa Walking Sticks," which he proudly had imprinted on ballpoint pens he ordered to promote himself. He decided to order pens instead of business cards when he attended a folklife conference as a crafts demonstrator and overheard an anthropologist speak negatively of business cards for anthropologists and folklorists. Often in festival demonstrations, Allen tells visitors the story of how he discovered his African connection, thus indicating the importance of this information to him.

In addition to his new perspective on the origins of his art, this exposure made him more aware of his work as art and the value of it. In Washington in 1981, he encountered another idea that would directly affect his work. At this time, collectors he met told him that his work was an art form that should be signed and dated. Therefore, in 1982, he began to woodburn his initials, "D. A." and a date on each cane. Interestingly, his method of dating varied during subsequent years, from the year only ("1982") to the abbreviated month and year ("Dec. 1983") to month-day-year in numerals ("8-7-88"). When I asked him why he just used his initials, he really had no reason for not putting his whole name. After this he began signing the canes "D. Allen." It was not until fall 1988 that I first observed his signing "David Allen" on the sticks, fully claiming the stick as his art. When I observed this change later, I was concerned that in questioning him on this, I had interfered in his art and made him more self-conscious of himself as artist. Yet at the same time, I had wanted to suggest he sign his work from the beginning; I had refrained from doing so, thinking I was pushing another aesthetic mode upon him.

With this growing awareness of the value of his carving, Allen has raised the prices of his work. His success in selling practically everything he makes and others' and my encouraging him to charge more also prompted him to raise his prices slightly. Although I was concerned about interfering on the economic side, I thought I was obligated to tell him what the market would bear since he spent many hours on each cane. When I met him in 1979, he gave away or sold the canes to family and people in the community for $4 or so; also, a local department store had a few for sale for him. Before this time, he occasionally would sell several sticks at once to community or family visitors from urban centers such as Houston. By 1983, his prices ranged from $15 to $40, and by 1989 from $25 to $75 or more for special sticks. He always seemed pleasantly surprised that he could get higher prices for his canes. When Reverend Kirkpatrick and I had told him in 1979 that he had a craft worth money, he did not really believe us. Reflecting his skepticism on how he first felt upon becoming involved in festivals and his amazement at his popularity and the value of his sticks, Allen states:

> When y'all came over, you were talking about the work I done on them. And he [Kirkpatrick] kept saying how I had a gold mine. I said, "I sho' is; if I can get it out of the house. . . ." To me it's still just something I can do. I mean I don't value what they're really worth. I don't have no idea what they're really worth. To me it's just a stick; I can do it, but he [Kirkpatrick] was telling me about how I could sell them and all that. And I thought I sell one once a year maybe, and I'm doing all right, but I didn't have no idea that people would see so much in them, that they would go as far as they went. (Allen 1987)

Modifications in Designs, Materials, and Techniques

As a result of this successful experience with marketing his walking sticks, Allen also made some modifications in his art form. Allen notes in an interview that he was motivated to produce more objects with wider variety: "It encouraged me to do more, to try something different, I started off with a few things, and the more I meet the peoples and they see me, the more I try harder to try to produce something different all the time. That set the stage for me to work that much harder" (Allen 1987). Thus again, he was influenced by his contact with the wider world and also had more money and time to put into the craft.

More specifically, this exposure and his push for variety have affected, to some extent, Allen's material and his techniques. In regard to materials, he was using hickory exclusively when I met him in 1979, but after 1981, he changed to different varieties of wood, including gum, cedar, and occasionally willow. As he explains it,

> Yeah, a lot of mine changed because when I started out, I was using mostly hickory. Since then I changed to different varieties of wood: gum, cedar, and different types of wood; I changed into for the simple reasons 'cause . . . the wood was softer; I was able to put more different designs in a softer wood, and since I been doing it and working with the festivals, I come up with a lot of different designs in the softer woods such as the snake wrapped around the stick. I hadn't been doing that. . . . The reason that I changed is that I had a demand for them. I had a demand for more snake types of stick. . . . The cedar or gum makes a more attractive stick, not any better; the hickory is stronger; it don't come any better. (Allen 1987)

Allen also needed the softer wood to do more intricate handles for his sticks, which he found to sell better: "I'm changing the design 'cause people look like they wanted more design in the handle part of the stick. So I put a change on them, and they're really selling. I'm still going to make more of my usual sticks" (Allen 1981). The new designs for his handles include heads of men, ducks, bunnies, pelicans, and more elaborate snakes. To complete the faces of these creatures, he also purchased black and white plastic eyes, which he learned about from his neighbor, Benny Holyfield, whom Allen had taught his art through a state folk artist apprenticeship. When I asked about his use of these instead of the usual rhinestones from his wife's jewelry, he complained he had used all the jewelry and was having difficulty finding more. After several customers told me that they did not like the new plastic eyes, I recalled one cane which had burned-in eyes, and I again questioned him about his new material and technique, asking if he had ever considered carving and burning or painting the eyes. He responded that he had not and that it would be a good idea. I reminded him of the devil cane he had made with burned eyes, which had used this technique accidentally. While making this cane, he had been using a propane torch to darken the head of the figure he termed a "devil," and mysteriously two spots on the face began to darken as if to form eyes. Allen saw this as a frightening omen that he should not carve such taboo figures. Since these eyes happened accidentally on a stick that he hastily sold, he had obviously not taken this as a viable technique at the time.

The change in emphasis from the shaft of the cane to the handle prompted Allen to get more tools for carving. He bought some electric carving tools and a woodburning set with the extra money from his cane sales. "Since I got into these different kinds of handles, I had to get me some more different kinds of tools to work with. I started with all these things because I can get in closer you know when I'm gonna work in here big knives won't work" (Allen 1981). The woodburning set gave him some new design options for the shaft as well and was more easily managed than the propane torch, which he still continued to use for darkening large areas. With the woodburning set, he began to draw rough figures on the shaft such as a man going fishing, cabins, trees, fences, and animals. While he has made several canes with such motifs, he continues to do his usual carving, often combining it with the woodburned drawings.

Allen's assessment of the market is that he must constantly strive for "something different"; he mentions this term so frequently that it underscores his own value of uniqueness and creativity: "Most of the walking sticks you see is straight. If I made mine that way, mine wouldn't be any different. The idea was to get something different to look different and draw the people's attention to seeing something different" (Allen 1987). Since he thinks it is important for him to sell, he feels that he must adapt his designs for the market: "I try to keep something new on the market all the time 'cause everybody [will] say he got the same thing. I've seen that before; I've seen something like that. But I come up with something like that [pointing to a new cane] and they get real excited" (Allen 1987).

Thus, Allen is interested in carving to meet general market and individual demand. This is exemplified by his repeated carving of canes with the coiled snake, probably his best selling design. He insists that he does not like snakes but that he likes to carve them because he can control the carved snakes, unlike the uncontrollable real snake. Actually, the coiled snake is a simpler design than many of his earlier canes, which required more carving. With the growing demand for his canes, he seems to have somewhat simplified the shaft designs and made the shafts thicker to lessen the amount of time needed to produce a stick. For example, on later sticks he more often put wider spirals or larger diamonds instead of closer, more intricate carving, which is much more frequent on his 1979–84 canes. Although the time of increased demand correlates with this change, he had bursitis at the same time, and later, an automobile accident made carving quite difficult for him and also required simplification of the designs.

Because his popularity has grown, he also has carved sticks on special commission. Some requests are for special combinations of his designs, but others are for new motifs. For example, after he demonstrated his carving at Centenary College's Meadows Museum in Shreveport, Louisiana, he was commissioned to carve a cane as a gift for a retiring art department chairman. Since the chairman had been designing a ceremonial mace for the university with the university flower, the customers requested that the cane finial feature the flower, a Yoncopin water lily, and the shaft, an alligator, a favorite animal motif of the recipient. Never having carved either design, Allen was given a quick sketch of the lily. He then went to the local library encyclopedia for a picture of an alligator. Instead of drawing the alligator as he told his customer, "I got it in my head and I came home and carved it out" (Godfrey 1989). Other customers saw the alligator cane and also wanted one, so Allen began to carve more alligators; he also improvised on his original design by carving a snake chasing an alligator up the stick. Both animals exhibit his original rhinestone eyes, red mouths, and propane-torch-darkened bodies, with diamond etchings on the alligator and circular carvings on the snake. With the success of the popular alligator design, he says that he is going to try to carve a crawfish, another popular Louisiana animal. These additions to his repertoire show Allen's sensitivity to the individual customer and the market and his interest in innovation.

The increased carving brought on by the demand for his sticks may have also caused physical side effects in Allen, which, in turn, also caused change in his work. After his trip to the Smithsonian festival in 1981, Allen had some trouble with his wrist and began to experiment with painting. However, he found that painting the shaft of the stick instead of doing so much intricate carving did not appeal much to him or the market, so he rarely uses paint now except for mouths of his figures. He also tried the new medium on a flat surface painting one of his familiar floral designs on a closet door. When I saw this work and became concerned about his wrist, I feared he would have to quit carving, so I gave him some new brushes and paints with which he experimented briefly. When his wrist improved so that he could continue carving at his old rate, he decided to go back to his canes and tackle the painting later because he could not really get interested in it.

Allen may have been influenced by other carvers he met at festivals; however, any such influence has been minimal. At the New Orleans Jazz and Heritage Festival, Allen met Hugh "Daddy Boy" Williams, a black carver from New Orleans, who produced canes with erotic motifs, which he terms "x-rated," and animal motifs including monkeys, tigers, snakes, and alligators. Allen was quite amused by William's x-rated sticks, but said he would never carve this type of stick because it was not appropriate for him, a devout Baptist. He also met an Anglo-American basketmaker and wood carver, Jack Phillips, with whom he became quite friendly. Phillips, who traveled most of the time, periodically made it a point to stop by the Allens' to visit for a couple of hours. The two would exchange stories and ideas. Allen would often report Phillips's visits to me. Phillips once told me he had even given Allen an elephant-head handle stick with most of the carving already done. Allen evidently had completed the carving, set rhinestone eyes, colored it with his torch, varnished it, and sold it to me, with my thinking it his own creation. Phillips thought it was hilarious that Allen had finished it and sold it to me. After I heard this story from Phillips and asked Allen about it, he readily confirmed that he had received the roughly carved stick from Phillips, but that he had done all the major work on it. It seems he did not even consider telling me that Phillips had done the basic handle design even though he knew that I knew Phillips. With this interaction, it might seem that Phillips's techniques would have more repercussions on Allen's work; however, they did not. Allen has not even carved another elephant cane. While he had no misgivings about completing the cane of another person, he seems to be quite proud of his own unique ideas, which come through his imagination.

Psychological and Social Effects

In addition to affecting the form, technique, and perception of his work, Allen's experience in public folklife projects have had an impact on him psychologically and socially. Such attention may have positive or negative effects, according to Georges and Jones (1980:151): "While individual subjects often react negatively to or are adversely affected by fieldwork outputs, there are also instances in which subjects react favorably to and benefit from fieldwork outputs which describe them, their behavior, or the information of which they were the sources." By his own assessment, Allen falls into the latter category:

It was the best thing that could have happened to us [him and his wife] in our middle age because we got a chance to see things and meet peoples and talk to peoples and go places that you ordinarily wouldn't have been able to go. I enjoy demonstrating for the peoples and talking to them, and they ask questions, and I'm able to give them answers to the best of my ability of how I got started and all that. . . . I enjoy traveling, and I enjoy the food. And you know, like when we went to Washington, they give us a day to go shop, and I enjoyed that—to be able to buy what I want. You know, there are mighty few times in a lifetime, when you're born poor and raised poor, you don't get a chance for somebody to hand you some money and go get what you want. It wasn't a hardship or nothing. (Allen 1987)

Indeed, such travels and opportunities are not normally available to minorities in lower socioeconomic brackets—Graburn's fourth-world "peoples without countries of their own, peoples who are usually in the minority and without the power to direct the course of their collective lives" (1976:1). These are the people F. D. Kirkpatrick termed "victim[s] of unrecognized culture" (1970:57). When I met him, Allen was disabled, retired, and living on a pension in a then unpainted bungalow in the "quarters" of the small North Louisiana town of Homer. Typically, in such rural areas of the South, lower-class, uneducated blacks and whites alike might be termed fourth world, for they have little, if any, power and little change of escaping their situation. To have the opportunity for free travel, to be paid for demonstrating a skill, and to be given a national market for sales of work are remarkable avenues not ordinarily available to such people. Since Allen is naturally outgoing and loves to talk, he doubly enjoyed his festival experiences, which allowed him to talk to hundreds of people a day as both a celebrity and an authority on a particular art form. This social interaction, along with the economic gain from his experience, served to empower him. In a follow-up interview, Allen reveals his sense of irony and amazement that a mere stick of wood could take him on such a long journey:

As far as the sticks have taken me—I wouldn't have dreamed to Washington, D.C., and all over the state of Louisiana. Ain't no way, if anybody had told me, it'd be like trying to tell me fifty years ago I would be able to sit here and see something on T.V. like that, "Oh, there ain't no way," but that's the same way the stick did. If they'd told me in '79 or whenever that in '81, I'd be goin' to Washington, D.C., with this stick, "Uh-uh, not me," you know. But I still couldn't believe it; I kept thinking I'd find out I was dreaming. (Allen 1987)

Allen's incredulity reflects his view of the importance of this experience.

Some of Allen's interactions with people at festivals have been especially meaningful to him and have given him great spiritual satisfaction, thus raising his self-esteem. Allen recounts one such experience, which he regards as a blessing:

> Since we been traveling, I like being able to help a few peoples. If they didn't have enough money to get what they want, I would let them have it for what they have. I enjoy doing that. I met a little boy once, and him and his grandmother's down at Natchitoches and . . . he had five or six dollars, and they come around, and they looked, and she told him, "Well, you ain't got enough." He wanted to know did I run a sale after everything was about over. I said "Naw."
>
> That last evening he came back, and he said, "You still ain't running no sale?"
>
> I said, "No." I said, "How much money has you got?" I think he had five or six dollars. Well, I done been blessed; I said "Pick you out the one over there you like."
>
> He said, "You mean it?"
>
> I said, "Yeah," and he didn't try to get the best one; he picked out a little old ugly one to me.
>
> I said, "You like that one?"
>
> "Yeah, I like that."
>
> I said, "I tell you what I'm goin' do; I'll make a deal with you."
>
> He said, "What's that?"
>
> "If you keep it in the family if you live, and show it to your children, I'll let you have it for what you got." He told me that was a deal, boy! And he was so happy, and his grandmother, she was so happy till she had tears in her eyes, and I felt like I gained more from that one stick than all the rest of them I made money off of. That stick was valued more to me, I mean what he gave me meant more to me than the rest of the money of the people that was able to pay that big money. 'Cause I felt like I had hope [helped] somebody; it wasn't some collector that come along with plenty of money. . . . This little fellow had taken all he had; I don't know how long he had taken to save it, but he'd taken all he had, and I let him have it, and that was something I enjoyed. (Allen 1987)

Along with awarding him financially so that he is able to help others less fortunate, his experience has developed his own pride in himself and made him realize that he has a valuable heritage to pass along.

In this same spirit he has donated some of his carving to the Ford Museum in his home town of Homer. Marking his newly gained celebrity status in the community, the museum reciprocated by having a special mural of Allen drawn larger than life above his canes on exhibit. Ironically, the mural dominates one side of the museum—the same building that was once a women's department store where Allen used to work as a porter. Allen's comments on visiting the museum with its mural indicate the intense importance of this local recognition: "Now I goes back there and I look at the same place where I worked and back here on the wall, and I thought it was an honor to me [for them] to recognize me enough to do that for me. That's the reason I want to continue to contribute stuff to them, you know" (Allen 1987).

That local recognition has also validated Allen's work for his own family:

> Another thing that made me happy is they [the museum] carried the little kindergarten down there and they all recognized me—the little children. Yeah, they carry them down there every year and give them a tour through there. And they say, "I know him."
> And my little grandbaby, she said, "That's my paw-paw."
> And they go, "No that ain't your paw-paw."
> And the teacher had to explain, "Yeah, that's her paw-paw," and that made me feel good—my grandbaby seeing me and saying that's her paw-paw. I would hope down through the years she would carry her kids in there and say, "That's your great paw-paw"; maybe down through the years they might carry theirs, and get to be great-great-great paw-paw, and say, "That's what he made, them sticks he made. Maybe some young child can go in and get an idea that I can do something I'd like to build. . . . That's why I want to continue to make something to leave at the museum, realizing that I ain't gonna be here always; I want to leave something behind. If it don't do nothing else, it'll be something I did and where that stick has carried me to and somebody will remember. (Allen 1987)

Without the public folklife relationship, Allen would probably not have been honored in such a manner. With the local museum's celebration of him, Allen's fame has come full circle from local anonymity to regional, state, national, and finally local and family recognition. Now the local museum can offer Allen more extended attention than the ephemeral folk festival or itinerant folklorist. Such community recognition is often the most deeply appreciated since it is usually the hardest to win.

The community response is not always favorable, however, when a member receives so much attention. When asked about this, Allen commented: "Well, I think at first, when we started getting television appearances and traveling, I think they thought we was goin' to kinda get a little beside ourselves, but we stayed just like we was; we were thankful and thanked the peoples and thanked the Lord for bringing us that far, and we stayed, we maintained ourself as we were with the community, and so they fell back in line" (Allen 1987).

Allen's recognition seems to have inspired ideas more than jealousy among community members. Most interesting was Allen's next door neighbor, Benny Holyfield, who saw his success and was motivated to learn the craft. Allen graciously showed him the basics. Having a great deal of woodworking experience, Holyfield caught on fast, and he and Allen received a state folk artist's apprenticeship for Allen to work with him and some young boys who were interested in the canes. For two years, Allen had a companion to look for wood for the canes. However, Mr. Holyfield died suddenly of a heart attack in late 1984, cutting the relationship short and leaving Mr. Allen depressed and grieving for a time. However, not even the community envy and personal loss his experiences have wrought seem to have soured Allen on his public folklore experience.

Ultimately, Allen is extremely proud of all his recognition and awards and carefully puts all mementos, symbols of each experience, in his "book," as he terms his growing pile of scrapbooks, which he frequently takes to festivals to recount his experiences. He stores news articles, festival programs, certificates, and name tags alike, treasuring each, and hoping one day that his grandchildren will be proud of their grandfather.

His identity has now become so intertwined with his stick making that when he was badly injured in an automobile accident in December 1985, the newspaper of the nearby town of Haynesville featured the photo of the accident with the red-ink caption, "Cane Carver Injured." Although his injury prohibited him from carving for several months, his love of his work and its rewards motivated him to regain use of his left arm. With his new identity and community status, he is assured that he and his work will not be forgotten.

And Miles to Go

Of all Allen's recognition, he seems to value the national festival experience the most since it has taken him the farthest in his journey, both in geographical distance and national and local recognition. His good fortune with his sticks has left him optimistic about his chances for even greater achievement. One hopes that he will continue to thrive even if left to his own and his community's promotion. He continues to find ideas everywhere, even in an "African-looking" sculpted wood figure a neighbor found in a trash heap and brought to him because "he thought about I worked with wood and brought it to me to see if I could do anything with it" (Allen 1987). Allen repaired the damaged piece with plastic wood as best he could and set it near his carving area in the small dining room.

At age sixty-two, thanks in part to his changed image, Allen sees himself as still developing his potential and having more miles to go on his journey:

> If I got that far with them first ones [sticks], what'll happen if I can come up with, I don't know, something like that old fellow over there [the African sculpture]. What'll happen if I can come up with something like him on top of a stick; I don't know: I don't think it's no limit to what I can do with a piece of wood. And that's what pushed me. If I got that far with that, I may get overseas with something. Anyway, I'm so thankful to have gone as far as I have, I still got a drive to go further. (Allen 1987)

This statement may be evidence of perhaps the greatest effect of public folklore on Allen, for it reflects his empowerment—his positive self-image, his hope for a promising future, and his belief in himself and his ability.

The transformations wrought by Allen's public folklore experience have been far-reaching, from his self-esteem to his domestic life to his higher community status to his concept of himself as an artist. Even with these changes, his basic life-style remains much the same. Since there is always a demand for his work, much of his time is devoted to making the sticks, yet he also continues his traditional activities such as gardening and fishing and continues to take part in community and church activities. Even though he may be better off financially now, he still lives in his little bungalow, now somewhat refurbished with sheetrock and some new furniture. And although the majority of his canes are sold outside his community, he still gives canes to some older people in the community just as he did when I met him.

The transformations in the art form itself include changes in tools and materials to accommodate easier carving and adaptation of forms. His process of carving was altered somewhat with his new carving tools and wood-burning set, but he only occasionally uses these. Authenticity does not seem as much an issue here since he selected and improvised his tools from those he knew from whittling and other woodwork. As noted, his materials have widened to include a wider variety of softer woods than hickory, but he had used hickory originally since it was stronger and retained its bark—improvisational and functional rather than traditional reasons. Even with the change in materials, the later canes still look much the same as the earlier ones. The greatest change in the canes is in the simplification of designs on some of the sticks. This is due in part to greater demand for certain designs, the growing numbers of sticks carved, and his physical problems with his wrist and hand. Since his original sticks were not based on other community prototypes, we cannot judge his work historically, except to say that it continues to exhibit tremendous continuity with other such African American carvings. While his art form has been modified by his experiences, the changes are compatible with his personal aesthetic of improvisation and his unique vision.

The fact that Allen emphasizes making "something different" by drawing on his imagination indicates that he regards this quest for innovation to be an important characteristic of his work; it pleases both him and his customers. Even with innovative designs inspired by customers and other outside influences, his canes continue to bear his distinctive touch—light and dark colors, glossy varnish, detailed eyes and mouths on faces, combined motifs, and strong figurative carving. Ultimately, his quest for stylistic uniqueness through improvisation is a characteristic of African American and African art (Vlach 1978; Perry 1989; Ferris 1989). Therefore, marketing in Allen's case does not undermine the authenticity of his work as much as might be feared.

Much to my relief, his outgoing, persevering, creative, philosophical, and spiritual nature has supported him throughout what could have been to some stressful public folklore experiences. My worries about the stress that festivals and the public world wreak on his health, with his high blood pressure and other problems, still continue each time I recommend him for a presentation. Yet I continue to recommend him because he is an excellent public presenter, and he enjoys the role. Given our long acquaintance, I also now feel obligated to help him to market his carving and refer him for other public folklore experiences whenever I can. This long-term involvement and friendship with folk artists, in turn, can become a difficult obligation for the folklorist, who continues to provide service long after paying contracts have expired, but it seems part of the price and the reward of cultural intervention.

While public folklorists may have misgivings at times about their cultural intervention, folk artists such as David Allen provide encouragement for our endeavors. In summing up his successful experience, Allen remembers our first contract through Kirkpatrick and attributes his success to both his sticks and the people who discovered and promoted him. While to him, a folklorist is somewhat akin to a talent scout, his statement validates the role of the public folklorist, striving to present and preserve folk culture:

> If it wasn't for the sticks, I wouldn't have been there. You just don't go out on the street and bring people in and say here he is. . . . To think it all started from the sticks, and not only that it really started from somebody caring enough to get out and hunt the people with the talent, that be able to do something, and recognize those people enough to bring them out to where they'd be exposed to the public and let somebody know about them instead of being born here and die here and be forgotten. That's the whole thing. (Allen 1987)

NOTE

A version of this paper was presented at the 1987 American Folklore Society Conference. I wish to thank Archie Green for encouraging me to write this article and for his suggestions. Thanks also go to Michael Owen Jones for his comments and sources.

REFERENCES

Allen, David. 1979, 1981, 1984, 1985, 1987, 1989. Personal interviews.

Camp, Charles, and Timothy Lloyd, 1980. "Six Reasons Not to Produce a Folk Festival." *Kentucky Folklore Record* 26 (1,2):67–75.

Carey, George. 1976. "The Storyteller's Art and the Collector's Intrusion." In *Folklore Today: A Festschrift for Richard M. Dorson*, edited by Linda Degh, Henry Glassie, and Felix J. Oinas. Bloomington: Indiana University Press.

Degh, Linda. 1969. *Folktales and Society: Story-Telling in a Hungarian Peasant Community*. Translated by Emily M. Schlossberger. Bloomington: Indiana University Press.

Ferris, William. 1989. "Black Art: Making the Picture from Memory." In *Black Art Ancestral Legacy: The African Impulse in African-American Art*, edited by R. V. Rozelle, A. Wardlaw, and M. A. McKenna, pp. 75–86. Dallas: Dallas Museum of Art.

Georges, Robert A., and Michael Owen Jones. 1980. *People Studying People: The Human Element in Fieldwork.* Berkeley: University of California Press.

Glassie, Henry. 1972. "Folk Art." In *Folklore and Folklife,* edited by Richard Dorson, pp. 253–79. Chicago: University of Chicago Press.

Godfrey, Judy. 1989. Personal communication, June 30.

Graburn, Nelson H., ed. 1976. *Ethnic and Tourist Arts: Cultural Expressions from the Fourth World.* Berkeley: University of California Press.

Gregory, H. F. 1981. *Doing It Right and Passing It On: North Louisiana Crafts.* Alexandria, Louisiana: Alexandria Museum.

Jones, Michael Owens. 1975. *The Hand Made Object and Its Maker.* Berkeley: University of California Press.

Joyce, Rosemary. 1986a. " 'Fame Don't Make the Sun Any Cooler': Folk Artists and the Marketplace." In *Folk Art and Art Worlds,* edited by John Vlach and Simon J. Bronner, pp. 225–41. Ann Arbor; UMI Research Press.

_____, ed. 1986b. *Marketing Folk Art. New York Folklore* 12 (1–2): 43–119.

Kirkpatrick, Frederick Douglass. 1970. "Statement of Rev. Frederick Kirkpatrick, President, Many Races Cultural Foundation, New York City." In *United States Senate Hearing before the Subcommittee on Education of the Committee on Labor and Public Welfare on S. 1591 to Establish an American Folklife Foundation,* pp. 55–60 (May 18). Washington: U.S. Government Printing Office.

———. 1979. Personal interview with David Allen.

Naisse, Andy. 1987. "Aspects of Visionary Art." In *Baking in the Sun: Visionary Images from the South,* pp. 8–27. Lafayette, Louisiana: University Art Museum.

Perry, Regenia A. 1989. "African Art and African-America Folk Art: A Stylistic and Spiritual Kinship." In *Black Art Ancestral Legacy: The African Impulse in African-American Art,* edited by R. V. Rozelle, A. Wardlaw, and M. A. McKenna, pp. 35–52. Dallas: Dallas Museum of Art.

Roach-Lankford, Susan. 1984. "David Allen: Walking Stick Carver." *ArtSpectrum,* December, pp. 12–13.

Sandmel, Ben. 1990. "Louisiana Lagniappes." *Spirit: The Magazine of Southwest Airlines,* October, pp. 42–45ff.

Staub, Shalom. 1988. "Folklore and Authenticity: A Myopic Marriage in Public Sector Programs." In *The Conservation of Culture,* edited by Burt Feintuch, pp. 166–79. Lexington: University Press of Kentucky.

Vlach, John Michael. 1978. *The Afro-American Tradition in Decorative Arts.* Cleveland: Cleveland Museum of Art.

Presenting Folklife in a Soviet-American Cultural Exchange

Public Practice during *Perestroika*

RICHARD KURIN

To the extent that the study and representation of folklore is an art, folklorists are artists. Folklorists try to shape their own practice as well as the presentations of others whose cultures they seek to represent. In this creative practice, ideas of folklore and folklife, authenticity, tradition, community, art, and performance have to be constructed, again and again, in variegated forms to audiences of scholars, the lay public, bureaucrats, government officials, and even the "folks" themselves (Staub 1988). Most familiar to scholars in the field are the monological constructions of folklore in books and journal articles, occasionally followed by review, commentary, and debate among colleagues at professional meetings, in publications, and in the classroom. Just as interesting, and in desperate need of critical attention, are the ways in which folklore is constructed in public practice (Kirshenblatt-Gimblett 1988 and this volume). In public practice the consequences of our ideas about folklore, some commonly held, others vigorously debated, are likely to become ap-

parent (Santino 1988). It is through practice, whether in mounting a festival presentation (McCarl 1988) or in a courtroom arguing a case (Clifford 1988), that the interests and understandings of social groups are juxtaposed with those of folklorists in dialogical, even multilogical ways and subject to debate and feedback (Bauman and Sawin 1991; Kirshenblatt-Gimblett 1991; Kurin 1991). And it is through practice that the knowledge of folklorists is brought to bear on matters of cultural and human rights policies (Whisnant 1983; Loomis 1983; Whisnant 1988; Kurin 1989).

This chapter examines how folklife, folklore, and related concepts have been defined and enacted in a cultural exchange program between the Smithsonian Institution Office of Folklife Programs (OFP) and the U.S.S.R. Ministry of Culture. This program, initiated in 1986 and still continuing, has involved a variety of projects including the production of festival programs, the publication of sound recordings, and the conduct of field research. The overall program has been marked by institutional collaboration and frustration, conceptual dissonance and resonance, and adaptations and transformations in the understanding and practice of public folklore. The exchange is not only revealing of differences in perspective between Smithsonian and Soviet cultural specialists, but also of broader internal debates within both the United States and the Soviet Union.

PRESENTING AND CONTEXTUALIZING THE EXCHANGE

The Smithsonian Institution-Soviet Ministry of Culture exchange program consists of a series of interrelated projects including Soviet participation in the "Musics of the Peoples of the Soviet Union" program at the Smithsonian's 1988 Festival of American Folklife on the National Mall; American participation in the 1988 International Folklore Festival held in Moscow; documentary recordings—*Musics of the U.S.S.R., Tuva: Voices from the Center of Asia, Bukhara: Musical Crossroads of Asia,* and *Shashmagan: Music of Bukharan Jews in Brooklyn*—on Smithsonian/Folkways Recordings; a

Members of the American delegation to the 1988 International Folklore Festival in Moscow assemble for a parade across Red Square. Photo by Nicholas R. Spitzer, courtesy Folklife & Folkways Archives, Smithsonian Institution.

collaborative field research project, "Soviet and Soviet American Folklife Research and Presentation"; American participation in the 1990 International Folklore Festival in Kiev; and Soviet participation in the 1990 National Folk Festival in Johnstown, Pennsylvania. These projects are supported by protocols between the two institutions, official visits, numerous meetings and communications. Taken together, the program represents an ongoing dialogue about folklife—its definition, importance, and place in the cultural life of the United States and the U.S.S.R.

The initial impetus for the exchange program came from Smithsonian Secretary Robert McC. Adams, who, in 1985, had invited key staff to propose possible collaborative activities with the U.S.S.R., then in its early stage of *glasnost* and *perestroika*. Peter Seitel, then director of OFP, wrote to Secretary Adams suggesting that several Soviet scholars be invited to the Smithsonian to observe the 1986 Festival of American Folklife and meet with American Scholars on the Smithsonian's Folklife Advisory Council. A Soviet delegation of folklorists, ethnologists, and semioticians was proposed, signaling a desire to put collaboration with the Soviets on a scholarly footing. This also reinforced to a secretary relatively new to the institution the view that OFP was at heart a scholarly organization and implicitly countered an alternative view of OFP as merely a producer of large-scale public performances.

Many Smithsonian museums and offices were interested in collaborative activities with the Soviet Union. Bill Fitzhugh, in the Department of Anthropology, had long been working with the Soviet Academy of Sciences on the "Crossroads of Continents" project to research and exhibit cultural materials from both sides of the Bering Strait. As a result of Secretary Adams's initiative, however, collaborative activities were to develop between many Smithsonian units and the Ministry of Culture. OFP relationships with the Academy of Sciences, the Folklore Commission, and several other organizations have also emerged in the course of our work with the ministry.

At a meeting in October 1986 in Washington, Yevgeniy Zaitsev, deputy minister of culture, and his delegation heard presentations from several Smithsonian museums and offices. OFP described its mission and suggested that a Soviet scholarly delegation visit Washington for the 1987 Festival of American Folklife. Zaitsev invited OFP scholars to visit Moscow in 1988 for the first in a planned series of biennial folklore conferences and festivals. I wrote a lengthy internal memorandum in November, presenting the possibility of long-term joint research on folklife in the United States and the U.S.S.R. that might result in the production of side-by-side "living exhibition programs" in the two nations in some future year.

OFP wanted to position scholars of folklore, ethnology, ethnomusicology, and related fields at the forefront of any collaborative project with the Soviet Union. This ensured that proposals would be developed from ethnographically based understandings of folk culture. OFP did not want to consider proposals conceiving of folklore as theatrical performance, as is often found in the U.S.S.R. In April 1987, Secretary Adams carried this point to the Soviet embassy in Washington and then to U.S.S.R. Minister of Culture Vasily Zakharov in Moscow, stating that the Smithsonian's OFP "has the mission to study and present unmediated forms of living folk cultural traditions."

Minister Zakharov indicated to Secretary Adams that the Soviet Union intended a substantial, permanent expansion of its folklore programs and was heartened by possibilities of collaborating with the Smithsonian in this area. Following this meeting, Seitel issued an official invitation "to two of our Soviet colleagues in folklore studies to attend the 1987 Festival of American Folklife." He stated, "I hope the specialists you select will be interested in the analysis of folk culture and of its scholarly, research-based presentation to general audiences for both educational and entertainment purposes."

Ralph Rinzler, then the Smithsonian's assistant secretary for public service and the founding director of OFP, followed up with a letter and visit to Alexander Potemkin, the cultural counselor at the Soviet embassy. In an effort to make sure that the Soviets knew what we were talking about when we meant folklife and its research-based presentation, Rinzler discussed the visit of Igor Moiseyev to the Smithsonian's 1976 Festival of American Folklife. Moiseyev had developed and popularized the genre of Soviet and Eastern European "folkloric ballet," or theatrical folklore. It is a genre characterized by large dance troupes, purposefully colorful costumes, highly choreographed movement, orchestral music, theatrical sets, and complex staging. It is usually performed on stages in auditoriums or stadiums for seated, ticketed audiences. Music, dance, sets, and costumes may be loosely based upon or inspired by ethnographic reality, but highly valued innovation and artistic control are vested in a professional staff. Rinzler wrote to Potemkin, "Moseyev spoke with enthusiasm of our unmediated or uninterpreted presentation which in fact differs from his own theatrical interpretation of folk traditions."

In June, we received word that two Soviets, Alexander Demchenko, the director of cultural education programs at the Ministry of Culture, and M. N. Nalepin, a folklorist at the Academy of Sciences, would be sent to Washington. Demchenko was in charge of amateur groups in communities across the Soviet Union who dress in costume and perform the folk dances and songs of their region. Nalepin studied American folk talks in their written form. Over a two-week period Demchenko and Nalepin met with Bess Hawes, director of the National Endowment for the Arts Folk Arts Program, and Alan Jabbour, director of the American Folklife Center of the Library of Congress, among others. They toured Baltimore neighborhoods with Maryland folklorist Charles Camp, the Adams Morgan neighborhood of Washington with Seitel and Smithsonian folklorist Alicia Gonzalez, and rural Virginia with folklorist Charles Perdue. They spent ample time observing the Festival of American Folklife, which included programs on the folklife of Michigan, the cultural conservation of language, and musics of the Washington metropolitan area. They also visited Sisterfire, a feminist performing arts festival in nearby Maryland. They had numerous meetings with OFP staff and stayed at the hotel with festival participants.

Demchenko and Nalepin talked about three levels of folklore—theatrical, amateur, and ethnographic. The latter was what real peasants and tribespeople traditionally did or do. These forms of folk tale, folk music, craft, ritual, and performance were generally considered to be dying out. Folklorists, ethnologists, and ethnomusicologists conducted historical and analytic studies of these traditions. Theatrical folklore was staged entertainment, supervised by choreographers, and artistic directors. It was not authentic folklore, but rather inspired by peasant and tribal life. Amateur folklore was community based and even research based, as enthusiasts from a particular area would join together with a common interest in understanding, preserving, and identifying with the traditional culture of their nationality or region. Their activities typically consisted of singing and dancing, making costumes, and perhaps even demonstrating the crafts and occupational skills of a previous era. Demchenko oversaw, and through his ministry department, supported the activities of these groups through budgetary allocations, publications, and sponsorship of festivals.

Demchenko, and perhaps Nalepin as well, were not all that concerned with reinforcing divisions between these types of folklore. Ethnographic, amateur, and theatrical folklore all had their place and were all legitimate forms of human expression. Further, they were interrelated. Theatrical folklore looked to ethnographic folklore for its inspiration. This was done out of respect for traditional cultural forms and mirrored creative practices in Russian literature and classical music. Theatrical folklore troupes also recruited members from local amateur groups interested in their region's folklore. Amateurs were motivated by strong feelings for their cultural heritage. These groups grew out of community interest and their expressions sought, in a literal way, to recreate traditional ethnographic forms of music, song, dance, and dress. These recreations took place in a society different from that which had originally given rise to those expressions. Amateur groups were preserving those parts of their culture that could be enacted and also give them a sense of identity. Preserving all of one's culture for its own sake did not make much sense to Demchenko or Nalepin. No one seriously expected contemporary people to enact daily routines of a bygone era by using ancient methods of getting food and making things when modern means were more efficient. Those who did were, indeed, traditional.

From our discussions, his visits to different Washington-area communities, and observations of the Festival of American Folklife, Demchenko understood our idea of folklife as, he called it, "a slice of life." For him, we were concerned with ethnographic folklore as contemporary people lived it in daily life. More problematic were our ideas of tradition, authenticity, community-based culture, and cultural conservation, particularly in their application. As Demchenko observed in the Festival's Michigan and metropolitan Washington programs, many of the musicians and craftspeople did not appear to be very authentic or traditional. A Washington-area gospel choir had a musical director and regularly scheduled performances in town. The blues musicians played professionally in bars and clubs and produced records for sale. Craftspeople made objects such as Ukrainian-style Easter eggs not only for home, but also for sale. For Demchenko, tradition referred to the received past. A traditional practice was authentic to the degree it replicated its original or socially solidified (articulated or reified) version. The problem for the Smithsonian's festival or any other was that if we were to seek the authenticity of tradition in a literal identity between contemporary and historical practice, we would have a difficult time in finding anything that was truly authentic. And even if we did, the social system within which the practice was embedded would be different now from how it had been in the past. We would be left with quaint survivals, stripped of their original meaning and social functions. If cultural conservation, as advocated by American folklorists, meant perserving these survivals, it would seem to run against the grain of cultural evolution and to the detriment of the very people we wanted to help.

OFP has operated with a more dynamic idea of tradition. OFP has used the ideas of "root" and "evolved" traditions to speak about and illustrate continuities and changes in aesthetic forms, occupational practices, and ways of knowing. While tradition may be viewed as a natural, received object by culture bearers (and some scholars), OFP's focus on living exemplars and practitioners has long recognized the process of traditionalization—the culturally negotiated way in which the present is connected to the past. While in this sense all traditions are invented and continually reinvented (Handler and Linnekin 1984), questions of authenticity still remain. Who is making or remaking the tradition, and for whom? And to what extent do enactments of the tradition exhibit a historical connection with the aesthetics, knowledge, and skills of the subject community? OFP has stressed the importance of a community of practice and value in assessing questions of authenticity. Festival research guidelines and presentations tend to stress the practices of culture bearers recognized as traditional and exemplary within their own community. Festival participants are encouraged to illustrate in-group performances, skills, and knowledge rather than those directed toward out-groups. Presentational contexts and selection of repertoire are construed to emphasize local or communal aesthetic and cognitive control over cultural practice, rather than the reception and imitation of the aesthetics and knowledge of others. For OFP, authenticity is a matter of both cultural continuity and community control (Vennum and Spitzer 1986). Conserving culture is a matter of a community being empowered to bring forth aesthetic, cognitive, normative, manual understandings in contemporary life—to gain some measure of control over technological, economic, social, and cultural change.

The value we, in our discussion with Demchenko, placed on the importance of considering community-based cultural practice in researching and presenting folklife was juxtaposed with our perceptions of state-run and state-controlled folklore in the Soviet Union. Demchenko argued that many of the amateur folkloric groups under his purview were indeed based in communities, controlled by members, and motivated by their own interests, values, and sense of ethnic, regional, or national identity. For Demchenko, much of the diversity of Soviet cultures was preserved through the performances, club activities, festivals, and amateur studies conducted by these groups. For me, Demchenko was arguing that the state had effectively penetrated and become the community. What happens when the culture of the state becomes the culture of the community? Rather than encouraging diverse cultural streams, state control of folklore resulted in cultural homogenization characterized by particular Russian and Communist party standards. American folklorists, I suggested to Demchenko, have a parallel problem—the penetration of commercial and popular culture into local, regional, and ethnic communities. In the United States, commerce and the marketability of cultural production often become the arbitors of local taste, knowledge, and value. Folklorists, even those employed by agencies of central power and to some extent supporting the cultural edifice of the larger social order, nonetheless encourage cultural diversity, pluralism, and equity rather than cultural homogenization, and community rather than state control over cultural production.

The discussions and conversations with Demchenko were important for understanding a letter of invitation he carried from Minister Zakharov to Secretary Adams. The letter announced the "commencement of the program of cooperation in the area of the folklore and the preservation and development of folk traditions" and formally invited an "American amateur folklore troupe of up to thirty persons to participate" in the International Folklore Festival in Moscow in August 1988. Minister Zakharov specified that "the troupe should have a performance program lasting no more than one hour, and should present upon request a special program, 'Man-Labor-Peace,' no more than thirty minutes in length and reflecting labor traditions and rituals." Minister Zakharov also asked for a "description of the creative accomplishments of the recommended troupe, their performance program, and promotional materials." He also invited the attendance of two Smithsonian staff who could acquaint themselves with the festival and the development of folklore work in the U.S.S.R.

Demchenko also proposed that the Smithsonian feature the Soviet Union at the 1988 Festival of American Folklife. Plans for Swedish participation in the 1988 festival had been abandoned just weeks before Demchenko's visit. A decision to mount a program on Soviet cultures would bring parity to the exchange and intensify our developing dialogue. We discussed a modest program that would concentrate mainly on traditional musics of the Soviet Union. So overstated was our concern for the "authentic" and "traditional" and the need to avoid both theatrical performers or amateur hobbyists that Demchenko responded (and I paraphrase), "If you want, I will bring the kind of people who will hunt squirrels, cook their fires, and eat on the Mall." OFP accepted Demchenko's proposal and Minister Zakharov's invitation, subject to funding.

OFP staff also immediately recognized potential problems in our mutual expectations. We informed Demchenko that the notions of a singular

American cultural representation, an amateur troupe, and a contrived program ("Man-Labor-Peace") to be presented in thirty-minute and hour versions implied a type of performance and group in which Smithsonian's
OFP had neither interest nor experience. This kind of spurious, contrived,
and packaged program, familiar to students of fakelore and folklorismus
(Dundes 1985), is popular at many international folklore festivals and
world's fairs or expositions. Such events, organized by such agencies as the
Conseil International des Organisations de Festivals de Folklore et d'Art
Traditionnels (CIOFF), tend to reify the identification of nation with a national folklore, which is almost always romanticized fakelore. If the ministry wanted a crisply choreographed presentation of American national
folklore, replete with national costume, square dance, and hillbillies, then it
would be better for them to seek a professional or semiprofessional troupe,
such as those that might perform a staged potpourri of "folk" dance Americana at Disneyland. If we were to participate in the Moscow festival, we
would send people such as would appear in the Smithsonian's Folklife Festival. We would send not a singular "American" group, but rather a group
referencing the diversity of American society. We would need to know
more about the range and coherence of the festival theme, but could certainly select participants whose repertoire included topical songs or performance items concerning peace, humankind, and occupational culture.
Demchenko accepted our participation knowing our concerns. Secretary
Adams wrote to Minister Zakharov, formally accepting the invitation and
promising to send "authentic folk performers to the International Folk Festival."

OFP also recognized possible difficulties for the Smithsonian's festival.
With Demchenko we agreed to host between thirty and forty "authentic
folksingers, musicians, and dancers demonstrating traditional, nonstylized
performances." We also agreed to work in tandem with Soviet folklorists
and ethnomusicologists to decide on the genres to be represented, generate
field documentation of musicians, and make final program selections. We
at the Smithsonian wanted to avoid receiving "an amateur troupe" with
characteristics parallel to those suggested in Minister Zakharov's invitation
of an American group. Unknown to us were Demchenko's thoughts on the
matter, for we were essentially asking him to step outside of his own program at the ministry, and indeed perhaps outside the bounds of the Ministry itself to formulate and sponsor a group such as we had in mind.

In the fall of 1987, OFP staff began to formulate ideas about the genres
and themes to be represented by the Soviet group coming to the Smithso-

nian festival and the American group going to Moscow. For the Soviet musicians, we decided that an illustration of the richness and diversity of Soviet musical culture was quite appropriate for a modest initial program. Most Americans identified the Soviet Union as Russia. A program spanning several republics and suggesting regional, ethnic, and religious diversity paralleling and even exceeding that of the United States was deemed to be a strong one. Consulting with Soviet specialist Nick Schidlovsky, and Margarita Mazo, a Soviet émigré with a doctorate from Leningrad and a former Harvard ethnomusicologist then in residence at the Wilson Center, we developed a detailed list of traditional musical genres from throughout the Soviet Union.

The genres were major ones in the cultural life of the regions and were, we thought, presentable on the Mall. In a letter to Demchenko, we specified that "all groups or individuals should be community-based artists who have learned in a traditional way and who perform in an authentic nonstylized manner. It is understood that we will depend on our Soviet scholarly colleagues to identify and document groups and individuals." Included in the documentation we asked for were sound recordings with accompanying logs, still photos, slides or video of the musicians in performance contexts and a written report describing the genres and styles, the social context of contemporary performance, the historical background of the tradition, the biographies of the performers, the repertoires of musicians, and translations of selected songs. We also suggested that Rinzler and Mazo visit Moscow in November to confer with Demchenko, Nalepin, and other scholars, such as one of Mazo's former teachers, ethnomusicologist Eduard Alexeev, vice chairman of the Folklore Commission at the Soviet Composers Union.

Our offer on how to proceed was accepted, as was the trip of Rinzler and Mazo. Rinzler and Mazo had a hectic week-long trip in Moscow, meeting with officials and scholars and learning about the work of various institutions including the Folklore Commission, the Moscow Conservatory of Music, the Gnesin Institute, the All Union Art Research Institute, Melodiya Records, and the Moscow Ensemble of Folk Music. Rinzler was impressed by the serious scholarship at many of these organizations. Scholars carried out field expeditions, generally produced descriptive, analytic, and theoretical works, attended conferences, and occasionally recorded performances of folk performers when in town. He noted strong collections of field material and the penchant for those interested in folk music to be trained through performance instruction. Presentation of traditional material was largely accomplished by these organizations through the pressing of records through Melodiya. What most impressed Rinzler in Moscow was the powerful style and delivery of the Soviet songs he heard on field tapes while visiting these organizations. He noted that it would be difficult to select contemporary American groups matching that vocal power.

Rinzler and Mazo met with Demchenko and Moscow festival director Tamara Gavrilova to discuss the American side of the exchange. The Soviets clearly wanted a delegation to represent the participation of the United States as one of many nations in the festival. The group's performance should address the stated festival theme, they said. Beyond that, they would leave the internal structure of the group up to the Smithsonian. Our concerns about mediated and stylized performance, traditionality, and authenticity were not issues for the Moscow festival.

With Demchenko as key anchor person, Rinzler and Mazo made arrangements with several folklorists and ethnomusicologists who would help identify and document musicians who might then travel to Washington to participate in the Smithsonian's festival. Demchenko agreed to rely upon such specialists, although several suggestions for including some youth ensembles were lightly made. The ministry and the specialists agreed to develop preliminary recommendations for the Smithsonian to look at by January.

In the spring, the Smithsonian did receive such recommendations and some tapes, but little other documentation. Nonetheless, the groups represented genres originally suggested, and from what we could ascertain, seemed to be appropriate for participation in the Smithsonian festival. We anticipated that there would be some battles in the U.S.S.R. over the groups to be presented. We were, as we later found out, correct. Some people in the ministry took the position that the Smithsonian could not possibly want "real peasants" to perform in Washington. They were sure we were trying to embarrass the Soviet Union. While other nations would be represented at the Smithsonian's festival by superb, highly trained, artistic troupes, the Soviet Union would be made to look foolish by having peasant women and Siberian tribesmen. The folklorists and ethnomusicologists countered that the Smithsonian's festival was more ethnographic and only had as participants authentic, traditional folk practitioners. Apparently Demchenko and Nalepin, bolstered by Alexeev and other scholars, held out. In the end the Soviet contingent was indeed composed mainly of people from the represented communities who had maintained their traditions and their local aesthetics without benefit of formal training or schooling. There were however cases that were harder to classify, and later Nalepin intimated that the selections represented a middle level of community-based group. The Azeri group played *mugam*, a regional genre that is locally and historically supported by a schooled and formal tradition. The Yakut *homuz* player had become a professor in his native Siberia and wrote about the instrument; he was not a shaman, but used the drum in some of his performance. The Estonians played a bagpipe type of instrument made from a fox and had learned traditionally through their family, but they were also fairly active on the amateur folklore festival circuit.

Upon Rinzler's return to the United States, OFP staff continued to work on the selection of an American contingent. We wanted to send a diversity of American groups to Moscow to present traditional, community-based material, as we had indicated to Demchenko. Rinzler, OFP staff—Peter Seitel, Diana Parker, Nick Spitzer, and Tom Vennum—and Joe Wilson, director of the National Council for Traditional Arts, contributed ideas about our delegation of performers. We finally ended up with a group larger than the Soviets wanted, but one that we successfully argued was justified given the diversity of material to be presented. Included in the group were Piedmont bluesmen Cephas and Wiggins; the Sioux Indian Badland Singers; Los Pleneros de la 21, a Puerto Rican *bomba* and *plena* band from New York City; the African American *a cappella* group Sweet Honey in the Rock; bluegrass performers the Johnson Mountain Boys; Washington D.C.'s H. D. Cooke Girls Double Dutch Jump Rope Team; and Cajun musicians Eddie Lejeune, Lionel LeLeux, and Bobby Michot.

Discussions about the composition of the American group amongst organizers in Washington paralleled discussions about the Soviet group in Moscow. Just as there were disagreements in Moscow, so too did Americans argue with each other. Rinzler suggested that we select American groups with strong, "strident" sounds to match the vocal quality of the Soviet groups. He also particularly liked the idea of having a children's group demonstrate a nonmusical form like jumping rope. This would attract the participation of Soviet children and audiences and also illustrate a genre not generally presented as folklore in the U.S.S.R. Several OFP staff and advisors felt that the choice of Sweet Honey in the Rock was problematic as they were too stylized and less traditional than others in the group. This might send the wrong message to the Soviets about what we meant by folklife. Other OFP staff countered that Sweet Honey in the Rock grew out of contemporary civil rights and women's movements as an expression of larger, more diffuse nonlocal communities. Sweet Honey's repertoire was indeed broad, ranging from traditional sacred music to contemporary stylizations. Sweet Honey illustrated the living, adaptable, and transformable element of traditional music. The group respected received African American traditions, and by using and adapting them in contemporary circumstances of community struggle and advocacy, made them their own. Its members were very conscious of their music and its social implications, and they could not be easily placed in such other categories as entertainers, revivalists, or hobbyists. Sweet Honey was also quite experienced in performing in a wide variety of circumstances around the world and in local communities throughout the United States. Their presence in the group, their versatility and experience would help as we faced uncertain performance situations in the U.S.S.R. Just as we were able to appreciate the arguments and issues facing our Soviet colleagues, so too did they become aware of ours. In Moscow, Sweet Honey's inclusion provoked discussion among American and Soviets about the defining features of folklore and how to assess traditionalized expressions of contemporary social movements.

In addition to sending the American contingent to Moscow, we decided to mount a small music stage program featuring these groups at the 1988 Festival of American Folklife. That way they could not only meet each other, but also meet the Soviet musicians at the festival whom they might see again in Moscow.

THE SOVIET MUSIC PROGRAM AT THE 1988 FESTIVAL OF AMERICAN FOLKLIFE

The Soviet groups recommended and selected by Soviet and American scholars arrived in Washington one day before the beginning of the festival. The contingent consisted of the Georgian men's choir, Elesea; women from the village of Podserednee in southern Russia; an Uzbek group from Fergana; an Azerbaijani *mugam* ensemble; Tuvan throat singer Genadii Chash; an Estonian instrumental duo; Lithuanian and Ukrainian women soloists; and a Yakut *homuz* player from Siberia. They were accompanied by Anatoli Kargin, a folklore theorist with the Ministry of Culture's scientific wing; Alexander Medvedev, head of the Russion Folklore Commission; and Izali Zemsovsky, a renowned ethnomusicologist and student of the eminent folklorist Vladimir Propp.

Presentations were made on two stages, one larger with seating for five hundred under a tent; and a smaller, more intimate outdoor platform with bench space for about one hundred. Each group in the Soviet contingent had blocks of stage time, from twenty minutes to an hour, to present material several times a day, depending upon their needs as negotiated by performers, Soviet and American scholars, and Smithsonian staff. The smaller stage was used more for demonstrations, workshops, and discussions. American scholars of Soviet musics—Ted Levin, Margarita Mazo, Zev Feldman, and Marjorie Balzar—helped present the performers by supplying background and historical and biographical information to audiences, translating questions and answers. Sometimes they would demonstrate musical techniques, for example when Levin showed the audience how to produce the sounds of Tuvan throat singing. Because Zemsovsky knew English, he also served as a presenter to the American audiences. Stuard Detmer, a fluent Russian speaker, aided by other staff and two dozen volunteers, looked after the daily needs of Soviet musicians.

Presentations were supplemented by phototext sign panels and maps, which provided background information on the peoples and cultures of the Soviet Union, types of musical genres, music and the life cycle, music and ritual, and other topics. Program books with articles by Mazo (1988) and Levin (1988) were also available for sale to the public. These provided further information on Soviet musics and cultures, and on the performers. Finally, the Smithsonian also sold a Folkways Records cassette, *Musics of the Soviet Union* (1988), with documentary notes.

Presentations at the festival are fairly informal, characterized by largely spontaneous choice of repertoire, announcers and presenters the audience can see, openly viewed set changes, gaps in the program, and considerable interaction between performer and audience. Whether or not the Soviet groups were prepared for this, they adapted exceedingly well. The biggest exception was the costuming. Most of the performers had quite elaborate costumes. We asked about these costumes and their appropriateness, the contexts back home in which they were worn, and so on. Some would be worn on special celebratory occasions, others in performances for outgroup audiences. Given the hot, humid Washington summer, we indicated that the costumes (particularly the Siberian furs) were not all that necessary, especially day after day. The clothing they would wear back home in performing for each other or singing together was fine with us. Indeed, either due to the Washington weather or to our suggestions, the Soviet costuming progressively lightened up over the course of the festival, becoming less uniform, less complete, and more casual.

Other types of presentations took place as the Soviet contingent assumed a measure of control over the festival program site and the festival format. One day the Russians from Podserednee set up a wedding feast under some trees, appropriated staff and volunteers, and sang wedding songs and danced, somewhat for the public, somewhat for themselves. Similarly, the Georgians made use of several vats of wine they had brought with them. They coerced some local Georgians to help cook and prepare a marvelous wedding feast table. A festival aide, fluent in Russian, and our housing coordinator were roped into playing bride and groom. The Georgians used the mock wedding event (at which the bride and groom basically just remained seated as props) to toast, sing, and drink. Visitors to the Mall came upon this as marginal guests, observing others quite busy indulging themselves in wine, song, and oratory.

Various types of cross-cultural performance also occurred at the festival. For the Massachusetts program, Italian and Portuguese Americans enacted a saint's day procession, similar to those mounted in the North End of Boston. Four saint's day societies from the Boston area participated. They trucked the sacred statues of their saints to the Mall in Washington to be carried, worshipped, and honored in the procession. Each of the saints was installed in their shrines—wooden structures also transported to the Mall from Boston. On the plot of land devoted to the Massachusetts program, we erected the thirty-foot high and fifty-foot wide decorated cardboard and wood band shell used by Italian Americans for saint's day concerts in the North End. We installed street decorations and hung lights from jury-rigged scaffolding along a Mall pathway. More than two hundred band members from the four different societies came to the Mall to play their music and process with their saints. Some ten thousand people joined in the parade of the saints down the Mall, through the festival site. At one point, the procession, consisting of the carried statues of St. Anthony, the Madonna, Cosmas, and Damian, four marching bands, and thousands of people, moved past the Soviet area on the Mall. OFP staff was unsure how the Soviet musicians would react. The women from Podserednee broke into traditional songs used to greet the saints. They hadn't sung them for quite some time, and no doubt the Italian and Portuguese Americans had never been greeted in such a fashion. Some of the Russian women prayed and asked for blessings, touching the statue-icons. The Russians sang, even the folklorists sang, and everybody danced and hugged and cried.

Similar interactions ensued as Soviet women danced to the music of

Greek Americans and sang during our semiprivate clambake, hosted by Massachusetts Quakers. Intimate interchange also occurred for instance when musician Mike Seeger, who had been filming Yakut mouth organ player Ivan Alexeev all day, was asked to join him on the small stage for a Siberian-Appalachian version of dueling jaw's harps.

THE AMERICANS AT THE 1988 INTERNATIONAL FOLKLORE FESTIVAL IN MOSCOW

The American contingent that traveled to Moscow for the International Folklore Festival included performing groups and a support staff. The support staff was organized to help frame presentations, provide translations to audiences, and look after the technical and housekeeping needs of the group. The staff included Smithsonian Deputy Assistant Secretary for Public Service James Early, who served as spokesman for the group and presented an overview of American cultures at performances; me; ethnomusicologist and Soviet specialist Ted Levin, who translated, coordinated our participation, and made presentations during performances; Simon Carmel, a folklorist who knew Russian and Russian sign language and interpreted for deaf audiences for performances; Elaine Hyman, a Russian speaker who helped translate and coordinate the group; translator and logistics coordinator Stuard Detmer; sound engineer Peter Reiniger; and Smithsonian scholars Bernice Reagon (who also led Sweet Honey in the Rock) and Nick Spitzer, who documented our presentations and experiences through photos and recordings for a Radio Smithsonian program. In addition, we also carried with us forty thousand flyers with program notes in Russian describing the groups and traditions represented, and masonite signs, in English and Russian, presenting photos and text material on American cultures. Short of building our own context-sensitive performance sites, we were equipped with a full complement of techniques for presenting, framing, and interpreting the represented traditions.

Our group stayed at the Olympic Village on the outskirts of Moscow with other groups from capitalist countries. Socialist-country delegations and those of Soviet republics and "fraternal" nations stayed in a downtown hotel. Given our distance from downtown Moscow and the central festival venues (Gorky Park and various concert halls), we generally left the village early in the morning to return late at night. This meant we had to carry with us instruments, signs, brochures, and equipment all day.

During his previous trips to Moscow, Levin had negotiated with festival organizers to ensure that we would have venues where our whole group could put on an uninterrupted performance of several hours on our own stage with our own equipment. We would also have to participate in the various ceremonial parades, opening and closing concert, and special events. We had, as we learned, very little prior knowledge of these events and almost no control over their conceptualization and the structure surrounding our participation. The larger framing of the festival and hence how we were presented was not in our hands. We also learned that CIOFF was working with the Soviet Ministry of Culture to organize the festival. CIOFF is a federation that presents and promotes folklore internationally. It is recognized by the United Nations, with each nation entitled to one membership. Most memberships are centered in ministries of culture, and some reside with various types of national organizations with some or no governmental affiliation. CIOFF's folklore festivals have as their stated goals the encouragement of brotherhood among and understanding between cultures. They tend to be large spectacles of a theatrical character that reify notions of national culture and make grandiose claims about humanity and art. They are much like the ceremonial pageantry accompanying the Olympics (MacAloon 1984).

This was made apparent on the first day of the festival. We were told to dress in national costume and then report to buses for the journey to Gorky Park. The costumes and the youthfulness of the participants from France, Spain, and the United Kingdom, and other nations indicated that we would be in the midst of a theatrical event, involving the participation of amateur folklore clubs, dance academy people, and the like, or as a Soviet musician called it, a festival for "souvenir folklore." When we got to Gorky Park and saw a large sign announcing our participation in the festival, this became more certain. The sign indicated that we were the "Smithsonian Folk Ensemble," representing the United States, and that Ted Levin was our "artistic director."

At Gorky Park we were asked to take our place for a rehearsal of the opening ceremonies parade of participants. We were given a standard to bear as we marched in the parade. The standard had a cloth banner decorated with a Northwest Coast American Indian eagle motif and the letters "США" (The Russian abbreviation for "U.S.A.") inscribed on its top. We had not brought an American flag, so our hosts provided one. Along with the other twenty-five nations, contingents from the Soviet republics, and local groups, we rehearsed our march into a large plaza in Gorky Park. Later that afternoon, we participated in the opening promenade, some of our musicians playing percussion instruments as we marched up on a large stage and were announced to Soviet television cameras, assembled official-dom, and the other participants. The show featured stylized performances of Soviet youth groups backed by prerecorded music. In front of the stage, water plumes in the Gorky Park fountain rose and fell to the beat of the music. A well known Russian "folksinger" sang salutes to the event, and officials, including Minister Zakharov and Politboro member Lichachev, gave speeches. Each national and republic contingent stood in an assigned space in the Gorky Park plaza. The arrangement of groups in lines and columns suggested to me the symbolic orderly arrangement and contain-ment of national cultures under the rubric of international folkloric under-standing, an example of what many (Oinas 1975; Herzfeld 1982; Dundes 1985) have seen as folklore being used in service of the state, and now, the global order. At the end of the ceremonies the orderly array of the groups broke down as hundreds of musicians played their instruments, people sang, and members of different groups intermixed in a myriad of dances. From one perspective this could be viewed as programmed spontaneity—a demonstration of the disordered "folk" prone to happy celebration. From another it allowed individuals and groups of artists to control their own participation, to be curious and explore the art of numerous others. The Girls Double Dutch Team, for example, demonstrated various jumproping routines, an art unfamiliar to participants at the festival. They soon had many others from Siberia, Eastern Europe, and Russia trying their feet at jumproping, observing the girls' skills, and asking questions about the tra-dition.

On that first day we also found out that we were to provide a five-minute performance for the televised three-hour opening concert on a large stadi-um stage. Festival organizers wanted our "whole troupe" to do a brief per-formance. We suggested instead that the Badlands Singers, representing the first Americans, perform at the powwow drum, since we were not a singular troupe. The six members of the Badlands group demonstrated their beating of the drum, calls, and the dancing of Ben Gray Hawk in the rehearsal. The Soviet artistic director for the opening concert found this performance problematic. It did not have the choreography and theatrical air of perfor-mances by the other larger troupes and failed to fill the stage. A Siberian Yakut troupe had just rehearsed its very stylized performance before the In-dians, and the artistic director suggested that the troupe stay on the stage to provide background to the Badlands group. They did, and we tried it. There was still not enough movement to please the artistic director, who then suggested that the Yakuts, dressed in their stage outfits, sway to and fro in background, waving their hands. This he liked.

The opening concert was tightly organized, strongly choreographed, and visually impressive. The ten-thousand-seat stadium was populated by festival participants and constituted a "backstage" to a performance for television cameras. Various troupes processed on cue to the stage, which was framed by the festival's emblems and decorated with snow-flake-patterned backdrops derived from traditional textile motifs. The show was run with directions and theatrical presentations developed for the concert stage. Traditional artists were used occasionally as props or tokens. An older Russian woman was set to one side of the stage to weave on an old loom and was, at intervals, the subject of a panning camera. Another presentation used about thirty seconds of jaw's harp performance and throat singing to help identify the home region of the troupe, and then made way for a large ensemble and Moiseyev-like production. Indeed, any doubts we had about the character of the festival were dispelled when Moiseyev himself appeared on stage to deliver salutary remarks about the importance of folklore and the festival.

We were included in various other outdoor and concert hall presentations and asked to do five-, fifteen-, or thirty-minute performances. Almost always we identified one or two of our groups for such performances and insisted on verbal introduction and presentations, sign language translation, and the passing out of our program notes. The one exception was for the closing concert, where we were to present, as a troupe, a performance reflecting the theme. We seized on the peace theme, and guided by Reagon's tuteledge and experience, managed a group rendition of "Down by the Riverside" to an appreciative audience. This particular performance was framed by large video screen projections of a collage of American images—Bob Dylan in concert, civil rights marches, and touristic views of American cities—prepared by our Soviet hosts. On the whole, our experiences fitting into the concert-stage format, as defined in terms different from our own and discounting our ability to exercise control, were quite trying. We continually ran into the constraints of being initially perceived mistakenly as the other choreographed ensembles had been and having to adjust to the demands of television production and a concert-hall ethos of theatrical production. This even extended to technical requirements, as sound systems were geared not for bluesmen or gospel singers but to theatrical productions, for example, omnidirectional hanging microphones with no on-stage monitors.

We did have several venues where we had a stage to ourselves and put on a half day's performance, as we might do at the Smithsonian's festival. In these cases our groups had time to develop their material and exhibit a selection of their repertoire. Presenters and performers talked, explained, interpretated, and otherwise—through audience participation, for example—conveyed some sense of the history and social context of their art. Informal bluegrass and blues jam sessions, jumproping, drumming, and other activities often occurred off stage with interested Soviet visitors and festival participants from other groups.

Our most successful venue was a low-tech lengthy, and gripping performance at a "house of culture" in Leninski Prospekt, a collective farm town some forty miles outside of Moscow. When we arrived, we were met by local resident members of an amateur folkloric troupe and greeted with Russian song and the traditional gift of bread. Adeptly led by Bernice Reagon and Sweet Honey in the Rock, we reciprocated in song and gifts. We toured the farm during the day, viewed the home of Lenin, ate with community leaders, and in the evening gave our performance in the equivalent of a school auditorium. Townspeople had either seen some of our previous performances on television, heard us on the radio, or read about the U.S. group in the newspapers. The turnout of perhaps one thousand people overflowed the auditorium—uniformed guards had to lock the front door. Our group was energized by the attention from local working-class people and the homey feel of the place. Program notes were snapped up, the audience hung on the words of background presentations, studied bluesmen Cephas and Wiggins, stomped their feet to the Cajuns, cheered the Double Dutch girls, and danced to Los Pleneros. The event was emotionally moving and culminated with townspeople dancing on stage and in the crowded aisles with each other and members of the American contingent.

In addition to the performances, members of our group met on several occasions with Soviet scholars and officials. A formal conference on folklore failed to materialize as the Soviet Folklore Commission pulled out of the event, its scholars arguing that the Moscow festival was too theatrical, disconnected from the city's populace and the people represented. Alexeev, among many others, found little in the festival suggesting their own ethnographic experiences and was critical of the festival's attempt to "put folklore on the concert stage." These Soviet folklorists and ethnomusicologists found the festival's presentation of culture to be a diversion from the more serious issues of cultural identity and human cultural rights facing the larger society. Nonetheless some small meetings and demonstration workshops were held in Gorky Park; for example, Cephas, Wiggins, and Spitzer talked about the blues, demonstrating aspects of the tradition and discussing issues of style, repertoire, and performance context with Soviet folklorists and ethnomusicologists.

While the festival was clearly not organized on the same principles as our own, we did manage to communicate to many people the power and diversity of American grass-roots performance traditions. We received a great deal of attention from the media. And while we might have been uncomfortable with the grand spectacular and theatrical nature of the festival, its lack of framed educational presentation and intimacy, we could not deny that folklore, for the Soviets, occasioned significant government support and occupied significant cultural space in the U.S.S.R. How often in the United States are traditional musics aired on television to reach mass audiences, and how well are they presented? Network television treatment of traditional culture is extremely limited, and programs such as "Hee Haw" present stereotypic refractions of regional culture as entertainment. The Soviet festival and the infrastructure upon which it was based represented the mobilization of massive resources in the service of regional, ethnic, and cultural heritage. U.S. government resources for such purposes seemed quite meager in comparison.

Some of us reviewed our thoughts on the Moscow festival with Demchenko. Many of our criticisms resonated with those heard by the ministry from Soviet audiences and scholars. U.S. participation, intimated Demchenko, had served as a catalyst for more discussion about alternative models of inclusion and presentation under the folklore rubric.

CONTINUING THE FESTIVAL PRESENTATIONS

Following these public performance programs, both the Smithsonian and the Ministry of Culture explored other forms of collaboration. Anthony Seeger, director of Smithsonian Folkways Records, and I visited Moscow and Kiev in May 1989 to discuss joint research and recording possibilities with the ministry, Melodiya Records, and the Folklore Commission. This led to the issue of a recording, *Tuva: Voices from the Center of Asia* (1990), on Smithsonian Folkways based on work by Levin, Aleexev, and Zoya Kirgiz. We also visited Kiev to review planning for the 1990 International Folklore Festival, which was continuing along the Ministry of Culture plan of biennial folklore conferences and festivals. We were assured that the Second International Festival would host traditional performers in addition to the theatrical and amateur troupes but were surprised when asked to attend "auditions" by the local organizers. During the summer of 1989, Alexeev and Kargin visited the Smithsonian's festival in Washington to work on the contours of a joint research project between the two nations. Kargin also wanted to secure American participation in the Kiev festival. In exchange, the Smithsonian's OFP endorsed the proposal of the National Council of Traditional Arts (NCTA) to have a Soviet contingent participate in the 1990 National Folk Festival, to be held in Johnstown, Pennsylvania. In December 1989 Kargin and ministry liaison Vladimir Selivestrov visited Washington to firm up agreements on research and festival exchanges and to visit the site of the National Folk Festival.

The Second International Folklore Festival was held in Kiev in May 1990. A symposium, cosponsored by the Ukraine Academy of Sciences and UNESCO, titled "Folklore in the Contemporary World," was held in conjunction with the festival.

The Smithsonian sent an American contingent to Kiev, which included tap dancer Lavaughn Robinson; Union Station, bluegrass band; dancers and chanters of the Kanakole *hulahalau*; a Tex-Mex duet, Jimmy Santiago y Su Conjunto; and the New Orleans Young Tuxedo Brass Band. Performers were aided by Presenter Joe Wilson, Coordinator Richard Kennedy, Sound Engineer Reiniger, Translator Detmer, and me. Scholars of Soviet cultures Mark Slobin (Wesleyan, president of the Society for Ethnomusicology), Margarita Mazo (Ohio State), Bill Noll (Harvard), Richard Dauenhauer (Alaska), and Ruth Thomasian (Project Save) would participate in the symposium and help develop a longer term collaborative research project proposed by the Smithsonian and the Ministry of Culture.

Although some of the Americans had written papers and wanted to formally present them to the symposium, they were left out of the program. The symposium was generally of uninspired quality. Despite the theme, there was a general lack of coherence to the papers. The presentations were rather staid, poorly translated, and rarely generated discussion. The final plenary session, ostensibly scheduled to sum up results, was used to host a men's choral group, dressed in tuxedos, performing medieval chants. It was rather bizarre for me, but, as several Soviet colleagues confided, considered rather normal. Many conferences were held, expectations were low, argument and substantive results infrequent.

The Kiev festival seemed to be a replay of the Moscow festival, with the same types of domestic and international groups. Again, the American contingent was the exception. Unlike other groups, we were internally diverse, did not have choreographed, highly stylized performances, insisted on interpretative presentations to frame performance, had program notes to give to audiences, and were composed of people from the societies or communities bearing the traditions represented.

Unlike the Moscow festival, we were housed in a nicer, downtown hotel, had more, better food to eat, had greater flexibility in participating in the festival schedule, and seemed to be listened to when we complained. We did cause our hosts some trouble because we were more egalitarian than expected. The Soviets had arranged for scholars to be treated differently from performers—the former getting single rooms facing the main street, the latter getting double rooms facing back streets. Scholars and performers were supposed to have separate buses for tours, separate tables for meals, and so on. The American contingent ignored these distinctions, causing problems for Soviet festival personnel and hotel staff.

In Kiev we had come prepared for the type of marching and Olympic-like spectacle we expected to encounter in a CIOFF-produced festival. We had seven members of the Young Tuxedo Brass Band, who generally performed while parading in the streets of New Orleans. Their renditions and remarkable presence led the rest of the American group, which fell in behind them on the parade route through downtown Kiev, much to the delight of several hundred thousand spectators. As we began to enjoy the parade and get into the spirit, Edward DiLima, one of the Hawaiian hula dancers, lifted an umbrella and danced in front of the band, as is done in New Orleans. We did have an American flag this time, but festival organizers asked us not to fly it. They wanted the festival to be "nonpolitical" and were apparently worried about the flying of the Ukrainian national flag (as opposed to the state, Communist flag) and the flags of the Baltic republics. We acceded to their wishes. As we later saw, the Baltic republics did not.

We marched into a stadium where scores of international contingents, Soviet republics, and Ukrainian folklore groups were assembled. A crowd of about twenty thousand cheered, the stadium scoreboard sent out messages, television cameras were everywhere. It was an impressive spectacle, with each group parading around the stadium track and sections of the audience cheering on cue and displaying various stylized patterns with hand-held cards. The music we played and the traditions members of the group had nurtured did not seem important to the audience or the organizers—we could hardly be heard. We were cheered for being American and being in Kiev to participate in the festival.

After taking our assigned seats, we heard and watched the opening ceremonies. We saw rock musicians described as "folk artists," heard "folk music" composed by professional and renowned composers, and witnessed a
wonderfully costumed, beautifully choreographed depiction of Ukrainian
folk culture involving a cast of thousands, several orchestras, massive fire-
works, horses, riders, and hot-air balloons. This was the height of folklore
as theatre, displayed to millions over Soviet television.

Our stay in Kiev involved a lot of sightseeing, and while our group liked
and appreciated this, we were frustrated by not having the opportunity to
play our music, sing our songs, and dance our dances for the people of
Kiev. For our first performance we were given five minutes on stage after
having waited for several hours. Our second performance was to be in the
town of Kanyev, three hours south of Kiev. We thought this would be a
great opportunity to bring American musics to the people of the rural
Ukraine. In Kanyev, after lunch downtown, we were told by the Ministry of
Culture official that we would be taken ten miles out of town to an exclusive Dnieper River site to perform for amateur folklore groups from Finland, Latvia, and the Ukraine. We were in the center of town, there were
plenty of people around, why not just play right there? Despite the reluctance of ministry and local officials, the Young Tuxedo Brass Band, then
Union Station, then Jimmy Santiago y Su Conjunto played their music. We
attracted a large, if surprised crowd and passed out notes explaining the
music.

We later did go to the out-of-town site. The audience consisted of only
the other folkloric groups also participating in the Kiev festival, as well as
Mrs. Silkova, the deputy minister of culture of the Soviet Union. She left,
however, before a stunning presentation of Hawaiian chant and hula, and
an intimate join-in and dance bluegrass performance.

On returning to Kiev, Joe Wilson and I met with the Soviet festival organizers. Our needs, we said, were simple. We wanted enough time to
frame and present our material so that Soviet people would know or understand who in America does these things and why. We wanted to engage
our audiences and effect an intimacy with them so they could appreciate
the artistry of the traditions represented in the group. The organizers told
us to perform on a stage in a Kiev park the next day.

The next morning it was drizzling, so we were forced to perform in-
doors at a park pavilion, which was, alas, hosting a numismatic show and
market. No one was expecting us. Across the street was a complex of very
tall apartment buildings. A member of the Young Tuxedo Brass Band, sug-

gested we "march through the projects" with the jazzmen in the lead, making music and drawing a crowd. We took up Big Al's suggestion. People in the apartments looked out their windows and came out on balconies. Some tossed down coins and flowers. During pauses, Detmer yelled up to people and told them to come to the pavilion for a full performance. We were enacting the anti-spectacle of the opening ceremonies, a low-tech, do-it-yourself, capture-the-audience performance. It was difficult, but it worked.

Following this, many of our group's musicians decided to "just do our stuff on the streets" of Kiev. We set up an area outside of our hotel for jazz, string, and conjunto sessions. I don't think the festival organizers knew what to make of us, and we stopped traffic down Kiev's main road several times. But we reached audiences and engaged people who stayed for hours to get a sense of the aesthetics and texture of several American musical traditions.

Our performances in subsequent days in Kiev's central park and on the factory floors and in the social halls of the Leninski Shipyards were more in this style. Each of the American groups had adequate time to present their performance. The audiences were close up and intimately involved. Performers or presenters were able to talk about the traditions and pass out explanatory material. We did not, however, participate in a "costumed street carnival evening" (which featured large air-filled cartoon characters on floats) and the festival's closing ceremonies.

At a dinner celebrating the closing of the festival, Richard Kennedy, upon being publicly asked by the minister of culture of Uzbekistan if the United States would participate in the next International Folklore Festival, scheduled for Tashkent in 1992, replied most appropriately and ambiguously, "*Insha allah*," a phrase well known by Muslims and others in central Asia. It might mean "God willing," "I hope so," "Perhaps," "It's out of my control," or "I don't know."

We did discuss the festival with Demchenko and Deputy Minister of Culture Silkova and informed them that the participation of the Smithsonian was unlikely if the festival was going to follow the same CIOFF model. I had covered the ground previously with Demchenko—the Kiev festival had many of the same problems as the Moscow festival. I was somewhat angry and frustrated by the Kiev experience (as were others in our group) and was quite direct in speaking with Silkova. The festival located folk culture in a fictionalized, disembodied, yet idealized past. It avoided any serious treatment or presentation of the culture of contemporary people, even

Kiev's urban street culture. It was too big, too diffuse, and had no educational value. It failed to address real issues of identity, cultural continuity, control, and practices bearing on various cultural policies. The presentational mode was an entertainment spectacle with no attempt at interpretation, intimacy, or educational engagement. Almost all the delegations were made up of dance academy personnel or amateur enthusiasts who bore little relationship to the carriers of the traditions represented—or more likely, misrepresented through stylization.

Silkova first argued that "every nation had the right to present folklore in their own way." Surely the United States was not telling the Soviet Union how it should deal with folklore. Later she proposed that the festival was successful because it offered a "good time for every one during a difficult period of transition in the Soviet Union." It was a happy, entertaining, diversionary spectacle. Authenticity, scholarship, and presentation were not really their concerns. Finally, she said, Soviet organizers were "not yet ready for the real folklore."

In this discussion I did not want to discount the fact that the festivalization of "traditional culture" was meaningful to many people. I did want to stress that forms of folklore were to be found in the daily life of Kiev's people. We discussed contemporary forms of Soviet urban folklore—stories about standing in line and occupational folklife—as examples of cultural expressions that had no place in the festival but were, nonetheless, types of folklores that might resonate with and address broad social concerns. The ministry, I argued, needed a new policy of "cultural *perestroika* and *glasnost.*"

Joe Wilson, director of NCTA, did want the "real thing" in folklore and spent some time in Kiev and Moscow trying to make sure that the ministry would send a contingent of performers to the United States suitable for participating in the National Folk Festival held in Johnstown, Pennsylvania, August 31–September 2, 1990. Wilson, in conjunction with the Smithsonian's OFP, had requested the ministry to compose and send a contingent of authentic, traditional performers from a number of specified genres. Again, enforcing our own notion of folklife and trying to clearly signal what we wanted from the ministry, we had written, "As you know from last year, we are not like Western Europeans in our appreciation of folk arts. We prefer the real folk to folk imitators in every case. So the artists you suggest to us do not need to be young, pretty, and wonderfully costumed. It's okay if they are older and have lines of experience in their face."

I confirmed arrangements for Soviet participation in the National Folk Festival during a subsequent trip to Moscow in August. NCTA welcomed a Georgian men's choir, a Russian vocal group, Tuvans, and others to its festival, where they performed admirably and fit in quite well, helped by translators, presenters, and festival organizers.

SOVIET AND AMERICAN FOLKLIFE RESEARCH AND PRESENTATION PROJECT

Based upon the success of the performance programs and their continuation, scholars and officials associated with them were able to generate enough interest, and funds, to initiate a long-term collaborative research project. This project grew out of possibilities foreseen from the very first contacts, to in-depth discussion between OFP staff and Soviet scholars, to gatherings of folklorists and ethnomusicologists from the two countries and the signing of a formal protocol in Kiev.

The Soviet American Folklife Research and Presentation Project builds on the facts that approximately 10 percent of the U.S. populace has its roots in regions of the Soviet Union and that both the United States and the Soviet Union are modern, technologically advanced nation states with populations that exhibit considerable cultural diversity. The project examines how various root traditions having their origin in the Soviet Union have continued and been transformed both in Soviet society and in the American context. The first phase of the project joins Soviet and American folklorists, ethnomusicologists, cultural anthropologists, and scholars from related fields in teams to carry out field research and analyses on American communities having their origin in the Soviet Union and on cognate Soviet communities in the U.S.S.R. In the two pilot projects, Ted Levin worked with Atanazar Matyakubov of Tashkent State Conservatory to study Bukharan Jewish musical culture in long-lived Jewish communities of Bukhara, Uzbekistan, and in a more recently formed Bukharan Jewish immigrant community in New York City. Margarita Mazo worked with Dr. Serafima Nikitina of the Soviet Academy of Sciences and Irina Pozdeva of Moscow University to examine language use, narrative, and music among Molokans in Stravapol, Russia, as well as in Oregon, Los Angeles, and Fresno, California. Projects currently underway involve research on Ukrainians in Boston and in Lvov, and native peoples in Siberia and in Alaska. Future projects are being developed for Armenians, Russians, and others. The research should result in scholarly articles and monographs, documentary recordings and videos, and a living cultural exhibition to be mounted in Washington at the Festival of American Folklife in 1993 and in Moscow the following year, assuming funding can be found.

As of this writing, several scholarly articles have been drafted. The first set of Smithsonian Folkways documentary recordings have been published. It is too early, perhaps, to determine if and how the language and analytic categories of Soviet and American scholars will affect the type of work being done and its interpretation. Field research and initial publications have thus far been highly empirical, exploratory, and documentary. But patterns, resonances, and dissonances, if there, should begin to emerge as more activities are taken up and those initiated begin to mature and generate interpretations and syntheses.

The project also reveals institutional considerations in the two countries. While a formal protocol exists between the Smithsonian and the Ministry of Culture, neither can implement it without the cooperation and expertise of other institutions and individuals upon whom they can call. The Smithsonian lacks any scholar or curator with expertise in Soviet or Soviet American cultures and has had to call upon Mazo, Levin, Slobin, Dauenhauer, Thomasian, Noll, and others for advice and participation. OFP has also had to raise funds for the project through internal Smithsonian grants, external grants, and in-kind support. The limitations involved in this have made OFP painfully aware of the difficulty of conceptually occupying itself with another country without the scholarly presence necessary to understand not only the folk cultures of the place, but its official, bureaucratic, and academic cultures as well. The project's potential for generating intriguing research and policy ideas has enabled OFP to successfully justify Smithsonian support for a position and funds to support the project, though Congress has not yet appropriated funds.

The project has necessitated similar actions in the Soviet Union. The ministry has had to call upon some of the scholars and organizations under its general purview to work on the project and provide fiscal support, for example, Kargin and the Russian Research Institute, Alexeev in his capacity at the Cultural Arts Institute, and Melodiya Records. The ministry has also had to team up with the Academy of Sciences, the Composers Union, and others in coordinating, funding, and supporting project scholars and other costs. While this has occasioned some thought within the ministry about its own limitations, it has also led to increased flexibility and greater awareness of research-based cultural exchange activities.

CONCLUSION

In July 1990 the new minister of culture of the U.S.S.R., Nikolai Gubenko, asked for the resignation of ministry staff and reappointed those who he felt would help realize his vision of a new ministry. Motivated by *perestroika* and attendant democratic movements in the U.S.S.R., this new ministry would encourage and support the cultural creativity of grassroots organizations rather than dictate a cultural canon. The new ministry would seek out a diversity of ethnic, regional, religious, and other groups previously excluded from support and encouragement. The new ministry would encourage internal and external collaborative efforts and seek to firm up financial support of cultural activities through self-financing and other "entrepreneurial" means. Among the changes effected at the ministry was a reorganization that took folklore out of the realm of theater and associated it with cultural policy concerns and issues of ethnic and national identity.

This new orientation and the impact of our cultural exchange program was made explicit when Minister Gubenko visited Washington in November 1990. In a meeting at the Smithsonian the folklife exchange was summarized and reviewed. I noted the way in which American folklorists have attempted to define their field in relationship to cultural policy concerns, particularly the encouragement, understanding, and public presentation of cultural diversity. I noted that the question of national culture and ethnic diversity was a major historical and continuing issue in the United States, and of obvious major contemporary importance in the U.S.S.R. Minister Gubenko agreed, and thought that our joint program could help in dealing with the issue, though it was so large, complex, and vital to the future of his nation.

Minister Gubenko also presented an interesting proposal for joint large-scale, year-long, multivenue, artistically broad-ranging festivals (on the model of the Festival of India in the U.S. and the U.S. in India) in both countries. One component of the Soviet festival would be devoted to traditional culture. As indicated in Minister Gubenko's proposal, "This would consist of various programs to show the folklore of the peoples of the U.S.S.R. (*previously they showed psuedo-folklore, staged by state controlled choirs and groups, now we can show authentic folklore groups)*" (my emphasis). Minister Gubenko also indicated that the programs should show "multinational culture and the fate of cultural traditions during the Soviet era. It is important to show the unvarnished truth of our cultural reality and to reveal the drama of our national culture."

Our own language for presenting folklore and folklife had returned full circle. The negation of the ministry's previous state support for folklore activity may overlook real achievements in the conservation of culture, as Alan Lomax has reminded me and Soviet colleagues on several occasions. The encouragement of amateur groups has inculcated people with a sense of regional, ethnic, and national identity, brought folk aesthetics into mainstream consciousness and public view, and nurtured an interest in and respect for traditional culture among a sizable segment of Soviet youth. Yet the shift, away from theater and folklore as entertainment to folklife as real life, entwined with contemporary issues of identity, style, and cultural and political rights, seems both timely and well grounded. As with other developments in the Soviet Union, one can only hope that our colleagues and friends see the leaks in the categories and ideas that we espouse, which, perhaps because of our own regard for rhetorical excess, we seem to transmit with such certainty to others.

REFERENCES

Buaman, Richard, and Patricia Sawin. 1991. "The Politics of Participation in Folklife Festivals." In *Exhibiting Cultures: The Poetics and Politics of Museum Display*, edited by Ivan Karp and Steven Lavine. Washington D.C.: Smithsonian Institution Press.

Clifford, James. 1988. *The Predicament of Culture: Twentieth Century Ethnography, Literature, and Art.* Cambridge: Harvard University Press.

Dundes, Alan. 1985. "Nationalistic Inferiority Complexes and the Fabrication of Fakelore: A Reconsideration of Ossian, the Kinder-und Hausmarchen, the Kalevala, and Paul Bunyan." *Journal of Folklore Research* 22 (1):5–18.

Handler, Richard, and Jocelyn Linnekin. 1984. "Tradition, Genuine or Spurious." *Journal of American Folklore* 97 (385): 273–90.

Herzfeld, Michael. 1982. *Ours Once More: Folklore, Ideology and the Making of Modern Greece.* Austin: University of Texas Press.

Kirshenblatt-Gimblett, Barbara. 1988. "Mistaken Dichotomies." *Journal of American Folklore* 101:140–55.

———. 1991. "Objects of Ethnography." In *Exhibiting Cultures: Poetics and Politics of Museum Display*, edited by Ivan Karp and Steven Lavine. Washington, D.C.: Smithsonian Institution Press.

Kurin, Richard. 1989. "Why We Do the Festival." In *Festival of American Folklife Program Book*, edited by Frank Proschan. Washington, D.C.: Smithsonian Institution Office of Folklife Programs.

———. 1991. "Cultural Conservation through Representation: Festival of India Folklife Exhibitions at the Smithsonian Institution." In *Exhibiting Cultures: The Poetics and Politics of Museum Display*, edited by Ivan Karp and Steven Lavine. Washington, D.C.: Smithsonian Institution Press.

Levin, Theodore. 1988. "Soviet Asia: A Multi-Ethnic Non-Melting Pot." In *Festival of American Folklife Program Book*, edited by Thomas Vennum, Jr. Washington, D.C.: Smithsonian Institution Office of Folklife Programs.

Levin, Ted, and Otanazar Matykubov. 1991. *Bukhara: Musical Crossroads of Asia.* Smithsonian/Folkways Recordings SF 40050. Washington, D.C.: Smithsonian Institution Office of Folklife Programs.

———. 1991. *Shashmaqam: Music of Bukharan Jews in Brooklyn.* Smithsonian/Folkways Recordings SF 40054. Washington, D.C.: Smithsonian Institution Office of Folklife Programs.

Loomis, Ormond. 1983. *Cultural Conservation: The Protection of Cultural Heritage in the United States.* Washington, D.C.: Library of Congress.

MacAloon, John. 1984. *Rite, Drama, Festival, Spectacle: Rehearsals toward a Theory of Cultural Performances.* Philadelphia: Institute for the Study of Human Issues.

Mazo, Margarita. 1988. "Song in Rural Russia." In *Festival of American Folklife Program Book*, edited by Thomas Vennum, Jr. Washington, D.C.: Smithsonian Institution Office of Folklife Programs.

McCarl, Robert. 1988. "Occupational Folklife in the Public Sector: A Case Study." In *The Conservation of Culture: Folklorists and the Public Sector*, edited by Burt Feintuch. Lexington: University Press of Kentucky.

Musics of the Soviet Union. 1988. Smithsonian/Folkways Recordings SF 40001. Washington, D.C.: Smithsonian Institution Office of Folklife Programs.

Oinas, Felix. 1975. "The Political Uses and Themes of Folklore in the Soviet Union." *Journal of the Folklore Institute* 12:157–75.

Santino, Jack. 1988. "The Tendency to Ritualize: The Living Celebrations Series As a Model for Cultural Presentation and Validation." In *The Conservation of Culture: Folklorists and the Public Sector*, edited by Burt Feintuch. Lexington: University Press of Kentucky.

Staub, Shalom. 1988. "Folklore and Authenticity: A Myopic Marriage in Public Sector Programs." In *The Conservation of Culture: Folklorists and the Public Sector*, edited by Burt Feintuch. Lexington: University Press of Kentucky.

Tuva: Voices from the Center of Asia. 1990. Smithsonian Folkways Records SF 40017. Washington, D.C.: Smithsonian Institution Office of Folklife Programs.

Vennum, Thomas, and Nicholas Spitzer. 1986. "Musical Performance at the Festival: Developing Criteria." In *Festival of American Folklife Program Book*, edited by Thomas Vennum, Jr. Washington, D.C.: Smithsonian Institution Office of Folklife Programs.

Whisnant, David. 1983. *All That Is Native and Fine*. Chapel Hill: University of North Carolina Press.

———. 1988. "Public Sector Folklore As Intervention: Lessons from the Past, Prospects for the Future." In *The Conservation of Culture: Folklorists and the Public Sector*, edited by Burt Feintuch. Lexington: University Press of Kentucky.

Crossover Dreams

The Folklorist and the Folk Arrival

DANIEL SHEEHY

n the film *Crossover Dreams*,[1] the sophisticated and socially aware Panamanian salsa musician Rubén Blades stars in the role of a frustrated salsa singer and songwriter who spends his nights running from one forty-dollar-a-show gig to another. The character he plays is talented and relatively successful at what he does, but as hard as he tries, he cannot "make it big." He eventually yields to the temptation of a recording company agent's promises of big money and instant fame. All he must do is "cross over" to the vogues of mainstream non-Latin pop music. He changes his name, appearance, and music to meet the expectations of an Anglo audience, he dumps his Latin fiancée for a fast blonde, and he replaces his best friend and long-time salsa trumpet player sideman with a white rhythm and blues saxophone player. The record company propels him to notoriety for a few weeks, but when sales of his "crossover" music plummet, he loses his recording contract. His records than sell for $1.99 each, his old fiancée (whom he wants back) marries a boorish Anglo dentist, the Latin club

owner refuses to hire him back, and he loses his self-respect.

As if the message of the film were not clear enough, in a subsequent interview with the *Albuquerque Journal* a writer asked Blades about the crossover possibilities of his music, that is if there were ways he could transform it to appeal to the American popular music audience. He answered, "I'm not eager to cross over. Cross over to what? The idea is not to cross over but to find people who will meet you halfway. . . . That way I don't abandon my background. That way I don't soften the way I think, the way I feel, to please another group of people. . . . I don't think that works" (Steinberg 1986:1). I admired his integrity and let his words and the film's moral fade into memory. A couple of weeks later, though, a series of real-life events brought their importance to my own work crashing back into mind.

I had been asked to put together two Latin American music performances to be part of a major festival of traditional arts in Philadelphia to mark the bicentennial of the signing of the United States Constitution.[2] I invited two trios of musicians, one native to Veracruz, Mexico, and the other of Paraguayan origin. Both were comprised of first-generation immigrants; both consisted of one harpist and two guitarists, and in each case, the individual musicians had considerable experience performing in public.

On the day of the festival, the Mexican trio had a number of things working against them. All three had spent most of the night before traveling from their homes in Los Angeles, Fort Worth, and Denver; their flights arrived late, and one musician got lost in the Philadelphia airport. They literally were rushed to the stage three minutes before they were scheduled to perform. Despite all this adversity, they presented a forty-five-minute set of exciting, impeccably performed *sones jarochos,* traditional music from Veracruz, complete with commentary between *sones* that gave the audience the sense of the music's connection to a particular accent of Spanish, a certain region, and a cultural background different from their own. The audi-

Los Pregoneros del Puerto, *jarocho* musicians from Veracruz, Mexico, now living in the United States, conclude their appearance at Carnegie Hall's Weill Recital Hall in New York for the Folk Masters concert and radio series. Fall 1990. Photo by Jack Vartoogian.

ence, mainly non-Latins mixed with a variety of local Hispanics, were delighted, and many returned for their second performance later that evening.

The Paraguayan trio had driven up that morning from their homes in Washington, D.C., and arrived at the festival site a couple of hours early. Together, we went over the Paraguayan *guaranias, polcas, canciones,* and the *galopa* that they were planning to perform. Fifteen minutes into their forty-five-minute performance, though, they abandoned all forms of Paraguayan music and launched into a series of hackneyed Mexican tunes, including "Cielito Lindo" and "Rancho Grande," in an obvious, heartrending attempt to please the multicultural audience. The audience responded with polite, token applause, and those who were acquainted with Paraguayan music (or Mexican music, for that matter) were disappointed. In the words of one of the Veracruz musicians, "¿Por qué hacen eso? Eso no tiene chiste." ("Why do they do that? There is nothing special about it.") Well, Rubén Blades had been right. They had tried to cross over to what they perceived as the expectations of the cultural "outsider" audience, they had abandoned their background, and it did not work.

Both the success and the failure of what had happened brought into relief something that I had already felt, but never quite so deeply—the fundamental importance of the role of the folklorist[3] in "transcontextualizing," if you will, or transferring the folk musician from a traditional context to a public, nontraditional setting. I and a few others had worked with the leader of the Veracruz group, José Gutiérrez, for ten years. When he had immigrated to Los Angeles in 1975, he could find no venue, no audience, not even a particular reason to perform his own tradition of music. As I got to know him, I came to realize that José was one of the most accomplished and respected performers of his own regional folk music in or out of Mexico. In Los Angeles, he could find no substantial audience for *música jarocha,* so he went to work assembling saunas and playing Mexican popular favorites two nights a week in a Hollywood restaurant.

José was clearly a stagewise musician, and after we began working together, it took only a few tests of the repertoire and the ways of presenting *sones jarochos* to mainly non-jarocho[4] audiences to settle on a presentation with which he felt comfortable and to which the audiences responded well.[5] At his request, I began helping him get performance opportunities, negotiate contracts on occasion, and find the venues and wider audiences that he wanted and deserved. Through all this, I constantly shared with him my knowledge of his tradition's history and my sense of the special value he had as a representative of that tradition in the context of the United States. This information sharing, as I look back on it, worked toward arming him against the damaging effects of culture shock and sharpened his sense of purpose in performing his traditional repertoire.[6]

Spreading the word of his availability to concert organizers and Mexican American cultural organizations and locating other jarocho musicians living in the United States took years. José went on to be a musician-in-residence at the University of Washington, a regular teacher at the Centro Cultural de la Raza in San Diego, guest artist at the annual conference of the Asociación Nacional de Grupos Folklóricos, and a frequent concertizer throughout California and the United States. He took on many Mexican American students, and in a modest way, he has helped open a niche of musical option for Mexican American musicians in southern California.

In Philadelphia, the value of all the time and effort that José, I, and others had put into the trio's performance was clear. On that stage, they were in command. To paraphrase Blade's words, they did *not* abandon their background, they did *not* soften the way they expressed themselves to please another group of people, and it *did* work. They did not cross over but rather developed a way to "package" themselves to cultural outsiders in order to best express the essentials of who they were and what they did. And through their ability to use the medium of the stage as a cultural translating device, they brought the audience closer to *them* by making *them* (the audience) feel more confident.

In the case of the Paraguayans' performance, the importance of the folklorist was also clear—in fact, painfully clear because of its absence. I had not done my job. I did the fieldwork, located the artists, and learned about their tradition, their individual backgrounds, and their repertoire, many of the things normally done for the purpose of scholarship. I had not, however, gone beyond that to arm the musicians with the confidence they needed to stay with what they did the best when they went on stage. I asked them to go up on the stage and "be themselves" and then I abandoned them to the mercy (or mercilessness) of show business.

Even though the folklorist's place in bringing folk musicians to public attention is an old one, we have seldom articulated a historical perspective, the issues implicit in cultural representation, the strategic benefits of performance events for cultural conservation, and the specialized roles and demands for the folklorist. Only a few people working as folk cultural advocates have taken it upon themselves to enter into a close, long-term collaboration with individual folk musicians. This type of symbiotic relationship, though, had been going on for a long time. Since at least the 1930s, folklore activists such as John Lomax, Alan Lomax, Bess Lomax Hawes, Ralph Rinzler, Guy Carawan, Mike Seeger, and a few others have worked to bring outstanding folk musicians to the attention of the broad American public. Out of a sense of social and cultural justice, or democratic ideals, or sheer enthusiasm for the genius of the traditional musicians they encountered, they introduced their fellow Americans to the likes of Huddie Ledbetter, Jelly Roll Morton, Memphis Slim, Bessie Jones, Doc Watson, and many other musicians well-known to millions of Americans. Many musicians, once known to but a few, became important communicators of their cultural group's values, worldview, life-style, and potential for creating expressions of beauty. I think it is fair to say that the public impact of these collaborations has been great, and they have done much to bring traditional arts, artists, and even communities the respect they deserve, but all too often do not receive.

In the early 1960s, Ralph Rinzler, building on Charles Seeger's use of the terms "survival" and "revival" (Seeger 1977:332), coined a term that described the fruits of these collaborations the "folk arrival" (Paton 1967:38), whereby the revivalists who ran folk festivals brought survivals of traditional music to those events in the form of living traditional performers. The point made by "folk arrival" was that authentic folk musicians were being brought to urban stages that up to that time had been occupied mainly by their surrogates. Their surrogates took the form of stylistic imitators and those who incorporated elements of Anglo- or Afro-American folk music style into their own creative compositions and billed what they did as "folk music."

The work of a number of scholarly researchers in the 1960s and 1970s clearly showed potential for application to the presentation of folk artists in new contexts. Folklorist Alan Dundes has pointed out that traditional communities have their own forms of "oral literary criticism" and that these metatexts as well as performance context are essential to grasping the meaning of oral literature such as proverbs (Dundes 1966). The same, of course, holds true for music and other forms of expressive behavior. The sociologist Erving Goffman has elaborated on how socially determined conventions of frame of reference shape our perception of experience and give meaning to events occurring within those frames.[7] Richard Schechner has taken the notion of theatrical frames further, looking closely at the continuity and change of meaning in the restoration of behavior from the past or from another context (Schechner 1981). Understanding the relationship and dynamics between folk performer, audience, and the frames that shape their perception of each other is key to determining the goals, objectives, and techniques of staged representations of folk culture. It is a fertile ground for further research.

In terms of cultural strategizing, the empowerment of artists, which is precisely what this type of cultural conservation is—empowering artists to take command of the stage—involves two of the main strategies employed by folklore conservationists, "framing" and "feedback." Putting a traditional artist on a stage can be like putting a picture in a frame and hanging it on a wall. The symbol of the stage (or the frame) commands attention and says, "This is art, and you should give it special consideration." The artists and art form are often not unaffected themselves by this transition from the primary frame of the ordinary context to the new frame, with a different set of rules and conventions (Goffman 1974:21–22), of course. Commenting on the ethical dimension of applying new frames to old forms, Bess Lomax Hawes wrote, "On bad days, we tend to think of framing as the ultimate co-option of the innocent by a society that is determined to make a buck out of everything that it touches, turning every act into a packageable and saleable commodity. On good days, we hope that we are providing smaller cultures with a defense mechanism whereby they can protect their art forms and carry them into the future" (Hawes 1980:89). On the positive side, the stage in many cases *can* be a great equalizer and through its strength as a symbolic medium send a message that is one of the most important and fundamental we can send—art traditions from different cultures are not innately better than one another; they are merely different.[8]

Now, taking this metaphorical frame and turning it around so that the artistic expression is aimed back at the particular cultural community out of which it came results in what has been called "feedback" (Hawes 1980:89). Feedback techniques are usually part of the "in-reach" approach, aimed at putting the art form and artist in touch with the community from which it derived, working to make important connections between artists and their cultural peers in order to draw attention to and maintain the highest possible aesthetic standards within that community.

If we extend the idea of "folk arrival" to the audience as well as the artists and make a particular effort to bring in members of that community to the performance, this obviously can enhance the feedback effect. In fact, augmenting "cultural insider" audiences with "cultural outsiders" creates a variety of possible encouraging effects. Not only might the aesthetic standards of the insider audience be reified by the performers, but the performers might be bolstered by a sense that "other people" as well value their traditional arts.[9] Folk artists from smaller culture groups in a larger society often suffer from a "prophet in their own land" status, and the attachment of value from the larger society may increase their prestige within their own cultural group. The cultural mixing of audiences can have the result of expanding the dimension of the theatrical frame as well. The outsider audience may have a similar impact on the insider audience, as they might have on the performers. And the insiders, acting out their own, extra-theatrical, socially determined notion of frame for the "ordinary" setting (e.g., conversing with the performers, responsorial shouting in the style of an African American church congregation, or dancing) may end up being part of the performance in the minds of the outsiders, enhancing the outsider's own sense of the traditional performance context and giving greater meaning to the performance.

In terms of specialized roles, the training and experience folklorists possess can be particularly helpful in empowering traditional artists to take command of the stage setting. As fieldworkers, our skills are especially important in locating the appropriate artists, becoming aware of their aesthetic sensibilities, and discovering their representative value in terms of the tradition as a whole. As cultural analysts, we can determine the propriety and potential impact of singling out one or a few individuals for their cultural milieu and giving them heightened visibility. As explainers of cultural phenomena to others, folklorists are especially trained to understand, create, and shape the "frames" of "staged" cultural representation to best communicate the meaning of folk performance on the stage to audiences of cultural outsiders while allowing the artists to maintain their own integrity and the integrity of the tradition.

This role as explainer aims not only at shaping presentational frames, but also at providing the artist with knowledge of new frames. This may or may not be difficult. After all, folk performers frequently shift frames in their "natural" context anyway. The length of performance, choice of repertoire and texts, and attitude toward the listener/viewer may vary greatly depending on whether the setting is a dance, a family reunion, the solitude of a living room, and so forth, or if the audience consists of adults or children, men or women, friends or strangers.

At the same time, the particular aim of the folklorist's effort may require a change in approach from that used in academic settings in several different respects. One has to do with the relationship of the fieldworker with the artist. Unlike much folklore fieldwork, which requires only short periods of time with those being surveyed or interviewed, fieldwork with an eye toward developing artists' skills in presenting themselves involves a much greater personal commitment to the musician, a commitment of time and of real emotion invested over a lengthy period. In making this commitment, we take on a new role. We become more than fieldworkers, more than scholars; we become collaborators with another human being.

Another role the folklorist necessarily takes on is one basic to the stage—that of critic. Actually, in the traditional community setting, this role is not new. Aesthetic criticism is always present in the ordinary give-and-take between the artist and the surrounding community. The folklorist's perspective as critic, though, is a dual one. On one hand, his or her task is to give opinion on artistic quality from the viewpoint of traditional aesthetic values. On the other hand, the folklorist must judge appropriateness for the stage from the point of view of the concert audience and the special expectations that go along with the stage itself. Putting artists on a stage is like putting a sculpture on a pedestal for all to scrutinize; they must be able to hold up to this kind of close and focused scrutiny for the stage setting to work in their favor. Furthermore, when the musician goes on the stage, he/she will be representing more than just him/herself. What the audience sees and hears may be the only thing they have in their ken upon which to form an impression about the entire culture. It is the folklorist's responsibility, therefore, to the artists, to their cultures, and to the audiences, to know traditional standards of excellence, make quality judgments, and select the best available representatives of those standards who are at the same time compatible with the stage setting—no small responsibility, to be sure.

Opinions on matters of artistic quality are only as good as the expertise available to the person with the opinion, and the best expertise possible simply must be brought to bear in selecting artists and repertoire. If we do not possess adequate expertise and knowledge of repertoire in a tradition to be presented, we must either find someone who does or develop it ourselves.

Another need is expertise in the medium of the stage itself. To my knowledge, very few folklorists have actively collaborated with stage producers, directors, stage managers, set designers, lighting consultants, or other professionals trained in staging techniques. This is not to say that there have not been many successfully staged performances of folk material, because there have been. It could be, however, that in general we have unwittingly accepted a low set of expectations as to what can be done technically in presenting folk artists on stage. Have we limited our presentational models to the folk festival format? Have perceptions (right or wrong) of theater specialists as "elitists" or members of another "tribe" prevented us from seeking out their expertise?

An understanding of the literati-derived and Eurocentric medium of the stage could prove to be of immense importance in guiding the process of filtering out what does not work in that venue and enhancing that which does. For example, one of the main characteristics of stage performance, the psychic and interactive distancing of the artist from the audience, is one of the main traits that distinguishes European "art" music from most folk music. Some presentations of folk music can overcome this, and some cannot. Perhaps the re-creation of stage settings such as plazas, bars, or living rooms could provide a greater sense of traditional context and serve to better inform the audience and make the performers more comfortable. The stage has its own set of technical values and expressive techniques, and utilizing the skills of stage professionals could improve our efforts at translating traditional arts via the language of the stage to audiences.

In entering into collaboration with stage professionals, we should keep in mind that there are prevailing, specialized styles of theatrical presentation. The vocabulary and rhetoric of lighting for a Shakespearian tragedy will in all likelihood be much different from that intended for a Grateful Dead concert. An expert in one may know very little about the other. And it could be that neither works for our own particular purposes. This of course, is the point. We must teach as well as learn, and strive, over the long term, to develop a greater knowledge and sensitivity on the parts of arts presenters and stage professionals to the needs of folk artists.

Finally, I would like to share one observation that has to do with the approach to audiences. In their relationship to most concert goers, the folk arts have something very much in common with avant-garde artistic creations—they challenge the audience members to understand them for what they are, and not to operate comfortably from previously formed aesthetic assumptions. With some success, avant-garde artists have conditioned their audiences to expect this challenge and to rise to it. Audiences must be made to realize that, just as with avant-garde artistic forms, the traditional arts (or "rear-garde," as one arts administrator put it) have their own, carefully conceived, inherent value and offer a special challenge to be seriously understood for what they are, in their own aesthetic terms. If audiences can be put in this frame of mind, they would be much more likely to rise to that challenge and open themselves up to new artistic insights. If along with challenging them, we provide cultural outsiders with the right kind of information and attitudes with which to approach the performance, we empower *them* and we give them the ability and confidence to "meet the artists halfway," as Rubén Blades insisted be the case.

The past few years have seen new opportunities for advancing the "folk arrival." More performing arts programmers want to and are including "ethnic" and tradition-based material in their season's offering. According to statistics from the National Endowment for the Arts, based on data from nonprofit performing arts presenters, both the total number and the overall percentage of performances thought of as "ethnic dance" or "traditional arts" in the 1986–87 season nearly doubled from those of the 1982–83 season.[10] Both small and large presenters are actively seeking high-quality folk performances that would appeal to their audiences. In recent years, the NEA Folk Arts Program has been contacted by Carnegie Hall, the Brooklyn Academy of Music, Jacob's Pillow, the Kennedy Center, and many other "mainstream" professional presenters asking for suggestions of or support for folk performers. Opportunity is not only knocking; it is ready to drag us down the "stream" with it.

To conclude, in order to progress in our ability to present traditional performance, we need to keep four sets of roles and needs in mind: (1) those of ourselves as folklorists; (2) those of traditional artists; (3) those of audiences; and (4) those of other specialists who can assist the first three. As folklorists, we need to cultivate a better awareness of our own responsibility and potential value to traditional artists and their communities (upon whom, after all, we depend for our livelihoods). Better understanding our role in public presentation of traditional culture as "cultural translators," educators, and critics will help us better define those areas in which to improve our cultural strategies, techniques, and representational models. And inviting the collaboration of specialists in "stage translation" could help move us closer to Rubén Blades's, own dream—not of crossover, but of meeting each other halfway.

The folk arrival continues. The artists are ready, the audiences are ready, and the venues are waiting. Cultural information, stage skills, and a sense of purpose can empower traditional artists. Similarly, folklorists can be empowered to assist them. The real purpose in writing this article is, at least in some way, to do just that.

228 . . . . DANIEL SHEEHY

NOTES

My Arts Endowment colleagues Bess Lomax Hawes and Barry Bergey and editors Robert Baron and Nicholas Spitzer were of valuable assistance in refining the contents of this article, and for this I am grateful.

1. *Crossover Dreams* is a 1985 production of Miramax Films.

2. This was the International Village Fair, organized by folklorist Mick Moloney and hosted by the National Park Service and the city of Philadelphia.

3. By "folklorist," I mean to include anthropologists, ethnomusicologists, or anyone else with appropriate training, experience, and attention to folklore. My own academic training was in ethnomusicology.

4. Jarochos, natives of the state of Veracruz in East Mexico, constitute a minute percentage of the population in Los Angeles among the first-generation Mexican immigrants, who are for the most part from the western and central Mexican states. One explanation of the origin of the term "jarocho," put forth by historian José Luís Melgarejo Vivanco in *Breve historia de Veracruz* (Xalapa, México: Universidad Veracruzana, 1960), is that colonial militiamen in Veracruz often were armed only with *jaras*, or "sticks," and thus were called "jar-ochos."

5. "Working together" may sound too formal. We soon became friends and later, *compadres*. I am his son's godfather.

6. This notion derived from an unpublished letter from Alan Lomax to his sister, Bess Lomax Hawes, in 1988 concerning the potential benefits and strategies of folklorists working in the American territories in the Pacific.

7. Erving Goffman puts forth an insightful and thorough discussion of "framing" in his book *Frame Analysis: An Essay on the Organization of Experience* (1974).

8. A convincing case for the cultural relativity of musical value is found in anthropologist/ ethnomusicologist John Blacking's monograph *How Musical Is Man?* (1973).

9. The appreciation of a group's traditional music by cultural outsiders in some cases may have the opposite effect. Manuel H. Peña argues that *rejection* of accordion *conjunto* as dé-classé music by upward-striving middle-class Mexican Americans strengthened it as a symbolic representative of blue-collar interests, often in conflict with those of the middle class. (Peña 1985:109–10)

10. Oral communication in August 1987 from Joel Snyder, administrator of the Inter-Arts Program of the National Endowment for the Arts.

REFERENCES

Blacking, John. 1973. *How Musical Is Man?* Seattle: University of Washington Press.
Dundes, Alan. 1966. "Metafolklore and Oral Literacy Criticism." *The Monist* 50:505–16.

Goffman, Erving. 1974. *Frame Analysis: An Essay on the Organization of Experience.* New York: Harper and Row.

Hawes, Bess Lomax. 1980. "Folk Arts." In *1980 National Endowment for the Arts Annual Report.* Washington, D.C.: National Endowment for the Arts.

Paton, Sandy. 1967. "Folk and the Folk Arrival." In *The American Folk Scene: Dimensions of the Folksong Revival,* edited by David A. DeTurk and A. Poulin, Jr., pp. 38–43. New York: Dell Publishing.

Peña, Manuel H. 1985. *The Texas-Mexican Conjunto: History of a Working-Class Music.* Austin: University of Texas Press.

Schechner, Richard. 1981. "Restoration of Behavior." *Studies in Visual Communication* 7 (3): 3–45.

Seeger, Charles. 1977. "Folk Music in the Schools of a Highly Industrialized Society." In *Studies in Musicology: 1935–1975.* Los Angeles: University of California Press.

Steinberg, David. 1986. "Salsa Star Adds Fire to Music." *Albuquerque Journal,* December 14.

Feet on the Ground, Head in the Clouds

Some Thoughts on the Training of Public Folklorists

JIM GRIFFITH

What we call public folklore seems to have always been an optional aspect of the professional folklorist's work, but it is only recently that it has become a viable, full-time professional specialty. Public folklore jobs vary widely, from intensely bureaucratic positions with state agencies to short-term contract fieldwork leading towards a festival, exhibition, or other presentation. Public folklorists supervise granting processes, engage in cultural mediation, initiate and organize presentational events, and do fieldwork and a host of other activities. Many public folklorists work for arts agencies, historical societies, or other branches of state or local government; others, myself included, work from within academic institutions. Each job seems to be unique in its demands, possibilities, and limitations, especially when the variables of regionality and the vitally important chemistry (or lack of it) between folklorist, community, and employers are worked into the equation.

For example, my job as director of the University of Arizona Library's

Southwest Folklore Center involves maintaining and augmenting an archive, acting as a sort of reference department for questions concerning regional traditional cultures, lecturing and doing media presentations, and producing educational events and materials such as festivals, exhibitions, booklets, and published recordings. I am not involved in granting, and operate pretty much independently. On the other hand, many of my colleagues who work in arts agencies hold highly bureaucratized positions with little opportunity for independent action. There are certain characteristics, however, that seem to distinguish public folklore work from that of the folklorist who works solely within an academic setting.

The most important of these can best be expressed in terms of focus and clientele; with our perception, in other words, of whom we are supposed to be communicating with. The academic folklorist communicates primarily with his or her students and with academic colleagues within the discipline. The public folklorist, on the other hand, communicates primarily with members of the general public and the community from which his or her data are drawn. Communication with colleagues tends to be not as much through publications, as it is in the case of the academic, but rather through lengthy conversations on the phone and at professional meetings and other gatherings.

One experience that many public folklorists seem to have had in common is the discovery that the job—whatever it may be—entails skills, knowledge, and abilities that were not even suggested during undergraduate and graduate training, much less emphasized. Cameras, computers, sound recording equipment, bureaucracies, the media, and other objects and institutions must be manipulated skillfully if the public folklorist is to succeed at the job. Audiences are not captive and must be attracted and retained by the intrinsic excitement of the presentation—and this while maintaining at least enough intellectual content to satisfy the academically trained public folklorist. This tension between pleasing one's intended au-

Los Ases, an all-Indian band in the Mexican mariachi style made up of members of the Yaqui and Tohono O'odham tribes, perform in the central plaza of Tucson. The group's performance was one of many presentations of southern Arizona's traditional arts during the 1989 "Tucson Meet Yourself," an annual festival. Photo by David Burkhalter.

dience and satisfying one's intellectual standards may well be one of the unique aspects of our work.

Other tensions exist as well: Frequently the public folklorist works in an environment in which he or she is the only person with postgraduate university training; frequently he or she discovers that his/her superiors are indifferent or even hostile to the notion of research. Projects must be completed and decisions arrived at quickly, and some of the criteria seem to be more political than intellectual or academic. Many of these tensions will be dealt with elsewhere in this book, but they must be noted here as a frequent condition for the work.

Is there any training that makes this work easier, more "doable"? My own answer, based on my particular experience, is both negative and affirmative. On the one hand, I find that I never have precisely the knowledge and skills I feel I need to get a specific job done; on the other, over the ten years I have been in my present position I feel I have drawn on everything I had ever learned, been, or done in the more than forty years preceding. It is not that I am advocating that the public folklorist "know everything about everything"; it is simply that the job permits (and frequently demands) that a wide range of knowledge, skills, and aptitudes be brought into play. The remainder of this article will deal with some of these attributes as I understand them from my experience in the field and from conversations with colleagues.

KNOWLEDGE

Certain things can be learned in a classroom situation—are perhaps best learned in that setting. Important among these is an understanding of basic cultural theory. Public folklorists frequently engage in activities that have the effect of changing certain aspects of the communities they deal with. It is important that they possess some shared model of the functioning of complex societies such as ours and some familiarity with the body of anthropological theory concerning culture change.

Public folklore has generated its own literature. Much of this involves lively debates, which often examine critically many of the basic activities of the field. The public-folklorist-in-training should be well grounded in this literature. It addresses questions that in my personal experience tend to arise on an almost daily basis. These can be extremely complex, partaking of a baffling combination of the theoretical and the practical.

Vital ethnographic knowledge can also come from the classroom. The more the public folklorist knows about the various groups he or she will work with, the easier it is to get going on the work. This knowledge can and often must come from self-directed reading projects, but the greater stock of orderly data, especially bibliographic data, the worker already has at hand, the better.

Related to this is the vital area of what I call stylistic and repertoire literacy. By this I simply mean familiarity with a wide range of expressive genres. If we are to be dealing with traditional art forms, it is imperative that we have a real understanding of those arts and the range of styles and repertoires they encompass. The public folklorist needs to have heard a lot of talk, listened to a lot of music, looked at a lot of art, and retained and considered what he or she has experienced.

Let me combine much of the above into a single example. I am often asked to recommend a mariachi band to perform at festivals, parties, and other occasions in the Tucson area. The local mariachi scene includes working-class groups that perform in bars and restaurants and which are made up of professional musicians, a middle-class group who perform extensively in cross-cultural concert settings, youth groups composed of high school students who put their earnings in a fund towards college and university scholarships, a university-sponsored student band, and a group of Spanish-speaking Native Americans who have been playing the music all their lives. Each band will provide a distinctive performance, and each will broadcast different social messages to different segments of the population. In each case my choice is a judgment call, based on a wide range of considerations involving the music, the nature of the group seeking a band, and an array of other considerations. I am able to make these decisions the way I do—I am aware that such decisions exist—because I was trained to look at art in its cultural context and because I am familiar with the mariachi tradition and repertoire and the ways in which that tradition is expressed in southern Arizona.

SKILLS

Certain skills can be introduced in a formal didactic setting as well, although most can be truly learned and perfected only through practice. Most important among these for the public folklorist is fieldwork. A thorough grounding in field-collecting techniques and the theoretical and ethical questions associated with fieldwork are essential to the practice of public folklore. Course work offering guided and monitored field experience, combined with an opportunity for reading, reflection, and discussion concerning the issues raised by that experience, would seem essential.

Essential skills of data gathering such as photography and sound recording, which demand familiarity with specialized equipment, can also be taught, but the successful application of those techniques must come with practice. My personal opinion is that more than competence is needed here. If the public folklorist's job is to present the work of traditional artists (and that is often a part of my job, through recordings, exhibitions, and publications), the documents (i.e., photographs or sound recordings) presenting that work must be of the highest possible quality to show respect both to the artist and his or her tradition.

Of course it is possible, and often desirable or even necessary, to hire professional photographers or recordists to do the documentation work on major projects. But this can have its disadvantages. These can be economic: There isn't always money to pay professionals on all projects. There can be other disadvantages as well. An excellent photographer, for example, may well have his or her own aesthetic or other agendas that can differ from that of the public folklorist who is directing the project. I personally buy strongly into the old adage that "if you want something done right, you should do it yourself." This is admittedly not always practical or even possible. But at the very least, an understanding of the technological and aesthetic processes involved in various kinds and styles of documentation can make negotiation with professionals much easier.

Another set of skills that can be at least introduced in a classroom situation involves grant writing, grant evaluation, and by extension bureaucratic "doing" in general. One course I know of has students write grants and then become members of a granting panel with the task of allocating a sum of money considerably less than the sum total of the grant requests. This involves some painful learning, to be sure, but not as painful as it would be in a real situation. A complaint frequently heard from public folklorists working on their first jobs is that graduate school in no way prepared them for the formal and bureaucratic demands of their work.

Communications skills as well can be taught in the classroom but must in the final analysis be learned through doing. Much of my work depends upon various kinds of communication—I must speak and write eloquently and clearly to many different kinds of people: my employers, my colleagues, members of the communities with whom I work, the media, and the "general public." My personal experience is that upon leaving graduate school I had to learn how to write all over again—that for the purposes of papers and theses I had developed a style that, while readable, was certainly uninviting. Faced with an audience who had no need to read or listen unless they wanted to, I found I needed a new set of skills to communicate with them.

I must emphasize that popular writing does not mean sloppy or unsophisticated writing. It means interesting, clear writing, which like other skills must be learned and polished by constant doing. Much of my job involves public education, and the public, unlike registered students, will not stick around for an experience unless it is an enjoyable or at least an interesting one. I am constantly reminded of a comment made to me by the late Leslie Keith, a fine bluegrass fiddler and a superlative traditional country showman, to the effect that the world was full of fiddlers who could "play it." That wasn't enough, he would say; you have to be able to "sell it" as well.

Another aspect of "selling it" moves into the area of showmanship. It helps to be able to design an exhibition, concert, festival, or lecture so that it will be appealing. Once again, some of the time there will be professionals to do the work or help out, but these professionals may have their own agendas, and it helps to understand their work at the very least. I have had a strong hand in designing and hanging all but one of the twelve museum exhibitions I have been involved in. Sometimes that was due to the realities of having two tiny offices collaborate on an exhibition. It was also by preference and a strong desire to control the message that the exhibition sent to its viewers.

For the same reasons, I prefer to do much of the emcee work at the concerts and festivals I produce. I find it important to act as mediator between audience and performers to be sure that I have done all I possibly can to ensure a respectful, intelligent, and appreciative response to the artists whom I have invited on stage. And I design the concerts carefully so as to set off the different performing groups from each other and provide a varied, interesting experience for the audience.

That I am able to do this is to a great extent a result of my work as an entertainer, performer, and coffeehouse programmer before I ever was a public folklorist. And this brings up yet another general category of skills important within our craft—those primarily gained through work experience.

In talking with colleagues about this article I frequently heard phrases like "most of what I know about public folklore work I learned in the restaurant industry" or "as a supermarket checkout clerk." As I understand these comments, they are an attempt at getting at the importance of some of the lessons one learns in almost any workplace, especially where one has to deal with the public as well as with fellow workers and supervisors. One of these lessons involves negotiation.

Many public folklorists find themselves continuously negotiating—with their employers, with potential project sponsors, with various kinds of special-interest organizations, with the communities and artists with whom they work. Frequently the public folklorist has aims that differ from those of many individuals within the agency in which he or she works. Even presenting the work of a folk artist to the public frequently involves negotiation. I suspect many of us have horror stories of failed attempts at such negotiation—frequently occasions when we were so immersed in our work and our enthusiasm for the particular artist or art form that we did not even realize that negotiation was necessary. I know I have my share, which is one reason for my personal desire to control as much as possible of the presentation process.

One horrible example should suffice. In the late 1970s I was contacted by a group of women who were starting up a gift shop in a local museum. They expressed their interest in selling local folk art and asked me if I knew any quilters who might be interested in selling their work. My thoughts immediately turned to a local African American woman whose quilts I had seen a few weeks before. I knew she was a prolific quilter, needed the money, and was in the habit of selling her work within her neighborhood at fifteen dollars a quilt. After checking with her, I gave her name to the gift shop committee. After a few weeks, I saw the quilter and asked her how things had gone. She looked a bit puzzled as she told me that "the ladies" had indeed visited her but had not been interested in buying any quilts. I then spoke with one of the committee members and learned that they had decided not to use the woman's quilts because "they weren't traditional." On further inquiry, I learned that, while "traditional" quilts were made from natural fabrics of subdued colors and featured hand sewing throughout, the quilter in question had shown them her "Trip around the World" quilt, which she had recently entered in the county fair. (It had not won a prize.) It was made of hot pink and turquoise-blue polyester, with the help of a sewing machine. Other quilts were equally mystifying: They featured "loud" colors, and the patterns frequently "didn't come out." That is, they did not exhibit the tight, symmetrical sense of control that is such an important feature of many European American quilts.

It is easy to reconstruct what had happened. The quilter was solidly within her African American aesthetic tradition, producing exciting quilts for everyday use in situations that might well require frequent washing and drying. The prospective buyers were looking for quilts that fit into the familiar, historic, European American pattern with which they were familiar. In a sense, utilitarian folk art was offered to prospective dealers in cultural icons. The result: disappointment and confusion on both sides. There is a chance that, had I worked with both parties involved, explaining the difference in traditions and perhaps even accompanying the buyers, things would have turned out differently. After all, I, rather than the artist or the consumer, am the one who is trained as a cross-cultural mediator. That's what I was hired to do, and unless I am there to do it, and do it well, I'm not doing my job.

Let's balance that tale of failure with a short description of a successful project. In the mid-1980s I was a member of the committee responsible for producing a powwow on the local district of the Papago Indian reservation. At a meeting, several committee members wondered out loud what specifically Papago events could be included in the powwow. Being aware that there had been a Papago fiddling tradition until recently and that several fiddlers still lived in the area, despite the fact that accordion-based bands had replaced the traditional fiddle bands at dances about twenty years previously, I suggested a fiddle contest. After being given the go-ahead, I then went to the fiddlers I knew and asked them if such a contest sounded like a good idea. The response being favorable, I then asked what a Papago fiddle contest should be like. "White people do it this way," I said. "How should Indians do it?" As the contest developed, it was between fiddle bands rather than individual fiddlers, run to Papago standards, with Papago musicians as judges, and announced in Papago. Four bands showed up for the first contest, and everyone had a good time. The contest remained an annual feature of the powwow until 1990. Since the first contest, more bands have gotten back together, three commercial tapes have been produced of this previously unrecorded music, fiddle music is once more heard at village feasts, and one band was invited to the 1990 Festival of American Fiddle Tunes in Port Townsend, Washington. The total cost of the project was approximately $300 a year in prizes and flyers, and a lot of time spent negotiating and attending to details.

Along with negotiation skills comes what I see as necessary attributes—patience and the ability to concentrate on a larger agenda. If I am forced to work with a bunch of folks whom I consider (however accurately) to be insufferable racists, it is far less important that they know my opinion of them than it is that I achieve as much as possible of my agenda. This sort of situation and the challenges it brings seems at times to be a constant feature of public folklore work. It involves the need for a good deal of patience, alternative phrasing of ideas, and negotiations. It can also involve some private screaming, cursing, and wall-kicking on the part of the folklorist. But these skills, often best learned in the public-service workplace, are essential to the success of our work.

Other learned skills come in useful as well. I find my lifelong experience as a musician to be of great value, not just because I can establish rapport with other musicians by playing with them (which can be a useful field-collecting technique), but also because I understand without being told some of the concerns that musicians seem to have in common. Another way of phrasing this is that I know how musicians like to be treated. By the same token, I am no sort of a craftsperson, and my work in documenting and presenting craftspeople has suffered accordingly. I do not always know the "right" questions to ask, the proper things to look for and document.

APTITUDES

This final area is admittedly a bit hazy. I approached it already when I spoke of patience and willingness to set priorities as an important thing for public folklorists to possess. The intense nature of the work, which in my case often involves long days and seven-day weeks, means that it is not a kind of work that is easy to pick up and set down, as one can do with some jobs. The work brings with it tremendous stress because the public folklorist frequently stands in a position of mediator or interpreter between mutually uncomprehending or even hostile groups within the greater society. Deadlines bring other kinds of stress, as does the overload that I personally find inevitable in a situation in which one does the necessary projects and then fills up the rest of one's time with the most interesting ones—at which point an opportunity inevitably turns up that simply can't be turned down!

All this is leading up to the importance of commitment. In addition to the stresses and long hours I just mentioned, I should add that few public folklore positions pay very well, and that at present there does not seem to be much opportunity for economic advancement within the field. Tenure is nonexistent in most jobs that I know of. So one important attribute for the public folklorist is a high degree of commitment. (Youth helps, too.) To descend for the moment to slightly less dignified language, if you don't believe passionately in the value of the work, the crap you frequently get handed becomes hard to take. Public folklore is not a very practical avenue for professional, social, or economic self-advancement, no matter how exciting and rewarding the work may be for many of us who are in it.

Several colleagues have mentioned to me that the work demands total engagement and that it is essential to have wide experience as a human being to respond to its challenges and opportunities. Steve Siporin put it very eloquently when he told me, "There is something about the whole person which is the best instrument" for public folklore (telephone conversation, April 25, 1989).

CONCLUSIONS

So how does one translate all this into a curriculum or set of recommendations for the training of public folklorists? It obviously isn't easy. A few colleges and universities offer courses in "applied" or "public-sector" folklore. One such series was described by Steve Siporin in the *Public Programs Newsletter* (1989:6). It consisted of three courses: an experimental course in which students designed programs and evaluated each other's grant applications, a more theoretically oriented course in which various issues involving public folklore were discussed, and the folklore program's regular fieldwork course. This strikes me as a useful beginning. Experience and skills are emphasized, with additional time for thought and reflection on the underlying issues behind their application. Siporin has had several years experience as a folk arts coordinator in Idaho, and I recognize the influence of this experience in his design.

However, as Siporin is the first to point out, these three courses do not a public folklorist make. My advice to the student entering the field would be as follows: Take this or a similar series of courses. Get all the practical work under your belt that you possibly can. Do field projects; apply for practica and internships; go for a wide range of contract jobs, doing different kinds of things in different parts of the country, if possible, for different kinds of agencies. Arm yourself with several models for any given activity—festivals and concerts are tools, after all, and the tool must vary with the demands of the job. Try to experience a variety of folk arts in their appropriate cultural contexts. My personal advice would be against taking a folk arts coordinator job with a state agency directly upon leaving graduate school. If economic and other factors permit it, a few short-term contract jobs should go far in giving the recent graduate some of the skills and experience necessary for the more exacting task with an agency.

Ours is a complex, demanding, and challenging profession, filled with many kinds of contradictions. Steve Siporin said it as well as I have ever seen or heard it said when he remarked, "Public folklore work requires folklorists to have their feet on the ground and their heads in the clouds" (Siporin 1989:6).

NOTE

I have discussed this article with the following public folklorists: Robert Baron, Michael Korn, Robert McCarl, Joanne Mulcahey, Blanton Owen, Steve Siporin, and Elaine Thatcher. Many ideas suggested by these colleagues have been incorporated without specific credit given. The errors are my own.

REFERENCE

Siporin, Steve. 1989. "Teaching Public Folklore." *Public Programs Newsletter* 8(1):6.

Part 3

Recovering a History
of Public Folklore

The Foundations
of American Public
Folklore

ROGER D. ABRAHAMS

The study of folklore was initiated by a group of scholar-scientists concerned with large public questions. The American Folklore Society, the national body that arose to carry out this study, was formed in the late 1880s by individuals who had achieved a high sense of moral endeavor before and during the Civil War and who carried this social perspective into the discussion of technological and industrial modernity. The study of folklore emerged out of an environment in which the uses of knowledge to address questions of life quality was in constant discussion.

While no common perspective on the moral dimension of life in the face of technological developments was clearly articulated by the founders of the AFS, the very ways in which the science of folklore as it was proposed and practiced during that era had an important public dimension. The university was not yet fully established as the most congenial environment in which such study might be pursued. The idea of education in a

new republic was often conceived as a public enterprise best carried out by popular institutions that could collect and disseminate knowledge through public lectures, in sermons, in reading circles and discussion clubs, and through shared facilities such as libraries and museums. Knowledge, it was felt, should be made available to society in a truly democratic nation.

While a number of early members of the AFS argued in favor of scientific inquiry, what was meant by such calls is not clear. Science came to be associated not only with a style of investigation but also with the establishment of a system by which criteria might be developed for accrediting professions. In the first decades of the AFS, folklorists made claims for scientific accuracy; intensive fieldwork produced significant texts, which were rendered as closely as possible to the spoken word, when rendered in print in as accurate a fashion as possible.

Folklore did not only produce disinterested scientists devoted to recording in objective fashion the traditions of otherwise unrepresented peoples facing the behemoth of modern culture. To be sure, the founders of the AFS were concerned with social questions that developed from the homogenizing tendency of technologically powerful culture makers and users. But they were also human beings who had a great regard for the power of institutions to establish cultural priorities and the power base from which scientific study might be launched.

Folklore study was launched by such men as Francis James Child, William Wells Newell, and Franz Boas, who had been trained at major universities and who were made increasingly aware of the politics of institutions carrying out scientific research. Newell was not a trained academic pursuing a career. He imagined a scientific society as a gathering of those heeding the same quasi-religious calling as he had himself experienced in a personal search for his own sense of profession. Boas was more the careerist. He had university training but had been denied access to position and employment. He had been forced to recognize that scientific study had

William Wells Newell was an independent scholar whose career included service as a Unitarian minister and a tutor in philosophy at Harvard. He established a private school in New York City and discovered a lively tradition of singing games among schoolchildren. Newell was one of the founders of the American Folklore Society in 1888. Photo courtesy Harvard University Archives.

to be organized within already established institutions, such as museums or universities, for individuals to find a place of importance in which to carry out research and to have it published in such a way that it would be recognized as significant.

In the late nineteenth century most of the scientific disciplines that now have university departments, societies, and journals were fighting for professional status. This meant not only achieving a place in the curriculum, but also developing a public understanding of the scientific usefulness of the discipline, and through this, obtaining opportunities for carrying on research and publications with the help of public moneys.

Scientific disciplines begin to emerge with the coming together of a self-selected group of investigators interested in a discreet body of data, who, through active discussion achieve a common understanding of how those data should be addressed and consequently begin to develop shorthand means by which these materials are approached and discussions carried out. Today these matters are institutionally organized. Professional societies have developed journals written in set styles of presentation that privilege certain kinds of data as well as modes of argument and presentation. Academic institutions enter into this process by rewarding those who carry out this research and subscribe to these styles of presentation. Thus are developed the professional standards by which these materials are presented and their value debated. But this was not the only way in which research and publication was carried out in the nineteenth century. Nor was the university the only center for the pursuit of knowledge.

Perhaps folklore did not become established as a separate discipline within academia at this time because the university in the late 1880s was in the process of becoming the training ground for professionals—the new class of technical knowledge managers who were just then coming into ascendancy in American life. After a prolonged period in which colleges had served the old family elites, providing in the main training in theology and the classics, the university had taken an egalitarian turn, one that has come to be called a meritocracy.

This appeal to talent and training, of course, produces a new kind of elite, one based on training for a career. As Burton J. Bledstein has detailed this development, the very idea of "profession," which to that point had been a synonym for a "calling," now was more firmly attached to the notion of making a career, using one's training for earning an income as part of the track of upward mobility (Bledstein 1976).

A profession was defined by the relationship between practitioners and clients or patients. The professional, having undergone a period of training and indoctrination, then received not only a degree but also certification, often in the form of a license to practice. The client, in such a system, comes to depend on the services of the professional, services delivered in mystified terms that are emblematic of the esoteric knowledge come by in the course of the training. This process, of course, was earliest worked out for law and medicine, but each profession followed the same pattern of developing tools, jargon, and a credentialing system. This process encouraged the narrowing of acceptable fields of knowledge, thus setting out disciplinary boundaries so that the hegemony of the accepted professionals might be put into place. An important feature of this process was the rejection of "the amateur investigator" at every level.

Each of the modern disciplines went through a period in which rival groups made representations for themselves, seeking thereby for the sanction to organize the field nationally, and by this, to establish scientific relations with practitioners of the field elsewhere. All of the sciences seeking to study living humans in groups were involved in this struggle. The ones who most firmly established themselves—anthropology, psychology, and sociology—all endured the formation of rival groups seeking representational status from the practitioners of the field. And, of course, folklore was involved in this discussion.

The founders of the American Folklore Society found themselves in something of a quandary on the disciplinary character of their designated area. To begin with, so long as folklore was studied as preliterature, the perspective that emerged from European comparatism as it was carried to America by Child and Crane and the early work of Newell, there were questions about establishing the importance of the materials of tradition to the point where they assumed canonical status. Child inherited the work of Percy, Ritson, and Scott as well as that of the continental ballad scholars. Ballads had achieved a kind of weightiness dictating that work in that area of research be taken seriously. The ballad, along with the epic, proverb, superstition, wonder tale, and fable, carried messages of past usages that endowed the form itself with a kind of in-built antiquity—instant authenticity, if you like. These characteristics Susan Stewart designates as "distressed" in the sense that the form itself is "antiqued"—"stressed and pitted for the antique look" of contemporary advertisements for furniture reproductions (Stewart 1991).

Such forms as myth, legend, and *Märchen* had also received serious treatment in the hands of the comparative philologists in the wake of the work initiated by the Grimms. But these were not American forms of pre-literature as far as the members of the Society had been able to ascertain. If there were genres of vernacular American lore, they were expected to emerge from groups who were hardly in power at the time: rural mountain Anglo-Americans, Afro-Americans, Indians, and Hispanic and Francophonic peoples on the continent. Thus the relation between indigenous vernacular language and lore, on the one hand, and the nation-state, on the other, was far from fully established.

In Europe, the study of folklore had developed out of an ardent antiquarianism based on observations of class-structure underscoring the distinctions between peasant and aristocrat. But when folklore came to be studied on this side of the Atlantic, most of those who called themselves folklorists made different assumptions about the materials of tradition and their relationship to the contemporary world. For here the very idea of a peasantry was anathema, and the social stratification that called for a differentiation between a nonliterate peasantry and sophisticated culture, on the one hand, and between European oral traditions and those of preliterate groups like American Indians or Africans, on the other, was simply rejected out of hand by those who moved in the late 1880s toward the formation of the American Folklore Society.

Such an elaboration of the definition of folklore was central to the agenda of the new Society and the discipline it was seeking to outline and direct. For practical as well as scientific reasons, Newell found himself in fruitful conversation not only with his mentor, the literary comparatist Francis James Child, but also with Franz Boas and a number of other ethnologists who had been working with still-living traditions among groups of American Indians (Bell 1973:15). For the nascent organization to gain some sense of itself, it was necessary to discover the common ground between the literary scholars interested in recorded evidences of the oral traditions of the past and the anthropologists who were carrying out the fieldwork among the living.

Moreover, Newell himself had found his niche as a folklorist when he began collecting singing games from the middle-class children in the school he had established in New York City. He discovered that there was a lively tradition of singing games with an ancient British lineage. Thus, he was hardly inclined to limit the study of folklore to the relics of the European past, having witnessed traditional practices in action. Newell, by all accounts the one who brought together the principals and formulated the direction the Society would take, placed "the folk" in a position much closer to the historical present than his colleagues in folklore in Europe were willing to do.

The organization also included in its original list of members representatives of a wide number of cultural entities. While not a great deal of emphasis was placed on ethnic Americans, clearly the lore of more recent immigrants was to be included in this project. For example, in the outline of how local folklore societies might view their mission, it was noted:

> A local society, in a country composed of so many elements has only to attend to the composition of its own city, to find interesting themes for research. How many nationalities, and in what proportions, enter into the life of the town? Where do these immigrants live, and in what manner? What were their habits at home, and with what rapidity do they become amalgamated with the American body politic? What is their distinctive racial character; what are their peculiar ideas and traditions? The German, Irishman, and French Canadian, the Bohemian and Russian, the Armenian and Japanese, bring to our doors the spectacle of the whole civilized and semi-civilized world, with all its rich developments of national costume, customs, and superstitions, religions, philosophies, and economical conditions; to study this extraordinary spectacle, to turn from the world of books to that of life, will be the inclination of the observer who is led to attend to the ethnography of the races with which he is daily brought into contact. (Newell 1885:237–38)

The tradition of a vibrant and living folklore of the present, then, has been the dominant position of American folklorists for at least a century. As Michael Bell has noted: "To Newell, oral traditions were survivals only in the sense that they, like all cultural artifacts, had a history" (1973:15).

If anyone had cause to think of himself as a member of the American elite, it would have been Newell, for he came of the oldest New England clerical stock and was raised in the Cambridge of James Russell Lowell, Oliver Wendell Holmes, and Henry Wadsworth Longfellow. A radical Yankee persuasion percolates through Newell's works that allies him with the Common Man. While he and his friends and neighbors were abolitionists, working for the Sanitary Commission during the Civil War, he later would exhibit strong aestheticist inclinations in line with the Pre-Raphaelite style that identified the best of the past with the trecento in Europe.[1]

However, by the age of forty-nine, when he made the personal commitment to organize the American Folklore Society, Newell had come to the view that to be American was to associate oneself with common values and common sense. He had developed a pragmatic, egalitarian ideology, which he argued should infuse folklorists' thinking, at least in America. Newell, as the prime mover in organizing the AFS, was empowered to speak out for the emerging discipline. His social philosophy—in line with that of his neighbors, teachers, and friends in and around Boston in the 1850s and 1860s—was presented in speeches given in the first five years of the Society's existence. He argued successfully that folklore was to be discovered in the old-fashioned attitudes and practices of everyday life in a land in which the Common Man has always been revered.

Newell well recognized how different was the American vision of folklore study. He made the bravest and most brazen statement of the AFS position in the face of Andrew Lang and others of the "Great Team" of British Folklorists at their International Congress in 1891: "English popular literature," Newell observed to his English hosts, "has been the property not only of the inferior portion of the community, but also the most intelligent class." In fact, the very notion of folklore had been misunderstood if it was supposed to be marked by class, he opined: "If the word *folk* is to be defined . . . as *plebs* or *vulgus*, it must be admitted that our own grandmothers belonged to the vulgar." "The folk," he remarked in an almost scampish manner, "must be taken to include (1) all savages; (2) the old-fashioned people; (3) the children; and (4) all of us where we are old-fashioned" (Newell 1892:47).[2]

While the "old-fashioned" dimension was here articulated in a tongue-in-cheek manner, Newell took the principles quite seriously when reformulating the definition of folklore from the American perspective for other audiences. In his most eloquent summary, he noted that folklore is to be equated with "oral tradition,—information and belief handed down from generation to generation without the use of writing." Such materials he related to common features of life in groups: "Such matter must express the common opinion, or it would not be preserved." Relating this to "the average rather than . . . the exceptional" individual, he summarized: "It must belong . . . to the folk rather than to individuals" (Newell 1890:134.)[3]

Newell aligned himself, unsurprisingly, with the party of Emerson, the man who had sent out a call for a culture of the commonplace American in his "American Scholar" speech of 1836. Says Emerson:

I ask not for the great, the remote, the romantic; . . . I embrace the common, I explore and sit at the feet of the familiar, the low. Give me insight into today, and you may have the antique and future worlds. What would we know the meaning of? The meal in the firkin; the milk in the pan; the ballad in the street; the news of the boat. (Emerson 1983:67)

Here Emerson set out a program and a perspective for the new age in this new country that explicitly rejected the past even while embracing the ideal of poetic comprehension of the best of human knowledge and experience. For "the sublime and the beautiful" Emerson would substitute "the near, the low, the common." And this new view would emerge from the uniqueness of the frontier experiences in acts of those "harnessing and provisioning themselves for long journeys into far countries." Such a realm of experience, not self-consciously realized in terms of their scholarly imaginative possibilities as the encounter with the wilderness was under way, became for Emerson the vivid stuff useful in resurrecting the spirit, producing new ways of elevating this new man through a "literature of the poor, the feelings of the child, the philosophy of the street, the meaning of household life" (Emerson 1983:67).

During this very period, of course, a great number of European polities were being formed through popular movements not unlike the American Revolution. And most of these countries, following the pattern of argument lined out by Herder and Schiller and codified by the Brothers Grimm, saw in language and customary practices the basis on which their national status might be asserted and maintained. This provided an ideological sponsorship for the collection and comparative study of customs, stories, songs, and other kinds of performance that constitute the body of materials that had been called popular antiquities but was renamed folklore in the middle of the nineteenth century.

The received notions of the history of folkloristics in North America would have our ideas, including our research concerns and priorities, as having come to us whole piece from our sister professional societies and members of the discipline in Europe. The social meaning of these developments is commonly read as emerging from nationalistic impulses. As Barbara Kirshenblatt-Gimblett phrases this approach, "The history of the discipline of folklore in Europe and America is largely a commentary on the tensions between national identity and state building. What colonialism is to the history of anthropology, nationalism is to the study of folklore" (Kirshenblatt-Gimblett 1988:143 and this volume).

The search for traditions is securely knit into the fabric of the search for national identities, even in the case of a country such as the United States, which first came into being through the act of rejecting the Old Country and its customary practices. This is not to argue that, in its North American apotheosis, the discipline of folklore became an agency of national identity through a developing sense of cultural unity. Rather, as a sense of national identity developed, the realization emerged that the pioneer experience itself and the War for Independence could be used as the basis for a new sense of tradition. As noted, Emerson was aimed in this direction from his earliest writings. His classic statement on the subject emerged in his essay "The Poet," where he called for an American genius who would reveal the vitality of life within our communities, in "our logrolling, our stumps and their politics, our fisheries, our Negroes and Indians," in the uniqueness of pioneering "the northern trade, the southern planting, the western clearing" (Emerson 1983:22; cf. Bluestein 1972).

Such words indicated that Emerson was responding to some of the same criteria for national traditions as his European correspondents: that out of a specific place or region will emerge an identity based on the genius of that locale. However, by the time that the American Folklore Society was conceived, such nationalistic proclivities had broadened. Now, while the materials sought out for study emerged from American populations and places, they were to be studied by following an international scientific agenda that drew attention not only to native invention but also to the flow of traditions between cultures.

Moreover, though many people had sent out a call to identify and collect the evidences of traditional practices in North America, there was far from any agreement on how the study should be carried out. There were those, such as Daniel Garrison Brinton, one of the most important figures in the scientific establishment at the time, who followed European notions that folklore should be approached simply as anachronistic evidences of past practices (Darrell 1988:68–69).

Hard-headed Progressive thinkers, such as John Wesley Powell and his colleagues at the Bureau of American Ethnology, accepted the general explanation of cultural development put forth by Social Darwinists (who were amplifying four-stage cultural development theories). These and other museum-based scholars had a vested interest in being able to present the human dimension of natural history in a single-line evolutionary pattern, for these ideas were the ones most easily presented in linear fashion in museum settings.

There were significant popular historians, such as Francis Parkman and Edward Eggleston, who also saw the course of history in terms of the inevitable transit of civilization, a perspective fully in line with Progressive thought (Skotheim 1966:48–65). Like other educators to the public, these historians saw an inevitable kind of development emerging as Europeans found a place in the New World and brought their scientific acumen to tasks-in-common (see Bronner 1988:21–25).

Literary figures, both inside and outside the academy, in addition, saw folklore as evidence of the aesthetic propensities of humankind, performing without the intermediacy of letters. However, such public educators found themselves at loggerheads with those who saw in progress a falling off of cultural vitality in the face of industrialization. They were firmly in the camp of what Jackson Lears has called "the anti-moderns" (Lears 1981:117–23, 141–59). Indeed, most of the group of AFS founders living in the Boston-Cambridge area were of this latter persuasion, including Newell.

For practical reasons, Newell subordinated his own aesthetic inclinations that he might find allies in forming the new organization. In the face of potential conflict over definitions arising from one or another view of cultural development, the founding group decided that all theories and most claims for national definition through tradition would be eschewed for the moment. (Here it is difficult not to see the influence of Newell's neighbors, Fredrick Ward Putnam, familiar to many in the antimodern camp, but a museum director well versed in the politics of culture of his time.) The group developed the diplomatic approach that no matter one's theory, everyone could agree that folklore was "fast vanishing" and therefore in need of fast gathering and publication.

Not only was the document chartering the AFS pluralistic, but the designation of those who were to be fit for study was shorn of the class bias by which it had been pursued in England and elsewhere in Europe. In these places, folklore was, in Richard M. Dorson's potent phrase, "past-minded and peasant-minded" (1982:72). It was explicitly not so in America. Indeed, not only was there no mention of the distinctions between the past and the present, nor between peasant and elite, but Newell also spelled out in some detail how close to folk culture he himself felt.

This did not mean that he subscribed to any theory of culture in which folk cultures were to be valued for their own sake, except as records of past ways of thinking. He thought that folk expression was going to be inexorably swept away in the face of the tide of civilization; his task, the one he espoused for the discipline in general, was for the collection of lore as the evidence of the human capacity for memory. As he put it, "Man is memory; the more memory, the more humanity." This human record was not always a pleasant one, but in need of being maintained, not for the sake of some putative past, but for the future, especially for those cultures under siege, such as that of Afro-Americans, that they can remember the stages through which they have passed (Newell 1982:187).

The espousing of a scientific perspective by the founders of the AFS, then, should not be underscored at the expense of the values that they felt they represented. For as Boas, the most scientifically trained and institutionally inclined, said of Newell, on his death:

> The strongest appeal of his sympathies lay in the light shed upon the fundamental values of culture by a close study of beliefs, customs, tales, and arts, of foreign races; in the ability given by this study of appreciating the strength and weakness of our own culture and its tendency to correct the overbearing self-sufficiency of modern civilization. (Boas 1907:64)

To be sure, this encomium may simply reflect what Boas wished to see in Newell's work. On the other hand, Newell was a member of a community made up primarily of antimodernists and belonged to the Dante Society, among many other organizations, a group which projected that figure as the essence of the "distinctively pre-modern sensibility."[4]

A strong moral element, then, is evident in the work of the founding members of the AFS from the outset, along with the sense that in representing tradition, folklorists not only were engaged in the pursuit of truth, but also the use of such knowledge in a continuing critique of modernity. I believe that this critique remains one of our enduring strengths, one derived from the strength of belief in the value of human diversity.

From our beginning as a nation we were confronted with questions of how to relate to the past. Founded on an act of rejection of our paternity, Americans were forced to confront the problems attending a giving up of the cultural patrimony. The desire to declare our independence culturally as well as politically led to the development of a self-conscious search for a usable past, one based on the uniqueness of the common experiences of becoming American.

Inevitably, folklorists were affected by this search. Indeed, as individuals came together to form the American Folklore Society, they were called upon, as a part of their statement of disciplinary purpose, to dedicate themselves to collect and study American materials without accepting European ways of carrying out such a project, without subjecting such thinking to scientific scrutiny.

While the group surrounding Newell urged an anti-modern perspective, other folklorists found themselves attracted to the Social Darwinistic style of discourse, which depicted the process of culture-building as a dimension of "the progress of mankind." As Simon Bronner has argued, the earliest members of the Society bought into this view and saw themselves therefore as providing evidence for what to them was the self-evident progress of humanity. The colonial and pioneer experiences were interpreted as evidence of the inevitability of this move (Bronner 1988:25).

Bronner, in urging this position, privileges the work of the Philadelphia and Washington, D.C., group of folklorists, especially Daniel Brinton and Stewart Culin, John Wesley Powell and James Mooney. Newell, even while allied with the medievalists, thought of himself as serving the cause of civilization to the extent that through the pursuit of knowledge, the vulgarities of racialist thinking could be cast off, and Americans could look forward to being members "of the one kinship sufficiently wide" to encompass the many new Americans—"the human race" (Newell 1982:188). But both Boas and Newell developed their thinking in direct opposition to the vulgarizing tendencies of Social Darwinist thinking.

While the founders of the Society did not spell out their convictions for diplomatic reasons, they quite clearly conceived of the new discipline as tying past and present together to criticize the agency of progress and its apostles. As such, they joined with the voices attempting to encounter the forces of modernity in Europe, those involved in the "folk school" and the "arts and crafts" movements.

A great many questions faced the fledgling discipline late in the nineteenth century, not least of which was whether the ways of describing the materials would remain rooted in a language available to the general public or would be rendered in an esoteric manner as a way of making the field more apparently scientific and rational. This matter was complicated by the inherent divisions in the AFS membership and the strong desire of a number of the most important members to obtain scientific status for the discipline. To do so would have resulted, among other things, in the creation of a special section of the American Association for the Advancement of Science. This was, in fact, the way in which a number of disciplines found widespread acceptance (Bledstein 1972:84). A number of the AFS founders were members of that body, but for reasons that can only be inferred from the record, any attempt to do this did not succeed.[5]

The primary movers in the chartering of the Society—Newell; his teacher, Child; and his new acquaintance, Boas—in their opening statement announced that the "principal object" of the group would be "to establish a Journal, of a scientific character, designed. . . . [f]or the collection of the fast-vanishing remains of Folk-Lore in America, . . . [and f]or the study of the general subject" (Newell et al. 1888:3). Child, the first teacher of literatures in English at Harvard, had established his professional scientific credentials already through the publication of the earliest volumes of his *The English and Scottish Popular Ballads.* Newell, after casting about for his own sense of profession and finally finding it as a collector of children's games, undoubtedly saw the Society as a way of paying homage to his teacher. Boas, trained in the German scientific method as a geographer, brought to the task the presumption that any professional society would call for the establishment of scientific credentialing. He had a personal stake in the diplomatic success of the organization, for as a German scholar looking for institutional connections in the United States, he needed an important place in the American Folklore Society as a means of establishing himself within American intellectual life.

From a scientific perspective, the materials of tradition are taken for granted, at least as they are collected and rendered through print and other media of record. Such an argument proceeds: Our objective is to organize these materials and to discern their patterns of composition and transmission. Finally, those arguing this position would seek to recognize the meanings of the lore. Such a perspective on the discipline encourages folklorists to offer alternative theories of how meaning is achieved through the performance and maintenance of items of traditional usage.

The master narrative of the genesis of the discipline in North America, from this perspective, centers on the war between the literary and the anthropological "schools" of analysis (Zumwalt 1988). Moreover, it is a tale that would underscore defeat—specifically in the failure of folklore study to achieve independent institutional (especially academic) status. But this is not the vision of the discipline or the profession as I read the early record of the AFS and the ways in which this group, along with state and local folklore societies, developed in the last century. Rather, I see a more pragmatic and experience-centered perspective as central to the American way of doing folklore, one in which lore is not to be separated in meaningful ways from the lives of the carriers of these traditions. There was from the outset a concern with the ways in which traditional communities and their lifeways might be dignified through receiving ardent notice by folklorists;

and out of this, many of our ancestors felt, a useful notion of what it means to be an American might be forged.

The Cambridge organizers of the AFS originally came together because of their interest in matters medieval. They were concerned with the place of the holdovers from the premodern past as they were confronted by the outbreak of industrialization and other aspects of modernity. Coming primarily from a class of socially aware—if privileged—people, the architects of the Society did not simply attempt to take an area of scholarship that had been carried out by amateurs and professionalize it with scientific methods of analysis. They introduced such scientific methodology with the explicit purpose of ridding the world of some of the fallacies of racist thought even while they attempted to discover what was unique about America from the traditions that had been maintained or developed because of the specific cultural confluences that had occurred here, and the socially open quality of the American experiment.

This principle of social openness is observable in many ways in the formation of the discipline. The American Folklore Society was not only founded with the idea that the lore of all Americans was fit subject for collection and analysis. It set forth an agenda of research arising from the most troubling social questions of the times.

Newell and his colleagues formulated an approach that American folklorists have been able to follow ever since. By building into their understanding of the folk many groups still very much in existence, they constructed a nonantiquarian folkloristics that nonetheless paid homage to traditions and to the past. While their approach looked forward to the elimination of racial distinctions as ones that will dictate social orderings, they nonetheless recognized that each group would need an understanding of the uniqueness of its past to address the future successfully.

These ancestral folklorists provide us today with the beginnings of an answer as to how, as social scientists and humanists, we might maintain a sense of connection with the peoples that we study even as we obtain intellectual distance from them so as to make objective and valid observations about their traditions. Now we are able, as well, to ask how we may use such insights as a way of dignifying the lives of those bearers of tradition who had managed to persist in the face of the forces of nationalism and modernity. These attitudes and values continue to provoke questions and provide strategies for folklorists today, especially those public folklorists who find themselves serving tradition-bearing populations as they contend with the postindustrial world.

NOTES

I first began to work out some of these matters in discussions with Dick Bauman as we worked on "American Folklore and American Studies" (Abrahams and Bauman, with Kalčik 1976). I have treated some of these matters more fully elsewhere, in Abrahams 1988a and 1988b. My thanks to Michael Bell and others who have let me bore them on this subject: Simon Bronner and William McNeill; and the others of the Folklore History Section of the American Folklore Society, Rosemary Zumwalt, Alan Dundes, Archie Green, and Nick Spitzer (who have had to rearrange my prose too often); to Bob St. George especially for arranging a conference in which I could try out some of these thoughts; to Xan Griswold for weighing in with a strong editorial hand; to my wife, Janet, who has heard this argument many too many times; and to my students who have patiently worked through the materials of so many of the early members of the AFS.

1. I have this point from Michael Bell's manuscript, *William Wells Newell and the Foundations of American Folklore Scholarship*, chapter 1, "The Making of a Folklorist," which reviews the surviving records of Newell's life, including a travel journal of 1883, written jointly by himself and his sister and some of her friends traveling together, in which he is identified in these terms (Bell n.d.) I am indebted to Mike Bell for sharing this manuscript with me as well as for many discussions with me on the subject.

2. The last part of the quotation, Newell says, "are the words of the President of the American Folklore Society," who at that point was Otis T. Mason. See Mason's very different use of these words in his presidential address (Mason 1891). Throughout this period, Newell was reporting this new perspective as being the accepted one as far as American folklorists were concerned. That it was not so readily accepted on this side of the Atlantic is unsurprising. See here, Bell (1973:7–21, especially 16).

3. For a thorough explication of this statement, see Bell n.d., chapter 3, "By Folklore Is Understood . . ." For a contrary view that underscores the continuing indebtedness of American scholars to the British and European antiquarian models, see Dundes (1966).

4. T. J. Jackson Lears gives a capsule history of the Dante Society, emphasizing the centrality of Charles Eliot Norton, Child's boyhood chum and one of Newell's mentors (Lears 1981:156). However, Norton was not a founding member of the AFS, indicating that by 1888 he and Newell had diverged in their interests. Perhaps he found the founding document too egalitarian and potentially antielitist for his tastes, for by that time he had eschewed totally, it would seem, any argument espousing common culture as the American norm.

5. Perhaps Brinton, the most important folklorist on that body, would not entertain this move because he conceived of folklore as the study of popular antiquities; see Darnell (1988:68–71).

REFERENCES

Abrahams, Roger D. 1988a. "The American Folklore Society: One Hundred Years of Folklore Study and Presentation." In *Program Book of the Festival of American Folklife*. Washington, D.C.: Smithsonian Institution.

————. 1988b. "Rough Sincerities: William Wells Newell and the Discovery of

Folklore in Late-Nineteenth Century America." In *Old Roots, New Roots: Folklore in the American Experience*, edited by Jane S. Becker and Barbara Franco, pp. 51–76. Lexington, Massachusetts: Museum of Our National Heritage. Revised for *Folk Music Journal* 5, no. 5 (1989): 608–19.

Abrahams, Roger D., and Richard Bauman, with Susan Kalčik. 1976. "American Folklore and American Studies." *American Quarterly* 28:360–77.

Bell, Michael J. 1973. "William Wells Newell and the Foundation of American Folklore Scholarship." *Journal of the Folklore Institute* 10.

———. n.d. *William Wells Newell and the Foundation of American Folklore Scholarship*. Manuscript.

Bledstein, Burton J. 1976. *The Culture of Professionalism: The Middle Class and the Development of Higher Education in America*. New York: W. W. Norton.

Bluestein, Gene. 1972. *The Voice of the Folk: Folklore and American Literary Theory*. Boston: University of Massachusetts Press.

Boas, Franz. 1907. "Memorial Meeting at the First Church, Cambridge, Massachusetts, March 10, 1907." *Journal of American Folklore* 20 (76):61–66.

Bronner, Simon J. 1988. "The Use of Folklore in the Shaping of American Ideology, 1880–1900." *International Folklore Review* 6:21–25.

Darnell, Regna. 1988. *Daniel Garrison Brinton: The "Fearless Critic" of Philadelphia*. University of Pennsylvania Publications in Anthropology, no. 3. Philadelphia.

Dorson, Richard M. 1982. "The State of Folkloristics from an American Perspective." *Journal of the Folklore Institute* 19.

Dundes, Alan. 1966. "The American Concept of Folklore." *Journal of the Folklore Institute* 3:136–42. Reprinted in his *Analytic Essays in Folklore*, pp. 28–34. The Hague: Mouton, 1975.

Emerson, Ralph Waldo. 1983. "The American Scholar." In *The Portable Emerson*, edited by Mark Van Doren. Vol. 1, *Nature, Addresses, and Lectures*, pp. 49–70. New York: Viking.

———. 1983. "The Poet." In *The Collected Works of Ralph Waldo Emerson*. Vol. 3, *Essays: Second Series*. Cambridge: Harvard University.

Frederickson, George. 1965. *The Inner Civil War: Northern Intellectuals and the Crisis of the Union*. New York: Harper.

Kirshenblatt-Gimblett, Barbara. 1988. "Mistaken Dichotomies." *Journal of American Folklore* 101:140–55.

Lears, T. Jackson 1981. *No Place of Grace: Antimodernism and the Transformation of American Culture, 1880–1920*. New York: Pantheon.

Mason, Otis T. 1891. "The Natural History of Folklore." *Journal of American Folklore* 4:97–105.

Newell, William Wells. 1890. "The Study of Folklore." *Transactions of the New York Academy of Sciences* 9.

———. 1892. "Lady Featherflight." In *Papers and Transactions of the International Folk-Lore Congress, 1891*. London.

————. 1895. "Folklore Study and Folk-Lore Societies." *Journal of American Folklore* 8.

————. 1982. "The Importance and Utility of the Collection of Negro Folk-Lore." Reprinted in *Strange Ways and Sweet Dreams*, by Donald J. Waters. Boston: G. K. Hall.

Newell, William Wells et al. (unknown). 1888. "On the Field and Work of a Journal of American Folklore." *Journal of American Folklore* 1.

Skotheim, Robert Allen. 1966. *American Intellectual Histories and Historians.* Princeton: Princeton University Press.

Stewart, Susan. 1991. "Notes on Distressed Genres," *Journal of American Folklore* 104:5–31.

Stocking, George W., Jr. 1968. *Race, Culture and Evolution: Essays in the History of Anthropology.* Chicago: Free Press.

————, ed. 1974. *The Shaping of American Anthropology, 1883–1911: A Franz Boas Reader.* New York: Basic Books.

Zumwalt, Rosemary Lévy. 1988. *American Folklore Scholarship: A Dialogue of Dissent.* Bloomington: Indiana University.

. Feasts of Unnaming

Folk Festivals and the Representation of Folklife

■ ROBERT CANTWELL

> They were all dressed up for a party, but were never
> introduced to any of their supposed hosts.
>
> Richard Bauman et al., *The 1987 Smithsonian
> Festival of American Folklife: An Ethnography
> of Participant Experience* (1988)

Folk festivals are occasions in which folk culture and official culture embrace one another: the one to win honor from the attention of cultural institutions allied with education, science, commerce, or government, the other to disseminate the influences of folk culture into the popular imagination and, by way of advocating and sustaining it, into the commercial marketplace or public policy. A folk festival thus reframes folk culture as an element of a legitimate, polite, or elite culture, typically under the auspices of institutions representing these interests—a school, university, or museum, a municipality, a historical site, a public park—and with the sponsorship of various establishments, foundations, corporations, governments, agencies, and the like.

Yet a folk festival is typically not one event, really, but the scene of many events, formal and informal, public and private, prescribed and sponta-

NATIONAL FOLK FESTIVAL

SOUVENIR PROGRAM
June 14th to 21st

15c

TEXAS CENTENNIAL EXPOSITION at DALLAS

neous, a social, political, and aesthetic phenomenon of almost incomprehensible complexity whose energy reaches, through its impact on individual souls, not only into local communities, but also into arts agencies, preservation societies, academic departments, state and local governments, commercial institutions, and folk communities themselves to disturb the surface and sometimes redirect the channels in which our cultural history flows. In the great public festivals such as the Smithsonian's Festival of American Folklife or the National Folk Festival, public audiences constituted both by particular local communities and visitors from distant parts can encounter folk artists, craftspeople, cooks, storytellers, and musicians representing a startling variety of the world's ethnic, regional, tribal, occupational, and voluntary cultures normally present to them only as names or at best as musical recordings, photographic images, caricatures, or as the subjects of books—or never known to them at all.

In this laboratory of cultural negotiation—a negotiation that for many may occur only in imagination—artistic power can overcome almost absurd cultural differences; private idealism can be restored; class antagonism can be quelled and the old incessant cravings put to rest; neglected parts of personality may assert themselves, and even erotic force, in one way or another, find expression. At the Festival of American Folklife, as Alan Lomax once exclaimed, America falls "in love with itself"—and even "tired old Washington sometimes is beautiful when the American people gather to sing and fall in love with one another again" (Lomax 1968).

At the same time, as a recent study of the Festival of American Folklife suggests (Bauman et al. 1988), the reframing of folk culture by high cultural institutions can for festival participants be deeply confusing and potentially painful. Ethnographers at the Michigan section of the 1987 Festival of American Folklife discovered, not surprisingly, that festival participants in many instances did not understand what a folk festival was supposed to be or why they had been invited to one, and in contriving their various performances and demonstrations found "a lack of consensus and explicit-

The cover of the program book for the 1936 National Folk Festival invokes images of ethnicity, antiquity, and modernity. The festival, founded in St. Louis in 1934, was being held in Dallas in conjunction with the Texas Centennial. Courtesy National Council for the Traditional Arts.

ness" among the festival staff to guide them (Bauman et al. 1988:9). Some men and women who had some understanding of the concept of "folk" were insulted to be so regarded, not only because several of the participants had had professional training or held advanced degrees, but also because they perceived the designation as implicitly degrading. Some were embarrassed to be viewed as such by audiences whom they mostly perceived, and mostly correctly, to belong to the social classes above them. Some rejected membership in the cultural group with whom the festival had identified them, while others struggled with the question of their own role—were they guests, hirelings, or honorees? In ways seldom acknowledged by public folklife presenters, most of the participants came with well-developed and fully articulated political and personal aims: to wield political influence in some area of importance, to expand a clientele, to accomplish a specific project of work, or simply—and perhaps most tellingly—to earn some money. Many found their personal needs, such as an opportunity to clean up for an evening reception after a day in the sun, neglected, and occasionally experienced the habits of other participants, from other cultural groups, as grossly discourteous or intrusive. Nearly everyone felt strongly the honor conferred by an invitation from the Smithsonian—but in one or two cases, only to meet, upon their return to their home communities, the resentment and jealousy of people who had not been so honored. On the whole, it seems, folk festivals have occurred in an intellectual tradition that cannot wholly credit the human competence of the participant nor thoroughly conceive his or her fundamental cultural difference.

Historically speaking, the public folk festivals of the post–World War II period, which include various university concert festivals such as those at Chicago and Berkeley, the Newport, Philadelphia, and Monterey folk festivals, the new National Folk Festival, and, particularly for this discussion, the Smithsonian's annual Festival of American Folklife, can be understood as outgrowths of the 1960s "folk revival." "Folk revival" is the name we assign, somewhat misleadingly, to the sudden explosion in the commercial popularity of folk song and folk music in the years when John Kennedy presided over the nation's cultural and political reawakening. With their repertoires supplied by extant folk song anthologies, field recordings such as those deposited at the Library of Congress, and esoteric record albums, their musical backgrounds often squarely rooted in the original rock and roll of the 1950s, young men and women of college age or slightly older, now familiar names such as Bob Dylan; Joan Baez; the trio Peter, Paul, and Mary; and the Kingston Trio, whose best-selling recording of the Appalachian murder ballad "Tom Dooley" widely popularized the movement, won considerable fame both as interpreters of folk songs and as original songwriters, spreading their music, their social and political attitudes, and their often dashing personal styles throughout the expanding college-age population. A complex mix of class alienation, political disaffection, arty bohemianism and messianic communalism, the folk revival was the reaction of postwar youth, newly conscious of itself as a group, against a cultural landscape regimented, spartanized, and bureaucratized by a war they could not remember and would never fully understand. It was a kind of unofficial cultural recovery program, innocently seeking a return on the promise that aspiring postwar families, in glad conspiracy with the postwar commercial establishment, had made to their children that life in America was something colorful, fulfilling, and fair.

We call the "folk revival" what we do because in the popular imagination, and on the historical surface, it seems temporarily to have lifted the oppressive weight of history and civilization upon old traditional musics. But in fact the gravitational force of folksong, folktale, folk crafts, and folk culture generally upon the minds of ordinary people, though it subsides and revives, has, historically speaking, always been there; it has been there for hundreds of years, well before there was even a word, in English, for "folklore." This has been particularly true in America, which was not only the native home of a complex and extensive aboriginal civilization, but also has been the adoptive home, from day one, of innumerable ethnic, religious, economic, regional, national, and minority groups from which have evolved, in the American setting, thousands of diverse folk communities, urban and rural, with many residual, syncretic, and emergent folk traditions. Among these is of course one of the world's most fertile and indomitable folk cultures, the African American, permanently locked, it seems, in a social, political, economic, and cultural symbiosis, often, sadly, a hostile one, with a racist official culture. There is, in America, scarcely a realm of human endeavor that has not enlisted the force of folklife, or representations of folklife, in its service.

Let us look briefly, by way of illustration, into the shallow prehistory of the folk revival. The Kingston Trio's "Tom Dooley" was not the first commercially popular folk song—not by a long shot. A folk song quartet, the Weavers, had made Woody Guthrie's "So Long It's Been Good to Know Ya" the best-selling song of the year in 1950 and sent several other folk songs to the hit parade; had show business blacklisting not scuttled their career they might have sustained their success until 1958 and recorded "Tom Dooley" themselves. And yet commercially popular folk music, strictly speaking, did not disappear from phonographs and radio stations between 1950 and 1958, for the rock and roll music that dominated the popular music of the period was, originally, a musically and commercially potent mix of African American jump, doo-wop, and other varieties generally called "rhythm and blues" by disc jockeys and record companies, and "rockabilly," a folk form of southern white dance music shaped out of the black influence upon commercial honky-tonk, bluegrass, and other kinds of "hillbilly" music, all of this a folk response to the sudden postwar urbanization of southern rural people, both black and white.

And why had the Weavers been blacklisted? Because certain political opportunists, notably Senator Joseph McCarthy of Wisconsin, had found it expedient to exploit a national paranoia, whose origins were in the presidential campaign of 1948, that the worldwide communist conspiracy promised after the war by Joseph Stalin had contaminated certain quarters of American life, including the labor movement, the intellectual community, and the entertainment and the art worlds. Not surprisingly, considering that they were often allied with all of these enterprises at once, the tiny cadre of left-inspired folksingers such as Pete Seeger who had performed at labor union, Communist party, Spanish Civil War relief, and other progressive functions were a conspicuous target for political witch-hunters. Blacklisting drove professional folksingers into the relative obscurity of college campuses, schools, summer camps, local recreational programs, and radio stations, where their influence upon young people would, ironically, almost guarantee a new folk revival, while many amateur enthusiasts, frightened by FBI investigations and wiretaps, packed up their guitars and banjos for good. At the same time, however, folksong was being introduced in the music curricula of elementary schools under the direction of the American Folklore Society, and folk stories and themes increasingly into popular entertainment: Remember Disney's Mike Fink and Davy Crockett?

The suppression of folksong was a peculiar and unexpected development, and, to the folk revivalists themselves, certainly a kind of betrayal, considering the ground swell of feeling for American life and culture, a kind of cultural patriotism, in which folk music and folklife during the Roosevelt era had allied itself with political action. In the economic and social emergency of the Great Depression, which to some was a kind of apocalypse, an apparent collapse of our social and economic system, the Soviet experiment did not seem conspiratorial to many young and thoughtful people; rather it appeared, from this distance at least, to embody the very ideals that to save itself American democracy urgently needed: an intelligently managed economy, a regulated industrialization, heroic measures in engineering and technology, and, above all, social justice; and these demanded that America learn something about itself, especially the ordinary people, above all the dispossessed and forgotten, who would be the designers and builders of a better democracy.

The New Deal brought the most concerted and multilateral documentation of American life and culture we have ever known. The Federal Writers' Project sent reporters into every state to record cultural life as it was actually lived, to collect not only what Ben Botkin, director of the project's folklore section, called "living lore," but also to take the testimony of living European immigrants and former slaves, as well as to depict, journalistically, the entire sense of life in given regions and urban districts. The Farm Security Administration sent writers and photographers into stricken agricultural areas to record the lives of men and women and children, and the circumstances in which they lived, in literary and photographic documents such as James Agee and Walker Evans's *Let Us Now Praise Famous Men*, which remain touchstones of America's image of itself as an agricultural, popular, and folk society. The Resettlement Administration engaged musicologist Charles Seeger to find ways, through the encouragement of indigenous musical resources, to foster the consolidation of communities around the project of economic and social self-help. Muralists glorified the working life in countless public buildings, and a vast pictorial record, in photographs and drawings, of American folk crafts, *The Index of American Design*, was initiated under government auspices. The Roosevelts themselves opened the White House in a series of nine concerts between 1934 and 1942, on one occasion with the king and queen of England in attendance, to traditional singers and musicians, including the North Carolina Spiritual Singers, organized by the Federal Music Project; a mountain string band called the Coon Creek Girls; an old sailor from Virginia, Dan Hunt, who sang sea chanties; and, because he and his father were the foremost collectors of them, Alan Lomax to sing cowboy songs.

Alan and his father, John, with a cumbersome wire-recorder built into the back of their car, had set out into the rural south in 1930, after a bank collapse had cost John Lomax his job, to search out what would become the mother lode of southern song, particularly of black song, in the holdings of the Library of Congress Archive of Folk Song. In the Angola State Prison they met a man called "Leadbelly," Huddie Ledbetter, who with his encyclopedic memory, siren voice, and engine-like twelve-string guitar became, after the Lomaxes had coordinated his release and brought him to New York, a living symbol of the black folk tradition, and as such was often misunderstood by well-intentioned but naive young radicals who had little acquaintance with the facts of black life in the rural South. Leadbelly and Woody Guthrie, whom leftist actor Will Geer had coaxed to the city in 1939, seemed to divide America's folk heritage between them, picturesque characters whose genius brought the cloudy idea of "the people," so fundamental to what was called "twentieth-century Americanism" during the days of the Popular Front, down to earth.

The folk revival began in the 1930s, then—under "the man who couldn't walk around," as his friend Josh White called him in a blues song. Well, not really. The Roosevelt administration had simply reached out into what by the 1920s had already become a brisk trade in the representation, as well as the commercial, political, and social exploitation, of folk culture. Pioneer record-company advance men such as Ralph Peer and Art Satherly, beginning in 1923, had begun to tap the immense resources in nineteenth-century social and display music, folk and commercial, still flourishing in southern folklife: now-familiar figures such as the Carter Family, the Stoneman Family, and Jimmie Rodgers won fame as performers and recording artists playing and singing traditional songs, of which they were both collectors and creators, to regional audiences. A parallel development was occurring on the vaudeville circuit, where singers such as Ma Rainey and Bessie Smith supplied the urban and rural African American marketplaces with a newly introspective blues and jazz music, opening the way for many black rural singers and guitarists such as Charlie Patton and Robert Johnson who left behind them on "race" records documents of prodigious musical and poetic genius. Commercial broadcasting, with its institution the radio barn dance, initiated by Nashville newspaper humorist George Hay's "Grand Ole Opry," brought traditional dance fiddling, minstrelsy, and the Saturday night play party, in performers such as Uncle Jimmy Thompson, Uncle Dave Macon, and Dr. Humphrey Bate and the Possum Hunters, to parlors urban and rural throughout the South and Midwest, recalling, with gentle satire, the old times before the First World War. This was a "folk revival" too.

Not all the activity in folk music was commercial. The intense concentrations of European immigrants in urban ghettos, the squalor and desperation occasioned by it, documented by such works as Jacob Riis's *How the Other Half Lives* (1890), had stimulated an anxious nativist movement among people who believed—their fears aroused by the lurid and monstrous ethnic stereotypes promulgated by newspaper cartoonists, pulp novelists, and the vaudeville stage—that the Anglo-American root stock and its values were threatened with extinction. This outlook was often conjoined with the related idea that the agent of extinction was the spread of commercial entertainment, including the aforementioned radio barn dances, but especially jazz, which to the nativist imagination was a poisonous brew of primitive racial elements both Negro and Jewish—what Robert Winslow Gordon, founder of the Archive of Folk Song, called "Hebrew Broadway jazz" (Kodish 1986:134). Modernity generally, or more precisely, its threat to the cultural hegemony of the Anglo-American middle class, in fact, was the enemy, and folk culture, understood as a survival from a more elegant and innocent, but above all more refined and respectable, past, might be a bulwark against it.

Class anxiety and ethnocentrism, then, occasioned by swift social and technological change, provided an atmosphere in which, in 1926, the regional office of the Ford Motor Company in Louisville sponsored a fiddlers' convention, bringing together the winners from local contests held at Ford dealerships in the middle South. Industrialist Henry Ford, an outspoken anti-Semite and isolationist, was, like John D. Rockefeller, inspired to memorialize the preindustrial artisan economy that his own enterprise had done much to abolish. While the Rockefellers were collecting folk art and underwriting its exhibit in New York and at Colonial Williamsburg, Ford was constructing his historical museum at Dearborn, Greenfield Village, which, like Colonial Williamsburg, would be a pseudoenvironment constituted from the relics of a renovated and rewritten preindustrial past. "Folk art," in this context, was really the folk objet d'art, with the craftsman or craftswoman herself quite eclipsed by it—precisely the condition of its "folk" status.

A new regional folk festival, music teacher Annabel Morris Buchanan's at White Top, Virginia, drew national attention when Eleanor Roosevelt visited in 1933; but another visitor, Charles Seeger, who came in 1936, was troubled by the strange parochial attitudes of a coterie of managers who seemed motivated as much by their contempt for what Buchanan called "crude modern folk productions with cheap tunes based on ancient Broadway hits," and a hatred of urban culture generally, as by a love for "the highest type of native material." They saw no contradiction in excluding from the festival local people who could not pay the forty-cent admission fee. "Elizabethan frankness may be tolerated," Buchanan wrote of her festival; but "vulgarity is barred. The folk festival is not concerned with prod-

ucts of the streets, nor of the penitentiaries, nor of the gutter . . . high standards cannot walk hand in hand with simon-pure democracy" (Buchanan
1937:30). Seeger called the affair "reactionary to the core," detecting in it a
veneration for Anglo-Saxon culture, which, with its apparent indifference
to actual mountain music and mountain people, was at bottom not musical at all, but social, the idol of a self-styled cultural aristocracy. "Not for
the mountain people alone," Buchanan intoned, "not for one region alone;
not for one class alone: the White Top activities, if they are to endure, must
be wrought slowly, carefully, measure by measure, for a *race* . . . for after
all, the White Top festival belongs to *the folk*. And we are *the folk*"
(1937:34).

Seeger was much better pleased by the Mountain Dance and Folk Festival, established in 1931 by local lawyer, collector, balladeer, banjo picker,
and square dancer, the "Minstrel of the Appalachians," Bascom Lamar
Lunsford, whom the Asheville, North Carolina, Chamber of Commerce
had enlisted to add a program of folk music and dance to its annual
Rhododendron Festival. Asheville's development boom, founded in a
feverish speculation in real estate, which in the previous decade had more
than tripled the town's population, was on the wane—and waning with it
was the hope that Asheville, "The Land of the Sky," might become the holiday, spa, and resort center of the East Coast (Jones 1984). Such was the occasion—but Lunsford's love of mountain people and culture was genuine,
and his understanding both of the tradition and of the concert stage profound. Lunsford located and invited to his festival many of the most interesting mountain ballad singers and musicians to have emerged in this century, including banjoists Obray Ramsey, Samantha Bumgarner, and Walter
Parham, and balladeers Cas Wallin and Pleaz Mobley, people whose vocal
and instrumental styles, the mountain origins of which no one could
doubt, had nevertheless enjoyed the pacifying influences of a prized first-
and second-generation literacy and the late-nineteenth-century parlor.

Conservative in politics and manners, and a former schoolteacher himself, Lunsford saw in the domestic music and social dance of his region a
reservoir of the old-fashioned rural gentility that a generation earlier had
flowed from the country schoolhouse, the law office, and Baptist pulpit, so
that virtually all of his participants represented in fact the culture of a particular socioeconomic class, a kind of mountain yeomanry, and Lunsford
himself a kind of local squire. He would not brook a hell-raiser or a rogue,
types not known either in folk music or in mountain society, and certainly not a convict or a tramp; normally he did not extend his hospitality

to the occasional visitors from the urban folksong movement, whom he saw largely as frauds. Often sheer personal regard, as well as an interest in the upcoming generation, not musicianship alone, determined who would appear on his stage—an indication that in spite of the far-flung audience and reputation it won over the years, the Mountain Dance and Folk Festival was at bottom the effort of a specific historical community, formed by a specific conjunction of regional, economic, and social factors then in de-cline, to turn the local real estate collapse into its own cultural opportunity.

Tourism provided the incentive for other festivals as well, such as the American Folk Song Festival, begun in Ashland, Kentucky, in 1930 by former Kentucky court stenographer Jean Thomas, the "Traipsin' Woman," whose experience in New York and Hollywood had taught her the commercial potential in bringing regional stereotypes to life, not only in her own gingham-clad Dogpatch persona, but also in a commercial icon of her own making named J. W. Day, a man whom she presented to the world, on records and in a book, as a blind Kentucky fiddler called "Jilson Setters," the "Singin' Fiddler of Lost Hope Hollow." All hope was not, however, lost: Setters, his sight miraculously restored, ultimately performed in England for George the Fifth.

Boosterism does not of course entirely preclude authenticity. The Kutztown, Pennsylvania, Folk Festival, conceived in 1933 by an Allentown newspaperman named William Troxell, or "Pumpernickel Bill," grew out of Pennsylvania Dutch community picnics and apple-butter boilings (Yoder 1974). Unlike the concerts at Ashland and Asheville, however, Kutztown was participatory, inviting the visitor to handle tools and chat with straw stackers, harvesters, shingle makers, soap boilers, and other traditional craftspeople and agricultural workers. Dialect speeches and ethnic humor nevertheless indicated that, like other festivals of the period, Kutztown was undertaken in the awareness of, if not entirely on behalf of, the gaze of the outsider. By the late 1950s, though, self-satire was replaced by seminars and panels in such matters as witchcraft, "powwowing," and the conduct of funerals, and the term "folklife," which the Smithsonian was to adopt for its own festival, was introduced to describe, more accurately than "folklore," the festival's focus upon the agriculture, domestic economy, and cottage crafts of the pre-automobile era.

But let's not forget the Rhododendrons, or Jilson Setters, or Pumpernickel Bill. What appear to be merely the occasions or expedients of these folk festivals are far more significant as signs of the essential and fundamental involvement of folk with official culture, the involvement that, because official culture absorbs all authority, prestige, and power into itself, providing social and political standards and proofs, opens culturally unincorporated tracts in which folklife may build according to its own codes. "Official culture" is—or at least the phrase implies it is—the sum total of those august institutions with which we identify our historical moment and level of civilization: the state, its governing bodies, its educational and business establishments, its corporate structure, commercial interests, its systems of transport, communication, production, and exchange, and so on—institutions that are, indeed, "official" because they are configurations of the forces that in any society shape all of its human processes and determine the sources of authority itself in human needs and wants.

The folk festivals at White Top, Asheville, Ashland, and Kutztown are bound up in various ways with these institutions, not only as expedients and occasions, but, more importantly, as forces in relation to which both the old local parochial culture and an embracing cosmopolitan culture understand themselves and the other—a fact that, in turn, shapes what each of these cultures is: what it values and devalues, the ways it addresses itself to itself and to the other, the ways in which that address shapes its own development. That such affairs should be bound up with tourism, and hence with travel, money, and, say, advertising and communication, is interesting because it suggests the deeper and more extensive forces that bring tourists and folk cultures together. We may suspect, for instance, that hard-surface roads, balloon-tired automobiles, and very likely radio are all implicated in the emergence of the folk festivals of the late 1920s and 1930s, just as interstate highway and jet air travel, and certainly long-distance telephone, form part of the understructure of the Festival of American Folklife and other public festivals of our epoch. Interesting, too, is the variety of ways in which festival organizers integrate folk culture with projects of a personal, political, or educational character, bringing intellectual, social, and economic resources and advantages to the husbanding and sometimes the engineering of folk cultural resources according to ideologies usually quite alien to ordinary people.

But the presentation of folk culture cannot not arise in a vacuum. The tacit system of shared understandings that makes any presentation intelligible—in this case, a ductile system of stock characters, stereotyped locales, old stage dialects, typical occupations and pastimes, and, above all, a fixed social and moral hierarchy—demands a tradition of *representation* in which and through which folk festivals have their meaning. The representation of folk culture, moreover, whether literary, popular, or social scientific, constitutes and frames the category of folk culture itself, opening in official culture a fictional space that reduplicates the cultural opportunity in which folklife has its existence. In that framework, folklife may be only a pure stereotype, a fantasy; but like any fictional frame, it can, with application, assiduous inquiry, and deep imagination, be penetrated—in fact, one can, like Alice into her mirror, disappear in it. As many folklorists have discovered, the careful field investigation of a folk community does, after time, gently do away with the conceptual frame that permitted the identification of the field to begin with, and gradually reveals particular people, with names, gifted and versatile people, with many kinds of social and cultural affiliations—not all of them, in the strict academic sense, "folk"—doing all kinds of interesting, real things.

Probably no society in the world is as fully represented to itself as ours. After the Civil War, and grounded in its technological, managerial, and productive requirements, began a sweeping and inexorable expansion, and a concomitant consolidation of forces of every kind that historian Alan Trachtenburg has called "the incorporation of America" (1982). Trade between the Northeast and the Ohio frontier had been briefly consolidated in early decades of the century by a system of canals—a fact important for the birth of our popular music, what was originally a folk form, blackface minstrelsy. In the decades after the war, however, the extension of the railroads into lumbering and coal areas, and into newly opened western lands, violently contracted the continent, opening to consciousness its vastness and variety, and at the same time blighting the old provincial life with obsolescence.

The developing transport network, with its sense of access, became simultaneously the superstructure of the vast telegraphic system of information processing, which lent lightning mobility to written communications between remote parts and urban centers—communications in turn amplified to godlike resonance by the steam-driven rotary press, whose massive productive capacity was readily served by the scope of rail distribution. The concentration and movement of capital and goods, the expansion of markets and of access to raw materials, the concentration of industry in urban centers and the formation of corporate monopolies, and, above all, the virtually universal ascendancy of print communications, markedly facilitated by the invention of the typewriter, the linotype, and the telephone: all of this, by the First World War, was plain fact—but far from a universally comprehended, not to mention an accepted fact.

At the center of the popular mythology of this epoch was the encounter of country and city, with its emblematic popular types, the hayseed and the city slicker, reiterated in popular and even literary fiction in a zillion different incarnations; the mythic journey of the period was of course from country to city. Think of Sherwood Anderson's George Willard, the young newspaper reporter of *Winesburg, Ohio*, whose ritual departure on the train to Chicago, leaving behind him a handful of sadly isolated and grotesquely provincial people, is his passage into manhood. There is no irony in the fact that Anderson himself had made this journey, and had peopled the fictional community of Winesburg with figures he knew in a Chicago boarding house. Winesburg, Ohio, with its idyllic pastoral name, had become itself little more than a boarding house, for America had become a nation of transients, and the old local community, with its intimate and personal interactions, its close economic interdependency, its social and cultural self-reliance—if ever such a community existed—had been replaced by a conceptual community of separates, their interaction and interdependency mediated by steam engines, electric wires, and printing presses.

The "incorporation" of America suggests of course a new unity and integrity, a transcontinental nation-state tied together by rails and wires, ever hungry for news of itself, as any community must be. But in linking us to one another technologically, such systems, we sometimes need to be reminded, also break us apart, transforming the individual into a tiny island of invisibility and powerlessness who can ratify his or her personal existence only by coupling it to massive collective projects and movements, or by somehow magnifying the personal—as a voice, as an image, as an action—until it has the visibility of "news," which is our name for the information that establishes and defines our connectedness to others. It is *voice*, literally and figuratively, the ability to exteriorize consciousness and win the attention of others to it, that secures our reality as social beings, without which we are scarcely human at all: Society is, after all, a field of conscious awareness differentiated by cultural codes that provide for the articulations of individual personality. In the period after the Civil War, America was a babylon of such voices, speaking voluminously in print to themselves and to each other, from, to, and within marginal communities and central ones, generating the panoply of ideas, images, narratives, and characters who became, imaginatively, the American civilization that apart from such representations could not be conceived at all.

Elite monthlies such as *Harper's* and the *Atlantic*, mass circulation weeklies such as *Ladies' Home Journal* and *McClure's*, local and regional newspapers and story-papers, the funnies, serial and dime novels, western pulp romances, ethnic and foreign-language tabloids such as the *Jewish Daily Forward*, joke books and dialect books, lithography, sheet music and product packaging, photography, and eventually, photogravure and half-tone reproduction brought the work of innumerable regionalists, local colorists, realists and naturalists, humorists, genre painters, book illustrators, and even song and tale collectors, some of America's first deliberate folklorists, into the popular imagination, furnishing it with a rich inventory of images of the American common life (Banta 1988). All of it was reportage—a message sent along the newly constructed lines of communication, marketing, and transportation from one enclave, locale, or center to another, its kinds distinguished not so much by the nature of the message as by the direction in which it traveled. The great proportion of it, of course, was romantic or sentimental, much of it simply a record of the covert shaping force of ruling ideas and values upon images of little-known and little-understood people. The superiority of the Anglo-Saxon "race," or, collaterally, of the white male, the subordinate role and innate inferiority of women, and so on—these were erected in pictures and stories of life among the Indians, on the plantation, in the ghetto, and out West in narratives whose subtext, in spite of exotic exteriors, was often simply an old story of masculine autonomy and female purity. The very term "stereotype" is borrowed, interestingly, from a printing process, for it is in the realm of print that the necessity of stereotype, as a means of organizing social information, becomes most urgent.

Some of it, though, we remember. Mark Twain's "The Celebrated Jumping Frog of Calaveras County" brought oral tradition into print. His Nigger Jim and Injun Joe and Pap owe a good deal to newspaper and minstrel-show stereotypes, but a moral complexity and penetration under the regionalist masks has given these characters continued life. The Atlanta newspaperman Joel Chandler Harris's Uncle Remus stories do considerable violence to schoolroom orthographical conventions in their effort to get across the Gullah dialect, but as a kind of proto-ethnography they do a creditable job and provide us with a fair record of a tale tradition whose roots have since been traced to West Africa. Frederick Douglass's harrowing narrative of his escape from slavery has the sloping, melodramatic contours of abolitionist oratory; but the report itself—of actual social conditions on the Maryland plantations, of actual cruelties exposed to keen psychological analysis, of work songs and field hollers as they actually struck the ear of one who remembered and felt them—rings appallingly true. *Forward* editor Abraham Cahan's story of Yekl the greenhorn's Americanization lies somewhere between social realism and a Yiddish folktale, but the collapse of traditional values under pressure of assimilation, with its consequences for men, women, and families, and the taxing adjustment to new conditions, are set in a context of convincingly human personalities. Greek American Lafcadio Hearn's lurid descents into the nocturnal underworld of Cincinnati's riverfront Bucktown are probably the best disclosures of the interaction of black and white on the folk level in the 1870s we are likely to get. And, to cite one more example, George Caleb Bingham's *The Jolly Boatmen*, actually an entire family of related paintings, much reproduced, of trappers on the Missouri River, is a masterpiece of composition and color, but also a document in which folkways, or their signs, have been carefully observed and recorded.

This traffic in the popular representation of folklife after the Civil War produced a number of pioneering collections and studies as well as fictions and fantasies. A classical scholar named William Francis Allen, who visited South Carolina and Arkansas as a government agent after the Civil War, became interested in black language and song, and with two others who had collected Afro-American songs, Charles Pickard Ware and Lucy McKim Garrison, daughter-in-law of William Lloyd Garrison, published the first collection of Afro-American folksong in 1867, *Slave Songs of the United States*. Harriet Beecher Stowe, author of *Uncle Tom's Cabin*, itself a virtual sourcebook of southern stereotypes, also published a collection of New England folktales called *Old Town Fireside Stories* in 1871. Another novelist, George Washington Cable, whose subject was the Creole culture of New Orleans and whose work had won the endorsement of the establishment periodical *The Century*, published two articles in that magazine in which he argued, first, that the banjo, commonly regarded as the signature instrument of the plantation slave, was actually little used in the South, and second that Negro songs had originated in Africa: issues over which folklorists still puzzle today. *The Century*, incidentally, had published both *The Adventures of Huckleberry Finn* and William Dean Howells's *The Rise of Silas Lapham* between 1884 and 1885.

The invention of America, or what Whitman called the "democratic nationality," did not of course commence with the invention of the steam-driven rotary press. Washington Irving had drawn upon Hudson Valley folktales for his "Rip Van Winkle" and "The Legend of Sleepy Hollow"; both of these have become, in a sense, allegories of the displacement of traditional culture by popular democracy. Revolutionary poets, educated in

Cicero, Horace, and classical rhetoric, inspired by Milton but trained to Dryden and Pope, attempted prophetic blasts of heroic verse such as radical republican Joel Barlow's *Columbiad* of 1807, on the future of the new utopia. Longfellow attempted it too, in historical narratives such as "Evangeline" and "Paul Revere's Ride," but especially in "The Song of Hiawatha," which he modeled on a national epic pieced together by folklore scholars, the Finnish *Kalevala*, using Ojibwa tales from Henry Rowe Schoolcraft's *Algic Researches*. Travelers and diarists, too, like Fanny Trollope, A. B. Longstreet, Caroline Kirkland, and Charles Dickens left discerning and sophisticated accounts of life on the old frontier.

But in the early nineteenth century the real office of defining the national character fell to tradesmen, artisans, frontiersmen, and adventurers, not to mandarin poets and novelists. The much-maligned, little-studied, and little-understood tradition of blackface minstrelsy, the single most popular and pervasive entertainment of the nineteenth century, was largely the property of this class. Layered with ironies comic and tragic, inscribed by suffering, an almost pathologically complex masking and unmasking ritual of dreamlike donning and doffing of constructed identities, minstrelsy ought to be taken as a paradigm of the elaborate process of cultural negotiation at the folk level from which new manifestations of the American identity are continually being formed. T. D. Rice, banjoist Joel Walker Sweeney, and the other "Ethiopian delineators" who brought black songs, dances, fiddle and banjo tunes, street cries, costumes, language, and gestures into the circuses and theaters of the 1820s and 1830s, many of them professional entertainers, were nevertheless largely footloose young men, many of Irish descent, moving along the edges and close to the floor of society in a condition of unending social and economic ambiguity. Minstrelsy provided them with a socially and culturally negotiable role as deliberate messengers and agents of the fertile cultural syncretism that had been transpiring along frontier river and canal routes and on the plantation for several generations.

Dan Emmett, the founder in 1842 of the Virginia Minstrels, the first blackface minstrel ensemble, gave us "Turkey in the Straw," "Old Dan Tucker," and "I Wish I Was in Dixie's Land" (not a martial song originally but a plaintive "walk-around" or cakewalk derived from the African American ring-shout). He was a blacksmith's son from the Ohio frontier, a fiddler with a headful of traditional dance tunes and hymns, a rudimentary literacy that permitted him to compose original words to them, and an education in frontier banjo playing from an enigmatic circus character named Ferguson, who if he was not racially African American was certainly one culturally. What the minstrels called "Ethiopian" was really neither African nor European but a folk-cultural creolization of Irish, Scots Irish, German, French, and African styles in language, music, gesture, bearing, in personality itself, an emergent indigenous type in whom Whitman recognized the "indescribable freshness and candor" and the "picturesque looseness of carriage" of the new American.

Whitman himself was a carpenter's son and a carpenter, who later tried his hand at newspapering. His "barbaric yawp," flooded with the babble of newspapers and of hundreds of popular books of poetry, fiction, and science, was a response to the dizzying sense of the expansion of access to the continent that constant exposure to images seemed to make possible. He saw them everywhere: "in paintings or mouldings or carvings in mineral or wood," he wrote, "or in the illustrations of books or newspapers, or in any comic or tragic prints, or in the patterns of woven stuffs or any thing to beautify rooms or furniture or costumes, or put upon cornices or monuments or on the prows or sterns of ships, or to put anywhere before the human eye." When the vast miscellany of American life came together in one place, as it did—significantly for our discussion—at New York's Crystal Palace Exhibition of 1853, Whitman was enchanted, and adopted as an important stylistic influence a popular poetic description of the fair (Zweig 1984:209). Whitman's supernaturally mobile imagination moved, with the enthusiasm of first-generation literacy, in a nation of representations, which, poetically transformed, became present to him, touched with a love and desire that took virtually everything and everyone for its object; and his voice, though we have not really heard it until now, he broadcast from what he knew was the "rooftop of the world," newly synthesized by organs of mass communication, whose culture he never learned to despise.

Its "incorporation," then, altered fundamentally the nature of community and identity in America. New affiliations, more virtual than actual, formed in new configurations of printed communications, and new identifications gathered around new lodestones of prestige and power. Freemasonry, associations, clubs, societies, organizations, parties, auxiliaries, and guilds accomplished social differentiation where commerce, mass production, and communication were introducing an unprecedented level of homogeneity on an unprecedented scale. "Ethnic" groups, as Werner Sollors (1986) observes, formed from communities often not connected in Europe but consolidated here by their contrastive relation to the Anglo-American elite; the "regional" and the "local" emerged as categories in a civilization no longer a loose federation of such communities but a dense urban commercial and technological nexus that seemed to marginalize them, categories embracing essentially every folk community that by definition remained economically and culturally unincorporated. Among these regions, locales, and ethnic groups was, for example, a population of leisured and literary middle-class women, which in regional writers such as Willa Cather, Kate Chopin, and Sarah Orne Jewett expressed itself not only as a consciousness of sexual oppression but also as a sensitivity to the details of social, domestic, and psychosexual culture—female culture—which male writers either satirized or tried to escape, or of which they were mostly ignorant. Print and its cheap reduplication in the post–Civil War decades helped to amplify the hitherto inaudible voice of the community of women, who as popular writers gradually rose to a position of cultural preeminence in the religious, social, and domestic life of the classes otherwise dominated by commercial men. The late nineteenth century was the age of the "New Woman," as political satirist Finley Peter Dunne dubbed her in 1898, asserting her sexual and economic independence and learning to translate it into social and political power and influence (Banta 1988).

The response to the newly commercialized and metropolitanized society, then, tended to divide along gender lines, and the uses of folklife that emerged around the turn of the century were to reflect that division. To many men and women comfortably accoutered in the material luxuries that industrial capitalism could produce, life had become, as Jackson Lears (1981) writes, something unreal, amorphous, and, in Nietzsche's word, "weightless," personal identity something shallow and vacillating, human drives dull and diffuse. In some sense these changes represented, in Ann Douglas's phrase (1977), a "feminization" of culture, particularly in the parlor and the parish house, the enclaves into which culture, understood as a special area of activity insulated from the marketplace, seemed to have retired; hence a masculine and "muscular" reaction, symbolized by hunter, soldier, explorer, and physical culturist Teddy Roosevelt, which laid emphasis upon male independence, strength, autonomy, and virility, stressing the self-sufficient outdoor life of the scout, the cowboy, the wilderness guide. It was Teddy Roosevelt's endorsement of John Lomax's *Cowboy Songs and Other Frontier Ballads* that hastened its popularity and inspired similar collections in a similar spirit such as Carl Sandburg's *American Songbag* and Robert Winslow Gordon's "Songs That Men Sing," a column he contributed to *Adventure Magazine*. This movement lingered in our culture until well after the Second World War in innumerable summer camps, scout troops,

YMCAs, outing clubs, and the like, many of which became repositories of revived folk crafts and folksongs and were among the contributory streams to the postwar folk revival. The ballad "Tom Dooley," for instance, had first been collected from mountain singer Frank Proffitt by a recreation director for the YMCA, folksinger and summer camp counselor Frank Warner; and the Kingston Trio learned the words to the song from a collection of folksongs published by the collegiate International Outing Club.

A parallel tradition developed among reform-minded women who found among the many varieties of socialism emanating from England an opportunity for personal fulfillment outside the home, a more spartan and rigorous existence than that of the kitchen, garden, or parlor, and a definite object toward which to direct their intellectual and spiritual energies. Socialism—represented by such writers as the Welsh industrialist-reformer Robert Owen, art and architecture historian John Ruskin, and the poet, designer, and printer William Morris—was and is a complex synthesis of utopian thought and romantic feeling occasioned by the profound bifurcation of the social order into antagonistic classes by industrialization. In general it sought to relieve the physical deprivation and psychic alienation of industrial labor and to raise the aesthetic standards of art and manufacture through various configurations of model communities and enlightened leadership. Morris, for example, took the medieval crafts-guild as his model, and with Ruskin and others shared the object of redefining, morally, the process of work itself as an agent of communal interdependency on the one hand and of artistic self-expression on the other.

Medievalism was a masquerade and a fantasy, an idealized realm of passion and color in a world whose passion and color seemed to have drained away. But socialism advanced the timely and potent hypothesis that social forms, power relations, and the culture that reproduced them formed around modes of production: a hypothesis whose immediate implication was that shifts in modes of production might bring about shifts in the organization of communities, and, still more fundamentally, that society, understood as a structure erected upon the basis of economic relations, might be reconstructed from the ground up—not merely as a political order secured by contract, but as a whole way of life: a culture. Hence medievalism and socialism were at bottom one idea, the substance and the structure of one deeply paradoxical idea that culture is, can, and must be deliberately produced, and that once produced tends to reproduce itself: produced, that is, by a powerful class whose power it is the purpose of culture to maintain. If bourgeois life had come to seem artificial, it sought its salvation in an artifice even more complete, laying claim to an omnipotence once thought to belong only to history, to nature, or to God.

In Jane Addams's Hull House, and throughout the settlement movement, these ideas, or ideas very similar to them, shaped and were shaped by the practical business of social service, but in an important new context: ethnicity. Ethnicity, again, was in America often a redefinition of otherwise highly diverse racial, cultural, social, and even linguistic groups according to nationality, mediating the relations between the European immigrant and the ruling Anglo-American order by means of a contrastive identity, which served them mutually, and a relational identity that distinguished national groups among themselves and differentiated them to Anglo-America. At Hull House, ethnicity was reconstructed symbolically in cultural remembrances, reenactments, and retrievals, including instruction in native language, literature, and the fine arts, and, most significantly for us, "folk festivals"—one of the earliest uses of the term—in which immigrant groups performed native music and dance for themselves and for one another.

In such symbolic reenactments ethnic identity at Hull House certainly lightened the heart and brightened the morale of dislocated and disoriented people urgently effacing their habits and customs in favor of the language and imagery of the fashion magazines, the newspapers, and the street. But a whole way of life could not of course be summoned up in a Hull House library or gymnasium. Ethnicity had become something specular and ceremonial, a representation among other representations that in the end fostered successful assimilation into the industrial work force by attaching itself to the occupational communities forming within factories and shops. Nevertheless it was a form of social identity that time has shown to be negotiable currency in our cultural economy, and a psychological mainstay against the vicissitudes of wage labor. It is likely, too, that ethnicity at Hull House, particularly as spectacle, lent something of its own color to the lives of earnest feminist reformers: For among the new Balkan and Mediterranean immigrants of the settlement period, many from areas of Europe little touched by industrialism, capitalism, or democracy, were nonliterate peasants pure and simple, the primitive "folk" originally imagined by German romantics such as Johann Herder and the Grimms who saw such people as the wellspring of national culture.

Ethnicity at Hull House, then, which in effect laminated national identity to folk culture symbolically reenacted, was an expression of that romantic idea. This was particularly true as the feminist reform movement extended from the liberal Northeast into Appalachia to create missionary and settlement schools, folk schools in the Scandinavian model, handicraft guilds and craft cooperatives in the tradition of William Morris: "psychic, educational, and cultural aid stations," writes David E. Whisnant in his admirable *All That Is Native and Fine*, "for the bruised and dislocated victims of advancing industrial capitalism" (1983:6). Among those social workers was Olive Dame Campbell, founder of the John C. Campbell folk school, on whose heels came the English folksong collector Cecil Sharp. But, as we noted in the case of the White Top Mountain folk festival, and as Whisnant explains at length, the quasi-religious idealism of enlightened crusaders such as Olive Dame Campbell could be almost indetectably poisoned by cultural manipulators for whom a vision of historical-cultural purity was part of an implicit, perhaps even an unconscious program of cultural totalitarianism. It is difficult not to admire, or to escape, the influence of men and women who believe strongly in what we believe and have a courage in their conviction that perhaps surpasses ours; but cultural evangelism, like its religious counterpart, is sometimes blind and deaf to what others actually believe, want, and need.

The first folk festival to address conscientiously, with clearly articulated social and political aims, the cultural diversity of American civilization, and to adopt that diversity as a structural principal, was Sarah Gertrude Knott's National Folk Festival, introduced at St. Louis in 1934 (Green 1975). Knott, like Annabel Morris Buchanan, was concerned about the leveling effects of commercial records and radio, and, like most folklore scholars, regarded folk culture as an endangered species; but, far from an exclusive commitment to a particular vision or strain of culture, with all the social and political allegiances such commitments imply, her outlook was generously, even exhaustively democratic, not shrinking from the historical moment but sensitively integrating its liberal ideals, from decade to decade, in the folk festival enterprise. Whether the preservation of traditional cultures, or the promotion of international understanding and tolerance, or, after the Second World War, the improvement of new leisure time occasioned by automation, and finally, in the postwar folk revival, anticipating what would become a complex theoretical discussion in the social science, a renewed interest in distinguishing between what she called "survivals" and "revivals" in folk tradition, Knott was able to ground her work in the ideological moment.

For Sarah Gertrude Knott, representation in a festival was as important culturally as it was politically in legislative bodies. Representation, she understood, was the primary medium of negotiation between official and unofficial culture; in a festival, moreover, representation took on, potentially at least, the imperative character of actual human relations, with their charge of moral, ethical, and emotional energy. "The festival reflected the broadened attitude of our people," she wrote during the Second World War, "and symbolized the democracy we claim and were fighting to protect. . . . We were more convinced than ever that interchange of folk expressions in festivals breaks down barriers, helps to eradicate racial and nationalistic prejudices, and lays a foundation for better understanding and stronger national unity" (Knott 1946:85).

Knott was a native Kentuckian and as a student at the University of North Carolina had been a member of the Carolina Playmakers under director Fred Koch. The Playmakers were part of a regional theater movement, inspired by the Abbey Theater in Dublin, that sought to erode the dominance of Broadway by appealing to native or "folk" materials, which the young playwrights imported into their vignettes, skits, plays, and pageants usually in picturesque stereotyped forms (Danker 1989). In 1929 she took a position as director of the Dramatic League in St. Louis, working with both blacks and European immigrant groups. Bascom Lamar Lunsford's Mountain Dance and Folk Festival, which she attended in 1933, inspired her to produce a festival at St. Louis—but her aim from the outset was diversity rather than uniformity. "Our national culture is being woven from the warp and woof of the variegated and colorful strains of many nations," she wrote. "No one would want to dull the richness of that pattern. How bleak indeed would be the cultural outlook for the future if we overlooked the distinctive, individual cultures in a universalized, standardized, regimented culture" (Knott 1946:93).

Early National Folk Festivals included Native Americans, British, Spanish, Irish, Scottish, French, German, and black singers, musicians and dancers, as well as the songs and music of occupational groups such as lumberjacks, miners, cowboys, canalmen, and sailors. Eventually her festival widened to embrace the folk traditions of Hungarians, Yugoslavs, Lithuanians, Poles, Greeks, Norwegians, Italians, Jews, Bulgarians, Chinese, Finns, Romanians, Filipinos, Portuguese, Russians, Czechoslovakians, and Spaniards, in recognition of the fact that "these newer groups are keenly aware of the value of folk activity in binding themselves together, in maintaining *esprit de corps* and national identity and spirit" (Knott 1961:189). A diversity of audiences was essential, too, so that she moved her festival from city to city—from St. Louis to Chattanooga to Dallas to Chicago to Washington to Philadelphia in the prewar years.

Knott's festival was the first to join the folk festival enterprise to folklore scholarship through teaching workshops, demonstrations, seminars, and lectures by noted collectors, folklorists, musicologists, and artists—indeed the entire folk arts community at one time or another seems to have rallied around her, including of course Bascom Lamar Lunsford, with whom she retained a lifelong association, and the "Traipsin' Woman," Jean Thomas, who brought "Jilson Setters" to perform. George Pullen Jackson, well known for his studies of southern shape-note singing, involved himself, as did Zora Neale Hurston, the black anthropologist and novelist who had studied under Franz Boas. J. Frank Dobie, the collector of Texas folklore; George Korson, a pioneer collector of coal-mining songs; Benjamin Botkin, the aforementioned federal folklorist and popular folklore anthologist; George Lyman Kittridge, Harvard editor of the Child ballads; John Lair, founder of the Renfro, Kentucky, Barn Dance; Arkansas folklore collector Vance Randolph; and Stith Thompson, compiler of the monumental *Motif-Index of Folk Literature*—all folklorists, academic or popular—became Knott's advisers. Even regionalist painter Grant Wood added his voice—an impressive, if diverse, group.

To appreciate the "colorful strains of many nations," of course, one's viewpoint must be beyond and above, rather than tangled in, the pattern in the cultural weave. This persistent blind spot in the panoptical ideology of cultural diversity remains its most vexing element. Knott's background was in theater, and her festivals, which like parallel festivals of the period, were essentially theatrical concerts with a visible emphasis upon picturesque promotional graphics heavily dependent upon ethnic and regional stereotypes, colorful pageantry and costume, and the sheer numbers of groups represented. In several days' time the National Festival program could saturate an audience's capacity for appreciation, requiring it to supply imaginatively the cultural contexts that had not been supplied in other ways and frustrating the passion for more thorough understanding and more intimate association that such performances usually inspire. In the National Folk Festival, the cornucopic outpouring of cultural voices met the relatively narrow limits of concert presentation. In the radio age, the fantastic diversity of a civilization now virtually stunned by the aural intensity and immediacy of its communications with itself seemed to urge a mastery of the diversity that theatrical presentation symbolically accomplished. But mastery, actual or symbolic, was utterly inimical to the festival's social and moral aims.

The National Folk Festival, which continues today under new auspices, the National Council for the Traditional Arts, led by Tennessee-bred producer and folklore specialist Joe Wilson, elevated the festival enterprise out of its milieu of cultural and political reaction on the one hand and sheer commercialism on the other and laid the groundwork of a festival ideology that could inform the relation of the folk festival both to its public and to public policy. Its problems arose out of Knott's ambition, idealism, and daring, and the still often elusive solutions to them engage all of the vital social, political, and aesthetic issues surrounding folklife and cultural life generally.

Both the Festival of American Folklife and the current National Folk Festival, and the increasing number of state and local festivals modeled upon them, follow Knott's example in seeking the guidance and participation of academic disciplines such as folklore and anthropology, which bear upon folklife and festivity and help in defining them. And in addressing the National Folk Festival's overriding problem, the theatrical insulation between participants and audience, both the Festival of American Folklife and the new National Folk Festival have been years in developing such counter-strategies as the construction of small community settings, modestly scaled performance and demonstration venues, discussion workshops, multiple staging, and, most significantly, the development of an "inner audience," which, through the natural influences that work in small assemblies, particularly the infectious and knowing enthusiasm of the cultural familiars within it, can encourage a visitor's more thorough participation and richer understanding.

In recent years the National Folk Festival, which had been sited at Virginia's Wolf Trap Farm Park near Washington from 1972 to 1982, has returned to Knott's practice of moving from city to city, mounting its exhibition in the postindustrial, multiethnic cities of Lowell, Massachusetts, and Johnstown, Pennsylvania, actually and symbolically joining, within the boundaries of an urban national park, the folk festival to kindred projects in historical preservation and local economic revitalization. Here the audience for various ethnic displays is formed from local ethnic communities, while local organizations such as the Lowell National Historical Park and the Laotian-American Organization of Lowell, or the Johnstown Area Heritage Association, assist in the planning and production of the event. In 1990 the National Council for the Traditional Arts, while moving its festival to Johnstown, continued in an advisory capacity to Lowell's local apparatus in hopes of converting the folk festival there to an annual community event (Wilson 1989).

The deeper social, economic, and political character of the folklife festival, however, begins to suggest itself when we place it in the context of the broader history of cultural exhibition, particularly through the Festival of American Folklife and its parent institution, the Smithsonian. For analogues in the history of international fairs and festivals we might look back, with the assistance of Robert Rydell's excellent history, *All the World's a Fair* (1984), at the great industrial and cultural exhibitions of the nineteenth century such as the Centennial Exhibition at Philadelphia in 1856 and Chicago's World Columbian Exhibition of 1893, both of which drew significantly upon the ideas of Smithsonian natural scientists and anthropologists as well as the material resources of the institution. These were not of course "folk festivals," but celebrations of technological and scientific progress, industrial might, the exploitation of the world's natural resources, the expansion of capital markets, and, above all, of Anglo-Saxon racial superiority—in short, festivals of colonialism whose anthropological theme, which reflected the period's rough conjunction of scientific and popular thought and ran comprehensively through the organization of the exhibitions, was the progress of humankind from its dark and savage beginnings to its zenith in European industrial civilization.

That the first of the great international exhibitions, Victoria's Crystal Palace Exhibition of 1851, and its sister event in New York two years later, took place under what was in effect a giant greenhouse is significant: Though its purpose was to exhibit England's primacy in steam engines, power looms, and other machinery, as well as the textile, iron, and other products manufactured by them, the glass canopy overhead, formerly an exclusive feature of the nobility's gardens, intimated that the exhibition's deeper purpose was, in some elemental sense, cultivation and nurture. That culture had become, by the 1870s, thoroughly machine driven, was a dismaying and colossal reality. At the Philadelphia Centennial Exhibition of 1876, an aging Walt Whitman, bound to a wheelchair by a stroke, lingered half an hour before the huge, insinuating Corliss Engine that silently presided over a brood of mechanical innovations including sewing machines, refrigerators, telephones, and the Westinghouse air brake, promissory notes of epochs to come. "Type of the modern," Whitman wrote that year, "emblem of motion and power—pulse of the continent. . . ."

Spencer Baird, assistant secretary of the Smithsonian under Joseph Henry, had sent John Wesley Powell and others on a pioneering expedition into the West to retrieve Indian pottery, weapons, tools, and the like for exhibit in the Smithsonian's section of the Government Building. Here Indian artifacts were mingled with a full-sized tepee and a sixty-five-foot Haida canoe alongside photographs and wax and papier-mâché figures of Indians that in their crass verisimilitude turned the romantic conception of the noble Red Man enjoyed by the novel-reading public into fear and revulsion. Living Indians had arrived from the West too, though not by invitation, and had made an encampment on the fairgrounds under the supervision of a Texas Scout and Indian fighter named George Anderson. African Americans were represented in a private concession operated by an Atlanta businessman, which presented "plantation darkies" singing and strumming the banjo and rattling the bones in a kind of outdoor minstrel show.

Ethnographic exhibition under the auspices of the Smithsonian, then, is nothing new. In a manner anticipating Secretary Dillon Ripley a century later, in fact, Joseph Henry sought to extend the institution's influence increasingly into public education and edification; in the twelve years after 1880, the Smithsonian erected industrial exhibits in Chicago, Philadelphia, New Orleans, Louisville, Cincinnati, Minneapolis, and Marietta, Ohio, as well as Berlin, London, Paris, and Madrid.

The structural parallels between the Festival of American Folklife, then, spreading itself out over the grassy Mall between the alabaster Capitol dome and the Washington Monument, and the Columbian Exhibition at Chicago in 1893, are all the more arresting. Overlooking Lake Michigan at the 1893 exhibition was a plaster-of-Paris White City of lakes and fountains, domes and columns, which shone with a vastness and glory reminiscent of the visionary cities of antiquity painted by Claude Lorraine or Thomas Cole. These utopian images, touched over the centuries by a sublime religiosity, and at least since Bunyan's City Beautiful an archetype of popular culture, left little doubt as to the nature of the hope and faith the official culture of the Age had placed in the scientific and technological Progress the White City was meant to consecrate.

Within the walls of the White City, several structures were either dedicated to or included exhibits of anthropological or ethnological import. The Anthropology Building itself was the work of Frederick Ward Putnam, of Harvard's Peabody Museum of American Archaeology and Ethnology, who had been placed in charge of the exhibition's anthropological exhibits. This was a thoroughgoing anthropological college, with a reference library, a laboratory, reference collections in religion and folklore, and exhibits of artifacts from around the world—Japanese and Indian toys and Mohammedan, Hindu, and Jewish ceremonial objects. In the Government Building, the Smithsonian's Bureau of American Ethnology, under anthropologist Thomas Wilson, assembled figurative groups—familiar to us now from our experience of natural history museums—of life-sized Indian families, framed on the nuclear model of the American middle class (see Haraway 1984–85), dressed in traditional costume and engaged in various labors in simulated natural environments. The government of Spain offered life-sized models of peasant women in costume in the Women's Building, where another Smithsonian scientist, Otis Mason, mounted an exhibit of the three "modern forms of savagery," American Indian, Negroid, and Malayo-Polynesian, in twelve groups of artifacts representing particular art forms.

The contributions of foreign governments were in several instances quite spectacular. Norway built a replica of a twelfth-century church, Spain a reproduction of the Valencian stock exchange, and Germany a kind of fifteenth-century city hall. The Sultan of Johore sent artifacts representing all of the ten or twelve distinct ethnic groups of his tiny state in British Indochina: models of the native dwellings of aboriginal Saki and Jacoons; a Malay audience hall, mosque, and palace, complete with kitchen and bath; the weapons and utensils of Malay and Chinese, a blacksmith's forge and tools, and costumes representing every social class from aboriginal hunter-gatherers to the robes worn by the Sultan's company of Chinese actors.

Interestingly, primitive arts and crafts in these exhibits were taken as indicators not of the accommodation a particular community has made to the conditions of life, but of the early stages in the history of civilization, a history that was simultaneously projected upon the racial categories of humankind that physical anthropology had posited. Crafts, then—technological development—during a period in which Thomas Huxley was popularizing the ideas of Darwin in America, were taken as a measure of human biological evolution. A visitor to the Anthropology Building, indeed, could participate in the advance of anthropological knowledge by volunteering for an examination by a physical anthropologist, who would determine his racial type!

Such vortexes of official culture as the White City naturally engender colonies of unofficial culture around them. The Philadelphia exhibition had generated a flimsy but festive "Centennial City" of beer gardens, ice cream parlors, peanut stands, pie stalls, fruit and sausage vendors, strolling players, brass bands, dioramas, and freak shows, which extended in ludic counterpoint the official program of science and machinery. At Chicago, flowing westward from the White City along a wide avenue of turf nearly a mile long, which today separates the campus of the University of Chicago from the black ghetto across 63d Street, was a mall called the Midway Plaisance.

Historian Hubert Howe Bancroft has given us a vivid recollection of it. "Entering the avenue a little to the west of the Women's Building," a visitor

> would pass between the walls of medieval villages, between mosques and pagodas, past the dwellings of colonial days, past the cabins of South Sea Islanders, of Javanese, Egyptians, Bedouins, Indians, among them huts of bark and straw that tell of yet ruder environment. They would be met on their way by German and Hungarian bands, by the discord of . . . camel drivers and donkey-boys, dancing girls from Cairo and Algiers, from Samoa and Brazil, with men and women of all nationalities, some lounging in oriental indifference, some shrieking in unison or striving to out-shriek each other, in hope of transferring his superfluous change from the pocket of the unwary pilgrim. Then, as taste and length of purse determined, for fees were demanded from those who would penetrate the hidden mysteries of the plaisance, they might enter the Congress of Beauty with its plump and piquant damsels, might pass an hour in one of the theaters or villages, or partake of harmless beverages served by native waiters. Finally they would betake themselves to the Ferris Wheel, on which they were conveyed with smooth, gliding motion to a height of 260 feet, affording a transient and kaleidoscopic view of the park and all it contains. (Quoted in Rydell 1984:60)

This officially unofficial folklife festival was an effort by Putnam and his associates to take advantage of what they knew was the attractive force of such commercial strips by introducing into it their own living ethnological exhibits. Some years earlier in Paris, at the International Congress of Prehistoric Anthropology and Archaeology, held in conjunction with the Paris Exhibition of 1889, a popular "colonial city" had presented upwards of two hundred Asians and Africans in simulated native villages. Within the White City, on the Shores of the South Lagoon, Native American representatives had built a Penobscot village; several Iroquois bark houses and a "long house," in which the visitor could meet Tuscarora and Seneca men and women from New York; a Navajo hogan that housed a native blacksmith and weaver; and an entire Pacific Coast village peopled by members of the

Kwakiutl tribe. Totem poles stood before these structures, and canoes drift-
ed by on the lagoon, while Franz Boas, one of the founders of modern anthropology, lurked about examining artifacts and conducting interviews
with the participants.

But stretching beyond the White City along either side of the Midway
Plaisance were the houses and shops of an astounding variety of exotic
peoples. Here, as a contemporary observer described it, was a Turkish village, with a bazaar, mosque, and theater; and an Arab encampment, where
a wedding, mock combats, and a traditional drama were in progress. A
Damascus house, with its domestic customs, lay hard by a Cairo street,
where two Sudanese families provided music, dancing, and soothsaying.
An Algerian and Tunisian village included a café and a "torture dance" in
which the dancer "ate live scorpions and broken glass, grasped red-hot
irons, and drew needles through his flesh, while apparently under the
influence of some drug" (Culin 1894–95:54).

A South Sea Village consisted of houses brought from Samoa, Fiji, and
the Wallis Islands, while in a Javanese Village over a hundred natives from a
colonial plantation engaged in batik dyeing, target shooting with bows and
blowguns, and kite flying. A wedding occurred here too, with attendant
festivity, as well as an actual funeral for several of the participants who had
succumbed probably to the violent physical and cultural dislocation, a fact
that did not prevent our commentator from observing that among the Javanese "good nature and merriment constantly prevailed, and life seemed a
perpetual holiday" (Culin 1894–95:59).

Best remembered of the Plaisance villages, however, because pioneering
work in African music was performed there by ethnomusicologist Henry
Edward Krehbiel, was a village of thirty thatch-and-plaster huts, entirely
enclosed by a high stockade—the Dahomey Village, inhabited by sixty-
nine men, women, and children from the French settlement of Benin on
the west coast of Africa, who on an open square in the center performed
native music and dances, ornamental painting and goldsmithing, and religious ceremonials—including the sacrifice of a bull. The Dahomey Village,
alongside settlements of Dakota Sioux, Navajo, Winnebago, Apache, and
Pueblo, arranged through Indian agents, occupied the far end of the Midway, while nearest the White City stood the German houses and two Irish
villages—an arrangement that one observer called "a sliding scale of humanity," descending from the Teutonic and the Celtic, through the Middle
Eastern and Asian, to the African and Native American (Rydell 1984:65)

Lest we laugh too derisively at the overt racism of some late nineteenth-century anthropological representations, let us recall that while ideologies come and go, the cultural traditions that gave rise to them, and the social experiences that continually drive them home, persist. The White City and the Midway Plaisance are merely momentary expressions of ideas, political and pastoral, that have been with us for centuries in thousands of varied embodiments, among which is the nation's capital itself; and, while most of us would like to think we have jettisoned the racist evolutionary assumptions of our grandparents, the social landscape around and before us, where difficulty, disadvantage, and outright oppression continually shape and reshape privilege and power along racial and cultural lines, sends our best convictions into an airy, abstract realm, which the passionate intensity of racial confrontation can blow away in an instant. They were not all racists, after all; an interesting young character called Sol Bloom, who installed the Midway Plaisance exhibits, found a "spiritual intensity" in Bedouin acrobats that exceeded the "emotional power of a Renaissance tapestry," and an Arabian sword-swallower whose level of culture to him was higher than that of Swiss peasants making cheese and chocolate. Bloom's head was clear—and it seems fitting that later in life he should have been one of the drafters of the United Nations Charter (Rydell 1984:62).

It is more than intriguing to place today's Festival of American Folklife in the context of these symbolic and ideological structures of the past. The nineteenth-century federal White City of Capitol and Monument now linger in remote and silent watchfulness on the margins of the National Mall while the festival draws onto the sunlit grass growing at the middle of things, into the social scientific as well as the touristic gaze, its own officialized Midway Plaisance. In the rotunda of the old Arts and Industries Building, hard by the Smithsonian Castle and the symbolic heart of the National Museum, an evening reception for festival participants, staff, officers, federal and foreign service dignitaries, and invited guests takes place amidst exhibits from the Philadelphia Centennial Exhibition of 1876. Science, industry, and technology in their modern forms are all there too—half hidden in the months of phone calls, the stacks of computer disks, the paperwork, xeroxing and faxing, the air and highway travel, the electrical and communication systems, and all the rest that it takes to produce a folklife festival. Even the Smithsonian's nineteenth-century anthropological paradigms survive in the institution's current initiatives in African American, Native American, and Pacific cultures.

Roger Abrahams has given us a powerful metaphor for understanding what, culturally, these structural and historical reconfigurations mean, particularly in the original nineteenth-century context of manufacture and trade. Trade, Abrahams observes, implies the crossing of frontiers and demands the creation of special zones outside the contexts of family and community in which people otherwise insulated from one another may come together for exchange. Typically the marketplace occurs "at the crossing points between two worlds," such as in the seventeenth-century suburban London "liberties" or unincorporated tracts outside the city gates, or on the borders between two precincts, or at international crossroads: a desert Palmyra or modern jetport with its unincorporated city beyond the last suburban tract.

The marketplace, Abrahams explains, is essentially cultural; though it may have evolved, anthropologically, from the festivals of tribal or communal societies, market society festivals, such as our national holidays, summer vacations, and long weekends, reflect the production calendars of complex market economies. At festival times, which are temporally as well as spatially unincorporated, situated between seasons, at moments when productive work is temporarily suspended, economic exchange retreats before the cultural exchange that is its social foundation, moving expressive activity dramatically into the center. The social hierarchy is inverted; an outpouring of symbols, effigies, and images bewilders perception; imitation, mimicry, and parody lift cultural identities out of their fixed positions in the social structure and bestow upon them the mobility and the appeal of commodities; sheer plentitude relaxes customary prohibitions, and a kind of erotic energy suffuses the festival space with the spirit of play and the promise of riches.

Though the Festival of American Folklife arises from a concentration of economic and political power, though for some participants its festive character is compromised by their hired status, though for others it represents an economic as well as a cultural and political opportunity, with its historical and institutional links to nineteenth-century anthropological exhibitions, and its place on the Mall outside the gates of the Capitol and on the summer holiday calendar, it is an essentially festive event. But what is the nature of this festivity, and what is its meaning for us, particularly in its symbolic movement into the center and onto what has been called the national front lawn, where in 1964, in one of his first actions as secretary, Dillon Ripley installed a carousel and turned the statue of Joseph Henry around to face the Mall? Why, indeed, as we approach the millennium, is the public folk festival, burdened as it is with discredited social and anthropological ideas, grounded in a thoroughly suspect concept, still invested with the dusky glow of old romance, aggravated by ideological conflict and class antagonism, a feature of the cultural landscape at all?

A folk festival, as I hope the foregoing discussion suggests, resituates, reconstrues, and recontextualizes, by means of public reenactment, displaced and decontextualized folk cultural performances. These are the variables—decontextualization, reenactment, and recontextualization—that determine the several kinds of folk festivals we have considered; and these variables, as we have seen, are themselves shaped by various motivating ideologies and interests; social, historical, technological, and other larger forces; and by the several modes of presentation available for folk-cultural display.

Let us consider, then, each of these factors in turn. The regional festivals of the 1920s annexed themselves to and assimilated certain local forms of presentation such as the singing convention, the camp meeting, or fiddlers' contest, or, as in Lunford's case, the annual Rhododendron Festival, mounted for tourists. At Kutztown, a seasonal celebration, the apple-butter boiling, provided the occasion and its structure. The present-day National Folk Festival has been linked to particular historical sites and national recreation areas and is exhibitory in character; other folk festivals have been more strictly theatrical, beginning with settlement house presentations and including of course Sarah Gertrude Knott's festival and most of the university-sponsored concert festivals of the postwar folk revival. The Festival of American Folklife provides perhaps the only real instance of a folk cultural exhibition whose models are the great exhibitions and world's fairs of mature industrial capitalism.

Each of these modes of presentation suggests particular processes of recontextualization and the audiences associated with them. All folk festivals are themselves contexts, of course, in which particular cultural performances are redefined and interpreted in relation to the other performances on the program, the total body of performances promulgating, though rarely articulating, a tacit theory of a particular folk culture or of folk culture generally. The regional folk festivals of the 1920s and 1930s strived for cultural purification or reinforcement, usually driven by certain ideological commitments arising from particular institutions such as a crafts cooperative, a settlement or folk school, or, as at Asheville, a business establishment. Where tourism or some other form of economic traffic—trade in local crafts, for example—is the object, recontextualizing, as in Jean Thomas's "Traipsin' Woman," may involve a deliberate gratification of the cultural stereotypes that tourists may be expected to bring with them. Or, as in the settlement house or folk school festival, recontextualization may consist, as we have suggested, in the construction of ethnicity: to enhance what Knott called "esprit de corps," to assist in the process of assimilation, and to acquaint the insulated middle class with the real culture of peasants and serfs. The new context here, of course, is life in the industrial working class.

In the case of theatrical and exhibitory presentations, recontextualization is more problematic. In Knott's festivals, and in the many concert presentations akin to hers, presenters seem to assume, probably accurately, that audiences are already furnished with whatever rudimentary cultural information may be required to make the performance intelligible. This may be some kind of formal or informal learning, a benign sentimental stereotype, or even something as simple as a belief in cross-cultural understanding or a love of the exotic. It is the aim of such festivals to validate and satisfy such beliefs and desires, which are all predicated upon a secure social standing and a tacit conviction of cultural centrality or even superiority. Various textual and oral mediators mounted in association with the performance, though, may promote and shape a recontextualization of the performance along educational or ideological lines.

"Cultural conservation," a policy initiative outlined in various federal documents and articles during the 1980s (Loomis 1983; Hunt and Seitel 1985; Kurin 1989), is one such ideology of recontextualization, in this case highly concrete and practical, one that aims to shape existing social, economic, and political structures in ways that will nurture the folk cultural performance, and with it the folk culture itself: by heightening awareness of itself in itself and in others, by strengthening cultural self-esteem, by opening potential markets for crafts and music, by preserving natural and cultural raw materials, by influencing favorable legislation, and so on. The synthesis "cultural conservation" represents, of the concepts of natural conservation, historical preservation, and economic revitalization, within the domain of federal authority, strikingly materialized at the National Folk Festival at Lowell, which attempted to summon various ethnic communities together around their own cultural performances in an architecturally preserved urban national park.

There is a close connection of course among a festival's mode of presentation, its interests, and the character of the folk performance itself. Performances mounted in conjunction with a regional celebration or local fair— a fiddlers' contest, for example—may be thoroughly traditional in themselves. But reframed as tourist attractions, they are assimilated to stereotypes; reframed as cultural recoveries, they are assimilated, say, to nativist, Anglo-Saxonist, socialist, populist, existentialist, or other ideological romances. What is "traditional," however, at a particular historical moment, may already have been constructed commercially, a generation or so earlier: by minstrel and tent shows and Wild West shows, by record-company advance men and concert promoters, by regional writers and local colorists, cartoonists and photographers, even by folklorists. Postwar revivalist concert festivals in the university and the Smithsonian's Festival of American Folklife have enjoyed a background of commercial, political, and academic constructions of folklore extending into the nineteenth century, with certain periods, such as the populist 1930s, contributing mightily to the concept as well as to the various claims made on its behalf.

A folk festival structurally reduplicates the social arrangements that make the concept of folk culture possible to begin with and in a variety of ways seeks to drive that concept home—and with it, its enabling social arrangements. We have already noted that a folk festival is itself a context; this fundamental recontextualization *must* occur—hence, always, a folk *festival*—because the concept of the folk cultural performance is implicitly *de*contextualizing. Whether romantic or reactionary, explicitly political or methodically academic, the concept of the folk cultural performance has already bracketed the many social, economic, technological, and especially the historical factors that join folk culture, and, more importantly, the people who bear it, inextricably to official culture, established institutions, and reigning technologies. By identifying, soliciting, organizing, and presenting the reenacted cultural performance, the folk festival formalizes that decontextualization so that recontextualization can occur under its own auspices and in the service of its own interests.

Because social differentiation and historical change have already created the conditions of the folk festival, it consequently may be said to be a kind of symbolic response to such differentiation and change: typically to reconcile or to resist it. In celebratory events, the anxieties occasioned by an aggravated economic inequality, say, or the emergence of a depersonalizing mass society, or the decline of social power in a particular class can be contemplated as joys; the grief attending the loss of tradition or community can be briefly recompensed. Nativist and Anglo-Saxonist festivals, for example, which may appear to have preserved traditional performances in contexts already in place, in fact occurred under the pressure of an anticipated or perceived decontextualization arising from disconcerting, even traumatizing, technological and social change—not only European immigration, which in Appalachia was a distant reality at best, but the entire modern world, the deep cultural ambivalence modernity inspired, and especially its apparent collapse in the Great Depression, which certainly inspired the idea of return to customary ways in newly modernized communities. Knott's later festivals have as their historical context the vast social, economic, and human catastrophe of global war: It is almost as if in her teeming festivals she was endeavoring symbolically to put the world back together again.

Finally we must consider social class itself and the cultural stereotypes that arise from and reinforce it as a psychosocial form of the process the folk festival recapitulates. In culturally heterogeneous societies the folk cultural performance, or its image, perceived across a social boundary and radically decontextualized in its passage, becomes the nucleus of a complex figure whose recontextualization, out of and on behalf of the perceiver's own cultural endowment, fixes and revalidates the distance that occasioned it (Cantwell 1991). That is the stereotype; and the process of its formation is precisely the process that the folk festival, by introducing itself at the moment of the transformation, seeks either to realize more perfectly or to radically disrupt.

The concept of folk culture finds itself embodied, and hence seeks a kind of fulfillment in cultures decontextualized by literal displacement—by immigration from abroad, say, or by country-to-city migration—communities in which cultural knowledge has been in a sense mentalized by its withdrawal from the practical field. Displacement need not be so literal, of course: The recent National Folk Festivals presented in Lowell, Massachusetts, and Johnstown, Pennsylvania, are addressed to groups whose ethnicity, long a coefficient of working-class social life, has been in a sense laid bare by the deterioration of the industrial base that originally grounded it. In these cases festival recontextualization mimics and in many cases seeks to influence the cultural process that any displaced community must undertake in new circumstances.

Hence the concept of community has in most respects displaced the concept of folk culture as the mainspring of folk festival planning and production, since sociologically speaking at least community at once constitutes and recontextualizes the folk cultural performance. The aim of folk festival, then, should be to identify, summon up, and perhaps in the end to reintegrate itself with community. In the community-oriented or community-based folk festival, the fixed categories and unilinear narratives of the old ethnology and folklore are gone; gone, too, are the strict identifications of the kinds of human communities with their specific historical manifestations in, say, certain nations or races. Such equations are of course axiomatic in the cultural mathematics of evolutionary narrative, folklore types, keys to mythology, and other idols of nineteenth-century social science.

Let us look, then, by way of conclusion, at the role of community in the Festival of American Folklife and the National Folk Festival. Communities are always formations, like whirlpools, rather than forms, like squares and circles. Some may arise under the pressure of insulation or enclaving—regional and ethnic groups, for example, bounded by the economy and the polity of a particular region in Mississippi or Kentucky, the Smithsonian's "featured states" in 1973 and 1974; by the binding force of a language such as Cajun French, for many years with Cajun music a conspicuous presence on the Mall; or by historical factors that drive particular groups into particular urban areas and industries. Some folk cultures arise out of their forced exclusion from official culture: African Americans, enslaved, economically and socially isolated, ghettoized; Native Americans, driven from native lands onto reservations—both compelled to forge syncretic cultures out of complicated and diverse legacies. Others are voluntary: labor unions, sister and brotherhoods such as the community of the hearing impaired, or enthusiast groups such as citizen band and ham radio broadcasters or Hawaiian hula dancers. Recently the Festival of American Folklife may have transgressed the bounds of public folklore practice by admitting a professional organization, the Association of American Trial Lawyers, to the festival as a folk community.

Some folk cultures, violently uprooted from one way of life without having yet accommodated, culturally, to the new circumstances, are in a state of becoming. These are protocultures—refugees, such as the Vietnamese and Laotians, mountain people such as the Hmong and Kmhmu, dislocated by war. In them we can observe a folk culture in transition, as, for example, Hmong embroiders, settled in church-sponsored communities in small-town neighborhoods, adapt to the American crafts economy by creating designs in our patriotic colors, or narratives of the war that drove them from their homes. Finally there are kinds of folk community that arise within certain webs of relation, embracing many different kinds of occupations, ethnic groups, economies and ecologies, and the rest: the Chesapeake Bay fishery, for example, or the California winery. Some associations seem purely natural, such as families, or children, or the elderly, all of them represented at different times at the Festival of American Folklife, and others purely economic—occupational communities such as cowboys, loggers, railroad workers, taxi drivers, or telephone workers, all of which have been represented over the twenty-five years of the festival.

A folk festival is "festive" because of the abundant multiplicity and simultaneity of performances: musicians playing, singers singing and dancers dancing, craftspeople crafting, sculptors sculpting, workers working, talkers talking, and children playing. In this theater the whole range of human ingenuity—crafts subsistent, domestic, preindustrial, and industrial—finds a specific form for presentation, ranging from potters' wheels and kneeling looms to temporary oil derricks and steel-girdered buildings. Open tents shelter Bengali effigy makers or Italian American stone carvers preparing finials for the Washington Cathedral; Chinese dragon dancers, Serbian string bands, Spanish bagpipers, Kentucky tobacco twisters, Lumbee Indian May Day players, a Finnish Laskiainen winter festival, Macedonian polkas, New Mexican adobe builders, Korean masked players, Philadelphia breakdancers, bluegrass bands, blues singers, tamburitza and mariachi and corridos and Cajun and zydeco and samba and reggae and a hundred other musics, as well as Lebanese, Mexican, and Ukrainian and Chinese and Ghanaian cooks—no list can even so much as suggest the number and variety of participants in twenty-five years of the Festival of American Folklife. They practice their art before small, often intimate audiences in whom the public and democratic spirit of the Mall often takes on a warmly communal character.

And *there*, in the festival's own "communities," fleeting as they are, but often unforgettable, whether it is an audience under canvas, or the community of participants that in its two weeks together works out its own set of codes and forms its own alliances, or in the community of volunteers that gathers around the festival and returns to it year after year, or of the staff with its ideas, its projects, its responsibilities and its inevitable office politics, or in the many combinations and permutations of all of these, that the purposes of the Festival of American Folklife are best achieved, when they are achieved—where the cultural recovery or recontextualization of the folk performance is, if temporary, more than didactic, theoretical, or imaginary.

It remains to be seen, however, whether the grand experiment on the National Mall, with its variegated public audience of tourists, suburbanites, students, civil servants, bureaucrats, legislators, executives, and professionals, as well as its tiny implanted "inner audiences" of Washington refugee, ethnic, and minority residents, will not eventually be displaced by localized events such as the National Folk Festival, the Cowboy Poetry Gathering at Elko, Nevada, the Conjunto Festival at San Antonio, Texas, and many other grass-roots events inspired by public folklore work. At Lowell, musicians, singers, dancers, and craftspeople of British, Irish, Swedish, Italian, Armenian, Polish, Greek, African, Caribbean, Portuguese, Brazilian, Puerto Rican, African American, Native American, Laotian, Vietnamese, Cambodian, French Canadian, Lithuanian, and Filipino heritage, all of them residents of Lowell or of other small cities in New England, performed both to the festival's audience of folk culture enthusiasts and their own families, neighbors, and friends. Such a festival strives for, and in a sense constructs, its own indigenity, building its cultural bowers in the ruins of the industrial age.

With each new contraction of history a new world comes closer to birth. Pilgrims from the obsolete but still prevailing age, its structures still standing and its business still transpiring all around them, colonize the unincorporated zones, bringing their old cultures with them, or fashioning new ones, their existence scarcely detectable until their new order has by ineluctable degrees displaced the old. The Dutch trading companies of the seventeenth century, for example, with their corporate organization, contractual ties, and written charters, a phenomenon of the merchant towns without legitimate place in the official discourse of the period, became, early in the seventeenth century, a metaphor for human society, and proto-forms of constitutional governments that would be secured by revolution against traditional power. Standing armies founded on protective armor and the rolling cannon, and the provision of them, prefigured the factory system, the bureaucracy, and mass society, whose consummation was the radio age, and whose apocalypse the atom bomb.

Our own folk festivals are footholds on a cultural future that we in the postmodern age, still defining ourselves in relation to the lost modernity, can but dimly discern. When he was an employee of Pan American Airways, in the early days of the jet age, Festival of American Folklife founder Ralph Rinzler was discovering what he calls, using an airline metaphor, "hubs" of alienated cultures flourishing around their imported expressive forms in taverns, clubs, theaters, and other spots, and at weddings, dinners, and other celebrations in New York, London, Paris, Istanbul, and other cities to which the airline took him.

Rinzler caught the scent, perhaps, of a new cultural synthesis of which his own early exposure to Library of Congress field recordings, and to the pioneer reformer-revivalist Pete Seeger, had been full of forebodings. A localizing of culture was following paradoxically from a new expansion of the global order. The new order, it seems, is not yet another "shrinking" or implosion of the planet, facilitating travel and communication, bringing distant places and people closer, a "global village" or world culture. On the contrary, it is an evaporation and precipitation, a kind of inundating cultural rain, an "information explosion" so vast that culturally it denatures information and levels the semiotic field. Culturally speaking, it is tantamount to no information whatever. It overcomes the power of human imagination to orient itself on its own terms and in its own scale and demands that we rediscover the basis of culture in immediate human interaction, conducted under the auspices of our God-given sensory and intellectual equipment, even while *as* cultures—and only as cultures—we are able to participate in the political and economic consolidation of a global civilization.

Though many may yearn for it, many struggling to create or to recreate it, the homogenous cultural community is precisely what most of us do *not* experience, and we would feel culturally suffocated if we did. In the information age, community no sooner forms than it deteriorates—and its deterioration is perpetual. In the evanescent, momentary reality between these impermanences culture springs forth out of acts of making essentially imaginative. The idea of the homogeneous cultural community, which in spite of recent theoretical refinements is still tinged with the old socialist romance, must ultimately give way to a concept of culture grounded not in specific social formations but in the agencies of psychic differentiation in which those formations are themselves grounded. That, I think, is what is indicated by the empty proliferation of the many names—endless lists of regional, national, ethnic, occupational, and other groups, musical varieties, material kinds, crafts types, and so on—without which neither the Festival of American Folklife nor the National Folk Festival can refer to itself or its history. These names speak of course to the perspicacity of fieldworkers, the wonderful diversity of people and their arts, the dizzying abundance of folk festival displays, and the bewildering process of planning and producing what is finally a mysterious and spontaneous social and cultural phenomenon well beyond the reach of mortal understanding. But they are, after all, only names, and, impressive as they are, do not say what the Festival of American Folklife or the National Folk Festival actually is or does.

A folk festival is not in the business of naming things, really, but of unnaming them—of reaching into the little structures of figurative compar-isons and self-serving judgments by which we at once admit and dismiss one another in our thoughts to pluck out the vague effigies, made from the scraps of our own culture's representations, that hold such structures to-gether. Bring them to the festival we will and must—they are simply images of unknowns, like the "x" in the equation, through which we assimilate the image of another and work out its value in our own known quantities.

But at the festival this cultural algebra becomes wholly inadequate to account for the chemistry of personal encounter. The sheer reality of the person, the rich exactitude of her presence, the keen imperatives of his art, empty our hopeless conceptions and bestow a gift of permanent love. If the festival has done its work—and it cannot always, of course—we can never think of him or her, or of culture itself, in the same way again. At the very least we will have felt the nagging unease that comes of being, at this time and place, who and what we are, and for one naked moment perhaps watch as outsiders as the gift of complete humanness falls into hands other than our own. For there is no Corliss Engine nor any merry Javanese to place us at the summit of history, seated on the throne of the human race.

The folklife festival is a practical investigation of the genesis of social ex-perience in a world where the boundaries between cultures are no longer geographical or political but personal, in which the person is in himself or herself culturally not one but many, capable of moving within and among many communities, in which "culture" itself has emerged as the force that secures the connection between reality and the individual soul. In this world folklife is not the culture of the rude peasant or the rustic moun-taineer but a very model of the ways in which we are at this moment learn-ing to reinvent our humanity.

REFERENCES

Abrahams, Roger. n.d. "The Winking Gods of the Marketplace." Manuscript.
Banta, Martha, ed. 1988. "Part Three, 1865–1910." In *The Columbia Literary Histo-ry of the United States*, edited by Emory Elliott. New York: Columbia University Press.
Bauman, Richard, Inta Gale Carpenter, Richard Anderson, Garry Barrow, Patricia Sawin, William Wheeler, and Jongsung Yang. 1988. *The 1987 Smithsonian Festi-val of American Folklife: An Ethnography of Participant Experience*. Bloomington: The Folklore Institute, Indiana University.

Buchanan, Annabel Morris. 1937. "The Function of a Folk Festival." *Southern Folklore Quarterly* 1, no. 1 (March): 29–34.

Cantwell, Robert. 1991. "On Stereotype." *New England Review* 13, no. 2 (Winter).

Culin, Stewart. "Retrospect of the Folk-Lore of the Columbian Exposition." *Journal of American Folklore* 7(8):51–59.

Danker, Fred. 1989. "Regionalism and the Uses of Folklife: The Carolina Playmakers." Paper delivered at the annual convention of the American Folklore Society, Philadelphia, October 21.

Douglas, Ann. 1977. *The Feminization of American Culture.* New York: Alfred A. Knopf.

Green, Archie. 1975. "The National Folk Festival Association." *John Edwards Memorial Foundation Newsletter* 11, no. 37 (Spring): 23–32.

Haraway, Donna. 1984–85. "Teddy Bear Patriarchy: Taxidermy in the Garden of Eden, New York City, 1908–1936." *Social Text* 2 (Winter).

Hunt, Marjorie, and Peter Seitel. 1985. "Cultural Conservation." In *Smithsonian Festival of American Folklife Program Book*, edited by Thomas Vennum, Jr. Washington, D.C.: Office of Folklife Programs, Smithsonian Institution.

Jones, Loyal. 1984. *Minstrel of the Appalachians: The Story of Bascom Lamar Lunsford.* Boone, North Carolina: Appalachian Consortium Press.

Knott, Sarah Gertrude. 1946. "The National Folk Festival After Twelve Years." *California Folklore Quarterly* 5, no. 1 (January): 83–93.

———. 1961. "Folksongs and Dances, U.S.A.: The Changing Scene." *Southern Folklore Quarterly* 25:184–94.

Kodish, Debora. 1986. *Good Friends and Bad Enemies: Robert Winslow Gordon and the Study of American Folksong.* Urbana: University of Illinois Press.

Kurin, Richard. 1989. "Why We Do the Festival." In *Smithsonian Festival of American Folklife Program Book*, edited by Arlene Liebenau. Washington, D.C.: Office of Folklife Programs, Smithsonian Institution.

Lears, T. J. Jackson. 1981. *No Place of Grace: Antimodernism and the Transformation of American Culture, 1880–1920.* New York: Pantheon Books.

Loomis, Ormond, ed. 1983. *Cultural Conservation: The Protection of Cultural Heritage in the United States.* Washington, D.C.: American Folklife Center, Library of Congress.

Lomax, Alan. 1968. Public speech, Festival of American Folklife, July 7.

Rydell, Robert W. 1984. *All the World's a Fair: Visions of Empire at American International Expositions, 1876–1916.* Chicago: University of Chicago Press.

Sollors, Wernor. 1986. *Beyond Ethnicity: Consent and Descent in American Culture.* New York: Oxford University Press.

Trachtenberg, Alan. 1982. *The Incorporation of America: American Culture and Society in the Gilded Age.* New York: Hill and Wang.

Whisnant, David E. 1983. *All This Is Native and Fine: The Politics of Culture in an American Region.* Chapel Hill: University of North Carolina Press.

Wilson, Joe, and Lee Udall. 1982. *Folk Festivals: A Handbook for Organization and Management.* Knoxville: University of Tennessee Press.

Wilson, Joe. 1989. "Welcome." In *51st National Folk Festival: Lowell, Massachusetts, July 28, 29, 30, 1989.* Program book. Lowell, Massachusetts: National Council for the Traditional Arts.

Yoder, Don. 1974. "25 Years of the Folk Festival." *Pennsylvania Folklife* 23:2–7.

Zweig, Paul. 1984. *Walt Whitman: The Making of the Poet.* New York: Viking Press.

Postwar Public Folklore and the Professionalization of Folklore Studies

ROBERT BARON

olklorists are ever aware of boundaries—crossing cultural boundaries in the field, dancing between disciplinary boundaries in the university, reaffirming or blurring boundaries between public and academic realms. During the emergence of folklore as an autonomous academic discipline in the postwar period, the relationship between its practice in the university and in nonacademic, public settings became a matter of great concern. Discourse among folklorists about this issue was of essential importance in defining the boundaries of the practice of folklore at a critical time in the molding of our discipline's professional identity.

The period between the end of World War II and the early 1960s in the United States has been generally acknowledged as a key period in the consolidation and professionalization of folklore studies. The number of university courses grew rapidly, folklore graduate programs were established, and efforts intensified to establish a unified body of theory for folklore. The marginalization of applied folklore and opposition to the populariza-

tion of folklore has been tied to a drive for the professionalization of folklore studies.[1] Richard M. Dorson's efforts to achieve the ascendancy of folklore as an autonomous academic discipline relied heavily upon the drawing of sharp boundaries between pure and applied folklore, folklore and "fakelore" (Kirshenblatt-Gimblett 1988 and this volume).

Within the historiography of the discipline, it is a given that Dorson's opposition to popularization and applied folklore had a strong impact upon the marginalization of public folklore. However, Dorson's well-known oppositional position should not obscure the involvement of many folklorists during the early postwar period in a far-reaching discourse about the relationship between the practice of folklore within and outside the university. Many folklorists participated in a spirited, often contentious discussion about popularization and the role of the folklorist in nonacademic uses of folklore. They discussed issues about the alteration and adaptation of folklore to new contexts, which should provoke a surprising shock of recognition from contemporary public folklorists. Their consideration of these issues occurred during a brief, but critically important period in the history of folklore studies, which was followed by a rapid fading of interest and marked antipathy to public folklore.

This essay explores a hidden chapter in the history of folklore studies, when public folklore was near the center of the discipline's concerns, and the period of reaction to public folklore that followed. The story of public folklore in postwar America should help illuminate the uneasy historical relationship of folklorists to public folklore, fill some gaps in the intellectual history of folklore studies, and expand our understanding of the course of its professionalization.

The close of the Second World War ushered in a period of intense social and cultural change in a nation ascending to the peak of its economic, political, and military power. Having triumphed over totalitarian fascism in a global conflict, the United States assumed a central role in molding a new

Folklorist Benjamin A. Botkin was president of the American Folklore Society (1944) and folklore adviser to the Federal Writers' Project in the late 1930s. He also served as the director of the Library of Congress's Archive of American Folksong. Botkin is shown here at the Library when his book *A Treasury of Railroad Folklore* (1953) was published. Photo courtesy of Gertrude Botkin.

world order. American involvement in the establishment of the United Nations reflected a widespread interest in accomplishing lasting world peace and international cooperation. During the early postwar years the shadow of the cold war also began to deepen. Anticommunism colored intellectual life in all fields, including folklore studies.

In a more suburban and urban nation, the disruption of old social formations intensified. Americans lived in a consumer society with an expanding middle class increasingly influenced by sophisticated marketing, advertising, and the penetration of mass media. Discretionary income could now be spent on consumer goods newly available following the frustrations of pent-up demand during the war years. Leisure time increased. The United States was ripe for new popular interest in folklore.[2]

In a nation undergoing rapidly expanding technological development, the reshaping of local cultures by the forces of modernity became more apparent, and nostalgic interest in American heritage, local history, and folklore went on the upswing. "Goodnight Irene," as sung by the Weavers, went to the top of the hit parade. Along with adaptations of folksongs that appeared in hit records, radio broadcasts and films used folk materials, folk museums were created, folksong and folktale anthologies reached wide readerships, and many teachers brought folklore into the schools. Folklorists found it harder to ignore a modernizing world spinning faster and faster around the enclaved, small-scale communities that they traditionally studied. In postwar America, interest in folklore spread far beyond a small, if growing, group of scholars concentrated in universities.

Wayland Hand, in his "Editor's Page" remarks in the *Journal of American Folklore*, gave us a sense of the tenor of the times as he encapsulated the challenges facing the professional folklorist and spoke to how the profession might respond to popular interest in folklore:

> The phenomenal increase of scholarly interest in folklore during the past decade, and the popular awakening to the possibilities of collecting, preserving, and interpreting the folklore of our great North American country create opportunities for leadership and impose upon the American Folklore Society responsibilities greater than it has ever borne. Our generation has seen folklore emerge from relative obscurity as an academic subject, where at best its value has been indifferently regarded, to a position of increasing importance and esteem. Convincing evidence of this development are the many courses and curricula in folklore which have been established recently in many of the major universities. . . .

Important as are the academic and scholarly aspects of folklore, nay as decisive as they are in the promotion of the discipline of folklore and a proper appreciation of it in American cultural life, they are overshadowed by the tremendous popular interest in the subject that has resulted from the utilization of folk materials in motion pictures, the theater, radio, music, and other media of entertainment,—not to mention the use of folklore in recreational programs and in education. . . .

It is distressing to note that much, if not most, activity in the entertainment aspects of folklore has been carried out quite independently of national and regional folklore societies and organizations, and without benefit of the research facilities of academic institutions and folklore depositories in our great libraries. Trashy performances can be laid quite as much to an ignorance of these facilities and services as to a willful yielding to box office expedients. As the leading coordinating agency in American folklore, the American Folklore Society will abdicate one of its most important duties if it does not take positive action to combat the many negative forces at work in the field of folk arts by insisting on greater fidelity to source materials, and by encouraging resort to them wherever found. Moreover, it should extend the hand of cooperation to local folk song, folk dance and folk festival groups with a view toward a more scientific study of the materials. Berating the efforts of these groups, or ignoring them is not enough! (Hand 1948:82)

During the late 1940s and early 1950s a number of other folklorists agreed that the widespread adaptation of folk materials by nonfolklorists called for a response from professional folklorists. They engaged in various efforts to identify issues of concern for the discipline regarding the uses of folklore and proposed strategies to foster the appropriate use of folkloric materials, grounded in the professional standards of the field. Many other folklorists shared Hand's interest in collaborating with nonprofessionals involved with the popularization and utilization of folklore.

"Utilization" served as a key word. The Committee on the Utilization of Folklore, chaired by Thelma James, defined this term. Reporting to the annual meeting of the AFS in 1946, the committee indicated that "the word utilization can be interpreted quite literally to mean the uses to which folklore materials are put" (Fifty-eighth Annual Meeting 1947:173).

The discourse about utilization among folklorists reflected the primacy of the text in the folklore scholarship of the time. Folklore was viewed as "materials," which, when used in new contexts, could be compared to more authentic, less-altered texts collected and published by folklorists. Their principal concerns included the authenticity of adaptations, the accuracy of the sources used in the materials, and the appropriateness of alterations of folk materials in new contexts. They contended that the professional responsibilities of folklorists included the provision of authentic materials and communication with popularizers about folklore scholarship.

In a 1946 report of the Committee on the Utilization of Folklore, James identified four points "which must be applied in all the areas in which folk materials may be or have been used," delineating them one by one:

> First involved is a definition of what constitutes true and pseudo-folk stuff; since this is most difficult to arrive at, and with the thought in mind that there is no gain in rethreshing straw, the Committee will canvass already formulated definitions and select or develop such a definition. Second, the source of the user's materials is important. (Did the items come to him through a straight oral tradition or through a literary recasting which may even have replaced or displaced the more antique oral tradition?) Third, is the user of the folk materials conscious of his sources? Fourth, to what extent, and in what ways, has he altered his materials, and to what extent has the medium in which he operates altered the folk materials? (Fifty-eighth Annual Meeting 1947:173)

The concerns of folklorists about the utilization of folklore were not limited to a formalistic interest in how texts were altered. Folklorists also recognized that the "use" of folklore in public presentations within new contexts resulted in new modes of transmission and functions for folk materials. They saw that by acting as agents for the presentation of folklore in new contexts they could contribute to the revitalization and perpetuation of traditions. During a symposium, "Making Folklore Available," at the Midcentury International Folklore Conference in 1950, folklorists engaged in spirited discussion of issues relating to their roles in the revival and revitalization of traditions and the consequences of their actions upon folk cultural processes.

Stith Thompson brought a distinguished international group of folklorists from both within and outside of the academy to Bloomington to discuss problems in folklore research. "Making Folklore Available" was one of four symposia at the conference, which occurred in midsummer in the Midwest at the midpoint of the twentieth century. Changing times clearly shaped a new perception of the folk and the survival of their traditions. Symposium participants recognized the transformative effects of mass communications, urbanization, industrialization, and schools upon the transmission and perpetuation of folklore in the contemporary world. Alan Lomax led off the initial discussion by calling for folklorists to act as advocates for the folk, whose traditions were endangered and in the process of actually being destroyed. He spoke passionately of the folklorist's responsibility to counter the forces threatening the survival of folklore:

> Malinowski . . . said that the role of the ethnologist is that of the advocate of primitive man. And it is my feeling that the role of the folklorist is that of the advocate of the folk. . . . We have seen the profit-making society smashing and devouring and destroying complex cultural systems which have taken almost the entire effort of mankind over many thousands of years to create. We have watched the disappearance of languages, musical languages, the sign languages, and we've watched whole ways of thinking and feeling in relating to nature and relating to other people disappear. We've watched systems of cookery . . . disappear from the face of the earth and I think we have all been revolted by this spectacle and in one way or another we have taken up our cudgels in the defense of the weaker parties.
>
> We have become in this way the champion of the ordinary people of the world who aren't backed up by printing presses, radio chains, and B29's. We believe in the oral tradition, we believe in the small cultural situation, we think that some of these folk of the world have something worth while culturally, morally, etc. (Thompson 1953:157–58)

Lomax spoke of radio and schools as essential media for disseminating and revitalizing folk traditions, anticipating the concept of cultural equity, which he formulated two decades later. He spoke approvingly of the increased presentation, on their own terms, of traditional ballads and country music on radio, noting that at first folklore had been presented through symphonic music on radio "because of this natural nationalistic desire for us to have, at once, a symphonic music based on our folk music" (Thompson 1953:160). He called for local folk traditions to be brought into the schools, which would help assure that they would continue to be part of ongoing cultural processes in their communities:

> In the same sense in public schools, it's not so important that every child in the nation sing "Skip-to-my-Lou" at nine o'clock in the morning. What is important is that the teachers in their own communities know that everywhere the children and their families are carriers of important literature and music and ways of living. And it is the job of the school to bring this material into the open and permit it to express itself, let the chips fall where they will.

> If the people have a chance not to be ashamed of their own material, if we stand just a little between them and the big powerful onslaught of commercial, heavily weighted culture, they will do their own job. The culture will work its own patterns out, and so the thing that's important for the teacher is to let the children and their people come into the schools through the avenue of folk culture, whatever there is in the neighborhood. (Thompson 1953:162)

Ruth Crawford Seeger also felt that school children should be provided with authentic folksongs, which they would use and make their own. She spoke of her experimentation with the use of folksongs in her child's cooperative nursery school, during which she used songs to suit the needs of the school's learning program. While she decided to provide songs in their authentic versions, Seeger, like others adapting folk materials to new audiences, felt conflicted in doing so. Although she provided folksongs with their "idiomatic pronunciation," she questioned whether such pronunciations would be "condescending," "citified," "unnatural" (Thompson 1953:193).

Seeger spoke about conflicts over the presentation of folksongs that rubbed up against the values of others involved with her progressive nursery school. Some of the other mothers were opposed to the use of songs that dealt with hitting. Seeger's response was consonant with her approach towards using authentic versions of folksongs appropriate to particular situations. When one child was "annoying another child and pulling his hair," they sang "Monday morning go to school, Friday evening home, Brother combs my sweetheart's hair as we come marching home" (1953:193–94).

Others attending the symposium suggested that the introduction of particular versions of folksongs in the schools could provide undue emphasis upon that version and skew local traditional processes of transmitting folklore. Herbert Halpert spoke of possible "danger": "If a particular version of a cowboy song gets into a song book used by the Boy Scouts or Campfire Girls, this then becomes the 'right way' of singing the song, no matter what the local tradition is." Halpert suggested that textbooks have supplementary notes indicating how a song is traditionally used, providing the example of an unaccompanied song, which, if sung otherwise, would be an adaptation to another condition (Thompson 1953:213). Halpert and Frances Gillmor suggested that local collecting could supplement particular versions codified in print or on recordings, with the local versions used for local purposes.[3]

Symposium participants discussing the use of folklore in the schools recognized the dilemma of balancing a folklorist's professional concern for the presentation of authentic versions with a consideration of the appropriateness of their use in particular circumstances and settings. Discussing folksongs with obscene content, Moritz Jagendorf suggested that nonobscene versions of folksongs should be published in school textbooks, with references to motif index numbers so readers could "perceive the changes that have been made" (Thompson 1953:216).

Stith Thompson expressed a radically different attitude towards the presentation of folklore in the schools. He contended that folklorists should not act as cultural arbiters to ensure the revival of older forms of folklore. Thompson questioned the artificial revival of traditions no longer widely practiced, which, perhaps, should be allowed to die (or stay dead) if they have no social purpose. In opposing intervention in ongoing folk-cultural processes, Thompson's position contrasted sharply with the point of view articulated at the beginning of the symposium by Lomax, an aggressive advocate for protecting and perpetuating endangered traditions. While not categorically opposed to the involvement of folklorists with the utilization of folklore, Thompson denied the inherent value of using folk materials in schools simply because they are folk materials:

> But I don't see that there is any special virtue in songs because they are folk songs. When we talk about putting the songs in the schools it seems to me the only criterion is that the song should be something that would be of use to the people in the schools. In this respect it seems to me folk songs must enter into direct competition with all other kinds of songs.
>
> Now when we are talking about putting folklore back in the schools I wonder if we would do the same thing about old beliefs which have died out, old practices that have long ago been abandoned. . . . I think most of us consider that some progress has been made by the sloughing off of superstitions and old practices. If we are looking at the general progress of society I think we should be very glad on the whole that our farmers depend primarily on instruction from the Department of Agriculture or a good agricultural school rather than on the practices of their great-great grandfathers. It is a very interesting thing from the antiquarian point of view to find out what they did, but the idea of putting that back into the schools seems to me, as it would seem to all of you, to be utterly false. So it is with a great many other aspects of folklore. I have my misgivings about some of it and about the replanting of something that has died out. There may well be times when even the putting back of a folk song will be just as futile. (Thompson 1953: 221–22)

Participants at the symposium countered Thompson's viewpoint by speaking of the inherent humanistic value of folklore and the importance of oral traditions for maintaining cultural heritages. While concurring that folklore should be made publicly available in the schools and elsewhere, they expressed varying, often divergent points of view about why and how it should be utilized.

A number of participants contended that folklorists should intervene to maintain folk traditions deemed worthy of perpetuation because they embodied appropriate values and aesthetic standards. Otto Andersson stressed the need for selectivity by folklorists in choosing folksongs to be presented in the schools. He indicated that folklorists should "select the good from the bad," selecting folk tunes that "express the same feelings that we have and that give the people in schools and communities a feeling of what they are and what they have been in the past" (Thompson 1953:222). Lomax saw the need for preserving folklore to be akin to that of preserving other kinds of good art:

> One of the answers . . . to Dr. Thompson's questions would lie in his own career. As a scholar of English literature he wouldn't object to anybody being interested in the literature of the sixteenth century and in propagating the best of it to the schools. The same thing applies at least to certain parts of folklore. It seems to me that we are all engaged in talking like teachers and educators rather than folklorists. What we are interested in seems to me not whether one tune or one version or one story continues, but whether this way of people's expressing themselves continues. Now, folklore has for a very long time been a sort of unofficial way for a great number of people to express their feelings about their fathers and mothers, as Mr. Halpert told us the other day, a way of projecting their dreams and hopes and aspirations, sometimes in relation to political and economic events and sometimes merely in relation to the problems of living in a particular culture. (Thompson 1953:223)

Lomax asserted that the key to maintaining traditional ways of expression lay in providing greater access for tradition bearers for the public performance of their traditions. Folklorists should not make choices of what to present, or perform the traditions themselves:

> Now, when *we* publish this material and when *we* broadcast it, we are substituting ourselves in the folk process. As folklorists, as teachers, as performers,

we are taking advantage of somebody else's creation to get up there and shine, whether it is in a book or a museum or in a classroom or in front of a microphone. But folklore lives in terms of ordinary people singing, dancing, telling stories. . . . If we want folklore to continue to live in the best way, what we should do is to find the best folk singers and storytellers that we can and get them heard everywhere. Let them carry the folklore for us. Whenever they get the chance, with an audience, whether it is through records, through films or in a classroom, on a public platform, in a movie, or in television, they win the day every time. They carry the whole folklore and its feeling inside themselves. (Thompson 1953:224)

Moritz Jagendorf, a New York City dentist and writer of popular books on folklore, defended the role of folklorists as revivalists and interpreters of folklore. He contended that Lomax "speaks as if folklore were something sacred, and distant from us." He and the participants at the conference were "part of the people," he said. A good storyteller "is a very rare thing": "I don't see any reason why we should be excluded from the pleasure of telling folk tales" (Thompson 1953:226–27).

Åke Campbell then expressed a concern articulated by Thompson earlier in the symposium, claiming that the proper role of a folklorist was an objective scholar engaged in interpretation and scholarship rather than advocacy. Campbell said that if "a renaissance of beauty" came, it was for the "people themselves and the artists" to decide when it would come and to act upon their interests. While the scholar can predict the coming of such a "renaissance" and teach people of the meaning of the renaissance, the scholar "must be the interpreter rather than the active propagator of the beauty that comes from the past" (Thompson 1953:229). Folklorists could appropriately act to advise and educate schools and educators about folklore when it is being presented in a school setting. While a "folklorist need not be himself a storyteller," he "ought to know the real truth about the folk tale or the folk song and its history. He should be there to answer the questions if anybody asks about it and so far as he knows he should give the truth about the history of the folk culture" (Thompson 1953:232).

Halpert felt that the field experience of folklorists impelled them to contribute to the perpetuation of a tradition, in light of the social and technological conditions of contemporary life, which had altered the involvement of communities with folklore. Speaking of his fieldwork in New Jersey, he compared his situation to that of a son, a "younger person who appreciated what the old people had." His informants' children, "who would normally have continued some, not necessarily all, of their parents'

tradition, had been cut off from it because of the schools, the radio—all
the outside forces that imposed themselves on these people who used to
live a moderately self-sufficient life" (Thompson 1953:240).

Disagreeing with Lomax, Halpert contended that the folklorist should
exercise selectivity in making folklore available and provide interpretation
about the traditions presented:

> I don't think you can offer these folk songs "straight." When I talk about
> songs I do try to tell people—and this is what Mr. Lomax is trying to do—
> something of what these songs mean. I'm not saying you can't present them
> just as art songs; if you are going to do that you will say, "This is a lovely
> song, learn it and love it." But I would rather say, "Here is a song; see if you
> like it. Here is something about that song." (Thompson 1953:241)

Toward the end of the symposium, Lomax and Thompson each came to
accommodate themselves somewhat to one another's viewpoints about the
role of the folklorist in making folklore available. While reasserting his emphasis upon providing access for tradition bearers to perform their traditions as they see fit, Lomax suggested that the decisions folklorists make
about intervening in the perpetuation of folk traditions should be conditioned by their understanding of cultural processes of transmitting and
maintaining folklore:

> It seems to me that instead of regarding it in a static way, as something we
> have picked up and used, what we folklorists ought to be after is to find out
> how the process works and to keep it going because we don't know what new
> values it can turn up at any time. As Mr. Halpert pointed out, we give folk-
> lore new meaning all the time; that is the meaning that the folk give it. We
> must keep it unrolling, unfolding, and then we can be sure that a healthy
> thing is continuing for all the people in all its many ways, also for Dr. Jagen-
> dorf and for his folk group too. But if we get on top and pick and choose too
> much, then we are likely to say, "These hillbillies shouldn't play accordions
> in Finland, shouldn't play steel guitars in the mountains." (Thompson
> 1953:244)

In his final words at the symposium, Thompson seemed to take pains to
say that he did not oppose the revival of folklore, but felt that folklorists
should approach revivals in a critical spirit:

> I must say that I did not realize that I was starting anything the other day
> when I made my remarks about misgivings concerning folklore revivals. We

seem to have found other people here who also have misgivings about revivals. My own point, of course, was that the misgivings were in the detail of revivals and not in the whole idea, though sometimes the whole general idea of reviving the thing that is dead may be a very doubtful procedure. Of course I wasn't talking about the revival of something that is still alive; I should make that very clear. (Thompson 1953:244)

The Midcentury International Folklore Conference provides clear evidence that discourse about the utilization of folklore involved a broad spectrum of folklorists who worked both within and outside of the academy. There was general acceptance, in principal, of involvement by folklorists in making folklore available to the public, even while there was disagreement about how and why they should be involved with such activities. During the early postwar period many folklorists welcomed collaboration with nonfolklorists involved in the utilization of folklore in education, recreation, and the arts. Professional folklorists were beginning to act in a concerted way, as Hand had suggested in 1948 in the *Journal of American Folklore.*

Some folklorists felt that the American Folklore Society could be engaged proactively to provide information about scholarly resources and ensure that accurate, authentic folk materials were provided to the public. Richard Dorson, concerned throughout his career with the distortion of folk materials through popularization, expressed these concerns early in his career as chairman of the American Folklore Society's Committee on Folklore in Education. Reporting on a conference on the teaching of folklore in grade schools held in Muncie, Indiana, in 1950, Dorson conceded, "At this level folklore must be a matter chiefly of entertainment and participation." For the professional folklorist, however, the "great danger from our point of view is that 'hokum' will be presented as folklore, and college instructors will be teaching the misinformed rather than the uninitiated" (Sixty-first Annual Meeting 1950:235).

Dorson felt that misinformation about folklore was widespread. He saw a need for authoritative publications about folklore designed for lay readers:

The general public has been badly misled about folklore through the commercialization and popularization of folk materials, and not only the public but librarians, school teachers and similar groups have no authoritative reference guides or manuals to help them out. I suggest that our Society consider issuing one or more pamphlets explaining to the nonspecialist the scope, aims and methods of folklore in America. The "Popular Studies in

Mythology, Romance and Folklore" issued by English folklorists at the end of the nineteenth century did just that for England with considerable success. The pamphlet, or pamphlets, should be popularly written, calm in tone, but positive in statement. They should provide the lay reader with a means for judging the merit of folklore books for himself, e.g., a sound book must indicate the sources of tradition. They should carry a brief, selective bibliography of books and articles. The first pamphlet can cover general points, and if it lays the way and others follow they can deal with specific topics, regions or problems. (Sixty-first Annual Meeting 1950:235)

Ralph Steele Boggs was the AFS delegate to the Second International Conference on International Educational Reconstruction, a meeting organized by UNESCO in 1947. In the flush of postwar idealism, he spoke of the possibilities for "peace through international understanding." Boggs suggested that folklore, which "represents our whole people, of whom it is a true reflection," could be sent abroad since it "localizes in different countries basic human cultural patterns that have long been traditionally current over the world." He recommended that the AFS compile a list of folklore societies and journals in the United States for widespread distribution abroad. He also suggested that the AFS consider compiling "folklore materials on color slides, films, recordings for radio and phonograph, etc. 'in the form of convenient packages' (to use the words of one mass media delegate) suitable for handling and distribution abroad" (Fifty-ninth Annual Meeting 1948:206–7).

The American Folklore Society only issued one publication during this period for the use of the general public and apparently did not issue any other kinds of folklore materials for professionals in other fields. A number in the AFS Bibliographical and Special Series resulted from the efforts of the Committee on Folklore for Children and Young People. Eloise Ramsey's *Folklore for Children and Young People: A Critical and Descriptive Bibliography for Use in the Elementary and Intermediate Schools* was published in 1952. All other public folklore activities resulted from the efforts of individual folklorists acting independently rather than through the collective action of the principal professional organization of folklorists. Benjamin Botkin published highly popular anthologies of folklore, Alan Lomax produced recordings and radio broadcasts of folk music, Louis Jones directed a folk museum—all continuing their involvement as activists in presenting folklore to the public begun during the previous, depression decade. A number of folklorists served diverse cultural groups within their communities to assist them in presenting their folklore. Among others, Frances

Gillmor and Alfred Shoemaker organized festivals of folk culture, Gillmor in Arizona with Hispanics and Native Americans, Shoemaker in Pennsylvania with the folklife of Pennsylvania Germans. The flourishing state folklore societies of the time also provided vehicles for folklorists to provide information and publications about folklore.

Folklorists provided opportunities for educating nonfolklorists about their field through courses and institutes attended by lay persons active in collecting and presenting folklore to the public. The most important of these were the Folklore Institute of America at Indiana University and the Seminars in American Culture of the New York State Historical Association. These courses and institutes served as major vehicles for public education about folklore studies, provided primary settings for interaction between university-based folklorists and lay persons involved with folklore, and facilitated the dissemination of information about successful undertakings in the popularization of folklore.

The nature of the student body at the 1946 Folklore Institute of America and the curriculum offered to them reflected the growing interest in folklore among nonfolklorists and the concerns of folklorists about meeting their needs. Students at the 1946 Institute included educators, folklore collectors, and artists who had dealt with folklore subjects as well as undergraduate and graduate students of folklore. The courses that summer included "Teaching and Presentation of Folklore" and "American Folklore and Folklore Techniques," both chaired by Wayland Hand; "Introduction to Folklore and the Folktale," chaired by Stith Thompson, the institute's director; and "American Indian Folklore," taught mainly by Erminie W. Voegelin, with special lectures by a number of folklorists, including Alan Lomax, John Mason Brewer, and Samuel Bayard. Students in the institute also learned about methodologies of collecting and archiving folklore and the state of folklore research in a number of genres and culture areas.

Folklorists on the front lines of the utilization of folklore lectured in "Teaching and Presentation of Folklore." Thelma James and Louis Jones spoke of extensive public folklore activities occurring in Detroit and upstate New York, respectively. James described Detroit as a city with great ethnic diversity and conflicts between ethnic groups, new immigrants, and African American and Southern Appalachian migrants. She viewed the purpose of public folklore work as the improvement of racial understanding. To these ends, she lectured visiting nurses on the folk customs of immigrants, provided curricular materials for schoolteachers, and advised the police department on the ethnic groups of the city through responding to their questions about particular communities and constructing an ethnic map of the city. James, like many university teachers of folklore before and since, required her students to collect folklore in their community as a course requirement. Her Wayne University courses were attended by teachers and other working people who used the folklore collected in the classes for their professional activities while adding to the store of knowledge about folk culture in Detroit (Folklore Institute of America 1946:Course 1, 6–10).

During the 1946 meeting of the Folklore Institute of America, Jones described his courses at the New York State College for teachers in Albany, which included graduate classes in extension courses and summer school. The students in his courses included primary and secondary schoolteachers as well as librarians and other nonteachers. They included rural residents and a large number of students whose parents had come from Europe within the past generation. Jones directed the course toward their professional needs and interests, with students encouraged to contribute to publications or other public presentations. Jones reported that students created a television script, assisted in archival work, prepared a collection of farm lore for publication in a pamphlet published by the Farmers' Museum, and created a child's anthology of folklore for use with retarded children (Folklore Institute of America 1946:Course 1, 1–5).

Jones also initiated the Seminars on American Culture as director of the New York State Historical Association. The seminars, which began in 1948, were attended by teachers, antique collectors, and other lay persons interested in folklore. The courses reflected Jones's folklife and social-history orientation. Their topics related to state and local history, the use of history in museums and historic preservation, and material folk culture and oral traditions (Jones 1982:24–26). In contrast to the Folklore Institute of America, which had a faculty comprised of folklorists, the faculty for the Seminars in American Culture included museum personnel and nonfolklorists with expertise in folk art as well as folklorists.

The broad-based efforts to effect collaboration between academic folklorists and nonfolklorists begun in the late 1940s did not last long. Many other folklorists came to share the strong reservations, misgivings, and ambivalence about the utilization of folklore expressed by Thompson at the Midcentury Conference. As the second half of the century dawned, individual folklorists continued to pursue their various efforts at utilizing folklore through courses, publications, recordings, and media activities. However, sharp conflicts about whether folklorists should be involved in nonacademic pursuits to utilize folklore burst into print, signaling a change in direction in the place of public folklore work in the folklore profession. During the 1950s and 1960s, folklore studies became centered upon establishing itself as an autonomous academic discipline with a firm foothold in American universities, professionalizing rapidly and pushing the utilization of folklore to the margins.

In his 1951 presidential address, "Conflict and Promise in Folklore," Francis Lee Utley acknowledged that the schism between "researchers" and "popularizers" represented one of the "disintegrative quarrels" now "making our Society function at only a small fraction of its potential" (1952:111). He made specific reference to the popularization of folklore through publications, an especially contentious topic at a time of strong attacks by Dorson on published examples of "fakelore." Utley recognized that popularization had a long history in folklore studies. He restated a concern previously made by other folklorists concerned with the fidelity of published texts to source materials, calling for scholarly rigor and careful annotations in publications. Utley spoke in terms intended to bridge a deepening schism:

> The cleavage is traceable to our competitive society, which rests personal prestige and survival on one's money-making job, rather than upon the crisscross of loyalties allied to traditional status. . . . Our art of popularization is rude in comparison to that of England, France and Germany. Can one conceive in this country a brilliant venture like the British Home University Library, with volumes by Sir Arthur Keith on *Man*, by J. Estlin Carpenter on *Comparative Religion*, and by W. P. Ker on *English Literature—Mediaeval*? Are not our own multifarious pocket books forced to borrow most of their best titles, like Tawney's *Religion and the Rise of Capitalism* from the British Penguin and Pelican series? These books do what most popular books in this country do not do—provide an important synthesis, full of ideas for the scholar, and full of the grace and graciousness needed by the intelligent amateur. Ben Botkin in a recent letter, after having read my title in the program, urged me to try to reconcile the views of Anna Gayton in her presidential address, and its strain, responsive to the recent efforts of the ACLS and the MLA, of "Research is not enough," with a review by Richard Dorson in the same . . . issue of JAF and its strain of "Popularization is not enough." He was right in assuming that I should touch on this conflict; wrong in hoping that I could thoroughly resolve it. As I say, economic reasons lie at the basis of the eternal struggle between free-lance and academic writers. My own axiom, which might lead at least to an *entente cordiale,* is that popularization, to be worth its salt, must be based upon fresh knowledge and not on the

preservation of cliches and errors in a vulgar pastiche of low commercial appeal. The publishers had better realize that there can be no popularization of something which does not exist, that there must be scholarship before it can be publicized. And they had better help that scholarship to see the light of day. . . .

In the field of folklore we have much raw material for popularization, and the Society must count among its honored members many men who have written books which sell. It is healthful to remember that the Grimms, Percy and Scott were popularizers as well as scholars. We niggle at them for their errors, for their doctored texts and their conflated ballad versions, for their outmoded records of the folk . . . I submit that our science would be nowhere without them. The way to approach the problem of conflated ballad-versions is not to draw a long face every time we see one in a Percy or a Lomax, but to insist that the present-day collector plainly record the raw data, text, music, and context, send it to the Library of Congress or publish it in a learned journal, and then do what he wants with it, with a brief and unobtrusive set of references in the back of the book, which bother no conceivable reader, and which, if they bother a publisher, should be made a point of minimal demand and outraged pride. (Utley 1952:115–16)

The most successful popularizer among folklorists at the time was Benjamin Botkin, whose treasuries of regional folklore sold many thousands of copies. These popular anthologies contained popular versions of traditional folklore materials designed to appeal to mass audiences. Botkin's alteration of traditional texts in these books excited much controversy among folklorists, with folklorists critical of the utilization of folklore focusing upon them as particular targets. Botkin was a former president of the American Folklore Society, who, since the 1930s, also wrote articles directed to his professional folklorist colleagues defending the application and utilization of folklore. Botkin recognized at the time of Utley's address that the divisions between "researchers" and "popularizers" had become personalized and that positions were beginning to harden. Botkin wrote in the column "Upstate, Downstate" in the *New York Folklore Quarterly* of a gathering at Moritz Jagendorf's house following Utley's address, where a spirit of reconciliation was present and he could manage to have a bit of optimism about the future (1951:78).

Botkin prefaced his account of the gathering at Jagendorf's house with a quotation from a review by Carl Carmer of a popular book on Christmas. Carmer wrote in the review of "splinter parties" in folklore who were causing a "rapid deterioration" of "public relations" in a field where "everyone who regards himself as a folklorist also regards himself as a lone wolf." Botkin echoed Carmer's sentiments, writing, "It is high time that folklorists realized that their internal squabbling and bickering, accompanied by much backbiting and sniping and open display of ill temper and bad manners, are doing their cause more harm than good, as far as the general public is concerned." He stressed the need for civility in the professional lives of folklorists and indicated that he was not making a "plea for mere geniality in criticism or for the elimination of healthy difference of opinion and controversy." Botkin also spoke positively of the "free meeting of minds and exchange of views" at the Jagendorfs' home during the MLA meetings:

> In the parlor after dinner, the hospitable doctor posed the following question to his three guests: "What do you think of the present widening of popular interest in American folklore? Is it good or bad, and should it be encouraged?" The gentleman from Indiana replied that, although he has his doubts and reservations about the value of much of the work being done in the name of folklore and while he himself is more interested in the science, there are both scientific and aesthetic folklorists; that the function of the latter is to make available aesthetically satisfying and reasonably faithful (to the spirit, if not always to the letter) versions of folk tales; that there is a good deal of scientific data that should not go beyond the confines of the learned journals and monographs; and that only the masterpieces (by master folk storytellers) should be made available to, and stand a chance of being accepted by, the schools. Turning to the subject of adaptations, the gentleman from North Carolina averred that, as long as the writer puts his cards on the table and does not presume to palm off literary versions as folk versions, the retelling of folktales has entertainment and even aesthetic value, and that with increased publication and reading there has been an improvement in standards and taste in the popular folklore field.
>
> Perhaps the improvement in social relations among folklorists holds the key to the improvement of their public relations. (Botkin and Tyrell 1951:79)

While the social relations at Jagendorf's house that evening may have been just fine, the internal conflict among folklorists was not to heal. "Researcher" folklorists might express tolerance of the work of popularizers and might admit that popular writing could be well grounded in scholarship; but discourse about the utilization of folklore was fading fast from the mainstream of folklore studies. The Midcentury International Folklore Conference and writings of leading folklorists had included discussion of the presentation, alteration, and adaptation of folklore to new contexts as fundamental issues of professional concern. During the 1950s these issues were discussed less frequently at meetings of the American Folklore Society and the pages of its journal.

The Committee on the Utilization of Folklore became inactive in 1950. Two other committees, each short-lived, continued to deal with aspects of the utilization of folklore. The Committee for the Encouragement and Development of New Folklore Societies and the Committee on Folklore for Juveniles and Young Children (later known as the Committee on Folklore for Children and Young People) were founded through the efforts of Thelma James. In a letter to MacEdward Leach, AFS president Ann Gayton complained that the AFS had "too many committees for a society the size of AFS." She wrote that she was "appalled at learning of these two new ones Miss James set up" (University of Pennsylvania Folklore and Folklife Department Archives, March 20, 1950). These committees reported to the 1950 meeting of the AFS with many suggestions for AFS activity in their areas of interest. Their recommendations were apparently not implemented, with the exception of Eloise Ramsey's 1952 bibliography, prepared for use in elementary and intermediate schools, During the early 1950s the Committee on Folklore in Education concentrated its efforts upon the teaching of folklore in universities, a redirection from a previous interest in primary and secondary education.

Through the remainder of the 1950s, some scholars analyzed the folk revival, reviewed popular books in the *Journal of American Folklore*, produced educational films and recordings, appeared on radio and television to explain folklore to the public, and performed as revivalist musicians with educational orientations.[4] However, the utilization of folklore and popularization increasingly became a minor concern for all but a handful of folklorists. Most folklorists became exclusively concerned with academic matters and viewed the application of folklore for uses in nonacademic settings as disjunct from their scholarly concerns.

The "utilization of folklore" disappeared from the folklorist's vocabulary in the 1950s. It was replaced by the term "applied folklore." Botkin is best known for his use of this term, which was apparently first used by Ralph Beals in 1950. In "Editor's Page" remarks in the *Journal of American Folklore*, he wrote, " 'Applied folklore' has been used somewhat nationalistically, either consciously or unconsciously, but at its best, has bolstered the egos of minority groups, given appreciation by majorities of minority group values and has broadened appreciation of the folk heritage by the wide diffusion of folk materials" (Beals 1950:360).

Beals seemed to view "applied folklore" as an alternative term for the utilization of folklore. A redefinition of applied folklore appeared in Botkin's article, "Applied Folklore: Creating Understanding through Folklore," which served as a kind of credo for his position. Botkin's use of the term had a distinctively different meaning from Beals's, reflecting the deepening gulf between academic folklorists and folklorists working outside of academic settings. Botkin defined applied folklore as "the use of folklore to some end beyond itself." He viewed the "applied folklorist" as a different kind of folklorist from the "pure folklorist." Applied folklore was to Botkin an interdisciplinary pursuit directed towards a socially useful end, to be distinguished from folklore studies centered upon folklore as an independent discipline. The applied folklorist stood "outside" of folklore as a discipline in serving the people who have created folklore:

> [But] as long as the folklorist stays inside of folklore and regards it "from the point of view of folklore itself," he remains a "pure" folklorist. It is only when he gets "outside" of folklore into social or literary history, education, recreation, or the arts, that he becomes an "applied" folklorist.
>
> As an applied folklorist I have always believed that while the study of folklore belongs to the folklorist, the lore itself belongs to the people who make it or enjoy it. As to the place of the study of folklore in the hierarchy of knowledge, we know it belongs both to the humanities and to the social sciences. But whereas a pure folklorist might tend to think of folklore as an independent discipline, the applied folklorist prefers to think of it as ancillary to the study of culture, of history or literature—of people. (Botkin 1953:199)

Folklore studies as an academic discipline in the 1950s was clearly on a trajectory towards recognition as an autonomous academic discipline rather than as the interdisciplinary field envisaged by Botkin. As the decade progressed, interest in the social utility of folklore rapidly diminished among university-based scholars. Botkin's approach, increasingly at odds with "pure folklorists," was characteristic of the folklore movement in New York State at the time, which Jones described as having the common quality of the "desire to return to the people themselves an awareness of their own traditions." Jones claimed, "We cared remarkably little what the rest of the folklore fraternity thought about this, and some of them were shocked, as though we were giving away to the great unwashed the secret password of the lodge" (Jones 1982:xviii).

Dorson's hostility toward Botkin and his fellow applied folklorists intensified the breach between "applied" and "pure" folklorists. Much has been written about Dorson's attitude toward applied folklore. As Archie Green notes elsewhere in this volume, Dorson began to express reservations about the work of popularizers during the mid-1940s and launched a full-scale attack on efforts to popularize and revive folklore in his 1950 article, "Folklore and Fakelore." Dorson recurrently attacked applied folklore and popularization throughout the 1950s and 1960s, with special scorn for Botkin. Until applied folklore reemerged as an area of interest among academic folklorists in the 1970s, Dorson criticized in the same breath applied folklorists engaged in popularizing folklore and popularization undertaken by nonfolklorists. In his later writing, Dorson concentrated on attacking applied folklore per se. Dorson's article "A Theory for American Folklore" in 1959 placed the activities of folklorists and nonfolklorists involved in popularization outside of the pale of serious folklore scholarship:

> Curiously, the one group in the United States who profess most concern with American traditions have least interest in its serious study. These are the popularizers, whose organ is the *New York Folklore Quarterly*, whose leading figure is Benjamin A. Botkin, the treasury manufacturer, and whose shrillest spokesman is Moritz Jagendorf, a writer of children's books.
>
> Folklore did not become big business until the 1940's, when Botkin began issuing his treasuries, Alan Lomax took to the air, and Burl Ives hit the night clubs. The cavernous maw of the mass media gobbled up endless chunks of folksiness and a new rationale appeared for the folklorist; his mission is to polish up, overhaul, revamp and distribute folklore to the American people. This he can do through the writing of juvenile and treasury folkbooks, the singing and recording of folk songs and the staging of folk festivals. (Dorson 1959:202)

Dorson joined with other folklorists during the 1950s and early 1960s in attempting to reorganize the AFS as a more exclusive body directed toward the interests of the professional, academic folklorist. The abolition of a large, diverse council and its replacement by a smaller executive board changed the structure of governance of the AFS. The elite Folklore Fellows group was formed, with selection based upon AFS activities and professional accomplishments (Williams 1975:224–25). As editor of the *Journal of American Folklore*, Dorson eliminated reviews and advertisements of books and records seen to "degrade" professional standards (Dorson 1963:10). He also led a failed effort to close the AFS to amateurs in order to "make our group a learned society comparable to the organizations of other disciplines" (Dorson 1975:236).

John Alexander Williams has interpreted the conflict over the popularization, utilization, and application of folklore as a struggle between "radicalism" and "professionalism." Williams saw the origins of the radical side of the struggle in a Washington-based group of the 1930s oriented toward progressive, leftist politics and embodying a functionalist approach to folklore. The radical dimension of their applied folklore was seen by Williams to have diminished in the 1950s and 1960s. He contended that a 1939 statement by Botkin in his article "WPA and Folklore Research: 'Bread and Song' " represented the agenda of the applied folklorists. In this article Botkin called for "breaking down on the one hand popular resistance to folklore as dead and phony stuff and on the other hand academic resistance to its broader interpretation and utilization" (1939:14). In his 1975 article, "Radicalism and Professionalism in Folklore Studies," Williams analyzed what he viewed as the success of the "radicals" in popularization and failure in breaking down academic resistance.

According to Williams, folklorists advocating "professionalism," led by Dorson, pushed for the advancement of folklore as an academic discipline, while fighting the popularization of folklore. Williams characterized them as embodying a "comparative" approach in contrast with the "functionalist" popularizers. In their antiradicalism they were seen to be ideologically at odds with these "functionalists." Williams associated their antiradicalism with their agenda of professionalizing the field as "one aspect of a drive for academic respectability that manifested itself chiefly as a search for money and status" (1975:225).

The divisions constructed by Williams break down upon review of the historical record. There is clear evidence to contradict Williams's claim that folklorists committed to the professionalization of the field were opposed to the utilization and application of folklore throughout the period between the depression and the 1960s. Between 1946 and 1952 many of the most prominent and active university-based folklorists in America accepted the utilization of folklore for nonacademic purposes and seriously considered how it might be best utilized and adapted to new contexts. These folklorists included Wayland Hand, Thelma James, Francis Utley, Herbert Halpert, and, yes, for a while, Stith Thompson and Richard Dorson.

It is bizarre of Williams to suggest that the postwar folklorists involved with the utilization of folklore and applied folklore were all, or even mainly, radicals. While some of these folklorists had, during the 1930s, used folklore as an "organizing tool in left-wing political and labor struggles" (Williams 1975:217), most either did not connect their folklore work to political activism or were far closer to the political center. Botkin in the 1950s was, as Green indicates in his essay in this volume, "committed to intercultural education and liberal social action." A reformist impulse towards the amelioration of social problems seems to have informed the work of Thelma James discussed earlier in this essay. James, in fact, inveighed against "folklore as propaganda," warning in the *Journal of American Folklore* of parallels between the use of folklore by fascists and by contemporary political activists espousing the "party line" and using folklore for "deliberate subversive or propaganda purposes" (James 1948:311).

Many folklorists involved with organizing folk festivals or educating lay persons in the utilization of folklore carried out their activities outside of any explicitly ideological framework. These folklorists engaged in the celebration of traditional community values and embodied an approach akin to consensus history. For example, the historical museum programming of Louis Jones at the New York State Historical Association and Farmers' Museum involved conservative representations of Anglo-American folk culture of the past.

Williams's association of the marginalization of applied folklore with the process through which folklore became established as an autonomous academic discipline represents a significant contribution of his essay. Drawing from sociological studies of the professionalization process, Williams described how folklorists achieved control over careers and determined professional status. The establishment of the AFS Fellows as a separate category of members "publicized and institutionalized" the "preferred career model" of professional accomplishment (Williams 1975:230). The restriction of access to AFS publications and the certification of research for the guidance of outside funding sources served to deny status and recognition to those not fulfilling the desired career models, the "quack" or "fakelorist." Access and recognition within the profession was tied to university folklore departments through the efforts of the builders of graduate programs, and to foundations, learned societies, and government agencies that shared an emphasis upon graduate degrees and other academically sanctioned markers of professional status (Williams 1975:230).

The boundaries of folklore studies as a profession became sharply delineated through the mechanisms of university-based programs and a professional association that defined academic standards and controlled access into the profession. Folklore studies had reached a point in its professionalization process where a number of folklorists perceived that success as an academic discipline required monopoly over its circumscribed field of study and restriction of involvement in the profession.

As the sociologist Jeffrey Lionel Berlant has indicated, professional groups may increase their chances of success in situations of conflict by varying the size of their membership, restricting or expanding it depending on the group's situation. Expansion of a group requires opening participation through tactics to attract new members, while "restriction" or "monopolization" involves the denial of membership in the group (Berlant 1975:46). In 1940 the response of the Committee on Policy to a need to expand and reorganize the AFS and make it more financially viable included a policy for the recruitment of new members, calls for closer cooperation with other folklore organizations, and "integrating the interests of amateur collectors with the work of the Society" (Fifty-second Annual Meeting 1941:77). In contrast, the Policy Committee in 1950 indicated that the "recent expansion in membership of the Society has been accompanied by some lowering of its scientific standards. The Committee wishes to emphasize that the goal of the Society is not merely to record traditions and oral literature, but to analyze these raw materials scientifically, relating and integrating them with other areas of human activity" (Sixty-second Annual Meeting 1951:211).

During the postwar period folklore studies initially became more open to amateurs and popularizers but then became increasingly monopolistic. Monopolization of folklore studies entailed squeezing out popularizers and orienting the profession more exclusively towards scholarship and away from utilization and collaboration with popularizers. While membership in AFS remained open to anyone, other monopolization tactics were employed to restrict and define professional status. The graduate programs for research and training in folklore socialized students into the profession and forged loyalty and commitment to a field that became their primary professional identity. The standard career model involved training through folklore graduate programs in preparation for college teaching, a career path that would not have been possible before the establishment of the first folklore graduate programs.

The postwar period from World War II to the early 1960s represented, as Williams correctly indicates, the key period in the professionalization process in folklore studies. As in other professions undergoing professionalization, a systematized body of knowledge was being developed, distinguishing folklore as autonomous from anthropology and literary studies. While this body of knowledge encompassed the utilization of folklore during the early postwar period, this dimension of folkloristics virtually disappeared during the 1950s, to reemerge in different terms during the early 1970s. Botkin's concept of applied folklore as an interdisciplinary field oriented toward socially useful ends ran counter to the movement to establish folklore as an autonomous discipline, which characterized the professionalization of the field during the 1950s and 1960s.

By any reckoning, folklore studies had professionalized to a considerable extent by the mid-1960s. But something was missing. In at least one very significant way, the full professional development of the field of folklore studies was not yet complete. Talcott Parsons has pointed out that the professional system has two branches. Through the "profession of learning," the first branch, the intellectual disciplines, engage in research and scholarship, and in transmitting this learning to others. The other branch of the professional system, the applied branch, is involved in the practical application of the intellectual disciplines. The application of a discipline involves the creation of technical competence in the mastery and use of an academic discipline. At the center of the institutional structures of all professional worlds is the university, where professional training occurs and where both theory and skills are learned, to be applied in the practice of a profession (Parsons 1968:536–47).

Sociologist Magali Sarfatti Larson has indicated that both "the producing of practitioners or researchers and the producing of knowledge pure and applied tend to become increasingly integrated and coherent within the modern university" (1977:50). Many intellectual disciplines have expanded and diversified the arenas in which their professions are practiced during recent decades. As the applied branches of professions have grown, the integration of theory and practice has become an important challenge for much of the professional world.

The integration of theory and practice has been problematic for folklore studies for four decades. During the years immediately following World War II, public folklore was integrated with the other academic concerns of many university-based scholars. As folklore studies became established as an autonomous academic discipline, the academic and public branches of the field became increasingly detached from one another. The professional development of folklore studies is incomplete, with the profession characterized by a poorly articulated relationship between its academic and public branches.

The value of public folklore was questioned or denied during the key period of the discipline's professionalization, as I have discussed. Training in skills to be applied in the practice of folklore outside of the university did not, of course, occur. As the profession became more bounded, what Everett Hughes characterizes as the "universalizing" of the practice of the profession was not accomplished. Such universalization enables the professional to "carry on his work in a wide variety of situations, so that his skill may meet the needs of any client whatsoever, or that his methods of investigation (in the case of a science) may be applied anywhere and at any time with equal validity" (Hughes 1958:62).

Training for the practice of folklore outside of academic settings has been problematic for many of our graduate programs, contributing to a lack of full integration of the profession at a time when the growth of the practice of folklore outside of the university has far outstripped the growth of its practice within the university. The legacy of folklore's professionalization experience during the postwar period lingers in a disjunction between the public and academic branches of the field. Unfortunately, the academic status of folklore remains somewhat marginal to the social sciences and the humanities, fostering continuing resistance of some academic folklorists toward the growing public dimension of the discipline. As Kirshenblatt-Gimblett has noted, "Even as academic folklore programs depend on the public sector both to recruit students and to absorb graduates, the academy (and I speak here of departments and curricula, not individual folklorists) continued to disassociate itself from applied folklore" (1988 and this volume).

Even while Kirshenblatt-Gimblett calls in her oft-cited article for folklorists to be "trained specifically for the public sector," she narrowly defines such training as encompassing a "critical knowledge of the history of the field and its essentially applied character." She characterizes folklore programs as trivializing the "applied sector" by treating it as a "largely practical, rather than intellectual undertaking" (this vol.:32). Kirshenblatt-Gimblett reduplicates the false dichotomies she decries in suggesting that training for the *practice* of public folklore is outside of the responsibilities of university folklore programs to train graduate students for the "applied sector."

Kirshenblatt-Gimblett wrote her article at a time when the public and academic sectors of folklore studies were becoming less disjunct and better integrated. Since the late 1970s an increasing number of university-based folklorists have consulted for public folklore projects and serve on funding panels for folk arts programs. The American Folklore Society now sponsors a public-sector internship, has many officers who are public folklorists, and includes a growing number of public folklore sessions at its annual meeting. During the past several years public folklorists have begun to teach university courses about public folklore. However, such courses in folklore doctoral programs have tended to deal with historical and theoretical issues in public folklore without also preparing the folklorist for the various dimensions of practice.

Academic preparation for public folklore should effectively integrate theory and practice while preparing students to actually apply the intellectual discipline of folklore in nonacademic settings. Such training should prepare students for the creation of ethnographically based representations of folklore through such media of public presentation as exhibitions, festivals, recordings; film, audio, and video productions; criticism and other publications for general audiences; and arts in education activities. Griffith discusses preparation for a broad spectrum of public folklore practice through both formal training and professional experience elsewhere in this volume. Preparing a graduate student for the practice of public folklore is essential to equipping him or her fully as a professional in the discipline, or, as Hughes puts it, "to carry on his work in a wide variety of situations" (1958:62).

By neglecting to train students for the practice of public folklore along with preparing them for academic pursuits, doctoral programs do not comprehensively train folklorists as practicing professionals. Some university-based folklorists remain ambivalent or hostile towards public folklore. Current graduate students speak of the devaluing of public folklore by some faculty members defensive about the academic status of the field. The curricula of doctoral programs continue to be structured as if all students will become university-based scholars, the realities of the current varieties of practice of folklore by folklorists and the academic job market notwithstanding.

So the relationship between the public and academic sectors continues to be uncertain and subject to conflict even as many academic and public folklorists forge better relationships. Through essays in this book and other recent publications, the history of public folklore is being recovered. Public folklore has a long and surprising intellectual legacy, which deserves to be restored to its rightful place in the history of the field and the field's discourse about itself. Through better understanding our past, we can better understand our place in a complex, ambiguous, and as yet unresolved relationship between academic and public folklore activities.

Knowledge, a sociologist colleague of mine once remarked, can be created, transmitted, and applied.[5] Contemporary folklorists create and transmit knowledge about folklore both through university-based activities and through public folklore research and programming. We must remember that the transmission and application of knowledge is constitutive of what we study in our life's work, folklore itself, and fundamental to our mission as professional folklorists.

NOTES

A previous version of this essay was delivered at the annual meeting of the American Folklore Society in Albuquerque, October 1987. I am grateful to Roger Abrahams, Archie Green, and Nicholas Spitzer for their comments and criticism. This essay is dedicated to Archie Green, who taught me long ago about the glory and necessity of struggle to accomplish public folklore.

1. The terms "applied folklore," "the utilization of folklore," and "public folklore" are used at different occasions in this essay to refer to the practice of folklore in nonacademic settings. The choice of one of three terms for particular parts of the essay has been determined by the term current at the time about which I am writing or the term used by a particular folklorist referred to in the text. Following from Cogswell and Green (see Green's essay elsewhere in this volume), "public folklore" is used as the most general term referring to the application, utilization, and practice of folklore in nonacademic contexts.

2. I am grateful to Archie Green for suggesting that a number of these aspects of American life in the postwar years set the stage for intensified interest in public folklore.

3. Two year's earlier, Melville J. Herskovits had written "The Collector's Obligation" in an "Editor's Note" of the *Journal of American Folklore*. He recognized that folklorists have different kinds of obligations toward the public and fellow scholars for collecting and presenting folklore. Toward the public, the folklorist has an obligation to "present his materials so that they will faithfully reflect the art, the social intent, the cultural values that gave rise to them." He contrasted the trained scholar's responsibility to record and present folklore that is both culturally representative and artistically exemplary, as well as multiple versions of items of folklore, with the attitude of amateur collectors: "The obligation of the folklorist toward his fellow scholars is essentially a problem of training and discipline. Those without training find it difficult to understand the importance of collecting *and presenting* many versions of a given tale; of taking down stories that may seem out of line with the culture; of recording the inartistic, the humdrum, the prosaic" (Herskovits 1948:391).

4. Bruce Buckley has provided a personal account of his involvement with public folklore during the 1950s. It describes his productions of early folklore television series and educational films and the activities of Indiana University folklore graduate students as revivalist musicians educating the public about folklore (Buckley 1989:3–7).

5. Conversation with Rocco Caporale, October 1987.

REFERENCES

Beals, Ralph L. 1950. "The Editor's Page." *Journal of American Folklore* 63:360.

Berlant, Jeffrey Lionel. 1975. *A Study of Medicine in the United States and Great Britain*. Berkeley and Los Angeles: University of California Press.

Botkin, Benjamin A. 1939. "WPA and Folklore Research: 'Bread and Song.' " *Southern Folklore Quarterly* 3:7–14.

———. 1953. "Applied Folklore: Creating Understanding through Folklore." *Southern Folklore Quarterly* 17:199–206.

Botkin, Benjamin A., and William G. Tyrell. 1951. "Upstate, Downstate." *New York Folklore Quarterly* 7:78–79.

Buckley, Bruce. 1989. "Forty Years before the Mast: Sailing the Stormy and Serene Seas of Public Folklife." *New York Folklore* 15:1–15.

Dorson, Richard M. 1950. "Folklore and Fake Lore." *American Mercury*, March, pp. 335–43.

———. 1959. "A Theory for American Folklore." *Journal of American Folklore* 72:197–232.

———. 1963. "Editor's Report, 1962" *Journal of American Folklore Supplement*, p. 10.

———. 1975. Comment on Williams. *Journal of the Folklore Institute* 11:235–39.

"Fifty-second Annual Meeting of the American Folklore Society: Reports of the Committee on Policy." 1941. *Journal of American Folklore* 54:76–77.

"Fifty-eighth Annual Meeting of the American Folklore Society: Report of the Committee on the Utilization of Folklore." 1947. *Journal of American Folklore* 60:173–74.

"Fifty-ninth Annual Meeting of the American Folklore Society: Report of the Delegate to the Second National Conference on International Educational Reconstruction." 1948. *Journal of American Folklore* 61:206–8.

Folklore Institute of America. 1946. *Informal Notes on Transactions and Lectures*. Second session, Indiana University, June 19–August 16.

Gayton, Ann. 1950. Letter to MacEdward Leach, March 20. University of Pennsylvania Folklore and Folklife Department Archives.

Hand, Wayland, 1948. "The Editor's Page." *Journal of American Folklore* 61:82.

Herskovits, Melville J. 1948. "The Editor's Page." *Journal of American Folklore* 61:391.

Hughes, Everett C. 1958. *Men and Their Work.* Glencoe, Illinois: Free Press.

James, Thelma. 1948. "Folklore and Propaganda." *Journal of American Folklore* 61:311.

Jones, Louis. 1982. *Three Eyes on the Past: Exploring New York Folk Life.* Syracuse: Syracuse University Press.

Kirshenblatt-Gimblett, Barbara. 1988. "Mistaken Dichotomies." *Journal of American Folklore* 101:140–55.

Larson, Magali Sarfatti. 1977. *The Rise of Professionalism: A Sociological Analysis.* Berkeley: University of California Press.

Parsons, Talcott. 1968. "Professions." *International Encyclopedia of the Social Sciences* 12:536–47.

Ramsey, Eloise. 1952. *Folklore for Children and Young People: A Critical and Descriptive Bibliography for Use in the Elementary and Intermediate Schools.* Bibliographical and Special Series of the American Folklore Society, no. 3.

"Sixty-first Annual Meeting of the American Folklore Society: Committee on Folklore in Education." 1950. *Journal of American Folklore* 47:235.

"Sixty-second Annual Meeting of the American Folklore Society: Report of the Policy Committee." 1951. *Journal of American Folklore* 64:210–11.

Thompson, Stith. 1953. *Four Symposia on Folklore.* Indiana University Folklore Series, no. 8. Bloomington: Indiana University Press.

University of Pennsylvania. Folklore and Folklife Department Archives.

Utley, Francis Lee. 1952. "Conflict and Promise in Folklore." *Journal of American Folklore* 65:111–19.

Williams, John Alexander. 1975. "Radicalism and Professionalism in Folklore Studies: A Comparative Perspective." *Journal of the Folklore Institute* 11:211–35.

Public Folklore

A Bibliographic Introduction

STEVE SIPORIN

> Then Jephthah collected all the Gileadites, and fought with
> Ephraim; and the Gileadites defeated Ephraim. Gilead
> seized the fords of the Jordan against Ephraim, and when-
> ever a fugitive from Ephraim would say, "Let me cross,"
> the Gileadites would say to him, "Are you an Ephraimite?"
> If he said, "No," they would say to him, "Then say 'Shibbo-
> leth.'" If he said "Sibboleth," seeing that it is not proper so
> to pronounce it, they would seize him, and slay him at the
> fords of the Jordan. Thus there fell at that time forty-two
> thousand of the Ephraimites.
>
> Judges 12:5–6

The story of the destruction of the Ephraimites is an ancient example of
the application of folklore, and it puts the history, literature, and dilemmas
of public folklore[1] in perspective. In the story, knowledge of the linguistic
habits of one group is applied by another group to destroy the first. Surely,
that was not what the members of the American Folklore Society Committee on Applied Folklore had in mind. In 1971, they defined applied folklore
as "the utilization of the theoretical concepts, factual knowledge, and re-

search methodologies of folklorists in activities or programs meant to ameliorate contemporary social, economic, and technological problems" (Byington 1989). But why think only folklorists utilize folklore publicly? And the amelioration of one group's problems may mean the oppression of others.

My reason for using the biblical example, however, is to remind us that applied, public-sector, or public folklore was not new in 1971, 1953,[2] during the New Deal, or in 1888; nor is it the invention of scholarship. Folklore is applied every day and always has been.

Nevertheless, as we actually use the idea within our discipline, public folklore is distinctive. From its origins within "applied folklore," it has always carried the idea of distance between the applier—a folklorist, anthropologist, or other manipulator of other people's culture—and the society in which the lore exists. Typical and often implicit in public folklore is the idea that the lore or folklore process is being applied in a historically atypical way. Different worlds are usually brought together—such as the worlds of folk and academic medicine (D. Hufford 1982), traditional performers and new folk music festivals (Wilson and Udall 1982), or local culture and the standardized curriculum and classroom (M. Hufford 1979). Application is no longer within the traditional context but rather in public places such as classrooms, parks, museums, and television.

The biblical example suggests two other potential aspects of public folklore: its assertion of group bonds and its power to manipulate. In the story, the application of folklore enables members of one group to kill members of another. We may take the story to symbolize the power one attains over others through understanding others' cultures: Folklore can be dangerous stuff. Thus, colonialism in the broadest sense—Whisnant's *All That Is Native and Fine* (1983) as a study in internal colonialism, for instance—and ultimately, ethics, are central, enduring concerns of public folklore.

The incubation of the study of folklore within the experiences of colonialism and nationalism is one good reason to begin a bibliographic intro-

Alice Cunningham Fletcher (holding a letter) at the Omaha Indian mission in the 1880s. She worked with the Smithsonian Institution's Bureau of American Ethnology and in 1905 became the first woman president of the American Folklore Society. Photo courtesy National Anthropological Archives, Smithsonian Institution.

duction to public folklore with Giuseppe Cocchiara's *History of Folklore in Europe* ([1952] 1981). Cocchiara placed folklore at the heart of Western civilization's intellectual tradition. He believed the study of folklore began with the discovery of America, with missionaries' descriptions of the newly discovered peoples (and with the impact of those descriptions on philosopher-essayists like Montaigne, Vico, and Rousseau), with colonialism, and with the idea of the noble savage, who made Adam and Eve contemporary. From the beginning there has been a tendency to romanticize "the folk," and Cocchiara showed this romanticizing to be a projection, through inversion, of European values upon others. Whether they were noble savages or mountain folk, new immigrants or former slaves, these personae became tools in Western civilization's critique of itself. As soon as folklore began to be seen as a subject fit for inquiry and scholarship, its public or applied dimension was simultaneously at work. As Barbara Kirshenblatt-Gimblett put it, "The folkloristic enterprise is not and cannot be beyond ideology, national political interests, and economic concerns" (1988:141 and this volume).

One perennially productive branch of folklore studies continues to deal with questions of folklore and its role in nationalism, politics, and ideology. William A. Wilson's book, *Folklore and Nationalism in Modern Finland* (1976), for instance, described the central role folklore, and especially folklore theory, had in the creation of a nation. Wilson has also written a key article summarizing the historical context and impact of Johann Herder, the figure most often cited as the first person to collect and utilize folklore for cultural, social, and political purposes (W. Wilson 1973). Wilson's concern was with the present, and he wrote, "The same stirring phrases about glorious national pasts and noble destinies that once moved Europeans to action are today to be heard echoing throughout Africa and Asia. . . . [T]he story of nationalism will continue to be an oft-told story and . . . folklore will remain one of its most important chapters" (W. Wilson 1973:833). Wilson's apprehensions about the political applications of folklore persist. In "Partial Repentance of a Critic: The *Kalevala*, Politics, and the United States" (1987), he discussed how his involvement in public folklore as a fieldworker, presenter, consultant, and NEA Folk Arts Program panelist and chair caused him to revise his earlier dichotomy between scholarship and ideology and to believe that "what one should be first and foremost is not necessarily a scholar, a patriot, or a special pleader—but a human being who responds humanely and sympathetically to the needs of other human beings" (W. Wilson 1987:86).

A special double issue of the *Journal of the Folklore Institute* (1975, vol. 12, nos. 2–3)—later republished with slightly different contents as a book entitled *Folklore, Nationalism, and Politics* (Oinas 1978)—was devoted to the use of folklore by political movements in a number of different countries and regions, including Albania, Bangladesh, Finland, Siberia, the Soviet Union, Turkey, and the Ukraine. Both collections contained Richard A. Reuss's article (1975), "American Folksongs and Left-Wing Politics: 1935–56," an important chapter in the historiography of American folklore. Other authors such as Herzfeld (1982), Kamenetsky (1972), March (1980), and Simeone (1978) have written about the political uses of folklore in Greece, Germany, Yugoslavia, and Italy, respectively. James R. Dow has made available to us the perspectives of German folklorists as they examine the role of folklore in Nazism (Dow and Lixfeld 1986; Dow 1987).

To jump from the politics of nationalism to the politics of American folklorists, the year 1971 marks a curious line of demarcation in the development of public folklore (then called applied folklore). A special issue of *Folklore Forum* (Sweterlitsch 1971b) published the papers presented at a meeting in Pittsburgh on applied folklore;[3] Richard Bauman's proposal for a Center for Applied Folklore was tabled by a vote of the membership at the annual American Folklore Society meeting in Washington, D.C.;[4] and Richard Dorson could still, somewhat innocently, attack the validity of applied folklore, saying, "We cannot afford much diversion from our primary responsibilities as scholars to seek and record the truth" (Dorson 1971:42).

At the meetings and in *Folklore Forum*, those advocating applied folklore spoke of "relevancy"[5]—a word of powerful connotations, now lost, in that era when the war in Vietnam, Cambodia, and Laos seemed to widen and "wind down" simultaneously, and when many of those now in public-sector positions were not sure if the university and learning were any longer "relevant." A popular bumper sticker, decrying perceived disloyalty to America, bluntly said, "Love it or leave it." Perhaps the study of folklore was one way a few members of that generation found to "love it" and still remain critical; public folklore emerged as a way to "love it" with action and activism.

The year 1971 and this special issue of *Folklore Forum* mark a boundary because within a remarkably short number of years public folklore would fulfill many of the grand hopes then expressed. Bauman's modest suggestion of $2.50–$3.50 in annual dues to defray the cost of the center would soon be dwarfed by the millions spent annually on public folklore through federal, state, local, and private funding. "The Folklore Boom" (Dorson

1978) was about to become visible—and it was to be a *public* folklore boom.

Robert Byington, one of the participants in the applied folklore discussions of 1971, comments that "the model the founders of applied folklore had in mind was, of course, applied anthropology" (1989). No doubt this was true, but it means that this group was not fully aware of the already existing public dimension in folklore's history. As Erika Brady notes, the expeditions of Major John Wesley Powell in the 1870s "represented an early experiment in applied folklore and anthropology" (1988). The interests if not always the methods (A. Green 1978:92) of applied anthropology and public folklore have often converged; the Bureau of American Ethnology publications and journals like *Cultural Survival Quarterly* and *Practicing Anthropology* display both parallel and intersecting concerns. A special issue of *Practicing Anthropology* entitled "Practicing Folklore," edited by Leslie Prosterman, surveyed contemporary areas of public folklore work in 1985.

Indeed, by 1971, public folklore, under other names, already had a distinguished history—a history temporarily suppressed by the interpretation of a dominant figure, Richard Dorson, who was disturbed by what he perceived as "the excesses to which well-intentioned folklore activists can go" (Dorson 1971:41).[6] As Archie Green points out (this volume), Dorson saw "applied folklore" as another disguise of his favorite enemy, "fakelore." But shortly even Dorson would relent and praise the development of festivals, folk artist directories, surveys, and other public projects (Dorson 1978).

Today the lines between public folklore and academic folklore are not as clearly, or naively, drawn as they were over twenty years ago, in 1971. Indeed, the division has been called "a mistaken dichotomy" (Kirshenblatt-Gimblett 1988 and this volume). Burt Feintuch has claimed that the history of the folklore discipline taught in the early 1970s turned "a blind eye to much of what folklore work has been and much of what folklorists have been doing in the last hundred years. . . . Throughout our history many American folklorists have seen their work as *both* public and private. . . . Much of what we today term 'public sector' folklore work has ample precedent from what is essentially the dawn of our profession" (Feintuch 1988c:70–71).

Besides the 1971 *Folklore Forum* special issue, there are other landmark collections of papers. A special issue of *Kentucky Folklore Record* (vol. 26 [1980]) entitled *Folklore and the Public Sector* consisted of the papers given at a conference convened to evaluate the state of public folklore.[7] This issue included fourteen articles by individuals working in a variety of public folklore roles. Two articles of enduring interest dealt with, and questioned, the then-dominant device of public folklorists, the festival (see Camp and Lloyd 1980:67–74 and Willett 1980:12–15). The roles of folklorists in new working contexts were considered by Harzoff, in a living history museum; and Rufty, in artists-in-schools programs. This special issue also included reports on local projects (Archbold 1980; Issacs 1980) and on two of the first permanent state folk arts programs, in Vermont and Florida (Beck 1980; Bulger 1980).

The development of state programs can be traced through a series of articles. Henry Glassie is sometimes considered the first state folklorist in the nation, in Pennsylvania. In a report for *Keystone Folklore Quarterly*, David Hufford described Glassie's work and then his own, as Glassie's successor (1969). Their projects read more like an extension of academic goals than a program designed to engage and serve the general public. They sought to create an archive and library, develop an annual conference, and write a bibliography. A different approach, which has succeeded in most states, was described in George Carey's article, "State Folklorists and State Arts Councils: The Maryland Pilot" (1976). Many of the recurring elements of folk arts programs initiated with NEA grants through state arts agencies were first described by Carey. There are, of course, other published reports on individual state programs.[8] Charles Camp evaluated the evolution of state folklore programs at two points in their rapid rise (Camp 1977, 1983a). Henry A. Willett has made three statistical surveys of state folk arts and folklife positions (Willett 1984, 1986, 1989).

The 1979 conference, "Folklore and the Public Sector," led to a "follow-up" conference in 1985.[9] The papers delivered were edited by Burt Feintuch into the first collection of essays in book form to deal with public folklore (1988a). This collection combined essays by activist public folklorists at the local, state, and federal levels,[10] who wrote about public folklore in the present, with essays by academic folklorists, who examined and reassessed the historical impact of public folklore in America.[11] This volume is noteworthy not only for the quality and range of its essays; its appendix, entitled "A Historical Archive," contains some of the key documents in the history of public folklore.[12]

These three publications of conference proceedings from 1971, 1980, and 1988, and others in specialized areas such as festivals or education, are evidence of public folklore's developing self-consciousness. The emergence of the *Public Programs Newsletter* in March 1983 was part of the same phenomenon. In the words of Jane Beck, its founding editor, the *Newsletter* would "serve as a way for us to communicate about what we are doing, our thoughts about it, our problems, and our successes" (Beck 1983:1). The *Newsletter's* genesis marked an important level in the growth of public-sector work. The number of working public folklorists had reached a critical mass, which could sustain, and required, its own "in-house" publication. The *Public Programs Newsletter* continues to feature reports on programs and projects, commentary on contemporary issues, and reflections on public folklore's past and future (A. Green 1985a).

Whatever recent work shows, there can be little doubt that public folklore's self-consciousness began with B. A. Botkin. His desire to give "back to the people what we have taken from them and what rightfully belongs to them" (Botkin 1939:10) is the ethical and moral basis of the entire public folklore enterprise.[13] He proposed a center for applied folklore (Botkin 1961) ten years before Bauman's proposal, and more significantly, even before Congress was considering the establishment of the arts and humanities endowments.

The burgeoning interest in public folklore in the 1970s and 1980s was the impetus for positive reassessments of Botkin's work (Hirsch 1984, 1987, 1988; Widner 1986). Hirsch, for instance, looked at Botkin's life work as an attempt "to reconcile romantic nationalism and cultural pluralism, literary and anthropological approaches to folklore, and scholarship and applied folklore" (Hirsch 1987:3).

Although discussions of public folklore refer to the New Deal as source and antecedent, much remains to be done in writing the history of folklore during the New Deal. Susan Dwyer-Shick's 1975 survey of folklore and folklorists in the WPA Federal Writers' Project focused on the contributions of John Lomax, B. A. Botkin, and Herbert Halpert, as well as the process by which the project operated. Dwyer-Shick's review (1976) of Mc-Donald (1969) and Mangione ([1972] 1974) evaluated the contributions of these works to a history of government support of folklore. She praised McDonald's work as "the most inclusive treatment . . . of this country's attempt to cope with the consequences of the worldwide social, economic, political, and technological changes during the post-World War I period" (Dwyer-Shick 1976:476).

John Vlach (1988) evaluated the contributions of the *Index of American Design*—the one New Deal federal arts project devoted to American folk art—noting its consistent failure to record accurately what it supposedly set out to record. The *Index* mainly served out-of-work artists, emphasizing the aesthetic rendering of preindustrial objects (mainly through water-colors) rather than the documentation of contemporary folk art in use. Items belonging to museum collections and bought in antique shops were recorded, but fieldwork was not undertaken. As Vlach writes, "Instead of preserving a record of objects tied to local communities, Index artists generally did renderings of artifacts safely ensconced in museums and private collections, things already in hand. . . . One can only wonder what messages the Index might have been able to send if its expressed goals had actually been pursued. Perhaps today the Index would be a powerful tool for cultural advocacy instead of 22,000 pictures of antiques" (Vlach 1988:9, 13). The *Index* has been valued by art historians and folk art collectors, providing them with a canon that, ultimately, has functioned to validate folk art market values.

James Agee and Walker Evans's *Let Us Now Praise Famous Men* ([1941] 1960), which grew out of Farm Security Administration work, succeeded where the *Index* failed. The *Index of American Design* did not become the useful reference tool it should have been, but Agee and Evans's work became one of the formative spiritual influences for public folklorists and, indeed, documentarians in general. In 1936, after preliminary fieldwork, Agee and Evans spent a month living with a tenant farm family in Alabama, documenting in great detail, with camera and written word, their lives and the lives of others in the area. The reasons for inspiration are rarely clear, but one can see the contributing factors here: the talent of the two artists, Agee and Evans; fieldwork, time spent living with their subjects; and the artists' passionate convictions and directness. As Walker Evans later wrote of Agee, "The families understood what he was down there to do. He'd explained it, in such a way that they were interested in *his* work. He wasn't playing" (Agee and Evans [1941] 1960:xi).

Equally important, and beginning in an even earlier era, are the Lomax family's contributions to public folklore in America. This special chapter—really an important book that needs to be written—can only be suggested here. Alan Lomax's 1972 article, "Appeal for Cultural Equity," for instance, was one of the most impassioned arguments ever made for cultural pluralism (A. Lomax [1972] 1985); if public folklorists share a common commitment, this article is its most succinct statement.

The Lomaxes' work, of course, does not begin or end with the cultural equity article. Bess Lomax Hawes, for instance, summarizes the approach of the National Endowment for the Arts Folk Arts Program in a Festival of American Folklife festival book (Hawes 1981). Her earlier collaboration with Bessie Jones, *Step It Down: Games, Plays, Songs, and Stories from the Afro-American Heritage*, a classic in the documentation of children's folk-lore, is also public folklore in the sense that it was designed for use in teaching. *Step It Down* is one of the few folklore books in which the "informant" gets credit as an author and the only one where the "informant" is named before the scholar.

Yetman (1967, 1970) wrote about John Lomax's decisive role in encouraging the Slave Narrative Collection, folklore's most significant contribution during the New Deal.[14] Lomax's earlier work with cowboy song and poetry (J. Lomax 1910, 1919) and the prestige that it had earned must have been real assets in convincing southern states to undertake this critical and daring effort.[15] Dwyer-Shick (1975:16) notes the likely resistance that might have come to requests for collecting Afro-American materials from Washington, D.C., in the 1930s and sees the selection of a white southerner to direct the folklore activities of the Federal Writers' Project—indeed this particular white southerner—as fortuitous indeed.[16]

John Lomax's populist pluralism and deep-seated sense of cultural responsibility continues in the work of his daughter Bess and in the collaborative work with his son, Alan (Lomax and Lomax 1936, 1960). D. K. Wilgus called John Lomax "the greatest popularizer and one of the greatest field collectors of American folksong" (Wilgus 1959:157). An unexpected side effect of the Lomaxes' work, though undocumented, was the "recruitment" of a new generation of academic and public folklorists.

Other kinds of action, conceived of as protecting and promoting Anglo-American folk culture, had preceded even the Lomaxes' efforts, but with less beneficial or enduring results. David Whisnant's *All That Is Native and Fine: The Politics of Culture in an American Region* (1983) is a thoroughly researched and powerful study of three long-term attempts, by outsiders, at cultural intervention in the Upland South.[17] Whisnant showed that even the best of intentions and plans can be ill conceived, based on questionable assumptions, and poorly carried out. At times, as Whisnant demonstrated, beneficent cultural intervention serves the ends of outside, economically exploitative interests and may even be derived from racist ideology (Whisnant 1983:237–46).

Barbara Kirshenblatt-Gimblett's article, "Mistaken Dichotomies" (1988 and this volume), continued the self-critical dialogue Whisnant so masterfully began. She questioned public folklore's possibility for independent, critical discourse in light of its role in advocacy and dependence on government funding. (The academy, of course, also depends on government funding and has its own restraints in style, genres, and results of discourse.) She suggested that folklorists wield power through the acts of defining and authenticating tradition. Kirshenblatt-Gimblett articulated some of the paradoxes in which public folklorists have found themselves as they deal with folk art. For example: "Not to pay fair market value is to exploit traditional artists, but to commercialize exchange is to risk the depletion of value" (1988:148). She worried that folklorists, "willingly or not, . . . contribute to rampant commodification of culture" (1988:149). Finally, she credited public folklore with "the potential to offer a critical perspective on the entire discipline" (1988:149), but claimed that current practice serves the status quo.

Since Kirshenblatt-Gimblett saw the academic-public distinction as a "false dichotomy" and the entire discipline as having an "essentially and inescapably applied character" (1988:141), her critique was aimed not at public folklore but at the folklore discipline as a whole. Her statements echo Betty-Jo and Henry Glassie's observation that "it seems strange that pure and applied research can be held as authentically distinct" (Glassie and Glassie 1971:31). Although many will disagree with some of Kirshenblatt-Gimblett's perspectives, few will argue with the spirit of her conclusion: "The time has come for folklorists to reassess their division of labor, to reexamine the split between the academic and applied traditions, and to close it" (1988:152 and this volume).

Besides the literature that accompanies festivals,[18] public folklore has generated a considerable literature *about* festivals. The definitive manual on how to produce festivals is Joe Wilson and Lee Udall's *Folk Festivals: A Handbook for Organization and Management* (1982). *Folk Festival Issues: Report from a Seminar* (Whisnant 1979) represents the dialogue of a meeting in Washington, D.C., March 2–3, 1978. The purpose of the meeting was

(1) to assemble and synthesize the reflections and insights of some of those who have had the broadest and deepest experience with traditionally oriented festivals during recent years; (2) to analyze and criticize the aims, recent history, accomplishments, and failures of such festivals; (3) to assess the possibilities and limitations of similar efforts in the future and to consider alternatives; and (4) to provide initial criticism of, and direction for, NCTA's[19] contemplated project on improving festivals. (Whisnant 1979:4)

The emphasis of the meeting was philosophic and programmatic rather than technical.

Some criticized the concepts behind folk festivals (Whisnant 1979; Camp 1976–77; Camp and Lloyd 1980; Willett 1980). Still, public folklorists continued to produce festivals and accompanying publications. Indeed, the Smithsonian Institution's Festival of American Folklife, beginning as a three-day event in 1967, grew to twelve weeks in length for the 1976 bicentennial. The festival has since become an institutionalized event, usually lasting two weeks each summer. The Festival of American Folklife's annual publication, a useful record of American folklife and a model for other festivals, has become more substantial in recent years. The more than twenty-five years of the Smithsonian Festival of American Folklife program books are a chronicle of the wide-ranging folklore fieldwork undertaken during this period. They have often provided a medium through which important ideas on cultural policy can reach the general public. (See, for example, Abrahams 1988; Auerbach 1988; Hawes 1981, 1984; A. Lomax [1977] 1985; Vennum 1989; and Vennum and Spitzer 1986.)

A positive result of the criticism of the festival format was the development of programming options. Beginning in the late 1970s, folk art exhibitions and catalogues became the preferred medium. The number of folk art catalogues produced by public folklore programs since that time is now large enough to warrant its own bibliography. Robert T. Teske (1988) reviewed ten state survey exhibitions from the period 1976–1986 and noted that the National Endowment for the Arts Folk Arts Program funded 107 folk art exhibitions during the same period. Public folklorists also took part in the debate between folk art collectors/dealers/curators, art historians, folklorists, and others about the nature of folk art (MacDowell and Dewhurst 1980; S. Jones 1986; Joyce 1986b; Posen 1986).

An early model of a folk art catalogue that had far-reaching influence was Suzi Jones's *Webfoots and Bunchgrassers: Folk Art of the Oregon Country* (1980). It set scholarly and artistic standards that others would soon emulate (Baron [1981] 1987:15–16). Its grounding in folk art scholarship, presented through object selection, Jones's captions and introductions, and Barre Toelken's essay "In the Stream of Life: An Essay on Oregon Folk Art" (1980), brought the folklore discipline's point of view eloquently to the public. Thus, the theoretical perspectives on folk art proposed by scholars like Henry Glassie (1972) and John Vlach (1978, 1980b) began to reach the public, the museum world, and academic disciplines other than folklore through exhibitions and catalogues created by public folklorists. Sometimes, public folklorists have used essays by their academic colleagues

(Toelken 1980; Vlach 1980a). But it is just as likely to find public-sector folklorists themselves in the role of essayist (Griffith 1988).

Public folklorists have also capitalized on their experience in festival production and contextual theory to combine festival and exhibit. Their purpose has been to bring the museum visitor closer to the native experience (Hall and Seemann 1987; especially Baron [1981] 1987:16–20; Santino 1988).

Some exhibitions focused on particular traditions: cowboys in Hawaii (Martin 1987) and the crafts of the Amana Colonies in Iowa (Ohrn 1988). But the state survey continued to be a significant form, as exhibitions from Wisconsin (Teske 1987) and Pennsylvania (Staub 1988b) demonstrated with insight and eloquence. Although state folk art exhibitions have been faulted for not making new theoretical contributions (Camp 1986), the two magnificent catalogues by Teske and Staub demonstrate that new theory is not all that counts. *The Grand Generation: Memory, Mastery, and Legacy,* by Mary Hufford, Marjorie Hunt, and Steven Zeitlin (1987), was a traveling exhibition and catalogue. The exhibit's content was not tied to a particular place, but as the introduction by Barbara Kirshenblatt-Gimblett suggests, it focused on generational and individual processes in creating folk art. Much of today's significant fieldwork and publication on American folk art is being done in the public rather than the academic programs.

Public folklorists have given folklore a new shape. Just as the festivals of the 1960s and 1970s utilized and expanded new theories based on performance, genre, and context, so too, the exhibitions and catalogues of the 1970s and 1980s have been public folklorists' vehicles for stretching the discipline. The introductory folklore class of the 1980s undoubtedly paid much more attention to material culture than its predecessor of the 1960s. Public folklorists deserve partial credit for this more balanced vision of folklore and folklife, which has changed the way all folklorists educate others about expression, creativity, and meaning.

The creation of folk art exhibitions, often through state agencies mandated to serve artists, has led public folklorists into yet another area: the marketing of traditional art. In *Marketing Folk Art,* a special issue of *New York Folklore* (1986, vol. 12, nos. 1–2), editor Philip Stevens, Jr., asked the question, "What role can folklorists play in developing marketing strategies that will at once improve the lot of folk artists *and* protect their traditional forms of expression from commercial exploitation?" (Stevens 1986:iv). He further noted, "There is a growing number of 'applied' or 'public sector folklorists' to whom the question [of marketing] is correct, vital, and immediate" (Stevens 1986:iv). Rosemary Joyce, the guest editor for the special issue, wrote an introduction, followed by articles dealing with the problems and opportunities presented by marketing.[20] Others, such as Blanton Owen (1984) and Lynn Martin (1986), have addressed the marketing of folk arts in the *Public Programs Newsletter*.

With a few exceptions, state folk arts and folklife programs have not created comprehensive guides to traditional life within their states' borders—something that might have been expected to grow out of earlier WPA emphases. (For examples, see Fisher 1939; Georgia Writers' Project 1972; Saxon 1945.) Some WPA works, such as Vardis Fisher's *Idaho Lore*, were literary rewritings of oral lore in a "folksy" tone and were misleading at best. One of the first post–WPA surveys of a state's folklore, Suzi Jones's *Oregon Folklore* (1977), was published with the help of the Oregon Arts Commission. *Oregon Folklore* is a survey of the state's verbal and material folklore by region and genre. Most state guides, however, tend to be more narrowly focused (Stanton 1989). Sometimes regions within states can be the subject, as with James S. Griffith's in-depth survey of "publicly accessible folk art" (1988:3). Griffith centered his attention on Tucson and environs, the area of his most extensive fieldwork over the past two decades.

The most thorough guide to any state's folklore is Nicholas R. Spitzer's *Louisiana Folklife: A Guide to the State* (1985). The twenty-three essays in Spitzer's book were written by nationally and locally known folklorists and other cultural experts. In addition to these essays—which range from "A History of Folklife Research in Louisiana," by F. A. de Caro, to "Folk Boats of Louisiana," by Malcolm Comeaux—there are descriptions of state offices dealing with folklife and nine appendixes on topics such as "Resources in Research, Preservation, and Presentation of Louisiana Folklife" and "Film and Video on Louisiana Folklife."

A few states and regions have published fieldwork guides (Brunvand 1971; Leach and Glassie [1968] 1973; Martin 1988). There are guides to folklife resources available for some states (New Jersey [Bartis, Cohen, and Dowd 1985] and Rhode Island [Bartis 1983], for example). The Washington State Folklife Council has recently published a major bibliography of that state's folklore and folklife (Walls 1987). In the area of public folklore reference, the American Folklife Center's *Folklife Sourcebook: A Directory of Folklife Resources in the United States and Canada* (Bartis and Fertig 1986) is invaluable. It informs the user about the locations of folklore archives, state folklore societies, and other organizations dealing with folklife. *The Folklife Sourcebook* also lists the addresses of all serial publications related to folklife, of recording companies, and of colleges and universities where one can study folklore and folklife.

Another major area of public folklore contribution has been the ideas and rhetoric of cultural conservation. Although this term can be used as a general term to describe *all* the endeavors of public folklorists—as in the title of Feintuch's collection, *The Conservation of Culture*—it grew out of a specific concern with preservation and planning. Betty-Jo and Henry Glassie wrote a pioneering article, "The Implications of Folkloristic Thought for Historic Zoning Ordinances," for the landmark *Folklore Forum* special issue on applied folklore (1971). In this article they argued for the inclusion of examples of folk architecture in preservation efforts to create a balanced architectural record: "The ideal is not the replacement of one myth with another, nor of the replacement of one taste with another. . . . Buildings of all kinds should be saved because of the real contemporary needs for material statements of history and beautiful cultural environments" (Glassie and Glassie 1971:35). They also advocated the value of diversity and other folkloristic perspectives for planning and zoning commissions. Robert T. Teske's 1979 article, "Folk Studies and Historic Preservation," arguing that folklife and historic preservation had a lot in common and could benefit from sharing their common perspectives, reflected a growing interest of the period.

The Glassies' and Teske's work did not take place in isolation. The National Historic Preservation Act of 1966 had laid the foundation for a historic preservation system. It mandated the National Register of Historic Places, the Advisory Council on Historic Preservation, and a grants program (Loomis 1988:184). The American Folklife Preservation Act of 1976 created the American Folklife Center, which was to "preserve and present American folklife through programs of research, documentation, archival preservation, live presentation, exhibition, publication, dissemination, training, and other activities" (Loomis 1983:106).[21]

Ormond Loomis's report, *Cultural Conservation: The Protection of Cultural Heritage in the United States* (1983), grew out of federal legislation and is a document that tries to synthesize and guide public policy. It developed the language and rationale for the inclusion of the "intangible" aspects of culture—nonmaterial items such as beliefs, narratives, and customs—along with the accepted material aspects such as archaeological sites and historic buildings. These cultural resources, Loomis felt, should be considered during the assessment of the impact of federal, state, and local development projects.

Specific efforts to apply the principles of cultural conservation were described for an urban setting in "The Folklorist and the Highway: Theoretical and Practical Implications of the Vine Street Expressway Project" (Camitta 1988); for a remote western valley in *The Grouse Creek Cultural Survey: Integrating Folklife and Historic Preservation Field Research* (Carter and Fleischhauer 1988); and for a "wilderness" in the industrial Northeast in *One Space, Many Places: Folklife and Land Use in New Jersey's Pinelands National Reserve* (M. Hufford 1986). *The Mississippi Delta Ethnographic Overview* (Spitzer 1979) was an earlier survey of ethnicity, cultural ecology, and conservation policies tied to the first national park (Jean Lafitte National Historical Park) to be dedicated to the representation of living traditional cultures. More recently, public folklorists contributed a "folklife resource study" section to an impact report entitled *Cultural and Paleontological Effects of Siting a Low-Level Radioactive Waste Storage Facility in Michigan: Candidate Area Analysis Phase* (Stoffle 1990).[22] The problem of cultural conservation has also begun to be discussed on an international level under the auspices of international organizations such as UNESCO (Honko 1984, 1985).

Several special publications concern themselves with folklore and education. They include *Folklore and Education*, a special issue of the *Journal of the Ohio Folklore Society* (new series, vol. 2, no. 2, summer 1973); *Folklore in the Schools*, an issue of *North Carolina Folklore Journal* (vol. 26, no. 1, May 1978); and *Perspectives on Folklore and Education*, a special issue of *Folklore Forum* (Bibliographic and Special Series no. 2, 1969). More recently, *New York Folklore* devoted a special section to "Folk Arts in Education," in which four essays described projects in four New York locations (Mundell 1987).

Teaching may not seem to be an "applied" topic at first glance, since academic folklorists are supposed to be educators primarily. Nevertheless, academic folklorists rarely write about teaching methods,[23] and as soon as one drops below the college freshman level, academic folklorists are hesitant to enter.

Eliot Wigginton's Foxfire project and books are in one sense a perfect example of "applied folklore."[24] That is, local folklore was used in the curriculum of a high school, not to study folklore itself, but because its inherent interest made it useful in the teaching of composition, reading, and journalism. This approach has had enormous success (Wigginton 1985).

In a related vein, Barre Toelken's article, "Cultural Bilingualism and Composition" (1971), suggested that educating the teacher about the students' traditional culture will facilitate—indeed may be essential to—learning. Thomas A. Green wrote in a parallel track, suggesting the value of using folklore to break out of ethnocentric habits (1969).

Some folklorists involved in public education have stressed misconceptions about folklorists and the inappropriate structure of artists-in-education programs as barriers to successful folklore projects (Coelho 1978; Rufty 1980). Others have explained the need to educate teachers and administrators, not just students, about the value of local culture. Mary Hufford's work in a neighborhood surrounding an urban school in New Jersey is a good example (M. Hufford 1979). Some states have developed curricular materials for use in their schools (Belanus 1985).

The use of folklore in both education and economic development can be a way of coping with social and economic problems. The hope of dealing with a broad host of social ills through folklore is a theme that links the public folklore growth of the post-1960s with Botkin's and others' WPA work of the 1930s. Kirshenblatt-Gimblett referred to this "larger enterprise" of public folklore as "the emancipatory potential of folklore as praxis, that is, how what we do as folklorists can be of socially redeeming value" (1988:142 and this volume). The desire to be of service to humanity ties together the many strands of public folklore interests. Sometimes the social problems are those of dislocation (Stekert 1971). Sometimes they are those of occupations and work (McCarl 1980; 1985a; n.d.). Robert S. McCarl's study of fire fighters was based on the premise that the changing demographics of Washington, D.C., fire fighters—from a predominantly homogenous white male group to a heterogeneous group including African Americans and women—required a more self-conscious transmission of knowledge and skills previously acquired informally (McCarl 1985a). McCarl developed a report (1980) to assist fire fighters in making this transition. He continues to publish his work through vehicles and organizations—such as the Brown Lung Association—that will directly reach and serve workers who have not had a voice in their own history or history in general.

This introductory bibliographic essay and accompanying bibliography has been an attempt, in a preliminary way, to survey a vast literature. That literature has roots in a wide variety of enterprises—the Bureau of American

Ethnology, the New Deal, cultural pluralism, and archeological and architectural preservation, to name a few. Today the roots have spread, and the
literature of public folklore is rapidly developing in many other areas, such
as public policy, law, the environment (Stoffle 1990), and international cultural conservation. There is an enormous media literature not touched
upon here—LPs, CDs, cassettes, films, videos, radio shows, and other media products. These items are just as central to the history, literature, and
impact of public folklore as anything here, but for the sake of coherency in
the space allotted, they have been set aside for now. It should be clear that
the field of public folklore is ready for a full-fledged, annotated bibliography. The whole discipline of folklore surely needs one.

NOTES

1. I use the term "public folklore" because it seems to be the most general, overarching, and
accepted term used today to cover a broad range of phenomena. I have retained "applied folklore" and "public-sector folklore" where it was appropriate historically. There is, however, a
difference between applied folklore and public folklore that is worthy of further exploration.
See Archie Green's article, this volume.

2. The year of Benjamin Botkin's article, "Applied Folklore: Creating Understanding through
Folklore" (Botkin 1953).

3. The preceding, regular issue previewed the controversy and summarized the issues (see
Sweterlitsch 1971a).

4. All elements of the proposal have long since been realized in other forms.

5. See Clements 1973, for example.

6. Kirshenblatt-Gimblett remarks that "not even during the activism of the New Deal, did the
public sector confront so vociferous an opponent . . . as Richard M. Dorson" (1988:140 and
this volume).

7. The conference, also entitled "Folklore and the Public Sector," was held at Western Kentucky University, Bowling Green, Kentucky, April 12–14, 1979.

8. See, for example, every issue of *Public Programs Newsletter* (from 1983 on).

9. "Folklife and the Public Sector: Assessment and Prognosis," organized by Burt Feintuch at
Western Kentucky University, Bowling Green, Kentucky, April 1985.

10. See, for example, the essays by Elaine Eff, "Birth of a New Tradition: A City Folklorist for
Baltimore"; Jane Beck, "Public Sector Folklore in Vermont"; and Ormond Loomis, "Links between Historic Preservation and Folk Cultural Programs."

11. See, for example, the essays by Erika Brady, "The Bureau of American Ethnology: Folklore, Fieldwork, and the Federal Government in the Late Nineteenth and Early Twentieth Centuries"; Jerrold Hirsch, "Cultural Pluralism and Applied Folklore: The New Deal Precedent"; and David Whisnant, "Public Sector Folklore As Intervention: Lessons from the Past, Prospects for the Future."

12. The documents consist of: "Letter from John Wesley Powell to S. F. Baird, April 2, 1880"; "Archive of American Folk-Song" (a report by Robert Winslow Gordon from 1932); "WPA and Folklore Research: 'Bread and Song' " (a reprint of Botkin 1939); "Preservation of Indian Lore" (Dell Hymes's 1973 letter to Senator Mark Hatfield in support of the American Folklife Preservation Act); and "P.L. 94-201—A View from the Lobby" (Archie Green's 1976 report to the American Folklore Society on the successful passage of the American Folklife Preservation Act).

13. Most of Botkin's publications would be appropriate additions to this bibliography, but space allows the inclusion of only a few of the most significant items. For bibliographies of Botkin's work see Jackson [1966] 1974:169–92 and Hirsch 1987:33–35.

14. See Botkin (1945a) Perdue ([1976] 1980), and Yetman (1970) for published texts from the Slave Narrative Collection.

15. *Cowboy Songs and Other Frontier Ballads* contained an introduction by President Theodore Roosevelt (J. Lomax 1910). By the mid-1930s, it had gone through several printings and was a popular book.

16. *Negro Folk Songs As Sung by Lead Belly* (Lomax and Lomax) was published in 1936.

17. The period covered is roughly 1890 to the early 1950s. The three case studies of cultural intervention deal with the Hindman Settlement School, founded in Kentucky in 1902; the lifelong work of Olive Dame Campbell, especially the John C. Campbell Folk School in North Carolina; and the White Top Folk Festival in southwestern Virginia, 1931–39.

18. There have probably been thousands of festival publications over the last fifty years. For examples, see the programs to the Festival of American Folklife (1967 to the present) and the National Folk Festival (1934 to the present). For the early history of the National Folk Festival, see J. Wilson 1988. Some publications are completely independent of the festivals that created them. The annual Cowboy Poetry Gathering in Elko, Nevada, for instance, has fueled the publication of a series of books of new cowboy poems and old classics (Cannon 1985, 1986, 1987, 1990; Edison 1985).

19. The National Council on the Traditional Arts, a nonprofit, private organization that sponsors the National Folk Festival, organizes tours of traditional performing artists and generally facilitates folk arts projects.

20. See Dewhurst and MacDowell 1986, Eff 1986, Zygas 1986, Teske 1986, Johnson 1986, Vlach 1986, and Walle 1986.

21. See also Green 1988b for the history of the passage of the bill.

22. The folklorists involved were Marsha L. MacDowell (coordinator), Laurie K. Sommers, Yvonne R. Lockwood, LuAnne Gaykowski Kozma, and C. Kurt Dewhurst.

23. But see Jackson 1984 for an exception.

24. See, for example, Wigginton 1972, the "original."

PUBLIC FOLKLORE BIBLIOGRAPHY

Abrahams, Roger D. 1988. "The American Folklore Society: One Hundred Years of Folklore Study and Presentation." In *1988 Festival of American Folklife Program Book*, edited by Thomas Vennum, Jr., pp. 46–52. Washington, D.C.: Smithsonian Institution.

Agee, James, and Walker Evans. [1941] 1960. *Let Us Now Praise Famous Men.* Boston: Houghton Mifflin.

Alexander, Charles C. 1980. *Here Lies the Country: Nationalism and the Arts in Twentieth-Century America.* Bloomington: Indiana University Press.

Archbold, Annie. 1980. "The Bowling Green-Warren County Folklife Project." *Kentucky Folklore Record* 26:75–76.

Auerbach, Susan. 1988. "Finding Folklife between the Freeways: Notes from the Los Angeles Folk Arts Program." In *1988 Festival of American Folklife Program Book*, edited by Thomas Vennum, Jr., pp. 57–59. Washington, D.C.: Smithsonian Institution.

Auser, Cortland. 1970. "The Viable Community: Redirections through Applied Folklore." *New York Folklore Quarterly* 25:3–13.

Baldwin, Sidney. 1968. *Poverty and Politics: The Rise and Decline of the Farm Security Administration.* Chapel Hill: University of North Carolina Press.

Baron, Robert. [1981] 1987. "Folklife and the American Museum." In Hall and Seemann (1987:12–26). Nashville: American Association for State and Local History.

Bartis, Peter T., ed. 1983. *Rhode Island Folklife Resources.* Washington, D.C.: American Folklife Center, Library of Congress.

Bartis, Peter T., David S. Cohen, and Gregory Dowd, eds. 1985. *Folklife Resources in New Jersey.* Washington, D.C.: American Folklife Center, Library of Congress.

Bartis, Peter T., and Barbara C. Fertig, eds. 1986. *Folklife Sourcebook: A Directory of Folklife Resources in the United States and Canada.* Washington, D.C.: American Folklife Center, Library of Congress.

Bauman, Richard. 1971. "Proposal for a Center of Applied Folklore." In Sweterlitsch (1971b:1–5).

Beck, Jane. 1980. "Vermont Folk Arts Project." *Kentucky Folklore Record* 26:77–78.

———. 1983. "First Newsletter." *Public Programs Newsletter* 1 (1): 1.

———. 1988. "Public Sector Folklore in Vermont." In Feintuch (1988a:83–94).

Belanus, Betty J. 1985. *Folklore in the Classroom.* Indianapolis: Indiana Historical Bureau.

Bible, The Complete. An American Translation. [1923] 1975. Translated by J. M. Powis Smith and Edgar J. Goodspeed. Chicago and London: University of Chicago Press.

Birdsall, Esther K. 1968. "Folklore Problems and Folklore Samplings of the American Guide Series." *Journal of the Ohio Folklore Society* 3:169–85.

Blaustein, Richard. 1980. "Furthering the Folk Arts in Tennessee: Some Observations." *Kentucky Folklore Record* 26:4–7.

Botkin, B. A. 1939. "WPA and Folklore Research: 'Bread and Song.'" *Southern Folklore Quarterly* 3:7–14. Reprinted in Feintuch (1988a:258–63).

———. 1945a. *Lay My Burden Down: A Folk History of Slavery.* Chicago: University of Chicago Press.

———. 1945b. "The Archive of American Folk Song: Retrospect and Prospect." *Library of Congress Quarterly Journal of Current Acquisitions* 2 (June): 61–69.

———. 1946. "Living Lore on the New York City Writers' Project." *New York Folklore Quarterly* 2:252-63.

———. 1953. "Applied Folklore: Creating Understanding through Folklore." *Southern Folklore Quarterly* 17:199–206.

———. 1958. "We Called It 'Living Lore.'" *New York Folklore Quarterly* 14:189–201.

———. 1961. "Proposal for an Applied Folklore Center." *New York Folklore Quarterly* 17:151–54.

Brady, Erika. 1988. "The Bureau of American Ethnology: Folklore, Fieldwork, and the Federal Government in the Late Nineteenth and Early Twentieth Centuries." In Feintuch (1988a:35–45).

Bronner, Simon J. 1984. Introduction to *American Folk Art: A Guide to Sources.* New York and London: Garland.

Brunvand, Jan Harold. 1971. *A Guide for Collectors of Folklore in Utah.* Salt Lake City: University of Utah Press.

Bulger, Peggy. 1980. "Defining Folk Arts for the Working Folklorist." *Kentucky Folklore Record* 26:62–66.

———. 1988. "Folklife Programs in Florida: The Formative Years." In Feintuch (1988a:71–82).

Byington, Robert. 1989. "What Happened to Applied Folklore." In *Time and Temperature*, edited by Charles Camp, pp. 77–79. Washington, D.C.: American Folklore Society.

Camitta, Miriam. 1988. "The Folklorist and the Highway: Theoretical and Practical Implications of the Vine Street Expressway Project." In Feintuch (1988a:206–16).

Camp, Charles. 1976–1977. "Perspectives in Applied Folklore: American Folk Festivals and the Recent Maryland Experience." *Free State Folklore* 3:4–15.

———. 1977. "State Folklorists and Folklife Programs: A Second Look." *Folklore Forum* 10:26–29.

———. 1983a. "Developing a State Folklife Program." In *Handbook of American*

Folklore, edited by Richard M. Dorson, pp. 518–24. Bloomington: Indiana University Press.

———, ed. 1983b. *Traditional Craftsmanship in America: A Diagnostic Report.* Washington D.C.: National Council for the Traditional Arts.

———. 1986. Review of Steven Ohrn, ed., *Passing Time and Traditions: Contemporary Iowa Folk Artists* and Steve Siporin, ed., *Folk Art of Idaho: We Came to Where We Were Supposed to Be. Journal of American Folklore* 99:97–99.

Camp, Charles, and Timothy Lloyd. 1980. "Six Reasons Not to Produce Folklife Festivals." *Kentucky Folklore Record* 26:67–74.

Cannon, Hal, ed. 1985. *Cowboy Poetry: A Gathering.* Salt Lake City: Peregrine Smith.

———. 1986. *Songs of Sage: The Poetry of Curley Fletcher.* Salt Lake City: Peregrine Smith.

———. 1987. *Rhymes of the Ranges: A New Collection of the Poems of Bruce Kiskaddon.* Salt Lake City: Peregrine Smith.

———. 1990. *New Cowboy Poetry: A Contemporary Gathering.* Layton, Utah: Peregrine Smith.

Carey, George. 1976. "State Folklorists and State Arts Councils: The Maryland Project." *Folklore Forum* 9:1–8.

Carter, Thomas, and Carl Fleischhauer. 1988. *The Grouse Creek Cultural Survey: Integrating Folklife and Historic Preservation Field Research.* Publications of the American Folklife Center, no. 13. Washington, D.C.: American Folklife Center, Library of Congress.

Celebration: A World of Art and Ritual. 1982. Washington, D.C.: Smithsonian Institution Press.

Christensen, Erwin. 1950. *The Index of American Design.* Washington, D.C.: National Gallery of Art.

Clements, William M. 1973. "Herder's *Humanitat:* A Theory for Applied Folklore." In *Studies in Relevance: Romantic and Victorian Writers in 1972,* edited by James Hogg, pp. 17–23. Salzburg, Austria: University of Salzburg.

Cocchiara, Giuseppe. [1952] 1981. *History of Folklore in Europe.* Translated by John McDaniel. Philadelphia: Institute for the Study of Human Issues.

Coe, Linda C. 1977. *Folklife and the Federal Government: A Guide to Activities, Resources, Funds and Services.* Washington, D.C.: American Folklife Center, Library of Congress.

Coe, Linda C., Rebecca Denney, and Anne Rogers. 1980. *Cultural Directory II: Federal Funds and Services for the Arts and Humanities.* Washington, D.C.: Smithsonian Institution Press.

Coelho, Dennis. 1978. "The Folklorist and the Folk Artists in Schools Program: A Case for Involvement." *Keystone Folklore* 22:1–14.

Culin, Stewart. 1890. "Folk-lore Museums." *Journal of American Folklore* 3:312–13.

———. 1924. "Creation in Art." *Brooklyn Museum Quarterly* 11:91–100.

Cultural Survival Quarterly. 1976 to the present.

Dewhust, C. Kurt, and Marsha MacDowell. 1986. "The Marketing of Objects in the Folk Art Style." *New York Folklore* 12 (1–2): 49–56.

Dorson, Richard. 1971. "Applied Folklore." In Sweterlitsch (1971b:40–42).

———. 1978. "Editor's Comment: The Folklore Boom, 1977." *Journal of the Folklore Institute* 15:83–90.

Dow, James R. 1987. "German *Volkskunde* and National Socialism." *Journal of American Folklore* 100:300–304.

———. 1988. Review of Helge Gerndt, ed., *Volkskunde und Nationalsozialismus. Referate und Diskussionen einer Tagung. Journal of American Folklore* 101:358–60.

Dow, James R., and Hannjost Lixfeld, eds. 1986. *German Volkskunde: A Decade of Theoretical Confrontation, Debate, Reorientation (1967–1977).* Bloomington: Indiana University Press.

Dwyer-Shick, Susan. 1975. "The Development of Folklore and Folklife Research in the Federal Writers' Project, 1935–1943." *Keystone Folklore Quarterly* 20 (4): 5–31.

———. 1976. "Review Essay: Folklore and Government Support." *Journal of American Folklore* 89:476–86.

———. 1979. "The American Folklore Society and Folklore Research in America, 1898–1944." Ph.D. diss., University of Pennsylvania.

Eaton, Allen. 1932. *Immigrant Gifts to American Life: Some Experiments in Appreciation of the Contributions of Our Foreign-Born Citizens to American Culture.* New York: Russell Sage Foundation.

Eaton, Allen, and Lucinda Crile. 1946. *Rural Handicrafts in the United States.* Washington, D.C.: U.S. Department of Agriculture in cooperation with Russell Sage Foundation.

Edison, Carol, ed. 1985. *Cowboy Poetry from Utah: An Anthology.* Salt Lake City: Utah Folklife Center.

Eff, Elaine. 1986. "Traditions for Sale: Marketing Mechanisms for Baltimore's Screen Art, 1913–1983." *New York Folklore* 12 (1–2): 57–68.

———. 1988. "Birth of a New Tradition: A City Folklorist for Baltimore." In Feintuch (1988a:95–105).

Evans-Pritchard, Deidre. 1987. "The Portal Case: Authenticity, Tourism, Traditions, and the Law." *Journal of American Folklore* 100:287–96.

Feintuch, Burt, ed. 1988a. *The Conservation of Culture: Folklorists and the Public Sector.* Lexington: University Press of Kentucky.

———. 1988b. "Introduction." In Feintuch (1988a:1–16).

———. 1988c. "The Folklorist and the Public." In *100 Years of American Folklore Studies: A Conceptual History*, edited by William M. Clements, pp. 70–74. Washington, D.C.: American Folklore Society.

Fisher, Vardis. 1939. *Idaho Lore.* Caldwell: Caxton.

Folk Arts Program Native American Grants: 1975–1986. 1986. Washington, D.C.: National Endowment for the Arts.

Folklore and Education. 1973. *Journal of the Ohio Folklore Society,* new series 2, no. 2 (Summer).

Folklore and the Public Sector. 1980. *Kentucky Folklore Record* 26, nos. 1–2 (January–June).

Folklore in the Schools. 1978. *North Carolina Folklore Journal* 26, no. 1 (May 1978).

Georgia Writers' Project. 1972. *Drums and Shadows: Survival Studies among the Georgia Coast Negroes.* Garden City, New York: Doubleday.

Glassie, Henry. 1972. "Folk Art." in *Folklore and Folklife: An Introduction,* edited by Richard M. Dorson, pp. 253–80. Chicago and London: University of Chicago Press.

Glassie, Henry, and Betty Jo Glassie. 1971. "The Implications of Folkloristic Thought for Historic Zoning Ordinances." In Sweterlitsch (1971b:31–37).

Green, Archie. 1978. "Industrial Lore: A Bibliographic-Semantic Inquiry." *Western Folklore* 37:71–102. Reprinted as *Working Americans: Contemporary Approaches to Occupational Folklife.* Smithsonian Folklife Studies 3. Washington, D.C.: Smithsonian Institution.

———. 1983. "Interpreting Folklore Ideologically." In *Handbook of American Folklore,* edited by Richard M. Dorson, pp. 351–58. Bloomington: Indiana University Press.

———. 1984. "Folklore and America's Future." *Kentucky Folklore Record* 30:65–78.

———. 1985a. "The Naming Tag 'Public-Sector Folklore,' A Recollection." *Public Programs Newsletter* 4 (1): 16–17.

———. 1985b. "Reflections on 'Keywords' in Public-Sector Folklore." *Practicing Anthropology* 1–2:4–5.

———. 1988a. "A Keynote: Stitching Patchwork in Public." In Feintuch (1988a:17–32).

———. [1976] 1988b. "P.L. 94-201—A View from the Lobby: A Report to the American Folklore Society." In Feintuch (1988a:269–81).

Green, Thomas A. 1969. "One Mile in Another Man's Moccasins." In *Perspectives on Folklore and Education.* Bibliographic and Special Series, no. 2. *Folklore Forum,* pp. 50–53.

Griffith, James S. 1988. *Southern Arizona Folk Arts.* Tucson: University of Arizona Press.

Hall, Patricia, and Charlie Seemann, eds. 1987. *Folklife and Museums: Selected Readings.* Nashville: American Association for State and Local History.

Halpert, Herbert. 1938. "Federal Theatre and Folksong." *Southern Folklore Quarterly* 2:81–85.

Harzoff, Elizabeth. 1980. "The Role of a Folklorist in a Government Sponsored Living History Museum." *Kentucky Folklore Record* 26:79–82.

Hawes, Bess Lomax. 1981. "Preserving Folk Arts: The National Endowment for the Arts, Folk Arts Program." In *1981 Festival of American Folklife Program Book*, edited by Jack Santino pp. 29–31. Washington, D.C.: Smithsonian Institution.

———. 1984. "Folk Arts and the Elderly." In *1984 Festival of American Folklife Program Book*, edited by Thomas Vennum, Jr., pp. 28–31. Washington, D.C.: Smithsonian Institution.

Henderson, Carole. 1973. "Folklore Scholarship and the Sociopolitical Milieu in Canada." *Journal of the Folklore Institute* 10 (1–2): 97–107.

Herzfeld, Michael. 1982. *Ours Once More: Folklore, Ideology, and the Making of Modern Greece.* Austin: University of Texas Press.

Hirsch, Jerrold. 1984. "Portrait of America: The Federal Writers' Project in an Intellectual and Cultural Context." Ph.D. diss., University of North Carolina at Chapel Hill.

———. 1987. "Folklore in the Making: B. A. Botkin." *Journal of American Folklore* 100:3–38.

———. 1988. "Cultural Pluralism and Applied Folklore: The New Deal Precedent." In Feintuch (1988a:46–67).

Honko, Lauri. 1984. "Do We Need an International Treaty for the Protection of Folklore? The UNESCO Process of Folklore Protection: Working Document, and List of Documents." *Nordic Institute of Folklore (NIF) Newsletter* 12 (3): 1–31.

———. 1985. "What Kinds of Instruments for Folklore Protection?" *Nordic Institute of Folklore (NIF) Newsletter* 13 (1–2): 3–11.

Hufford, David. 1969. "History and Work of the Ethnic Culture Survey and State Folklorist Program of the Pennsylvania Historical and Museum Commission." *Keystone Folklore Quarterly* 14:166–75.

———. 1971. "Some Approaches to the Application of Folklore Studies." In Sweterlitsch (1971b:6–9).

———. 1982. *The Terror That Comes in the Night: An Experience Centered Study of Supernatural Assault Traditions.* Philadelphia: University of Pennsylvania Press.

———. 1985. "Folklore Studies and Health." *Practicing Anthropology* 1–2:23–24.

Hufford, Mary. 1979. *A Tree Smells Like Peanut Butter: Folk Artists in a City School.* Trenton, New Jersey: The New Jersey State Council on the Arts and the National Endowment for the Arts.

———. 1986. *One Space, Many Places: Folklife and Land Use in New Jersey's Pinelands National Reserve.* Washington, D.C.: American Folklife Center, Library of Congress.

———. 1988. "Stalking the Native View: The Protection of Folklife in Natural Habitats." In Feintuch (1988a:217–29).

Hufford, Mary, Marjorie Hunt, and Steven Zeitlin. 1987. *The Grand Generation: Memory, Mastery and Legacy.* Washington D.C.: Smithsonian Traveling Exhibition Service and Office of Folklife Programs in association with University of Washington Press, Seattle.

Issacs, Susan. 1980. "The Role of Family Folklore in the Jewish Folklife Project of Cincinnati." *Kentucky Folklore Record* 26:8–11.

Jackson, Bruce, ed. [1966] 1974. *Folklore and Society: Essays in Honor of Benjamin A. Botkin.* Norwood, Pennsylvania: Norwood Editions.

———. 1976. "Benjamin A. Botkin (1901–1975)." *Journal of American Folklore* 89:1–6.

———, ed. 1984. *Teaching Folklore.* Buffalo: Documentary Research.

———. 1986. "Ben Botkin." *New York Folklore* 12 (3–4): 23–32.

Johnson, Geraldine N. 1986. Commentary on *Marketing Folk Art* issue. *New York Folklore* 12 (1–2): 85–87.

Jones, Bessie, and Bess Lomax Hawes. 1972. *Step It Down: Games, Plays, Songs and Stories from the Afro American Heritage.* New York: Harper and Row.

Jones, Michael O. 1970. "Folk Craft Production and the Folklorist's Obligation." *Journal of Popular Culture* 4 (1): 194–212.

Jones, Suzi. 1977. *Oregon Folklore.* Eugene: University of Oregon and Oregon Arts Commission.

———. 1980. *Webfoots and Bunchgrassers: Folk Art of the Oregon Country.* Salem: Oregon Arts Commission.

———. 1986. "Art by Fiat, and Other Dilemmas of Cross-Cultural Collecting." In *Folk Art and Art Worlds*, edited by John Michael Vlach and Simon J. Bronner, pp. 243–66. Ann Arbor: UMI Research Press.

Joyce, Rosemary O. 1986a. Introduction to special section, *Marketing Folk Art. New York Folklore* 12 (1–2): 43–48.

———. 1986b. " 'Fame Don't Make the Sun Any Cooler': Folk Artists and the Market Place." In *Folk Art and Art Worlds*, edited by John Michael Vlach and Simon J. Bronner, pp. 225–41. Ann Arbor: UMI Research Press.

Kallen, Horace. 1924. *Culture and Democracy in the United States.* New York: Boni and Liverright.

———. 1956. *Cultural Pluralism and the American Ideal.* Philadelphia: University of Pennsylvania Press.

Kamenetsky, Christa. 1972. "Folklore As a Political Tool in Nazi Germany." *Journal of American Folklore* 85:221–35.

Kaplan, Anne R. 1980. "The Folk Arts Foundation of America: A History." *Journal of the Folklore Institute* 17:56–75.

Kirshenblatt-Gimblett, Barbara. 1988. "Mistaken Dichotomies." *Journal of American Folklore* 101:140–55.

Kodish, Debora G. 1978. " 'A National Project with Many Workers': Robert Winslow Gordon and the Archive of American Folk Song." *Quarterly Journal of the Library of Congress* 35 (4): 218–33.

Leach, MacEdward, and Henry Glassie. [1968] 1973. *A Guide for Collectors of Oral Traditions and Folk Cultural Material in Pennsylvania.* Harrisburg: Pennsylvania Historical and Museum Commission.

Lewis, Mary Ellen B. 1974. "The Feminists Have Done It: Applied Folklore." *Journal of American Folklore* 87:85–87.

Lewis, Peirce F. 1975. "The Future of Our Past: Our Clouded Vision of Historic Preservation." *Pioneer America* 8:1–20.

Lomax, Alan. [1977] 1985. "Appeal for Cultural Equity." In *1985 Smithsonian Festival of American Folklife Program Book*, edited by Thomas Vennum, Jr., pp. 40–46. Washington, D.C.: Smithsonian Institution. Originally appeared in *The World of Music* 14 (1972):3–4, 9.

Lomax, John A. 1910. *Cowboy Songs and Other Frontier Ballads.* New York: Sturgis and Walton.

———. 1919. *Songs of the Cattle Trail and Cow Camp.* New York: Macmillan.

———. 1947. *Adventures of a Ballad Hunter.* New York: Macmillan.

Lomax, John A., and Alan Lomax. 1936. *Negro Folk Songs As Sung by Lead Belly.* New York: Macmillan.

———. 1960. *Folk Songs of North America.* Garden City, New York: Doubleday.

Loomis, Ormond H. 1983. *Cultural Conservation: The Protection of Cultural Heritage in the United States.* Washington, D.C.: American Folklife Center, Library of Congress.

———. 1988. "Links between Historic Preservation and Folk Cultural Programs." In Feintuch (1988a:183–95).

MacDowell, Marsha, and C. Kurt Dewhurst. 1980. "Expanding Frontiers: The Michigan Folk Art Project." In *Perspectives on American Folk Art*, edited by Ian M. G. Quimby and Scott T. Swank, pp. 54–78. New York: W. W. Norton and the Winterthur Museum.

Mangione, Jerre. [1972] 1974. *The Dream and the Deal: The Federal Writers' Project, 1935–1943.* Boston: Little, Brown.

March, Richard. 1980. "The Ideology of Folklore Festivals in Pre- and Post-War Yugoslavia." *Kentucky Folklore Record* 26:53–61.

Martin, Lynn J. 1986. "From Hawai'i." *Public Programs Newsletter* 4 (2): 4–7.

———. 1987. *Na Paniolo o Hawai'i.* Honolulu: State Foundation on Culture and the Arts/Honolulu Academy of Arts.

———, ed. 1988. *A Guide for Surveying Pacific Island Folk Arts.* Honolulu: Consortium for Pacific Arts and Cultures.

McCarl, Robert. 1980. *Good Fire/Bad Night: A Cultural Sketch of the District of Columbia Fire Fighters As Seen through Their Occupational Folklife.* Washington, D.C.: Fire Fighters Association, Local 36.

———. 1985a. *The District of Columbia Fire Fighter's Project: A Case Study in Occupational Folklife.* Smithsonian Folklife Studies, no. 4. Washington, D.C.: Smithsonian Institution Press.

———. 1985b. "Fire and Dust: Ethnography at Work in Communities." *Practicing Anthropology* 1–2:21–22.

―――. 1988. "Occupational Folklife in the Public Sector: A Case Study." In Feintuch (1988a:132–53).

―――. n.d. *While I Breathe, I Hope: Personal Accounts of Cotton Mill Workers with Brown Lung Disease*. Brown Lung Association.

McDonald, William F. 1969. *Federal Relief Administration and the Arts: The Origins and Administrative History of the Arts Projects of the Works Progress Administration*. Columbus: Ohio State University Press.

Meeting concerning the Pilot State Apprenticeship Program. 1985. Washington, D.C.: National Endowment for the Arts.

Meeting on Crafts and Public Funding Policies. 1986. Washington, D.C.: National Endowment for the Arts.

Mooney, Michael. 1980. *The Ministry of Culture*. New York: Wyndham Books.

Mundell, Kathleen, ed. 1987. Special section, "Folk Arts in Education." *New York Folklore* 13 (3–4): 1–48.

Netzer, Dick. 1978. *The Subsidized Muse*. Cambridge: Cambridge University Press.

Ohrn, Steven, ed. 1984. *Passing Time and Traditions: Contemporary Iowa Folk Artists*. Ames and Des Moines: Iowa Arts Council/Iowa State University Press.

―――. 1988. *Remaining Faithful: Amana Folk Art in Transition*. Des Moines: Iowa Department of Cultural Affairs.

Oinas, Felix J., ed. 1978. *Folklore, Nationalism, and Politics*. Indiana University Folklore Institute Monograph Series, vol. 30. Columbus, Ohio: Slavic Publishers.

Owen, Blanton, 1984. "To Market to Market to Sell a Folk Pig . . . or Not!" *Public Programs Newsletter* 2 (1): 16–18.

Perdue, Charles L., Jr., ed., Thomas E. Barden, and Robert K. Phillips. [1976] 1980. *Weevils in the Wheat: Interviews with Virginia Ex-Slaves*. Bloomington: Indiana University Press.

Perspectives on Folklore and Education. 1969. Bibliographic and Special Series no. 2. Folklore Forum.

Polemiton, Olga A. 1980. "Folk Crafts and Economic Development: A Viable Alternative." *Kentucky Folklore Record* 26:42–49.

Posen, I. Sheldon. 1986. "Storing Contexts: The Brooklyn *Giglio* As Folk Art." In *Folk Art and Art Worlds*, edited by John Michael Vlach and Simon J. Bronner, pp. 171–91. Ann Arbor: UMI Research Press.

Practicing Anthropology. 1978 to present.

Prosterman, Leslie, ed. 1985. *Practicing Folklore*, special issue of *Practicing Anthropology*.

Public Programs Newsletter. 1983 to present.

Reich, Wendy. 1971. "The Use of Folklore in Revitalization Movements." *Folklore* 82:233–44.

Reuss, Richard A. 1971. "American Folklore and Left-Wing Politics: 1927–1957." Ph.D. diss., Indiana University.

————. 1975. "American Folksongs and Left-Wing Politics: 1935–56." *Journal of the Folklore Institute* 12 (2–3): 89–111.

Rufty, Ruby. 1980. "Folklorists-in-Schools: Refining Public Expectation." *Kentucky Folklore Record* 26:50–52.

Santino, Jack. 1988. "The Tendency to Ritualize: The Living Celebrations Series As a Model for Cultural Presentation and Validation." In Feintuch (1988a:118–31).

Saxon, Lyle, Edward Dreyer, and Robert Tallant, eds. 1945. *Gumbo Ya-Ya: A Collection of Louisiana Folk Tales.* Boston: Houghton Mifflin.

Simeone, William E. 1978. "Fascists and Folklore in Italy." *Journal of American Folklore* 91:543–57.

Smithsonian Festival of American Folklife Program Books. 1967 to present.

Speer, Jean Haskell. 1988. "Unshared Visions: Folklife and Politics in a Rural Community." In Feintuch (1988a:154–65).

Spitzer, Nicholas R., ed. 1979. *The Mississippi Delta Ethnographic Overview.* New Orleans: Jean Lafitte National Historical Park.

————. 1985. *Louisiana Folklife: A Guide to the State.* Baton Rouge: Louisiana Folklife Program.

Stanton, Gary, 1989. *Collecting South Carolina Folk Art: A Guide.* Columbia: University of South Carolina.

Staub, Shalom. 1982. "The Work of the Office of State Folklife Programs." *Keystone Folklore*, new series 1:1–7.

————. 1988a. "Folklore and Authenticity: A Myopic Marriage in Public Sector Programs." In Feintuch (1988a:166–79).

————, ed. 1988b. *Craft and Community: Traditional Arts in Contemporary Society.* Philadelphia: Balch Institute for Ethnic Studies and Pennsylvania Heritage Affairs Commission.

Stekert, Ellen. 1971. "Focus for Conflict: Southern Mountain Medical Beliefs in Detroit." In *The Urban Experience and Folk Tradition,* edited by Américo Paredes and Ellen Stekert, pp. 95–127. Austin: University of Texas Press.

Stevens, Philip, Jr., ed. 1986. *Marketing Folk Art. New York Folklore* 12(1–2).

Stoffle, Richard W., ed. 1990. *Cultural and Paleontological Effects of Siting a Low-Level Radioactive Waste Storage Facility in Michigan: Candidate Area Analysis Phase.* Ann Arbor: University of Michigan.

Stryker, Roy, and Nancy Wood. 1973. *In This Proud Land: America 1935–1943 As Seen in the FSA Photographs.* Greenwich, Connecticut: New York Graphic Society.

Sweterlitsch, Dick. 1971a. "Applied Folklore: The Debate Goes On." *Folklore Forum* 4:15–18.

————, ed. 1971b. *Papers on Applied Folklore.* Bibliographic and Special Series, no. 8. *Folklore Forum.*

Tennessee Writers' Project. 1940. *God Bless the Devil: Liars' Bench Tales*. Chapel Hill: University of North Carolina Press.

Teske, Robert T. 1979. "Folk Studies and Historic Preservation." *Pioneer America Society Transactions* 11:71–80.

———. 1986. " 'Crafts Assistance Programs' and Traditional Crafts." *New York Folklore* 12 (1–2): 75–84.

———, ed. 1987. *From Hardanger to Harleys: A Survey of Wisconsin Folk Art*. Sheboygan, Wisconsin: John Michael Kohler Art Center.

———. 1988. "State Folk Art Exhibitions: Review and Preview." In Feintuch (1988a:109–17).

Toelken, J. Barre. 1971. "Cultural Bilingualism and Composition." *English for American Indians*, Spring, pp. 29–32.

———. 1980. "In the Stream of Life: An Essay on Oregon Folk Art." In S. Jones (1980:8–38). Salem: Oregon Arts Commission.

Vennum, Thomas, Jr. 1989. "American Indian Problems of Access and Cultural Continuity." In *1989 Festival of American Folklore Program Book*, edited by Frank Proschan, pp. 22–35. Washington, D.C.: Smithsonian Institution.

Vennum, Thomas, Jr., and Nicholas Spitzer. 1986. "Musical Performance at the Festival: Developing Criteria." In *1986 Festival of American Folklore Program Book*, edited by Thomas Vennum, Jr., pp. 101–4. Washington, D.C.: Smithsonian Institution.

Vlach, John Michael. 1978. *The Afro-American Tradition in Decorative Arts*. Cleveland: Cleveland Museum of Art.

———. 1980a. "Black Creativity in Mississippi: Origins and Horizons." In *Made by Hand: Mississippi Folk Art*, pp. 28–32. Jackson: Mississippi Department of Archives and History.

———. 1980b. "American Folk Art: Questions and Quandaries." *Winterthur Portfolio* 15:345–55.

———. 1986. Commentary on *Marketing Folk Art* issue. *New York Folklore* 12 (1–2): 88–90.

———. 1988. "The Index of American Design: From Reference Tool to Shopper's Guide." In *Wood and Wood Carvings from the Index of American Design*. East Hampton, New York: Guild Hall Museum.

Walle, Alf. 1986. "Mitigating Marketing: A Window of Opportunity for Applied Folklorists." *New York Folklore* 12 (1–2): 91–112.

Walls, Robert E., ed. 1987. *Bibliography of Washington State Folklore and Folklife*. Seattle: University of Washington Press.

Warren-Findley, Janelle. 1979–80. "Musicians and Mountaineers: The Resettlement Administration's Music Program in Appalachia, 1935–1937." *Appalachian Journal* 7 (1–2): 105–23.

Whisnant, David. 1979. *Folk Festival Issues: Report from a Seminar*. Special Series, no. 12. Los Angeles: John Edwards Memorial Foundation.

———. 1983. *All That Is Native and Fine: The Politics of Culture in an American Region.* Chapel Hill: University of North Carolina Press.

———. 1988. "Public Sector Folklore as Intervention: Lessons from the Past, Prospects for the Future." In Feintuch (1988a:233–47).

Widner, Ronna Lee. 1986. "Lore for the Folk: Benjamin A. Botkin and the Development of Folklore Scholarship in America." *New York Folklore* 12:1–22.

Wigginton, Eliot. 1972. *The Foxfire Book.* Garden City, New York: Doubleday.

———. 1985. *Sometimes a Shining Moment: The Foxfire Experience. Twenty Years Teaching in a High School Classroom.* Garden City, New York: Doubleday.

Wilgus, Donald K. 1959. *Anglo-American Folksong Scholarship since 1898.* New Brunswick, New Jersey: Rutgers University Press.

Willett, Henry. 1980. "Re-thinking the State Folk Arts Program (Or, Alternatives to the Festival)." *Kentucky Folklore Record* 26:12–15.

———. 1984. "A Survey of State Folk Cultural Programs." Washington, D.C.: Public Programs Section, American Folklore Society, in conjunction with the Folk Arts Program, National Endowment for the Arts.

———. 1986. "A Survey of State Folk Cultural Programs." Washington, D.C.: Public Programs Section, American Folklore Society, in conjunction with the Folk Arts Program, National Endowment for the Arts.

———. 1989. "A Survey of Public Folk Cultural Programs." Washington, D.C.: Public Programs Section, American Folklore Society, in conjunction with the Folk Arts Program, National Endowment for the Arts.

Williams, John A. 1975. "Radicalism and Professionalism in Folklore Studies: A Comparative Perspective." *Journal of the Folklore Institute* 11 (3): 211–39.

Williams, Michael Ann. 1988. "The Realm of the Tangible: A Folklorist's Role in Architectural Documentation and Preservation." In Feintuch (1988a:196–205).

Wilson, Joseph. 1988. "The National Folk Festival: 1934–1936." In *50th National Folk Festival 1988,* program book, pp. 6–15. Washington, D.C.: National Council for the Traditional Arts.

Wilson, Joseph, and Lee Udall. 1982. *Folk Festivals: A Handbook for Organization and Management.* Knoxville: University of Tennessee Press.

Wilson, William A. 1973. "Herder, Folklore, and Romantic Nationalism." *Journal of Popular Culture* 4:819–35.

———. 1976. *Folklore and Nationalism in Modern Finland.* Bloomington and London: Indiana University Press.

———. 1987. "Partial Repentance of a Critic: The *Kalevala,* Politics, and the United States." In *Folklife Annual 1986,* edited by Alan Jabbour and James Hardin, pp. 81–91. Washington, D.C.: American Folklife Center, Library of Congress.

Wolfe, Charles K. 1980–81. "The Blue Ridge Parkway Folklife Project." *Journal of the Virginia Folklore Society* 2:15–24.

———. 1983. "Folklife Festival: A Debate over Effect." *Tennessee Folklore Society Bulletin* 49:24–28.

Yetman, Norman R. 1967. "The Background of the Slave Narrative Collection."
American Quarterly 19:534–53.

———. 1970. *Life under the "Peculiar Institution": Selections from the Slave Narrative Collection.* New York: Holt, Rinehart and Winston.

Zygas, Egle Victoria. 1986. "Who Will Market the Folk Arts?" *Marketing Folk Art* issue. *New York Folklore* 12 (1–2): 69–74.